CUSTOM **PHIT** →

D1621830

The Pearson
Custom Program for CIS

Pearson Learning Solutions

New York   Boston   San Francisco
London   Toronto   Sydney   Tokyo   Singapore   Madrid
Mexico City   Munich   Paris   Cape Town   Hong Kong   Montreal

Senior Vice President, Editorial and Marketing: Patrick F. Boles
Editor: Ana Díaz-Caneja
Development Editor: Christina Martin
Operations Manager: Eric M. Kenney
Production Manager: Jennifer Berry
Art Director: Renée Sartell
Cover Designers: Blair Brown and Kristen Kiley

Cover Art: Jerry Driendl/Getty Images, Inc.; Steve Bloom/Getty Images, Inc.; "Cheetah" courtesy of Marvin Mattelson/Getty Images; "Tabs" courtesy of Andrey Prokhorov/iStockphoto; "Open Doors" courtesy of Spectral-Design/iStockphoto; "Compass" courtesy of Laurent Hamels/Getty Images; "Fortune Teller" courtesy of Ingvald Kaldhussaeter/iStockphoto; "Ladder of Success" courtesy of iStockphoto; "Global Communication in Blue" courtesy of iStockphoto.

This special edition published in cooperation with Pearson Learning Solutions.

Printed in the United States of America.

Please visit our web site at *www.pearsoncustom.com/custom-library/custom-phit*.

Attention bookstores: For permission to return any unsold stock, contact us at *pe-uscustomreturns@pearson.com*.

Pearson Learning Solutions, 501 Boylston Street, Suite 900, Boston, MA 02116
A Pearson Education Company
www.pearsoned.com

ISBN 10: 1-256-00362-X
ISBN 13: 978-1-256-00362-5

Attention Students

How to Find Your Student Data Files

Some projects in this book begin from a student data file that has already been started for you. The student data files can be accessed from the Custom PHIT Web site, www.pearsoncustom.com/customphit/datafiles

Because this is a custom book, student data file names are not always consistent with chapter numbers in your book's Table of Contents. Be sure that any student data file that you use exactly matches the file name cited in the chapter.

Files from www.pearsoncustom.com/customphit/datafiles

1 Decide where you want to store your student data files.

- If you are storing on the hard drive of your computer or on a network drive, you may want create a folder with an appropriate name on that drive.

- If you are storing on a removable storage device such as a USB flash drive, Zip® disk, or floppy disk, insert the device now.

2 From your Web browser, go to **www.pearsoncustom.com/customphit/datafiles**

3 Select the series and the book that is the source of the files that you need.

4 From the list of the available resources, point to the link for the files you need, and then click the active link.

5 In the displayed dialog box, click the command to **Save** and then click **OK**.

6 In the displayed dialog box, navigate to the location where you decided to store your files—either in a folder on your hard drive or network drive, or on your removable storage device.

7 Click **Save** to begin the downloading process. When complete you can close your browser.

8 As specifically directed in each project, navigate to the location where you have stored the student data files and then save and rename the file according to the instructions in the project.

Contents

why computers matter to you:

becoming computer literate

From Chapter 1 of *Technology in Action Complete*, Seventh Edition, Alan Evans, Kendall Martin, Mary Anne Poatsy. Copyright © 2011 by Pearson Education, Inc. Published by Pearson Prentice Hall. All rights reserved.

why computers matter to you:

becoming computer literate

After reading this chapter, you should be able to answer the following questions:

1. What does it mean to be "computer literate"?

2. How does being computer literate make you a savvy computer user and consumer?

3. How can becoming computer literate help you in a career?

4. How can becoming computer literate help you understand and take advantage of newly emerging careers?

5. How does becoming computer literate help you deal with the challenges associated with technology?

 Active Helpdesk

This chapter has no Active Helpdesks.

 Sound Bytes

- Questions to Ask Before You Buy a Computer
- The History of the Personal Computer

 Companion Website

The Companion Website includes a variety of additional materials to help you review and learn more about the topics in this chapter. Go to: *pearsonhighered.com/techinaction*

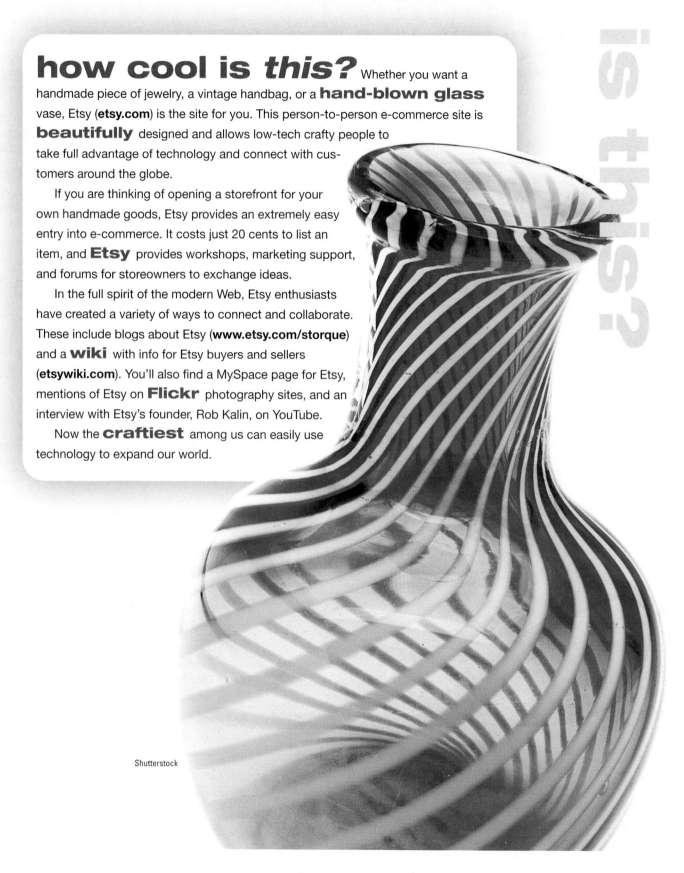

how cool is *this?*

Whether you want a handmade piece of jewelry, a vintage handbag, or a **hand-blown glass** vase, Etsy (**etsy.com**) is the site for you. This person-to-person e-commerce site is **beautifully** designed and allows low-tech crafty people to take full advantage of technology and connect with customers around the globe.

If you are thinking of opening a storefront for your own handmade goods, Etsy provides an extremely easy entry into e-commerce. It costs just 20 cents to list an item, and **Etsy** provides workshops, marketing support, and forums for storeowners to exchange ideas.

In the full spirit of the modern Web, Etsy enthusiasts have created a variety of ways to connect and collaborate. These include blogs about Etsy (**www.etsy.com/storque**) and a **wiki** with info for Etsy buyers and sellers (**etsywiki.com**). You'll also find a MySpace page for Etsy, mentions of Etsy on **Flickr** photography sites, and an interview with Etsy's founder, Rob Kalin, on YouTube.

Now the **craftiest** among us can easily use technology to expand our world.

Shutterstock

Why Should You Become Computer Literate?

It's safe to say that computers are nearly everywhere in our society. You find them in schools, cars, airports, shopping centers, toys, medical devices, and homes, and in many people's pockets. You interact with computers almost every day, sometimes without even knowing it. Whenever you buy something with a credit card, you interact with a computer. And, of course, most of us can't imagine our lives without e-mail. Even if you don't yet have a computer and don't feel comfortable using one, you still feel the impact of technology: Countless ads for computers, cell phones, digital cameras, and an assortment of Web sites surround us each day. We're constantly reminded of the ways in which computers, the Internet, and technology are integral parts of our lives.

So, just by being a member of our society, you already know quite a bit about computers. But why is it important to learn more about computers, becoming what is called *computer literate?* Being **computer literate** means being familiar enough with computers that you understand their capabilities and limitations (see Figure 1), and you know how to use them. Being computer literate means more than just knowing about the parts of your computer. The following are some other benefits:

- As a computer literate individual, you can use your computer more

wisely and be a more knowledgeable consumer.
- Computer literate employees are sought after in almost every vocation.
- Becoming computer literate will help you better understand and take advantage of future technologies.

In addition, understanding computers and their ethical, legal, and societal implications will make you a more active and aware participant in society.

Anyone can become computer literate—no matter what your degree of technical expertise. Being computer literate doesn't mean you need to know enough to program a computer or build one yourself. With a car for example, you should know enough about it to take care of it and to use it effectively, but that doesn't mean you have to know how to build one. You should try to achieve the same familiarity with computers.

Becoming a Savvy Computer User and Consumer

One of the benefits of becoming computer literate is being a savvy computer user and consumer. What does this mean? The following are just a few examples of what it may mean to you:

- **Avoiding hackers and viruses.** Do you know what hackers and viruses are? Both can threaten a computer's security.

Figure 1

Do you know what all the words in a computer ad mean? Can you tell whether the ad includes all the information necessary to make a purchasing decision?

Processor:	Intel i7-965 Extreme, Factory O'Cd to 3.73 GHz
RAM:	12 GB Tri Channel Corsair DDR3 (1066 MHz)
Video:	ATI Radeon HD 4870 X2 with 2048 MB
Audio:	Creative Labs X-Fi Elite Pro; HDA 7.1 surround channel sound
Network:	Native Gigabit Ethernet
Optical Drive:	Blu-ray burner
Storage Drive:	1 TB Serial ATA hard drive with support for up to 3 additional drives with RAID options
Ports:	10 USB 2 DVI and 1 S-Video 2 IEEE 1394 1 S/PDIF out
Physics Accelerator:	Ageia PhysX Card
Cooling:	Two-stage liquid cooling system
Portable Storage:	Bluetooth wireless 19-in 1-media hub with VoIP stereo headset
Operating System:	Windows 7 Ultimate 64-bit

NEW!

Being aware of how hackers and viruses operate and knowing the damage they can do to your computer can help you avoid falling prey to them.

- **Protecting your privacy.** You've probably heard of identity theft—you see and hear news stories all the time about people whose "identities" are stolen and whose credit ratings are ruined by "identity thieves." But do you know how to protect yourself from identity theft when you're online?

- **Understanding the real risks.** Part of being computer literate means being able to separate the real privacy and security risks from things you don't have to worry about. For example, do you know what a *cookie* is? Do you know whether it poses a privacy risk for you when you're on the Internet? What about a *firewall?* Do you know what one is? Do you really need one to protect your computer?

- **Using the Internet and the Web wisely.** Anyone who has ever searched the Web can attest that finding information and finding good information are two different things. People who are computer literate make the Internet a powerful tool and know how to find the information they want effectively. How familiar with the Web are you, and how effective are your searches?

- **Avoiding online annoyances.** If you have an e-mail account, chances are you've received electronic junk mail, or **spam** (see Figure 2). How can you avoid being overwhelmed by spam? What about *adware* and *spyware*—do you know what they are? Do you know what **software** (programs or instructions that tell the computer what to do) you should install on your computer to avoid online annoyances?

"Wow! I've got one from someone I know!"

Figure 2   www.CartoonStock.com

Understanding how to use e-mail effectively is just one example of what it means to be computer literate.

- **Being able to maintain, upgrade, and troubleshoot your computer.** Learning how to care for and maintain your computer and knowing how to diagnose and fix certain problems can save you a lot of time and hassle. Do you know how to upgrade your computer if you want more memory, for example? Do you know which software and computer settings can help you keep your computer in top shape?

- **Making good purchasing decisions.** Everywhere you go, you see ads like the one in Figure 1 for computers and other devices: notebooks (laptops), printers, monitors, cell phones, digital cameras, and GPS (global positioning system) devices. Do you know what all the words in the ads mean? What is *RAM?* What is a *CPU?* What are *MB, GB, GHz,* and *cache?* How fast do you need your computer to be, and how much memory should it have? Understanding computer buzzwords and keeping current with technology will help you better determine which computers and devices match your needs.

- **Knowing how to integrate the latest technology with your equipment.** Finally, becoming computer literate means knowing which technologies are on the horizon and how to integrate them into your home setup when possible (see Figure 3). Can you connect your notebook to a wireless network? What is *Bluetooth,* and does your computer "have" it? Can a device with a USB 2.0 connector be plugged into an old USB 1.0 port? (For that matter, what *is* a USB port?) How much memory should your cell phone have? Knowing the answers to these and other questions will help you make better purchasing decisions.

The benefits of being computer literate will help you in your career and in running your

Hewlett-Packard Company, TIMURA\Shutterstock, PRNewsFoto/D-Link Systems\AP Wide World Photos, Handout/MCT\Newscom, Apple/Splash News\Newscom, Belkin International, Inc., ExpressCard - PCMCIA, Sony Electronics Inc.

National Research Council concludes that by the year 2030 computers will displace humans in 60 percent of the current occupations. It will be more critical than ever for employees to have advanced skills. For more information about computers and the workplace, see the Technology in Focus section, "Careers in IT."

Becoming truly computer literate—understanding the capabilities and limitations of computers and what you can do with them—will undoubtedly help you perform your job more effectively. It also will make you more desirable as an employee and more likely to earn more and advance your career. So, let's begin with a look at how computer systems are used in a wide range of careers. Whether you become an employee in one of these industries or a user of its services, you will have a great advantage if you understand computer systems.

Figure 3

Can you identify all of these devices? Do you know how to get them all to work well together?

personal life. You'll be able to save money, time, and endless frustration by having a strong background in the basics of how computers and computer systems operate.

Being Prepared for Your Career

Computer careers are on the rise. Regardless of which profession you pursue, if computers are not already in use in that career, they most likely will be soon. **Information technology (IT)** is the set of techniques used in information handling and automatic retrieval of information. Information technology includes computers, telecommunications, and software deployment. IT careers are on the rise, and the seven fastest growing occupations are computer related. The changes technology is forcing on the workplace demand new skill levels from employees. A study from the

Computers in Today's Careers

We all are used to seeing computers at the checkout counter in stores, at the check-in area at an airport, and so on, but there are many ways that computers are being used that you probably weren't aware of. Before we begin looking at a computer's parts and how it operates, let's take a look at a whole range of industries and examine how computers are a part of getting work done. Whether you plan on a career in one of these fields or will just be a user of their products and services, your life will be affected by the use of computers in areas including

- Business
- Arts
- Education
- Law
- Agriculture
- Sciences

Retail: Working in a Data Mine

Businesses accumulate a lot of data, but how do they manage to make sense of all of it? How do they separate the anomalies from the trends? They use a technique known as **data mining**, the process of searching huge amounts of data with the hope of finding a pattern. For example, large retailers often study the data gathered from register terminals to determine which products are selling on a given day and in a specific location. This helps managers figure out how much merchandise they need to order to replace stock that is sold. Managers also use mined data to determine that for a certain product to sell well, they must lower its price—especially if they cut the price at one store and see sales increase, for example. Data mining thus allows retailers to respond to consumer buying patterns.

Did you ever wonder how Amazon or Netflix can suggest items that fit your taste? Or how such Web sites automatically display lists of items people bought after they ordered the camera you just picked out? Data mining can keep track of the purchases customers are making, along with their geographic data, past buying history, and lists of items they examined but did not purchase. This can be translated into extremely specific marketing, immediate and customized to your shopping experience. This is the motivation behind all of the "discount cards" that grocery stores and drugstores offer. In exchange for tracking your personal buying habits, they offer you some kind of special pricing. How much is your private information worth?

Business: Data on the Go

Did you know that United Parcel Service (UPS) handles more than 3.9 billion packages and letters a year? Just how does the "brown" company ensure that all its customers' packages get from points A to B without ending up forever at point C? The company uses a sophisticated database and a highly efficient package tracking system that follows the packages as they move around the world.

For UPS, package tracking starts when the sender drops off a package and the company creates a "smart label" for the package (see Figure 4a). In addition to the standard postal bar code and a bar code showing UPS customer numbers, this smart label contains something called a *MaxiCode*. The MaxiCode is a specially designed, scannable sticker that resembles an inkblot and contains all the important information about the package (class of service, destination, etc.). When the package is handled in processing centers, UPS workers scan the MaxiCode using portable handheld devices (see Figure 4b). These devices use **Bluetooth technology** (a type of wireless communication) to transmit the scanned data through radio waves to a terminal. This terminal then sends the data across a wireless network, where it is recorded in the UPS database.

To track package delivery, UPS carriers use delivery acquisition devices (see Figure 4c) that feature wireless networking capability, infrared scanners (to scan the smart labels and transmit the information back to the UPS database), and an electronic

a Editorial Image; LLC\Alamy Images **b** United Parcel Service **c** Mary Kate Denny\PhotoEdit Inc.

Figure 4

(a) Package tracking starts when the package is sent with the generation of a smart label, which includes the UPS MaxiCode. (b) Portable handheld devices allow UPS personnel to scan packages for accurate transfer of information. (c) Devices with built-in GPS systems are used to find directions to customers, capture customer signatures, and transfer information.

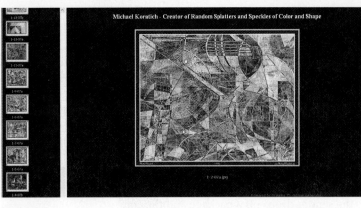

Figure 5

Artists like Michael Koratich display and sell their creations by using custom Web galleries such as this one (michaelkoratich.com).

pad to capture customer signatures. By capturing all of this data and making it available on its Internet database, UPS enables its customers to track their packages. UPS is also able to make informed decisions about staffing and deploying equipment (trucks, airplanes, etc.) based on the volume and type of packages in the system at any given time.

Arts: Shall We Dance?

Some art students think that because they're studying art, there is no reason for them to study computers. However, unless you plan to be a "starving artist," you'll probably want to sell your work. To do so, you'll need to advertise to the public and contact art galleries to convince them to purchase or display your work. Wouldn't it be helpful if you knew how to create a Web site like the one shown in Figure 5?

Using computers in the arts and entertainment fields goes far beyond using the Internet. Dance and music programs like the ones at the Atlanta Ballet and the Julliard School of Music use computers to create new performances for audiences. As shown in Figure 6, a live dancer can be wired with sensors that are connected to a computer that captures the dancer's movements. Based on the data it collects, the computer generates a virtual dancer on a screen. The

Peter Schaaf

Figure 6

A dancer is wired with light electronic sensors so that her movements can be digitized for computer analysis.

computer operator can easily manipulate this virtual dancer, as well as change the dancer's costume, with the click of a mouse. This allows artists to create new experiences for the audience.

Of course, not all artwork is created using traditional materials such as paint and canvas. Many artists today work exclusively with computers. Mastery of software programs such as Adobe Illustrator, Adobe Photoshop, and Adobe Flash is essential to creating digital art.

Other artists are pushing the envelope of creating art with computers even further. For example, through her series *External Measures,* artist Camille Utterback uses a computer to create a work of art that reacts to the presence—and the absence—of movement of the viewers in the gallery (see Figure 7). When no one is near the art piece, the image paints a small series of dots. However, as onlookers in the gallery move closer to the work, a camera mounted on the ceiling of the art gallery captures the onlookers' movements and dimensions. A computer with specialized software then uses this captured data to create smears of color and patterns of lines that reflect their movements. Because the image itself is created from the current and past movements and sizes of the gallery patrons, the work looks different each time it is viewed.

Video Game Development: A Long Way from Pac-Man

Revenues from video game sales in the United States are now larger than the movie industry's box office. Computer gaming topped $21 billion in 2008 and is projected to continue its rapid growth over the next decade. If you're a gamer, you know games must be creative to grab their audience. Large-scale games are impossible

Figure 7

Camille Utterback, "Untitled 5", from the "External Measures" series. Photo by Peter Harris, © 2007

Computers even figure directly into the development of artwork. Artist Camille Utterback develops interactive art that changes with the presence and movement of viewers in the gallery.

to create on your own—you must be part of a team. The good news is that because computer games are best developed for a local market by people native to that market, game development will most likely stay in the United States instead of being **offshored** (sent to other countries), as many other types of programming jobs have been.

You'll need an in-depth knowledge of computers to pursue a career in game programming or as a gaming artist. Mastering software animation tools, such as 3ds Max, will enable you to create compelling new worlds and new characters like those in the story-driven adventure game Metal Gear Solid 4 (see Figure 8).

Education: Teaching and Learning

Today's teachers need to be at least as computer savvy as their students. Computers are part of most schools, even preschools. In fact, at many colleges, students are required to have their own computers. Courses are designed around course management software such as Blackboard or Moodle so that students can communicate outside of class, take quizzes online, and find their class materials easily. Teachers must therefore have a working knowledge of computers to integrate computer technology into the classroom effectively.

The Internet has obvious advantages in the classroom as a research tool for students, and effective use of the Internet allows teachers to expose students to places students otherwise could not access. There are simulations and instructional software on the Web that are incredible learning

tools. Teachers can employ these to give students a taste of running a global business (see Figure 9) or provide the experience of dissecting a virtual human cadaver.

Many museums have virtual tours on their Web sites that allow students to examine objects in the museum collections. Often, these virtual tours include three-dimensional photos that can be viewed from all angles. So, even if you teach in Topeka, Kansas, you can take your students on a virtual tour of the Smithsonian Institution in Washington, D.C.

But what about when you want to take your students to visit museums in person? Today, technology is often used to enhance visitors' experiences at museums. New York's Museum of Modern Art, for example, offers PDA tours that provide visitors with additional information about the art they're viewing. By using a **personal digital**

Figure 8

Konami Corporation of America

Using powerful software, game developers can create complex worlds and characters to satisfy even the most demanding gamer.

Figure 9

Internet applications have become sophisticated learning resources. IndustryMasters.com allows students to compete online for domination of a global market while giving instructors the chance to introduce many business concepts.

assistant (PDA), a small device that enables users to carry digital information, you can listen to music that the artist listened to when he or she was creating a particular work or look at other works that reflect similar techniques or themes to those of the one you're viewing (see Figure 10). While looking at works by more modern artists, you can watch interviews with the artist explaining his or her motivation for the work. You can even use the PDA to contact other members of your group and direct them to specific works you want them to see. Knowing how

to use a PDA effectively may help make a museum tour even more memorable.

Computers in the classroom will become more prevalent as prices continue to fall and parents demand that their children be taught the computer skills they will need to be successful in the workplace. Therefore, as an educator, being computer literate will help you integrate computers constructively into lesson plans for your students and use technology to interact with them.

Law Enforcement: Put Down that Mouse—You're Under Arrest!

Today, wearing out shoe leather to solve crimes is far from the only method available to investigators trying to catch criminals. Computers are being used in police cars and crime labs to solve an increasing number of crimes. For example, facial reconstruction systems like the one shown in Figure 11 can turn a skull into a finished digital image of a face, allowing investigators to proceed far more quickly with identification.

One technique used by modern detectives to solve crimes employs computers to search the vast number of databases on the Internet. Proprietary law enforcement databases such as the National Center for the Analysis of Violent Crime database enable detectives to analyze a wealth of

Moeskau Photography

Figure 10

Multimedia tours using PDAs and wireless technology are commonplace in museums and galleries.

information about similarities between crimes, trying to detect patterns that may reveal serial crimes. Where the law permits, detectives can also use their knowledge of wireless networking to intercept and read a criminal suspect's e-mail messages and chat sessions when he or she is online, all from the comfort of a car parked outside the suspect's home.

Polhemus/Fast Scan

As detective work goes more high tech, so, too, does crime. To fight modern crime, a law enforcement specialty called **computer forensics** is growing. This specialty employs computer systems and techniques to gather potential legal evidence. The ability to recover and read deleted or damaged files from a criminal's computer is already providing evidence for trials.

© Digital Art/CORBIS All Rights Reserved

Figure 11

(a) The FastScan wand lets forensics teams quickly grab three-dimensional images of skulls. (b) Tissue rendering programs then add layers of muscles, fat, and skin to create faces that can be used to identify victims.

Every day, businesses across the world use complicated forecasting models to make predictions about their sales and inventory levels. Thanks to recent technological advancements, law enforcement officials might soon have access to specialized software that can forecast criminal activity, helping police officers take preventive measures to stop crime.

Don't believe it? Criminologists Jacqueline Cohen and Wilpen Gorr and computer scientist Andreas Olligschlaeger received funding from the U.S. Department of Justice to study police reports from Rochester, New York, and Pittsburgh, Pennsylvania. After entering data about criminal offenses, precinct staffing, and patrol routes, the researchers used trend spotting programs to analyze the data.

As a result, the program was able to predict criminal activity before it happened an astounding 80 percent of the time. The key to the analysis was identifying and studying leading indicators that trigger crime sprees. Whereas consumer researchers may look at consumer spending patterns and levels of disposable income, criminologists study soft crime statistics such as disorderly conduct and trespassing. Increases in these types of crimes indicate that serious crimes may soon be on the rise. When a trend is identified, patrols in the area can be stepped up to try to head off crimes before they occur. Building, analyzing, and fine-tuning such models will keep law enforcement officials busy for years.

Computers are also used in training law enforcement officers to be more effective. For example, the Federal Bureau of Investigation (FBI) and the Transportation Security Administration (TSA) use computer-based training to teach officers to recognize lies and evasive behavior. Dr. Paul Ekman has spent a career studying *microexpressions*, brief (1/25th of a second) flashes of emotion. When a person is being deceptive, microexpressions, which cannot be controlled, reveal true emotions in their body language. The Microexpression Training Tool software system (**paulekman.com**), a program developed by Dr. Ekman's company, trains users to recognize emotions like fear, disgust, contempt, and anger in these flashes of microexpressions (see Figure 12). You can try the online demo to see if you are a "natural," one of the rare people who can recognize and read emotion with no training.

Figure 12

The Microexpression Training Tool software trains law enforcement officials to distinguish true emotion from deception.

Paul Ekman Group, LLC.

You're probably already using your computer in many different ways to fit your lifestyle. Perhaps you're ripping your CD collection to MP3 files so that you can transfer them from your computer to your iPod. Maybe you're burning a CD of all your favorite songs for a party you're having. But wouldn't it be great if you could manage the music for your party straight from your computer, using the iTunes software? And what about that video of your friend's birthday party you shot last week? You've already imported it to your computer, edited it, and added a music track. But when your friends come over for the party this weekend, wouldn't it be fun to be able to show them the video on the TV in the living room instead of having them crowd around your computer monitor?

When in the future will you be able to do all this? Right now if you set up a digital home. Setting up a **digital home** means having an appropri-ate computer and digital devices that are all connected to a home network. Let's discuss the key components you need to get started with a digital living room, some of which are shown in Figure 13.

1. **A media computer:** A computer is the nerve center of any digital home, allowing you to interface with all the different digital devices you have connected to the network. For a Windows-based computer (see Figure 14), you should opt for a computer running the current version of Microsoft Windows 7 or Windows Vista as its operating system. A typical media PC includes the following components:

   a. **A TV tuner:** A TV tuner allows your computer to receive television channels from a cable connection and display them on your computer monitor. In fact, you can install more than one TV

Figure 13

You can create a digital living room with only a few devices.

Legal System: Welcome to the Virtual Courtroom

In courtrooms today, videos of crimes in progress (often captured by cameras at convenience stores or gas stations) are sometimes shown to juries to help them understand how crimes unfolded. But what happens if no surveillance camera recorded a crime? Paper diagrams, models, and still photos of a crime scene used to be the only choice for attorneys seeking to illustrate their cases. Now there is a much more exciting and lively alternative: computer forensics animations.

Computer forensics animations are extremely detailed and often lifelike re-creations that computers generate based on forensic evidence, depositions of witnesses, and the opinions of experts. Using sophisticated animation programs, similar to the ones used to create movies such *Up* and

Why Computers Matter to You: Becoming Computer Literate

Figure 14
Media Center in Microsoft Windows 7 allows you to manage all your media entertainment from your computer.

tuner on your computer, allowing you to receive multiple television channels at the same time.

b. **A radio tuner:** A radio tuner allows you to tune into Internet radio stations and record their broadcasts as digital files on your computer.

c. **Media software:** In addition to a computer and tuners, you'll also need software. Windows 7 includes software called Media Center, which functions as a digital video recorder (DVR), a video player, and a music player. You can use Media Center to view and organize the digital audio and video files on your computer. In combination with a TV tuner, digital video recorder software that is included as part of Windows Media Center allows you to turn your computer into a DVR similar to TiVo. Digital video recorders record TV programs like VCRs do, but they use your computer's hard drive to store the video. If you have multiple TV tuners installed in your computer, you can record several programs onto your computer's hard drive at the same time.

d. **Blu-ray, DVD, and CD players and recorders:** To make it easy to transfer your audio or video files from one device to another, high-definition recorders and DVD and CD players and recorders allow you to record files onto high-definition media (such as Blu-ray discs) or onto standard-resolution DVDs and CDs instead of your hard drive.

e. **A network adapter:** A network adapter is a special device that is installed in your computer and allows it to communicate with other devices on a network. For digital devices to communicate with each other, they need to be connected to a network.

2. **A network:** Unless you're going to view digital and audio files only on your computer, you will need a network to transfer files easily to other devices (such as televisions) in your home. A wireless network has an advantage over a wired network because it is easier to relocate devices on a wireless network. For example, suppose you rearrange your living room and need to move your TV to the opposite end of the room. If your TV was connected to a wired network, you might have to run a new cable or relocate the existing one. With a wireless network, you'd just move the TV and be done with it.

3. **A digital television:** Newer plasma and organic light emitting diode (OLED) televisions (see Figure 13) or high-definition TVs (HDTVs) are an important part of any digital home because they are the best way to show off all your digital entertainment (digital photos and so on). Note that even if you don't have a plasma or OLED television, as long as you bought your TV within the last five years or so, you can probably use it to display digital content. However, televisions are not usually ready to be integrated into a network right out of the box. For this, you need a digital media adapter.

4. **A digital media adapter:** A digital media adapter (see Figure 13) allows you to transfer media such as videos, digital photos, or MP3s from your computer to your other media devices, such as your plasma TV. Digital media adapters are also known as *media center extenders*. A digital media adapter allows you to integrate your TV into your home network. This device connects to your computer network (either wired or wirelessly) and then to your TV through specially designed audiovisual connectors.

5. **A universal remote:** A universal remote is a single remote control that works with any infrared controlled device (such as your computer, digital media adapters, amplifiers, or receivers) and allows you to access media such as MP3 files no matter where in the house it is stored. Universal remotes such as the Pronto from Philips (see Figure 13) come with software that allows you to program your own custom interface for the remote. You can even program macros that perform multiple commands with the press of a button.

With these devices installed, you can get the maximum benefit from your computer and all your digital entertainment devices. When you're in your living room, you can play digital music files stored on your computer (in the den) for the party you're throwing. You can also display the video of your friend's birthday party (downloaded to your computer) on the TV for your friends to see. And when you're in your room, you can watch the latest episode of *CSI*, which you recorded on your computer's hard drive, while your sister is listening to MP3 files stored on your computer on the TV in the living room.

Bolt, forensic animators can depict one side's version of how events occurred, allowing the jury to watch it unfold.

Of course, being able to display sophisticated multimedia, televise trials, or record witness testimony for archiving requires modern courtrooms to be wired. Those such as Florida's Ninth Judicial Circuit Court (see Figure 15) are on the cutting edge, complete with robot-controlled video cameras that pivot to record whoever is speaking on the microphone at the time. Video images can be streamed directly to a Web site for immediate viewing or stored for archival purposes. Meanwhile, the judge uses a touch-screen terminal to control the action in the courtroom, including turning on real-time closed captioning by linking in the court reporter's transcription terminal. Lawyers have access to wireless touch-screen handheld devices that allow them to access and display evidence they have stored on the

Computers in Today's Careers

13

Touch screens

Video cameras

Digital recording devices

Universal remote with touch screen

Figure 15

Courtrooms such as Florida's Ninth Judicial Circuit Court are on the cutting edge.

Ninth Judicial Circuit Court of Florida

courtroom's multimedia systems. Attorneys can also connect their own notebook computers to the system, and audio recordings of all proceedings are captured and available for immediate playback.

Outside the courtroom, lawyers and other legal professionals use vast online legal libraries and databases, such as LexisNexis, to research cases and prepare for court.

Agriculture: High-Tech Down on the Farm

You might think that ranching and farming are low-tech operations that have little use for computers and software. The growing season can't be changed by any computer program! Even so, new technologies are changing life on farms and ranches in many ways.

Ranchers face many challenges in modern meat production. For example, they must watch for and prevent diseases such as hoof and mouth, mad cow, and *E. coli* outbreaks. The meat you purchase can be introduced to these dangers at many different places in the processing chain, from the ranch to the supermarket.

Fortunately, outbreaks can be managed and minimized with the use of **radio frequency identification tags (RFID tags)**. These RFID tags are small versions of the roadway electronic toll systems used in many states to collect tolls automatically as you pass through the toll station. Each tag looks like a tiny button and is attached to a cow's ear. It contains a microchip that holds a unique sequence of numbers used to identify that animal. When the cow walks past a panel reader, its location is automatically recorded and tracked in a database.

If a cow is identified as having a disease, all of its recorded movements can be checked in the database that stores the RFID information. It is then simple to identify exactly which food lots that and other animals ate at.

Using RFID tags, potential crises can be averted or at least better controlled.

In cranberry bogs, computer technology is being used in some interesting ways. For example, cranberry crops easily can be destroyed by frost. In the past, growers had to race to protect the bogs of berries on cold nights by turning on water pumps to surround the berries with water and keep them from freezing. Today, growers use a Web-based system that can automatically control the pumps. It analyzes information about the time, the temperature measured near the berries, watering schedules, rainfall, and wind conditions, and then automatically turns the pumps around the bog fields on and off as needed.

Automotive Technology: Sensors and CPUs

An automotive technician is required to have knowledge of a range of tools—impact hammers, wrenches, pneumatic tools, lathes, and welding and flame cutting equipment. Individuals considering a career in automotive repair today require a sophisticated level of computer literacy as well (see Figure 16). Environmental trends and governmental regulation are driving auto manufacturers to develop vehicles that produce lower emissions as the push for more efficient cars and higher gas mileage continues.

These changes have increased the number of sensors and computer CPU (central processing unit) systems needed in a typical vehicle. The fuel injection and engine management systems possible today go far beyond what a simple carburetor can do. Several sensors measure everything from air pressure to air temperature, engine temperature, and throttle position, for example. The data from these sensors is then used to compute the precise amount of fuel to spray into the cylinders, resulting in less fuel waste and reduced pollution. The braking, transmission, and steering systems also are primarily controlled by computers and electronic components.

As consumers come to expect digital music systems, airbags, voice-controlled phones, and GPS navigation screens in their cars, the number of computer subsystems will continue to grow. In addition to these driver-friendly features,

Figure 16

These automotive technicians for BMW Sauber gather around their car before the start of the Malaysian Grand Prix. They need computer skills to run all of the electronic checks of automotive subsystems.

the computers in today's cars even alert drivers when it's time to take the car in for maintenance or repair.

As a result, automotive technicians must be able to update documentation through the Internet, use computer databases to learn about common problems and solutions, and use computer systems to interface with and run diagnostics on all the different automotive computer systems. The days of working on a car in the driveway with some screwdrivers and a socket wrench are fading quickly.

Medicine: Fact or Fiction?

In some movies set in the distant future, humans interface with computers just by thinking and looking at a screen or monitor. Until recently, such scenes took place only in movies. But since 2006, companies such as Cyberkinetics have been working to understand the human neural interface system. In testing the company's software, known as BrainGate, a man suffering from amyotrophic lateral sclerosis (ALS, which is also known as Lou Gehrig's disease), who no longer had any control of muscle movement, was able to control the movement of a robotic arm.

The BrainGate software translates his thoughts into commands to the robotic limb. The patient has had a tiny array of microelectrodes implanted in his brain

Figure 17

(a) The BrainGate Neural Interface is implanted in the patient's brain. (b) A signal converter recognizes patterns and then translates them into commands to a robotic arm.

(see Figure 17a). The computer equipment receiving data from his neural activity (see Figure 17b) identifies the impulses that the brain associates with physical movement (of his arm, for example) and then translates the instructions into commands to the robot. Patient Stephen Heywood explained, "After being paralyzed for so long, it is almost impossible to describe the magical feeling of imagining a motion and having it occur."

In addition to being an integral part of many medical research projects, computers are helping doctors and nurses learn their trades. Training for physicians and nurses

Photo courtesy of METI © METI

Figure 18

Patient simulators allow health care students to practice medical procedures without risk of injury or death to real patients.

can be difficult at the best of times. Often, the best way for medical students to learn is to experience a real emergency situation. The problem is that students are then confined to watching as the emergency unfolds and trained personnel care for patients. Students rarely get to train in real-life situations; when they do, a certain level of risk is involved.

Medical students now have access to better training opportunities thanks to a computer technology called a **patient simulator** (see Figure 18). Patient simulators are life-sized, computer-controlled mannequins that can speak, breathe, and blink (their eyes respond to external stimuli). They have a pulse and a heartbeat, and they respond just like humans to procedures such as the administration of intravenous drugs.

Medical students can train on patient simulators and experience firsthand how a human would react to their treatments. The best thing about these "patients" is that if they "die," students can restart the computer simulation and try again. Even the U.S. military is using patient simulators to train medics to respond to terrorist attacks that employ chemical and biological agents.

Even more exciting than patient simulators is the work being done on modeling complete human biological systems. The Physiome Project began as the brainchild of the Bioengineering Institute in Auckland, New Zealand. It now is a global **public domain** effort (not covered by copyright) in which bioengineers are creating realistic computer simulations of all systems and features of the human anatomy. (An example is shown in Figure 19.)

Although the Physiome Project's current system models a theoretical human's lungs, researchers hope to one day use computers to simulate a specific person's anatomical systems. With such a system, imaging scans (CTs, MRIs, etc.) of your body and a sample of your DNA would be fed into a computer, which would create an exact computer model of your body. This would allow doctors to experiment with different therapies to see how you would react to specific treatments. A great deal of work is still to be done before this refinement becomes a reality, and computer-literate medical professionals will be needed to make it happen.

Figure 19

The Physiome Project has an ambitious goal of creating a complete digital model of a human being. This goal will require the joint efforts of collaborators from all over the world.

Computational Bioengineering Laboratory

Surgeons are even using computer-guided robots to perform surgery. Surgeons are often limited by their manual dexterity and can have trouble making small, precise incisions. Robots can help. Robotic surgery devices can exercise much finer control when making delicate incisions than can a human guiding a scalpel. To use the robots, doctors look into a surgery control device where they manipulate controls that move robotic devices hovering over the patient (see Figure 20). One robot control arm contains a slender imaging rod that allows the doctor to see inside the patient when the rod is inserted into the patient. Doctors can now perform a coronary bypass by making two small incisions in the patient and inserting the imaging rod in one incision and another robotic device with a scalpel into the other. The ability to make small incisions instead of the large ones required by conventional surgery means less trauma and blood loss

© 2008 Intuitive Surgical, Inc.

Figure 20

(a) A doctor manipulates controls that move the robotic instrument tips inside the patient. (b) This shows what surgeons might see as they operate on the patient.

for the patient. Theoretically, surgeons do not even have to be in the same room as the patient. They could be thousands of miles away, controlling the movements of the robotic devices from a control station.

Medicine: The Chip Within

When you mention implanting technology into the human body, some people conjure up images of the Terminator, a futuristic cybernetic life form from the movie of the same name that looks human but is mostly machine. The goal of modern biomedical chip research is to provide technological solutions to physical problems and to provide a means for positively identifying individuals. Figure 21 shows a nerve cell on a silicon chip. The cell was cultured on the chip until it formed a network with nearby cells. The chip contains a transistor that stimulates the cell above it, which in turn passes the signal to neighboring neurons.

One potential application of biomedical chip implants is to provide sight to the blind. Macular degeneration and retinitis pigmentosa are two diseases that account for the majority of blindness in developing nations. Both diseases result in damage to the photoreceptors contained in the retina of the eye. (Photoreceptors convert light energy into electrical energy that is transmitted to the brain, allowing us to see.) Researchers are experimenting with chips containing microscopic solar cells that are implanted in the damaged retina of a patient. The idea is to have the chip take over for the damaged photoreceptors and transmit electrical images to the brain. Although these chips have been tested in patients, they have not yet restored anyone's sight. But biomedical chips such as these exemplify the types of medical devices you may "see" in the future.

One type of chip is already being implanted in humans as a means of verifying a person's identity. Called the VeriChip, this "personal ID chip" is about the size of a grain of rice and is implanted under the skin. When exposed to radio waves from a scanning device, the chip emits a signal that transmits its unique serial number to the scanner. The scanner then connects to a database that contains the name, address, and medical conditions of the person in whom the chip has been implanted.

Hitachi has a similar device, called the μ-chip (mu-chip), which is smaller than the period at the end of this sentence (see Figure 22). The μ-chip could be easily attached to, or ingested by, a person without his or her knowledge.

The creators of the VeriChip envision it speeding up airport security and being used together with other devices (such as electronic ID cards) to provide tamperproof security measures. If someone stole your credit card, that person couldn't use it if a salesclerk had to verify your identity by scanning a chip in your arm before authorizing a transaction.

Currently, nonimplant versions of identity chips are used in hospitals. When chips are attached with bands to newborn infants, the hospital staff can monitor the location of any baby instantly. Elevators and doors are designed to allow only certain people to enter with a specific baby, even if the hospital power is interrupted. Although the use of these tags is becoming more

Figure 21 Courtesy of Dr. Peter Fromherz/Max Planck Insitute of Biochemistry

Researchers are experimenting with implantable chips such as this one to repair nerve damage and restore movement or sensation to parts of the body.

Figure 22

Reuters/Eriko Sugita\Landov Media

No bigger than the period at the end of this sentence, the Hitachi μ-chip can hold digital information, which can then be read when it passes a detector.

commonplace, it remains to be seen whether the general public will decide that the advantages of having personal identity and medical data quickly available justifies having chips implanted into their bodies.

Science: Simulating Reality

Thanks to a partnership between the National Severe Storms Lab and the National Center for Supercomputing Applications,

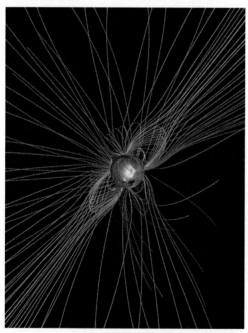

Figure 23

Courtesy of Ilia Iankov Roussev, Ph.D.

A simulation from the University of Michigan shows the structure of the magnetic fields around the sun and how they change in time.

tornado forecasting may be getting more accurate. Scientists have been able to create a model so detailed that it takes nine days for a supercomputer to generate it, even though the computer is executing four trillion operations each second. Simulations also can model the structure of solar magnetic flares, which can interfere with broadcasts on Earth (see Figure 23). By studying the data produced by these simulations, forecasters hope to improve their predictions about weather phenomena.

Other technological applications in the sciences are being used on some of the oldest sites on Earth. The ancient site of Pompeii has been under the intense scrutiny of tourists and archaeologists for decades. Sadly, all the foot traffic and exposure to the elements is eroding portions of the ruins. Today scientists are using three-dimensional scanners and imaging software to capture a detailed record of the current condition of the ruins (see Figure 24). The virtual re-creation of the ruins is so lifelike that archaeologists can study the ruins on screen instead of at the actual site. Using the scans as well as satellite imagery, aerial photography, and other data, scientists will eventually be able to re-create missing portions of the ruins in a virtual model. And scientists won't stop at Pompeii. This method will soon be used to make records of other decaying sites.

Media from the Discovery Channel's Pompeii: The Last Day, courtesy of Crew Creative, Ltd.

Figure 24

A digital re-creation of the ruins of Pompeii allows archaeologists to study the ruins without even being there, as well as re-create Pompeii as it looked before the devastation.

Sports Science: Compute Your Way to a Better Game

Want to be a world-class swimmer or baseball player? Getting an Olympic-caliber coach and training for hours every day are no longer enough. To get that competitive edge, you really need to use a computer.

That's right, computers are now being used to help athletes analyze their performance and improve their game. How does this work? First, video recordings are made of the athlete in action. The video is then transferred into special motion analysis software on a computer. This software measures the exact angles of the athlete's body parts as they progress through ranges of motion, such as the angle of a baseball player's left arm relative to his body as he swings the bat. Minor adjustments can be made on the computer regarding positioning of body parts and the force used in performing various movements. This helps baseball players, for example, enhance their performance by determining what adjustments they should make to hit the ball harder and farther.

The U.S. Olympic Training Center in Colorado makes extensive use of computers in training athletes such as swimmers. The major objective in training swimmers to swim faster is to reduce drag from the water and minimize turbulence, which also can slow down a swimmer. Software has been developed that simulates the way water flows around the parts of a swimmer's body when in motion. Coaches can use the software to experiment with small changes in the position of a swimmer's arms or legs and determine whether turbulence and drag are reduced. The coaches can then train the swimmers to use the new techniques to improve their strokes and speed.

Aren't planning on competing in the next Olympics or playing in the major leagues? How about improving your weekend golf game? Employees in golf shops are now using sophisticated motion-capture equipment to improve golfers' swings. To have your golf swing analyzed, golf shop personnel hook you up into shoulder, leg, and hip harnesses containing motion sensors. As you swing away at a variety of shots (drives, chips, and so on), computers capture information about the motion of your swing, comparing it to a database of the ideal positions of pro golfers (see Figure 25). Trainers then suggest adjustments you can make so that your

Figure 25

(a) High Definition Golf does a complete analysis on your swing and projects the flight path the ball would have taken. (b) It can also simulate many popular golf courses, like Pebble Beach.

Interactive Sports Technologies

Why Computers Matter to You: Becoming Computer Literate

swing more closely emulates that of successful golfers. Even weekend warriors can benefit from high-tech analysis.

Athletic equipment is also getting a technology boost. Even in a sport such as soccer, where not much equipment is involved, technology is making an impact. Adidas is developing a new soccer ball that contains an integrated circuit chip. When the company's Smartball crosses the goal line, it sends a radio signal to the referee's watch. The ball is not yet approved for World Cup play, but you can expect to see Smartballs showing up in professional soccer matches soon.

Nanotechnology: Careers Yet to Come

Have you ever heard of nanoscience? Developments in computing based on the principles of nanoscience are being touted as the next big wave in computing. Ironically, this realm of science focuses on incredibly small objects. **Nanoscience** involves the study of molecules and structures (called *nanostructures*) that range in size from 1 to 100 nanometers. It will provide numerous career paths and high-tech positions over the next several decades.

The prefix *nano* stands for one billionth. Therefore, a nanometer is one billionth of a meter. To put this in perspective, a human hair is approximately fifty thousand nanometers wide. Put side by side, 10 hydrogen atoms (the simplest atom) would measure approximately one nanometer. Anything smaller than a nanometer is just a stray atom or particle floating around in space. Therefore, nanostructures represent the smallest human-made structures that can be built.

Nanotechnology is the science of using nanostructures to build devices on an extremely small scale. Right now, nanoscience is limited to improving existing products, such as enhancing fibers used in clothing with coatings so that they repel stains, resist odors, or stop wrinkles. However, someday scientists hope to use nanostructures to build computing devices that will be too small to be seen by the naked eye. Nanowires (see Figure 26), which are extremely small conductors, could be used to create extremely small pathways in computer chips. Developments

Figure 26
Nanowires hold promise for use in constructing even smaller computing devices.

Mazur Group

such as this could lead to computers the size of a pencil eraser that will be far more powerful than today's desktop computers.

If you've ever watched *Star Trek*, then you know that *nanoprobes* (tiny machines that can be injected into the bloodstream) have already been envisioned. Nanotechnology researchers are now beginning to use carbon nanotubes to create devices that deliver medicine and information. We are still a long way from developing nanoscale machines, and some scientists don't think this will ever be possible. However, researchers are investigating the use of nanostructures to deliver precise doses of drugs on a

NASA Wants You . . . to Learn

As you read this chapter, hundreds of satellites are orbiting the globe and taking wonderfully detailed pictures of Earth. Until recently, these photos weren't available to the general public. However, thanks to NASA (and U.S. taxpayer dollars) and some savvy software developers, an application called World Wind is now making some 10 trillion bytes of imagery available to you. Do you need a picture of Mount Fuji for your science project or an aerial picture of your house for your PowerPoint presentation? Just download the software from learn.arc.nasa.gov, and you're ready to go. You'll find several terrific learning applications here as well. "Virtual Lab" lets you pretend you have your own scanning electron microscope, and "What's the Difference" takes you on a tour of the planets, complete with information about their composition and atmosphere and fly-throughs. With a few clicks, you can have interactive learning resources that open the world to you.

molecule-by-molecule basis within the human bloodstream. Universities and government laboratories are investing billions of dollars in nanotechnology research every year. If you have the background and interest in computing technology and science, this is the time to pursue an education in nanoscience.

Psychology: You Should Smile. . . Now

Science fiction shows and movies such as *Star Wars* have always been populated with robots that emulate humans, seemingly effortlessly. So, when will we have C-3PO, R2-D2, or the Terminator laughing at our jokes or bringing us our favorite snack when they recognize we're sad? It is a question that pushes us to explore the nature of being human and the nature of machines.

Psychologists and computer scientists are jointly conducting research to develop computer systems that respond to human affect and emotional expression, and to enable computer systems to develop social and emotional skills. **Affective computing** is computing that relates to emotion or deliberately tries to influence emotion. Most computers with which you are familiar can perform calculations and the tasks for which they are programmed much faster than humans can, but they fail miserably in telling a good joke or modifying their behavior based on your frustration. This wide gap in the computing abilities of computers versus their emotional abilities is the target of research in affective computing.

One project to emerge is the emotional social prosthesis (ESP) device, developed by a group at the Massachusetts Institute of Technology (MIT) Media Lab. The ESP system is

Figure 27

AP Wide World Photos

Robots with articulated joints that mimic human limbs can balance, stand, walk and even hug.

targeted at helping people who have autism. Autistic individuals can have extremely high intelligence but do not easily sense nonverbal cues such as facial expressions and tone of voice. ESP is a wearable system that isolates the movements and facial expressions of people, interprets what their mood and intention probably are, and communicates this information back to the user.

Another project at the Media Lab will help people who have difficulty maintaining focus on a specific task. This project centers on the creation of computer systems that can analyze a person's movements, watch their use of the mouse, and interpret the pressure patterns on the chair in which the person is seated. That data is then used to determine the individual's level of attention. The computer could then interrupt an individual who is beginning to lose concentration and refocus him or her on a certain task.

While engineers work to create computers that can understand us emotionally, psychologists and computer scientists are also working to evolve systems toward a more human appearance (see Figure 27). Teams at the University of Michigan, Ohio State University, and the French Institute of Computer Science Research are working on robots that move in a more human fashion. Their biped (two-legged) robot, named Rabbit, is able to walk, run, and climb stairs. It may lead to industrial robots that can tackle new tasks for us.

SOUND BYTE

The History of the Personal Computer

In this Sound Byte, you will explore the history of the personal computer, including the events that led to the development of today's computers and the people who made them possible.

Understanding the Challenges Facing a Digital Society

Part of becoming computer literate is being able to understand and form knowledgeable opinions on the challenges that face a digital society. Although computers offer us a world of opportunities, they also pose ethical, legal, and moral challenges and questions. For example, how do you feel about the following?

Figure 28

SparkFun Electronics

With cameras becoming smaller, you could unknowingly be under surveillance at any time. Should the government be allowed to install such cameras or should your privacy be respected?

- Since the tragic events of September 11, 2001, various nationwide surveillance programs have been proposed. Some programs include installing surveillance cameras in public places that could be considered attractive areas in which to stage terrorist activities. These cameras would be monitored via the Internet, possibly by volunteers. Should the government be allowed to monitor your activities in public places, à la George Orwell's famous book *1984,* to help keep the country secure?

- Advances in surveillance device technology (see Figure 28) are allowing these devices to become smaller and less noticeable. In certain jurisdictions, courts have upheld the rights of employers to install surveillance devices in the workplace (sometimes without needing to notify employees) to cut down on theft and prevent industrial espionage. Do you know if your employer is watching you? Do you think your employer should have this right?

- Many employees don't know that employers have the right to monitor e-mail and network traffic on the systems they use at work, because those systems are provided at the employer's expense for the sole purpose of allowing employees to do their jobs. Have you visited Web sites that you don't want your employer to know about (such as employment sites as part of a new job search)? Have you sent personal e-mail through your company e-mail system? Does your employer know about these activities? Should employers have the right to know?

These are just a few examples of the kind of questions active participants in today's digital society need to be able to think about, discuss, and, at times, take action on. Being computer literate enables you to form educated opinions on these issues and to take stands based on accurate information rather than media hype and misinformation. Here are a few other questions that you, as a member of our digital society, may be expected to think about and discuss:

- What privacy risks do biomedical chips such as the VeriChip pose? Do the privacy risks of such chips outweigh the potential benefits?
- Should companies be allowed to collect personal data from visitors to their Web sites without their permission?
- Should spam be illegal? If so, what penalties should be levied on people who send spam?
- Is it ethical to download music off the Web without paying for it (see Figure 29)? What about copying a friend's software onto your computer?
- What are the risks involved in humans attempting to create computers that can learn and become more human?
- Should we rely solely on computers to provide security for sensitive areas such as nuclear power plants?

As a computer user, you must consider these and other questions to define the boundaries of the digital society in which you live.

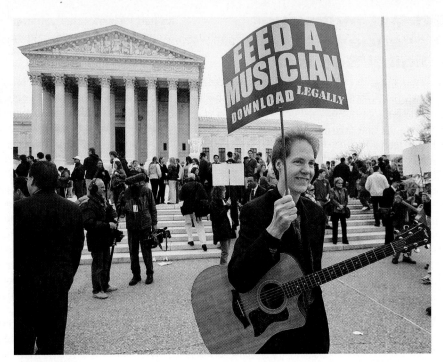

Figure 29

Does downloading music without paying for it hurt anyone? Or is it merely a cost absorbed by huge record companies? How will your choices create the music market you will experience in the future?

Gerald Herbert\AP Wide World Photos

Ethics: Knowledge Is Power—Bridging the Digital Divide

What would your life be like if you had never touched a computer because you simply couldn't afford one? What if there were no computers in your town? If you're like most people in the United States, access to computers is a given. But for many people, access to the opportunities and knowledge computers and the Internet offer is impossible. The discrepancy between the "haves" and "have-nots" with regard to computer technology is commonly referred to as the **digital divide**.

This discrepancy is a growing problem. People with access to computers and the Internet (that is, those who can afford them) are poised to take advantage of the many new developments technology offers, whereas poorer individuals, communities, and school systems that can't afford computer systems and Internet access are being left behind.

For example, in the United States, more teachers are using the Internet to communicate with parents than ever before. E-mail updates on student progress, Web sites with homework postings that allow parents to track assignments, and even online parent–teacher conferences are becoming popular. Unwired parents and students are left out of the loop. In the United States, children who do not have access to the Internet and computers won't be prepared for future employment, contributing to the continuing cycle of poverty.

But the digital divide isn't always caused by low income. Terrain can be a factor that inhibits connectivity (see Figure 30). In Nepal's mountainous terrain, for example, even though a village might only be a few miles away "as the crow flies," it might take two days to hike there because of the lack of roads. Volunteers, funded by a generous donor, have installed 12 outdoor access points complete with directional antennas to connect a series of villages to the Internet via a wireless network. The last access point in the connectivity chain connects to an Internet service provider 22 miles away. The villagers are now able to hold meetings, attend school classes, and access the Internet without trekking across miles of mountainous terrain. Unfortunately, this solution isn't available throughout all of Nepal . . . or even throughout some areas of the United States.

What is being done to bridge the digital divide? Organizations worldwide are working to raise awareness and to increase government involvement. Groups are sponsoring referendums that increase Internet capacity in schools, for example, and are urging state legislatures to provide additional funding for technology to struggling school systems. Community organizations are rising to the challenge as libraries and recreation centers work to provide free Internet access to the public.

You can help directly by donating used computer equipment to nonprofit groups that refurbish computers. These organizations repair and upgrade retired systems, and then distribute the systems to needy families at low cost. The Web site Techsoup (**techsoup.org**) maintains national resource lists that can help you find such organizations in your area. Some technology companies have programs in place to help with these efforts. The Microsoft Authorized Refurbisher (MAR) program, for example, supports refurbishers by allowing certain Microsoft operating systems and Office software to be installed for free on refurbished systems.

Getty Images/Digital Vision

Figure 30

Terrain (such as mountains) and remote locations (the Sahara, for example) can present barriers to conquering the digital divide.

summary

1. **What does it mean to be "computer literate"?**

   Computer literacy goes beyond knowing how to use a mouse and send e-mail. If you are computer literate, you understand the capabilities and limitations of computers and know how to use them wisely. Being computer literate also enables you to make informed purchasing decisions, use computers in your career, and understand the many ethical, legal, and societal implications of technology today. Anyone can become computer literate.

2. **How does being computer literate make you a savvy computer user and consumer?**

   By understanding how a computer is constructed and how its various parts function, you'll be able to get the most out of your computer. Among other things, you'll be able to avoid hackers, viruses, and Internet headaches; protect your privacy; and separate the real risks of privacy and security from those you don't have to worry about. You'll also be better able to maintain, upgrade, and troubleshoot your computer; make good purchasing decisions; and incorporate the latest technologies into your existing equipment.

3. **How can becoming computer literate help you in a career?**

   As computers become more a part of our daily lives, it is difficult to imagine any career that does not use computers in some fashion. Understanding how to use computers effectively will help you be a more productive and valuable employee, no matter which profession you choose.

4. **How can becoming computer literate help you understand and take advantage of newly emerging careers?**

   In today's world many changes are a result of new computer technologies. Understanding how today's computers function should help you utilize technology effectively now. And by understanding computers and how they work today, you can contribute to the technologies of tomorrow, like nanoscience and new medical technologies.

5. **How does becoming computer literate help you deal with the challenges associated with technology?**

   Although computers offer us great opportunities, they also pose ethical, legal, and moral challenges and questions. Being computer literate enables you to form educated opinions on these issues and to take stands based on accurate information rather than media hype and misinformation.

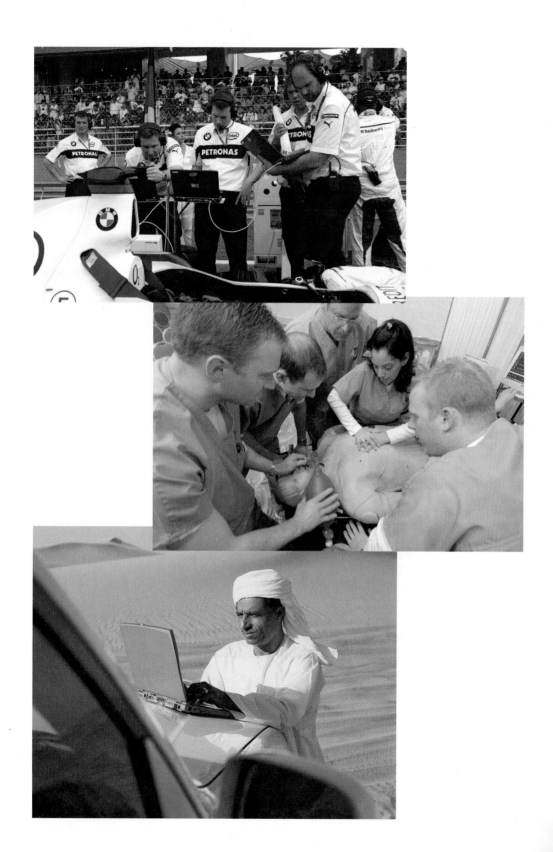

key terms

affective computing
Bluetooth technology
computer forensics
computer literate
data mining
digital divide
digital home
information technology (IT)
nanoscience

nanotechnology
offshored
patient simulator
personal digital assistant (PDA)
public domain
radio frequency identification tag
   (RFID tag)
software
spam

Why Computers Matter to You: Becoming Computer Literate

Word Bank

- affective computing
- Bluetooth technology
- computer forensics
- computer literate
- data mining
- digital divide
- digital home
- information technology (IT)
- nanotechnology
- offshoring
- patient simulator
- personal digital assistant (PDA)
- public domain
- radio frequency identification tags (RFID tags)
- spam

Instructions: Fill in the blanks using the words from the Word Bank above.

As technology advances continue, many fields of study are available now that were unheard of a few years ago. (1) _____, the study of incredibly small computing devices built at the molecular level, is providing major advances in the miniaturization of computing. (2) _____ is taking criminologists beyond what they could accomplish with conventional investigation techniques. And as the science of (3) _____ advances, computers will perform more and more like human beings in emotion and social cueing.

There are many reasons to become (4) _____, or to understand more about the capabilities and limitations of computers. Doing so can help you manage computer annoyances like unwanted e-mails, called (5) _____. You will also know how to upgrade your system to the latest standards, like the wireless (6) _____.

More and more aspects of how our homes are run are being coordinated through computers, giving rise to the term (7) _____. You may even find you enjoy computers so much you want to explore careers in (8) _____.

People who fail to keep up with the knowledge of how to use and maintain computer systems will fall to one side of the gap known as the (9) _____. When an entire country begins to fall behind in computer expertise, jobs are relocated to other, more tech-savvy countries. This shift of work is known as (10) _____.

becoming computer literate

Using the key terms and ideas you learned in this chapter, write a one- or two-paragraph summary for your school advisor so that he or she can use it to explain to students the importance of being computer literate in today's job market. Using the Internet, find additional examples of careers most people would not expect to require computer knowledge and show how computer literacy is still critical to success in those careers. Add these examples to your document to support your advice further.

Instructions: Answer the multiple-choice and true–false questions below for more practice with key terms and concepts from this chapter.

Multiple Choice

1. Which of the following is NOT a current use of computers in the legal environment?
   a. Creating animations that simulate a crime for use in the courtroom
   b. Tracking criminal behavior patterns
   c. Predicting criminal behavior patterns
   d. Conducting interviews with suspects

2. Art interfaces with technology by
   a. using a computer to generate images that respond to the environment.
   b. having computers suggest appropriate solutions to a dispute.
   c. using software that completes the plot of a story.
   d. having Web sites search for prospective clients for artists.

3. Affective computing is the science of relating computers and
   a. effective organizational skills.
   b. results-oriented outcomes.
   c. emotional and social skills.
   d. the calculation of interest rates.

4. Computer systems CANNOT be trained to understand
   a. the U.S. tax code.
   b. human emotion.
   c. a good joke.
   d. the perfect golf swing.

5. Automotive technology requires an understanding of computers to
   a. properly bill customers.
   b. control computerized pneumatic tools.
   c. keep carburetor settings at optimal positions.
   d. run sensors and CPU diagnostics for a vehicle's many computerized subsystems.

6. A device that tracks movement is
   a. a PSS.
   b. an RFID tag.
   c. a PDA.
   d. a patient simulator.

7. Criminologists use computer technology to
   a. reconstruct faces from bare skulls.
   b. create software programs that predict criminal activity.
   c. reconstruct deleted files from criminals' computers.
   d. All of the above.

8. IT careers
   a. are only about programming and software development.
   b. are many of the fastest-growing occupations.
   c. are on the decline.
   d. have largely been outsourced to India.

9. Computer forensics
   a. uses computer technology to gather potential legal evidence.
   b. helps identify the remains of bodies.
   c. investigates a suspect's home computer for evidence.
   d. All of the above.

10. Robotic surgery devices help physicians because
   a. they make incisions that are more accurate.
   b. the doctor does not have to be involved in the surgery.
   c. they monitor and make suggestions to the surgeon during the procedure.
   d. if the operation runs into complications, they can suggest creative alternatives.

True-False

_____ 1. Computer simulations are used for gaming purposes, but they are not yet accurate enough for criminal investigations.

_____ 2. Affective computing is the science that attempts to produce machines that make people comfortable because they look human in form.

_____ 3. Artists use computers for the business side of their work—for example, advertising or record keeping—but not for creative artistic work.

_____ 4. Ranchers tag their cattle and use computer systems to track and record their movements.

_____ 5. In many hospitals, infants are "chipped," or injected with a small, computerized tracking device, so that nurses can monitor their location and keep them safe.

Why Computers Matter to You: Becoming Computer Literate

1. Computer Literacy

In your college career, you'll be spending time understanding the requirements of the degree program you choose. At many schools, computer literacy requirements exist either as incoming requirements (skills students must have before they are admitted) or outgoing requirements (skills students must prove they have before graduating). Does your program require specific computer skills? Which skills are these? Should they be required? How can students efficiently prove that they have these skills? How often does the set of skills need to be reviewed and updated?

2. Computing and Education

Think about the schedule of courses you will be taking next semester. How many courses will require you to produce papers in electronic format? How many will require you to use course management software, such as Blackboard or Moodle? Will any course require you to use some specialty software product such as a nutrition monitoring program or a statistics training application? Do any require specialized hardware such as a scanner for your computer? How many require the use of collaborative meeting software?

3. Old Technologies Holding On

What courses and careers have not felt the impact of computer technology? Think of three courses that are taught effectively with no use of technology. Think of three careers that do not use computers in a significant way. Research and find the average salary and the rate of growth in these careers.

4. Using Biomedical Implants

If having such a chip implanted meant you would never need to carry cash or a credit card because your financial information was encoded on the chip, would you want one? If the chip could help instructors take attendance automatically in your class by reading your personal information, would that be an acceptable use? Would you consider using such a chip if it could be disabled whenever you wanted it to be or if only individuals you authorized had access to the information? Would you agree to have your chip communicate your financial information directly to the Internal Revenue Service (IRS)?

5. Campus Policing

In this chapter, the use of trend spotting programs to predict criminal activity was discussed. If existing criminal statistics are used to help identify trouble spots (such as wild parties) on your campus and the potential for serious criminal activity, is this the same as profiling? Does your campus police force have the right to take proactive steps to prevent crime based solely on developing trends? Should someone be held accountable if such information is not acted upon and a crime occurs?

1. Computer-Free Workplaces?

In this chapter, we listed several careers that require computer skills. How are computers used in the profession you are in or plan to enter? Can you think of any careers in which people do not use computers? Can you imagine computers being used in these careers in the future? If so, how? Are there benefits to having a "computer-free" zone in some aspects of some careers? How do computers affect creativity?

2. Medical Computing Applications

In their training and work, doctors and nurses rely on computers. What about patients? Does having access to a computer and computer skills help a patient find better health care options? Does having access to a computer help when filing an insurance claim? Does it help with finding the best doctor or hospital for a specific procedure? Explain your answers by giving specific examples.

3. Preparing for a Job

An office is looking for help and needs an employee able to manipulate data on Excel spreadsheets, coordinate the computer file management for the office, and conduct backups of critical data. How could you prove to the interviewer that you have the skills to handle the job? How could you prove you have the ability to learn the job?

4. Career Outlook

Which career fields are growing most rapidly? (Suggestion: Try searching at **ask.com**.) Which fields are growing fastest in the state where you live? What computer skills and knowledge do the top 10 career paths demand? What kinds of continuing training in technology can you imagine would be required as you progress in these careers?

5. IT Careers

Information technology (IT) careers are suited to a wide range of people at different points in their lives. Review that section and then answer the following questions:
a. Would an IT career have advantages for a single parent? How?
b. How might an IT career be able to help someone pursue a later career in a nontechnical field?
c. How might an IT career assist someone in completing a college degree?
d. Would an IT career be a good choice if you wanted geographic independence (i.e., the ability to live in a location different from your work)?

6. Job Skills Assessment

Frequently, job seekers are asked about their computer literacy when applying for a job.
a. How do you think computer skill levels are determined by employers? How should they be determined?
b. If your interpretation of "expert" doesn't match your prospective employer's definition, does that make you wrong?

Instructions: Albert Einstein used *Gedankenexperiments*, or critical thinking questions, to develop his theory of relativity. Some ideas are best understood by experimenting with them in our own minds. The following critical thinking questions are designed to demand your full attention but require only a comfortable chair—no technology.

1. Rating Your Computer Literacy

This chapter lists many ways in which knowing about computers (or becoming computer literate) will help you. How much do you know about computers? What else would you like to know? How do you think learning more about computers will help you in the future? How would you suggest measuring computer literacy?

2. Data Mining

This chapter briefly discusses data mining, a technique companies use to study sales data and gather information from it. Have you heard of data mining before? How might companies like Wal-Mart or Target use data mining to better run their business? Can you think of any privacy risks data mining might pose?

3. Nanotechnology

As you learned in the chapter, nanotechnology is the science of using nanostructures to build devices on an extremely small scale. What applications of tiny computers can you think of? How might nanotechnology affect your life?

4. Biomedical Chips

This chapter discusses various uses of biomedical chips. Many biomedical chip implants that will be developed in the future will most likely be aimed at correcting vision loss, hearing loss, or other physical impediments. But chips could also be developed to improve physical or mental capabilities of healthy individuals. For example, chips could be implanted in athletes to make their muscles work better together, thereby allowing them to run faster. Or your memory could be enhanced by providing additional storage capacity for your brain.

a. Should biomedical implant devices that increase athletic performance be permitted in the Olympics?
b. What about devices that repair a problem (such as blindness in one eye) but then increase the level of visual acuity in the affected eye so that it is better than normal vision?
c. Would you be willing to have a chip implanted in your brain to improve your memory?
d. Would you be willing to have a VeriChip implanted under your skin?

5. Affective Computing

Affective computing is the science that attempts to produce machines that understand and can respond to human emotions and social mores. Do you think humans will ever create a machine that cannot be distinguished from a human being? In your opinion, what are the ethical and moral implications associated with that development?

6. The World Stage

How might access to (or denial of) electronic information improve the education of a country's citizens? Could that affect who the world's next technology power will be? Could it eliminate third world status?

Promoting Future Technologies

Problem

People are often overwhelmed by the relentless march of technology. Accessibility of information is changing the way we work, play, and interact with our friends, family, and co-workers. In this Team Time, we consider the future and reflect on how the advent of new technologies will affect our daily lives 10 years in the future.

Task

Your group has just returned from a trip in a time machine 10 years into the future. Amazing changes have taken place in just a short time. To a large extent, consumer acceptance of technology makes or breaks a new technology. Your mission is to develop a creative marketing strategy to promote the technological changes you observed in the future and accelerate their acceptance.

Process

Divide the class into three or more teams.

1. With the other members of your team, use the Internet to research up-and-coming technologies (**howstuffworks.com** is a good starting point). Prepare a list of innovations that you believe will occur in the next 10 years. Determine how they will be integrated into society and the effect they will have on our culture.
2. Present your group's findings to the class for debate and discussion. Note specifically how the rest of the class reacts to your reports on the innovations. Are they excited? Skeptical? Incredulous? Do they laugh off your ideas, or do they become wildly enthusiastic?
3. Write a marketing strategy paper that details how you would promote the technological changes that you envision for the future. Note some barriers to acceptance the technology may have to overcome, as well as any legal or ethical challenges or questions you see the new technology posing.

Conclusion

The future path of technology is determined by dreamers. If not for innovators such as Thomas Edison, Alexander Graham Bell, and Albert Einstein, we would not be as advanced a society as we are today. Innovators come from all walks of life, and we must exercise our creative energies to keep them in shape. Don't be afraid to suggest technological advancements that seem outrageous today. In 1966, when the original *Star Trek* series was on television, handheld communicators seemed astounding and beyond our reach. Yet the dreamers who created those communication devices for a science fiction series helped to inspire a multibillion-dollar cell phone industry in the 21st century. The next technological wave may start in your imagination!

multimedia

In addition to the review materials presented here, you'll find additional materials on the Pearson IT Multimedia Library and the Companion Website (**pearsonhighered.com/techinaction**), which will help reinforce your understanding of the chapter content. These materials include the following:

Active Helpdesk

In Active Helpdesk calls, you'll assume the role of helpdesk operator, taking calls about the concepts you've learned in this chapter. You'll apply what you've learned and receive feedback from a supervisor to review and reinforce those concepts. The Active Helpdesk calls for this chapter are listed below and can be found on the Pearson IT Multimedia Library:

- This chapter has no Active Helpdesks.

Sound Bytes

Sound Bytes are dynamic multimedia tutorials that help demystify even the most complex topics. You'll view video clips and animations that illustrate computer concepts and then apply what you've learned by working through the Sound Byte Labs, which include quizzes and activities specifically tailored to each Sound Byte. The Sound Bytes for this chapter are listed below and can be found on the Pearson IT Multimedia Library:

- Questions to Ask Before You Buy a Computer
- The History of the Personal Computer

Companion Website

The *Technology in Action* Companion Website includes a variety of additional materials to help you review and learn more about the topics in this chapter. The resources available at **pearsonhighered.com/techinaction** include:

- **Online Study Guide.** This chapter features an online true–false and multiple-choice quiz. You can take these quizzes, automatically check the results, and e-mail the results to your instructor.
- **Web Research Projects.** This chapter features several Web research projects that ask you to search the Web for information on computer-related careers, milestones in computer history, important people and companies, emerging technologies, and the applications and implications of different technologies.

Technology in Focus:

The History of the PC

From *Technology in Action Complete*, Seventh Edition, Alan Evans, Kendall Martin, Mary Anne Poatsy.

The History of the PC

SuperStock\Jupiter Images

D o you ever wonder how big the first personal computer was, or how much the first portable computer weighed? Computers are such an integral part of our lives that we don't often stop to think about how far they've come or where they got their start. In just 35 years, computers have evolved from expensive, huge machines that only corporations owned to small, powerful devices found in millions of homes. In this Technology in Focus feature, we look at the history of the computer. Along the way, we will discuss some developments that helped make the computer powerful and portable, as well as some people who contributed to its development. However, we will start with the story of the personal computer and how it grew to be as integral to our lives as the automobile is.

Technology in Action

The First Personal Computer: The Altair

Our journey through the history of the personal computer starts in 1975. At that time, most people were unfamiliar with the mainframes and supercomputers that large corporations and the government owned. With price tags exceeding the cost of buildings, and with few if any practical home uses, these monster machines were not appealing or attainable to the vast majority of Americans. That began to change when the January 1975 cover of *Popular Electronics* announced the debut of the **Altair 8800**, touted as the first personal computer (see Figure 1). For just $395 for a do-it-yourself kit or $498 for a fully assembled unit (about $2,000 in today's dollars), the price was reasonable enough that computer fanatics could finally own their own computers.

The Altair was a very primitive computer, with just 256 bytes (not *kilo* bytes, just bytes) of memory. It didn't come with a keyboard, nor did it include a monitor or printer. Switches on the front of the machine were used to enter data in machine code (strings of 1s and 0s). Flashing lights on the front indicated the results of a program. User-friendly it was not—at least by today's standards.

Despite its limitations, computer "hackers" (as computer enthusiasts were called then) flocked to the machine. Many people who bought the Altair had been taught to program, but until that point, they had access only to big, clumsy computers. These people were often hired by corporations to program routine financial, statistical, or engineering programs in a workplace environment. The Altair offered these enthusiasts the opportunity to create their own programs. Within three months, Micro Instrumentation and Telemetry Systems (MITS), the company behind the Altair, received more than 4,000 orders for the machine.

The release of the Altair marked the start of the personal computer (PC) boom. In fact, two men who would play large roles in the development of the PC were among the first Altair owners. Recent high school graduates Bill Gates and Paul Allen were so enamored by this "minicomputer," as these personal computers were called at the time, that they wrote a compiling program

Why Was It Called the "Altair"?

For lack of a better name, the Altair's developers originally called the computer the PE-8, short for Popular Electronics 8-bit. However, Les Soloman, the *Popular Electronics* writer who introduced the Altair, wanted the machine to have a catchier name. The author's daughter, who was watching *Star Trek* at the time, suggested the name Altair. (That's where the *Star Trek* crew was traveling that week.) The first star of the PC industry was born.

Figure 1

Heinz Nixdorf Musuemsforum\ AP Wide World Photos

In 1975, the Altair was touted as the "world's first minicomputer" in the January issue of Popular Electronics.

(a program that translates user commands into commands that the computer can understand) for the Altair. The two friends later convinced the Altair's developer, Ed Roberts, to buy their program. This marked the start of a small company called Microsoft. We'll get to that story later. First, let's see what their future archrivals were up to.

The Apple I and II

Around the time the Altair was released, **Steve Wozniak**, an employee at Hewlett-Packard, was becoming fascinated with the burgeoning personal computer industry and was dabbling with his own computer design. He would bring his computer prototypes to meetings of the Homebrew Computing Club, a group of young

Figure 2 *Steve Jobs (a) and Steve Wozniak (b) were two computer hobbyists who worked together to form the Apple Computer Company.*

Figure 3 *The first Apple computer, the Apple I, looked like a typewriter in a box. It was one of the first computers to incorporate a keyboard.*

computer fans in Palo Alto, California who met to discuss computer ideas. **Steve Jobs**, who was working for computer game manufacturer Atari at the time, liked Wozniak's prototypes and made a few suggestions. Together, the two built a personal computer, later known as the **Apple I**, in Wozniak's garage (see Figures 2 and 3). In that same year, on April 1, 1976, Jobs and Wozniak officially formed the **Apple Computer Company**.

No sooner had the Apple I hit the market than Wozniak began working to improve it. A year later, in 1977, the **Apple II** was born (see Figure 4). The Apple II included a color monitor, sound, and game paddles. Priced around $1,300 (almost $4,700 in today's dollars), it included 4 kilobytes (KB) of random access memory (RAM) as well as an optional floppy disk drive that enabled users to run additional programs. Most of these programs were games. However, for many users, there was a special appeal to the Apple II: The program that made the computer function when the power was first turned on (the operating system) was stored in read-only memory (ROM).

Figure 4 *The Apple II came with a monitor and an external floppy disk drive.*

Previously, the operating system had to be rewritten every time the computer was turned on The friendly features of the operating system on the Apple II, such as automatic loading, encouraged less technically oriented computer enthusiasts to try writing their own software programs.

An instant success, the Apple II would be the most successful product in the company's early line, outshining even its successor, the **Apple III**, which was released in 1980. Eventually, the Apple II would include a spreadsheet program, a word processor, and desktop publishing software. These programs gave personal computers like the Apple functions beyond gaming and special programming, and led to their increased popularity. We will talk more about these advances later. For now, we will look at which other players were entering the market.

Enter the Competition

Around the time that Apple was experiencing success with its computers, a number of competitors entered the market. The largest among them were Commodore, RadioShack, and IBM. As Figure 5 shows, just a few years after the introduction of the Altair, the market was filled with personal computers from a variety of manufacturers.

The Commodore PET and TRS-80

Among Apple's strongest competitors were the **Commodore PET 2001**, shown in Figure 6, and Tandy RadioShack's **TRS-80**, shown in Figure 7. Commodore introduced the PET in January 1977. It was featured on the cover of *Popular Science* in October 1977 as the "new $595 home computer." Tandy RadioShack's home computer also garnered immediate popularity. Just one month after its release in 1977, the TRS-80 Model 1 had sold approximately 10,000 units. Priced at $594.95, the easy-to-use machine included a monochrome display and 4 KB of memory. Many other manufacturers followed suit over the next decade, launching new desktop computers, but none were as successful as the TRS-80 and the Commodore.

The Osborne

The Osborne Company introduced the industry's first portable computer, the **Osborne**, in April 1981 (see Figure 8). Although portable, the computer weighed 24.5 pounds, and its screen was just five inches wide. In addition to its hefty weight, it came with a hefty price tag of $1,795. Still, the Osborne included 64 KB of memory, two floppy disk drives, and preinstalled programs such as word processing and spreadsheet software. The Osborne was an overnight success, and its sales quickly reached 10,000 units per month. Despite the Osborne's popularity, the

Why Is It Called "Apple"?

Steve Jobs wanted Apple Computer to be the "perfect" computer company. Having recently worked at an apple orchard, Jobs thought of the apple as the "perfect" fruit because it was high in nutrients, came in a nice package, and was not easily damaged. Thus, he and Wozniak decided to name their new computer company Apple.

Figure 5

Personal Computer Development

YEAR	APPLE	IBM	OTHER
1975			MITS Altair
1976	Apple I		
1977	Apple II		Tandy RadioShack's TRS-80 Commodore PET
1980	Apple III		
1981		IBM PC	Osborne
1983	Lisa		
1984	Macintosh	286-AT	IBM PC clones

Jerry Mason/SPL/Photo Researchers, Inc.

Figure 6 *The Commodore PET was well received because of its all-in-one design.*

Figure 7 *The TRS-80 hid its circuitry under the keyboard. The computer was nicknamed "trash-80," which was more a play on its initials than a reflection of its capabilities.*

Photo Courtesy of The Computer History Museum

release of a successor machine, called the **Executive**, reduced sales of the Osborne significantly, and the Osborne Company eventually closed. Compaq bought the Osborne design and in 1983 produced its first portable computer.

IBM PCs

By 1980, IBM recognized that it needed to get its feet wet in the personal computer market. Up until that point, the company had been a player in the computer industry, but primarily made mainframe computers, which it sold only to large corporations. It had not taken the smaller personal computer seriously. In August 1981, however, IBM released its first personal computer, appropriately named the **IBM PC**. Because many companies were already familiar with IBM mainframes, they readily adopted the IBM PC. The term *PC* soon became

Photo Courtesy of The Computer History Museum

Figure 8 *The Osborne was introduced as the first portable personal computer. It weighed a whopping 24.5 pounds and contained just 64 KB of memory.*

the term used to describe all personal computers.

The IBM PC came with 64 KB of memory, expandable to 256 KB, and prices started at $1,565. IBM marketed its PC through retail outlets such as Sears and Computerland in order to reach the home market, and it quickly dominated the playing field. In January 1983, *Time* magazine, playing on its annual "man of the year" issue, named the computer "1982 machine of the year" (see Figure 9).

Other Important Advancements

It was not just the **hardware** of the personal computer that was developing during the 1970s and 1980s. At the same time, advances in programming languages and operating systems and the influx of application software were leading to more useful and powerful machines.

Roberto Brosan\Time Inc. Magazine

Figure 9 *The IBM PC was the first (and only) nonhuman object chosen as "man of the year" (actually, "machine of the year") by* Time *magazine. This designation, in* Time's *January 1983 issue, indicated the impact the PC was having on the general public.*

The Importance of BASIC

The software industry began in the 1950s with the development of programming languages such as FORTRAN, ALGOL, and COBOL. These languages were used mainly by businesses to create financial, statistical, and engineering programs for corporate enterprises. However, the 1964 introduction of **Beginners All-Purpose Symbolic Instruction Code (BASIC)** revolutionized the software industry. BASIC was a programming language that the beginning programming student could easily learn. It thus became enormously popular—and the key language of the PC. In fact, **Bill Gates** and **Paul Allen** (see Figure 10) used BASIC to write their program for the Altair. As we noted earlier, this program led to the creation of **Microsoft**, a company that produced software for the microcomputer.

Figure 10 *Bill Gates and Paul Allen are the founders of Microsoft.*

The Advent of Operating Systems

Because data on the earliest personal computers was stored on audiocassettes (not floppy disks), many programs were not saved or reused. Rather, programs were rewritten as needed. Eventually Steve Wozniak developed a floppy disk drive called the **Disk II**, which he introduced in July 1978. With the introduction of the floppy drive, programs could be saved with more efficiency, and operating systems (OSs) developed.

Operating systems were (and still are) written to coordinate with the specific processor chip that controlled the computer. Apples ran exclusively on a Motorola chip, while PCs (IBMs and so on) ran exclusively on an Intel chip. **Disk Operating System (DOS)**, developed by Wozniak and introduced in December 1977, was the OS that controlled the first Apple computers. The **Control Program for Microcomputers (CP/M)**, developed by Gary Kildall, was the first OS designed for the Intel 8080 chip (the processor for PCs). Intel hired Kildall to write a compiling program for the 8080 chip, but Kildall quickly saw the need for a program that could store computer operating instructions on a floppy disk rather than on a cassette. Intel wasn't interested in buying the CP/M program, but Kildall saw a future for the program and thus founded his own company, Digital Research.

In 1980, when IBM was considering entering the personal computer market, it approached Bill Gates at Microsoft to write an OS program for the IBM PC. Although Gates had written versions of BASIC for different computer systems, he had never written an OS. He therefore recommended that IBM investigate the CP/M OS, but no one from Digital Research returned IBM's call. Microsoft reconsidered the opportunity and developed **MS-DOS** for IBM computers. (This was one phone call that Digital Research certainly regretted not returning!)

MS-DOS was based on an OS called **Quick and Dirty Operating System (QDOS)** that was developed by Seattle Computer Products. Microsoft bought the nonexclusive rights to QDOS and distributed it to IBM. Eventually, virtually all personal computers running on the Intel chip used MS-DOS as their OS. Microsoft's reign as one of the dominant players in the PC landscape had begun. Meanwhile, many other programs were being developed, taking personal computers to the next level of user acceptance.

The Software Application Explosion: VisiCalc and Beyond

Inclusion of floppy disk drives in personal computers not only facilitated the storage of operating systems, but also set off an application software explosion, because the floppy disk was a convenient way to distribute software. Around that same time, in 1978, Harvard Business School student Dan Bricklin recognized the potential for a spreadsheet program that could be used on PCs. He and his friend Bob Frankston (see Figure 11) created the program **VisiCalc**. VisiCalc not only became an instant success, but was also one of the main reasons for the rapid increase in PC sales. Finally, ordinary home users could see how owning a personal computer could benefit their lives. More than 100,000 copies of VisiCalc were sold in its first year.

Daniel Bricklin

Figure 11 *Dan Bricklin and Bob Frankston created VisiCalc, the first business application developed for the personal computer.*

After VisiCalc, other electronic spreadsheet programs entered the market. **Lotus 1-2-3** came on the market in 1982, and **Microsoft Excel** entered the scene in 1985. These two products became so popular that they eventually put VisiCalc out of business.

Meanwhile, word processing software was gaining a foothold in the PC industry. Up to this point, there were separate, dedicated word processing machines, and the thought hadn't occurred to anyone to enable the personal computer to do word processing. Personal computers, it was believed, were for computation and data management. However, once **WordStar**, the first word processing application, came out in disk form in 1979 and became available for personal computers, word processing became another important use for the PC. In fact, word processing is now one of the most common PC applications. Competitors such as **Word for MS-DOS** (the precursor to Microsoft Word) and **WordPerfect** soon entered the market. Figure 12 lists some of the important dates in application software development.

The Graphical User Interface

Another important advancement in personal computers was the introduction of the **graphical user interface (GUI)**, which allowed users to interact with the computer more easily. Until that time, users had to use complicated command- or menu-driven interfaces to interact with the computer. Apple was the first company to take full commercial advantage of the GUI, but competitors were fast on its heels, and soon the GUI became synonymous with personal computers. Who developed the idea of the GUI?

You'll probably be surprised to learn that a company known for its photocopiers was the real innovator.

Xerox

In 1972, a few years before Apple launched its first PC, photocopier manufacturer **Xerox** was hard at work in its Palo Alto Research Center (PARC) designing a personal computer of its own. Named the **Alto** (shown in Figure 13), the computer included a word processor, based on the What You See Is What You Get (WYSIWYG) principle, that incorporated a file management system with directories and folders. It also had a mouse and could connect to a network. None of the other personal computers of the time had any of these features. For a variety of reasons, Xerox never sold the Alto commercially. Several years later, it developed the Star Office System, which was based on the Alto. Despite its convenient features, the Star never became popular, because no one was willing to pay the $17,000 asking price.

The Lisa and the Macintosh

Xerox's ideas were ahead of its time, but many of the ideas of the Alto and Star would soon catch on. In 1983, Apple introduced the **Lisa**,

Figure 12 *Application Software Development*

YEAR	APPLICATION
1978	**VisiCalc:** First electronic spreadsheet application. **WordStar:** First word processing application.
1980	**WordPerfect:** Thought even now to be the best word processing software for the PC, WordPerfect was eventually sold to Novell, and was later acquired by Corel.
1982	**Lotus 1-2-3:** Added integrated charting, plotting, and database capabilities to spreadsheet software.
1983	**Word for MS-DOS:** Introduced in the pages of *PC World* magazine on the first magazine-inserted demo disk.
1985	**Excel:** One of the first spreadsheets to use a graphical user interface. **PageMaker:** The first desktop publishing software.

Figure 13 *The Alto was the first computer to use a graphical user interface, and it provided the basis for the GUI that Apple used. However, because of marketing problems, the Alto never was sold.*

figure 14 *The Lisa was the first computer to introduce a GUI to the market. Priced too high, it never gained the popularity it deserved.*

shown in Figure 14. Named after Apple founder Steve Jobs's daughter, the Lisa was the first successful PC brought to market that used a GUI. Legend has it that Jobs had seen the Alto during a visit to PARC in 1979 and was influenced by its GUI. He therefore incorporated a similar user interface into the Lisa, providing features such as windows, drop-down menus, icons, a hierarchical file system with folders and files, and a point-and-click device called a mouse. The only problem with the Lisa was its price. At $9,995 ($21,530 in today's dollars), few buyers were willing to take the plunge.

A year later, in 1984, Apple introduced the **Macintosh**, shown in Figure 15. The Macintosh was everything the Lisa was and then some, and at about a third of the cost. The Macintosh was also the first personal computer to utilize 3.5-inch floppy disks with a hard cover, which were smaller and sturdier than the previous 5.25-inch floppies.

The Internet Boom

The GUI made it easier for users to work on the computer. The Internet provided another reason for consumers to buy computers. Now they could conduct research and communicate with each other in a new and convenient way. In 1993, the Web browser **Mosaic** was introduced. This browser allowed users to view multimedia on the Web, causing Internet traffic to increase by nearly 350 percent.

Meanwhile, companies discovered the Internet as a means to do business, and computer sales took off. IBM-compatible PCs became the personal computer system of choice when, in 1995, Microsoft (the predominant software provider to PCs) introduced Internet Explorer, a Web browser that integrated Web functionality into Microsoft Office applications, and **Windows 95**, the first Microsoft OS designed to be principally a GUI OS, although it still was based on the DOS kernel.

About a year earlier, in mid-1994, Jim Clark, founder of the computer company Silicon

Figure 15 *The Macintosh became one of Apple's best-selling computers, incorporating a graphical user interface along with other innovations such as the 3.5-inch floppy disk drive.*

Graphics Inc., Marc Andreessen, and others from the Mosaic development team developed the Netscape commercial Web browser. Netscape's popularity grew quickly, and it soon became a predominant player in browser software. However, pressures from Microsoft became too strong. In the beginning of 1998, Netscape announced it was moving to the open source market, would no longer charge for the product, and would make the code available to the public.

Making the PC Possible: Early Computers

Since the first Altair was introduced in the 1970s, more than a billion personal computers have been distributed around the globe. Because of the declining prices of computers and the growth of the Internet, it's estimated that a billion more computers will be sold within the next decade. What made all of this possible? The computer is a compilation of parts, each of which is the result of individual inventions. From the earliest days

Figure 16 *The Jacquard Loom used holes punched in stiff cards to make complex designs. This technique would later be used in punch cards that controlled the input and output of data in computers.*

Photo Courtesy of The Computer History Museum

of humankind, we have been looking for a more systematic way to count and calculate. Thus, the evolution of counting machines led to the development of the computer we know today.

The Pascalene Calculator and the Jacquard Loom

The **Pascalene** was the first accurate mechanical calculator. This machine, created by the French mathematician **Blaise Pascal** in 1642, used revolutions of gears, like odometers in cars do, to count by tens. The Pascalene could be used to add, subtract, multiply, and divide. The basic design of the Pascalene was so sound that it lived on in mechanical calculators for more than 300 years.

Nearly 200 years later, **Joseph Jacquard** revolutionized the fabric industry by creating a machine that automated the weaving of complex patterns. Although not a counting or calculating machine, the **Jacquard loom** (shown in Figure 16) was significant because it relied on stiff cards with punched holes to automate the weaving process. Much later, this punch-card process would be adopted as a means for computers to record and read data.

Babbage's Engines

Decades later, in 1834, **Charles Babbage** designed the first automatic calculator, called the **Analytical Engine** (see Figure 17). The machine was actually based on another machine called the **Difference Engine**, which was a huge steam-powered mechanical calculator that Babbage designed to print astronomical tables. Babbage stopped working on the Difference Engine to build the Analytical Engine. Although it was never developed, Babbage's detailed drawings and descriptions of the Analytical Engine include components similar to those found in today's computers, including the store (akin to RAM) and the mill (a central processing unit), as well as input and output devices. This invention gave Charles Babbage the title of "father of computing."

Meanwhile, Ada Lovelace, who was the daughter of poet Lord Byron and was a student of mathematics (which was unusual for women of that time), was fascinated with Babbage's Engines. She translated an Italian paper on Babbage's machine, and at the request of Babbage added her own extensive notes. Her efforts are thought to be the best description of Babbage's Engines.

The Hollerith Tabulating Machine

In 1890, **Herman Hollerith**, while working for the U.S. Census Bureau, was the first to take Jacquard's punch-card concept and apply it to computing. Hollerith developed a machine called the **Hollerith Tabulating Machine** that used punch cards to tabulate census data. Up until that time, census data had been tabulated manually in a long, laborious process. Hollerith's tabulating machine automatically read data that had been punched onto small punch cards, speeding up the tabulation process. Hollerith's machine became so successful that he left the Census Bureau in 1896 to start the Tabulating Machine Company. His company later changed its name to International Business Machines, or IBM.

The Z1 and the Atanasoff–Berry Computer

German inventor **Konrad Zuse** is credited with a number of computing inventions. His first, in 1936, was a mechanical calculator called the **Z1**. The Z1 is thought to be the first computer to include certain features that are integral to today's systems, such as a control unit and separate memory functions. These were important breakthroughs for future computer design.

In late 1939, John Atanasoff, a professor at Iowa State University, and his student Clifford Berry built the first electrically powered digital computer, called the **Atanasoff–Berry Computer (ABC)**, shown in Figure 18. The computer was the first to use vacuum tubes, instead of the mechanical switches used in older computers, to store data. Although revolutionary at its time, the machine weighed 700 pounds, contained a mile of wire, and took about 15 seconds for each calculation. (In comparison, today's personal computers can perform billions and billions of calculations in

Figure 17 *The Analytical Engine, designed by Charles Babbage, was never fully developed, but included components similar to those found in today's computers.*

Photo Courtesy of The Computer History Museum

15 seconds.) Most importantly, the ABC was the first computer to use the binary system. It was also the first computer to have memory that repowered itself upon booting. The design of the ABC would end up being central to that of future computers.

The Harvard Mark I

From the late 1930s to the early 1950s, **Howard Aiken** and **Grace Hopper** designed the Mark series of computers at Harvard University. The U.S. Navy used these computers for ballistic and gunnery calculations. Aiken, an electrical engineer and physicist, designed the computer, while Hopper did the programming. The **Harvard Mark I**, finished in 1944, could perform all four arithmetic operations (addition, subtraction, multiplication, and division).

However, many believe Hopper's greatest contribution to computing was the invention of the **compiler**, a program that translates

Figure 18 *The Atanasoff–Berry Computer laid the design groundwork for many computers to come.*

Ames Laboratory

English-language instructions into computer language. The team was also responsible for a common computer-related expression. Hopper was the first to "debug" a computer when she removed a moth that had flown into the Harvard Mark I and caused the computer to break down (see Figure 19). After that, problems that caused a computer not to run were called "bugs."

The Turing Machine

Meanwhile, in 1936, the British mathematician **Alan Turing** created an abstract computer model that could perform logical operations. The **Turing Machine** was not a real machine, but rather was a hypothetical model that mathematically defined a mechanical procedure (or algorithm). Additionally, Turing's concept described a process by which the machine could read, write, or erase symbols written on squares of an infinite paper tape. This concept of an infinite tape that could be read, written to, and erased was the precursor to today's RAM.

The ENIAC

The **Electronic Numerical Integrator and Computer (ENIAC)**, shown in Figure 20, was another U.S. government-sponsored machine developed to calculate the settings used for weapons.

Created by **John W. Mauchly** and **J. Presper Eckert** at the University of Pennsylvania, it was placed in operation in June 1944. Although the ENIAC is generally thought of as the first successful high-speed electronic digital computer, it was big and clumsy. The ENIAC used nearly 18,000 vacuum tubes and filled approximately 1,800 square feet of floor space. Although inconvenient, the ENIAC served its purpose and remained in use until 1955.

The UNIVAC

The **Universal Automatic Computer**, or **UNIVAC**, was the first commercially successful electronic digital computer. Completed in June 1951 and manufactured by the company Remington Rand, the UNIVAC operated on magnetic tape. This set it apart from its competitors, which ran on punch cards. The UNIVAC gained notoriety when, in a 1951 publicity stunt, it was used to predict the outcome of the Stevenson–Eisenhower presidential race. After analyzing only 5 percent of the popular vote, the UNIVAC correctly identified Dwight D. Eisenhower as the victor. After that, UNIVAC soon became a household word. The UNIVAC and computers like it were considered **first-generation computers** and were the last to use vacuum tubes to store data.

Figure 19 *Grace Hopper coined the term* computer bug *when a moth flew into the Harvard Mark I, causing it to break down.*

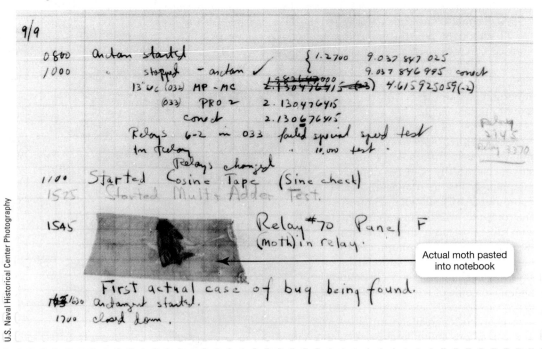

U.S. Naval Historical Center Photography

Transistors and Beyond

Only a year after the ENIAC was completed, scientists at the Bell Telephone Laboratories in New Jersey invented the **transistor**, which was another means to store data. The transistor replaced the bulky vacuum tubes of earlier computers and was smaller and more powerful than tubes were. It was used in almost everything, from radios to phones. Computers that used transistors were referred to as **second-generation computers**. Still, transistors were limited as to how small they could be made.

A few years later, in 1958, **Jack Kilby**, while working at Texas Instruments, invented the world's first **integrated circuit**, a small chip capable of containing thousands of transistors. This consolidation in design enabled computers to become smaller and lighter. The computers in this early integrated-circuit generation were considered **third-generation computers**.

Other innovations in the computer industry further refined the computer's speed, accuracy, and efficiency. However, none were as significant as the 1971 introduction by the Intel Corporation of the **microprocessor chip**, a small chip containing millions of transistors. The microprocessor functions as the central processing unit (CPU), or brains, of the computer. Computers that used a

Figure 20 *The ENIAC took up an entire room and required several people to manipulate it.*

Courtesy of Intel Corporation

Figure 21 *The Intel Itanium 2 is one of Intel's most powerful processors.*

microprocessor chip were called **fourth-generation computers**. Over time, Intel and Motorola became the leading manufacturers of microprocessors. Today, the Intel Itanium 2 chip, shown in Figure 21, is one of Intel's most powerful processors.

As you can see, personal computers have come a long way since the Altair, and have a number of inventions and people to thank for their amazing popularity. What will the future bring? If current trends continue, computers will be smaller, lighter, and more powerful. The advancement of wireless technology will also play a big role in the development of the personal computer.

looking at computers:

understanding the parts

looking at computers:

understanding the parts

how cool

is this?

how cool is *this?*

If you have ever thought about **customizing** the layout of your **keyboard**, this Luxeed Dynamic Pixel LED Keyboard is the one for you. If you're a gamer, you can program specific keys to control your game and to **glow** with different colors that indicate each key **action**. If you're not a gamer but just would like to add a bit of fun to your otherwise dull keyboard, you can **animate** colored scenarios to "play" on the keys, or create an **illuminated** pattern or design. With 430 LEDs, the Luxeed is capable of individually lighting each key in your choice of color.

The keyboard comes in either black or white. The keys of the white keyboard light up more brightly and have a semi-transparent look. The keys of the black keyboard can be set so just the letters light up.

Understanding Your Computer

You may already have learned a bit about computer literacy, so, you can see why becoming computer literate is so important. But where do you start? You've no doubt gleaned some knowledge about computers just from being a member of society. However, although you certainly know what a computer is, do you really understand how it works, what all its parts are, and what these parts do? In this section, we discuss what a computer does and how its functions make it such a useful machine.

Computers Are Data Processing Devices

Strictly defined, a **computer** is a data processing device that performs four major functions:

1. It *gathers* data, or allows users to input data.
2. It *processes* that data into information.
3. It *outputs* data and information.
4. It *stores* data and information.

What is the difference between data and information? People often use the terms *data* and *information* interchangeably. Although they may mean the same thing in a simple conversation, the actual distinction between data and information is an important one.

In computer terms, **data** is a representation of a fact, figure, or idea. Data can be a number, a word, a picture, or even a recording of sound. For example, the number 6125553297 and the names Derek and Washington are pieces of data. Alone, these pieces of data probably mean little to you. **Information** is data that has been organized or presented in a meaningful fashion. When your computer provides you with a contact listing that indicates Derek Washington can be reached by phone at (612) 555-3297, then the previous data suddenly becomes useful—that is, it becomes information.

How do computers interact with data and information? Computers are excellent at **processing** (manipulating or organizing) data into information. When you first arrived on campus, you probably were directed to a place where you could get an ID card. You most likely provided a clerk with personal data (such as your name and address) that was entered into a computer. The clerk then took your picture with a digital camera (collecting more data). This information was then processed appropriately so that it could be printed on your ID card (see Figure 1). This organized output of data on your ID card is useful information. Finally, the information was probably stored as digital data on the computer for later use.

Bits and Bytes: The Language of Computers

How do computers process data into information? Unlike humans, computers work exclusively with numbers (not words). To process data into information,

 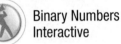

Binary Numbers Interactive

This Sound Byte helps remove the mystery surrounding binary numbers. You'll learn about base conversion between decimal, binary, and hexadecimal interactively using colors, sounds, and images.

Figure 1

Computers process data into information.

Looking at Computers: Understanding the Parts

computers need to work in a language they understand. This language, called **binary language**, consists of just two digits: 0 and 1. Everything a computer does, such as processing data or printing a report, is broken down into a series of 0s and 1s. Each 0 and 1 is a **binary digit**, or **bit** for short. Eight binary digits (or bits) combine to create one **byte**. In computers, each letter of the alphabet, each number, and each special character (such as the @ sign) consists of a unique combination of eight bits, or a string of eight 0s and 1s. So, for example, in binary (computer) language, the letter K is represented as 01001011. This equals eight bits, or one byte.

What else can bits and bytes be used for? You've probably heard the terms *kilobyte (KB), megabyte (MB),* and *gigabyte (GB)*. Bits and bytes not only are used as the language that tells the computer what to do, but also are what the computer uses to represent the data and information that it inputs and outputs. Word processing files, digital pictures, and even software are represented inside a computer as a series of bits and bytes. These files and applications can be quite large, containing thousands or millions of bytes.

To make it easier to measure the size of these files, we need units of measure larger than a byte. Kilobytes, megabytes, and

gigabytes are therefore simply amounts of bytes. As shown in Figure 2, a **kilobyte (KB)** is approximately 1,000 bytes, a **megabyte (MB)** is about 1 million bytes, and a **gigabyte (GB)** is around 1 billion bytes. As our information-processing needs have grown, so too have our storage needs. Today, many business computers can store up to a petabyte of data, and the Google search engine processes more than 20 petabytes of data per day—that's a lot of bytes!

How does your computer process bits and bytes? Your computer uses a combination of hardware and software to process data into information and enable you to complete tasks such as writing a letter or playing a game. An anonymous person once said that hardware is any part of a computer that you can kick when it doesn't work properly. A more formal definition of **hardware** is "any part of the computer you can physically touch."

Figure 2 | HOW MUCH IS A BYTE?

Name	Abbreviation	Number of Bytes	Relative Size
Byte	B	1 byte	Can hold one character of data.
Kilobyte	KB	1,024 bytes (2^{10} bytes)	Can hold 1,024 characters or about half of a double-spaced typewritten page.
Megabyte	MB	1,048,576 bytes (2^{20} bytes)	Can hold approximately 768 pages of typed text.
Gigabyte	GB	1,073,741,824 bytes (2^{30} bytes)	Approximately 786,432 pages of text; 500 sheets of paper is approximately 2 inches, so this represents a stack of paper 262 feet high.
Terabyte	TB	1,099,511,627,776 bytes (2^{40} bytes)	This represents a stack of typewritten pages almost 51 miles high.
Petabyte	PB	1,125,899,906,842,62 bytes (2^{50} bytes)	The stack of pages is now 52,000 miles high, or approximately one-fourth the distance from the Earth to the moon.
Exabyte	EB	1,152,921,504,606,846,976 bytes (2^{60} bytes)	The stack of pages is now 52 million miles high, or just about twice the distance between the Earth and Venus.
Zettabyte	ZB	1,180,591,620,717,411,303,424 bytes (2^{70} bytes)	The stack of pages is now 52 billion miles high. That's some 20 times the distance between the Earth and Pluto.

However, a computer needs more than just hardware to work: It also needs some form of software (computer programs). Think of a book without words or a CD without music. Without words or music, these two common items are just shells that hold nothing.

Similarly, a computer without software is a shell full of hardware components that can't do anything. *Software* is the set of computer programs that enables the hardware to perform different tasks. There are two broad categories of software: application software and system software.

When you think of software, you are most likely thinking of application software. **Application software** is the set of programs you use on a computer to help you carry out tasks such as writing a research paper. If you've ever typed a document, created a spreadsheet, or edited a digital photo, for example, then you've used a form of application software.

System software is the set of programs that enables your computer's hardware devices and application software to work together. The most common type of system software is the **operating system (OS)**—the program that controls the way in which your computer system functions. It manages the hardware of the computer system, such as the monitor and the printer. The operating system also provides a means by which users can interact with the computer. For the rest of this chapter, we'll explore hardware.

Your Computer's Hardware

Are all computers the same?

Considering the amount of amazing things computers can do, they are really quite simple machines. You learned in the previous section that a basic computer system is made up of software and hardware. There are two basic designs of computers. A **notebook computer** (or laptop computer) is a portable computer that is powered by

batteries (or a handy electrical outlet) and has keyboards, monitors, and other devices integrated into a single compact case.

A **desktop computer** is intended for use at a single location. Desktop computers consist of a separate case that houses the main components of the computer plus peripheral devices. A **peripheral device** is a component, such as a monitor or keyboard, which is connected to the computer. An **all-in-one computer** such as the Apple iMac (see Figure 3), the Dell XPS One, or the Gateway One houses not just the computer's processor and memory but also its monitor.

Are there other types of computers besides desktop and notebook computers?

Desktop and notebook computers are the computers that you will most likely encounter. Although you may never come into direct contact with the following types of computers, they are still important to our society:

- A **mainframe** is a large, expensive computer that supports hundreds of users simultaneously. Mainframes are often used in insurance companies, for example, where many people are working on similar operations (such as claims processing) all at once. Your college also may use mainframe computers to handle the multitude of processing needs throughout the campus. Mainframes excel at executing many different computer programs at the same time.

- A **supercomputer** is a specially designed computer that can perform complex calculations extremely rapidly. Supercomputers are used in situations in which complex models requiring intensive mathematical calculations are needed (such as weather forecasting or atomic energy research). The main difference between a supercomputer and a mainframe is that supercomputers are designed to execute a few programs as quickly as possible, while mainframes

Figure 3

The Apple iMac is an example of an all-in-one computer.

Courtesy of Apple

ZTS\Shutterstock

are designed to handle many programs running at the same time but at a slower pace.

- An **embedded computer** is a specially designed computer chip that resides inside another device, such as your car or the electronic thermostat in your home. Embedded computers are self-contained computer devices that have their own programming and typically neither receive input from you nor interact with other systems.

In the following sections, we look more closely at your computer's hardware (the parts you can actually touch). Each part has a specific purpose that coordinates with one of the functions of the computer—input, processing, output, or storage (see Figure 4).

Additional devices, such as modems and routers, help a computer communicate with the Internet and other computers to facilitate the sharing of documents and other resources. We begin our exploration of hardware by looking at your computer's input devices.

Input Devices

An **input device** enables you to enter data (text, images, and sounds) and instructions (user responses and commands) into the computer. The most common input devices are the keyboard and the mouse. A **keyboard** is used to enter typed data and commands, and a **mouse** is used to enter user responses and commands.

There are other input devices as well. Microphones input sounds, and scanners and digital cameras input nondigital text and digital images, respectively. A **stylus** is an input device that looks like a skinny pen but has no ink. Electronic pens are also becoming quite popular and are often used in conjunction with graphics tablets that can translate a user's handwriting into digital input.

Keyboards

Aren't all keyboards the same? Most desktop and notebook computers come with a standard **QWERTY keyboard** (see Figure 5). This keyboard layout gets its name from the first six letters in the top-left row of alphabetic keys on the keyboard and is the standard English-language keyboard layout. Over the years, there has been some debate over what is the best keyboard layout. The QWERTY layout was originally designed for typewriters and was meant to slow typists down and prevent typewriter keys from jamming.

Although the QWERTY layout is considered inefficient because it slows typing speeds, efforts to change to more efficient layouts,

Figure 4

Each part of the computer serves a special function.

Logitech Inc.

Figure 5

Most notebook and desktop keyboards share the same QWERTY keyboard layout.

such as that of the Dvorak keyboard, have not been met with much public interest. The Dvorak keyboard is an alternative keyboard layout that puts the most commonly used letters in the English language on "home keys," which are the keys in the middle row of the keyboard The Dvorak keyboard's design reduces the distance your fingers travel for most keystrokes, increasing typing speed.

How do notebook keyboards differ? To save space and weight, some of the smaller notebook keyboards (14" and under) are more compact than standard desktop keyboards and, therefore, have fewer keys. To retain the same functionality as a standard keyboard, many of the notebook keys have alternate functions. For example, many notebook keyboards do not have a separate numeric keypad. Instead, some letter keys function as number keys when they are pressed in combination with another key such as the function (Fn) key. The keys you use as numeric keys on notebooks have number notations on them so you can tell which keys to use (see Figure 6).

What if the standard keyboard doesn't work for me? Because users are demanding more portability from their computing devices, recent development efforts have focused on reducing the size and weight of keyboards. Flexible keyboards are terrific if you want a full-sized keyboard for your notebook. You can roll one up and fit it in your backpack. The virtual laser keyboard (see Figure 7) is about the size of a cellular phone. It projects the image of a keyboard on any surface, and sensors detect the motion of your fingers as you "type" on a desk or other flat surface. Data is transmitted via **Bluetooth** technology, which is a wireless transmission standard that facilitates the connection of electronic computing devices such as cell phones, smartphones, and computers to peripheral devices such as keyboards and headsets.

Gamers love keyboards such as the DX1 from Ergodex (see Figure 7). These keyboards allow placement of the keys in any position on the keyboard pad. The keys can be programmed to execute individual keystrokes or macros (a series of tasks) to perform specific tasks. This makes it easy for gamers to configure a keyboard in the most desirable way for each game they play.

How can I use my keyboard most efficiently? All keyboards have the standard set of alphabetic and numeric keys that you regularly use when typing. As shown in Figure 8, many keyboards for notebook and desktop computers have additional keys that perform special functions. Knowing how to use these special keys will help you improve your efficiency.

- The numeric keypad allows you to enter numbers quickly.
- Function keys act as shortcut keys you press to perform special tasks. They are sometimes referred to as the "F" keys because they start with the letter F followed by a number. Each software application has its own set of tasks assigned to various function keys. For example, the F2 key moves text or graphics in Microsoft Word but allows editing of the active cell in Microsoft Excel. Many keys are universal: the F1 key is the Help key in most applications.
- The Control (Ctrl) key is used in combination with other keys to perform shortcuts and special tasks. For example, holding down the Control (Ctrl) key while pressing the B key adds bold formatting to selected text. The Alt key works with other keys to execute additional shortcuts and special tasks. (On Macs, the Control function is the Apple key or Command key, and the Alt function is the Option key.)
- The Windows key is specific to the Windows operating system. Used alone, it opens the Start menu, although you use it most often in combination with other keys to perform shortcuts. For example, in

Figure 6

On many notebooks, certain letter keys can function as number keys.

Paul Sakuma\AP Wide World Photos

Martin Meissner\AP Wide World Photos

Ergodex

Figure 7

(a) The virtual laser keyboard projects the image of a QWERTY keyboard on any surface. Sensors detect typing motions, and data is transmitted to a computing device via Bluetooth technology. (b) The Ergodex DX1 allows keys to be relocated anywhere on the pad and reprogrammed easily, making the keyboard popular with gamers.

view e-mail, access Help features, or control your CD/DVD player. These buttons are not always in the same position on every keyboard, but the symbols on top of the buttons generally help you determine their function. Some desktop keyboards include USB ports to facilitate attaching other devices, such as mice.

Another set of controls on standard keyboards are the cursor control keys that move your *cursor* (the flashing *I* symbol on the monitor that indicates where the next character will be inserted). A cursor control key is also known as an *arrow key* because each one is represented by an arrow on standard keyboards. The arrow keys move the cursor one space at a time in a document, either up, down, left, or right.

Above the arrow keys, you'll usually find keys that move the cursor up or down one full page or even to the document's beginning (Home), or to the end of a line of text or

Windows 7 and Vista, pressing the Windows key plus the M key minimizes all windows.

What are some other features on keyboards? Some keyboards (such as the one shown in Figure 8) also include multimedia and Internet keys or buttons that enable you to open a Web browser,

Figure 8

Keyboards have a variety of keys that help you work more efficiently.

Input Devices

Keystroke Shortcuts

Did you know that you can combine certain keystrokes to take shortcuts within an application, such as Microsoft Word, or within the operating system itself? The following are a few of the most helpful Windows shortcuts. Use them to make more efficient use of your time. For more shortcuts for Windows-based PCs, visit **support.microsoft.com**. For a list of shortcuts for Macs, see **apple.com/support**.

Text Formatting	File Management	Cut/Copy/Paste	Windows Controls
CTRL+B Applies (or removes) **bold** formatting to selected text	**CTRL+O** Opens the Open dialog box	**CTRL+X** Cuts (removes) selected text from document	**Alt+F4** Closes the current window
CTRL+I Applies (or removes) *italic* formatting to selected text	**CTRL+N** Opens a new document	**CTRL+C** Copies selected text	**Ctrl+Esc** Opens the Start menu
CTRL+U Applies (or removes) underlining to selected text	**CTRL+S** Saves a document	**CTRL+V** Pastes selected text (previously cut or copied)	**Windows Key + F1** Opens Windows Help
	CTRL+P Opens the Print dialog box		**Windows Key + F** Opens the Search (Find Files) dialog box

Insert key inserts new text within a line of existing text. When toggled off, the Insert key replaces (or overwrites) existing characters with new characters as you type. Other toggle keys that switch between an on state and an off state include the Num Lock key and the Caps Lock key.

Are all conventional keyboards connected to the computer via wires? Although most desktop PCs ship with wired keyboards, wireless keyboards are available. Wireless keyboards are powered by batteries. They send data to the computer using a form of wireless technology that uses radio frequency (RF). A radio transmitter in the keyboard sends out radio wave signals that are received in two ways. In one, a small receiving device sits on your desk and is plugged into the back of the computer where the keyboard would normally plug in. In the case of Bluetooth-compatible computers, a receiving device is contained in the system unit. RF keyboards used on home computers can be placed as far as 6 feet to 30 feet from the computer, depending on their quality. RF keyboards that are used in business conference rooms or auditoriums can be placed as far as 100 feet away from the computer, but they are far more expensive than traditional wired keyboards.

document (End). The Delete (Del) key allows you to delete characters, and the Insert key allows you to insert or overwrite characters within a document. The Insert key is a *toggle key* because its function changes between one of two options each time you press it: When toggled on, the

Optical laser (sensor)

Wheel

Trackball

a

b

Mice and Other Pointing Devices

What kinds of mice are there? The mouse type you're probably most familiar with is the **optical mouse** (see Figure 9). An optical mouse uses an internal sensor or laser to detect the mouse's movement. The sensor sends signals to the computer, telling it where to move the pointer on the screen. Optical mice are often preferable to other types of mice because they have few moving parts, which lessens the chances that dirt will interfere with the mechanisms or that parts will break down. Optical mice also do not require a mouse pad, though you can still use one to protect your work surface from being scratched. Optical mice are most common now, but you may still find a mouse at

Figure 9

(a) An optical mouse has an optical laser (or sensor) on the bottom that detects its movement. (b) A trackball mouse turns the traditional mouse on its back, allowing you to control the rollerball with your fingers.

home or in school that has a rollerball on the bottom, which moves when you drag the mouse across a mouse pad. The movement of the rollerball controls the movement of the cursor that appears on the screen.

A **trackball mouse** (see Figure 9) is basically a traditional mouse that has been turned on its back. The rollerball sits on top or on the side of the mouse, and you move the ball with your fingers, allowing the mouse to remain stationary. A trackball mouse doesn't demand much wrist motion, so it's considered better for the wrist than an optical mouse. Mice also have two or three buttons that enable you to execute commands and open shortcut menus. (Mice for Macs sometimes have only one button.) Many mice have additional programmable buttons and wheels that let you quickly scroll through documents or Web pages.

Do notebook computers include a mouse? Most notebooks do not come with a mouse. Instead, they have an integrated pointing device such as a **touchpad**, a small, touch-sensitive area at the base of the keyboard (see Figure 10). To use the touchpad, you simply move your finger across the pad. Some touchpads are sensitive to taps, interpreting them as mouse clicks, while others have buttons beneath the pads to record mouse clicks. Other notebooks incorporate a **trackpoint device**, a small, joystick-like nub that allows you to move the cursor with the tip of your finger.

Are there wireless mice? Just as there are wireless keyboards, there are wireless mice, both optical and trackball. Wireless mice are similar to wireless keyboards in that they use batteries and send data to the computer by radio frequency or Bluetooth technologies. If you have an RF wireless keyboard, then your RF wireless mouse and keyboard usually can share the same RF receiver. Wireless mice for notebooks have their own receivers that

Trackpoint

Touchpad

Lenovo, Inc.

Figure 10

Touchpads and trackpoint devices take the place of a mouse on notebook computers.

often clip into the bottom of the mouse for easy storage when not in use.

Small, compact devices like the MoGo Mouse (see Figure 11) are designed for portability. The MoGo Mouse fits into a peripheral slot on the side of a notebook; this slot serves to store the mouse, protect it, and charge its batteries all at the same time. The MoGo Mouse is wireless and uses Bluetooth technology to transmit data to the notebook.

What else can I do with my mouse? Manufacturers of mice are constantly releasing new models that allow you to perform useful tasks with a few clicks of the mouse. On some mouse models, Microsoft and Logitech now provide features such as the following:

- **Magnifier:** Pulls up a magnification box that you can drag around the screen to enhance viewing of hard-to-read images (see Figure 12). This feature is often used by people with visual disabilities.

- **Customizable buttons:** Provide extra buttons on the mouse that you can program to perform the functions that you use most often to help you speed through tasks.

- **Web search:** Allows you to quickly highlight a word or phrase and then press the search button on the mouse to start a Web search.

- **File storage:** Includes a wireless USB receiver that contains flash memory

Figure 11

The MoGo Mouse is a portable mouse that stores and charges in a PC Card slot.

Newton Peripherals, LLC

Newton Peripherals, LLC

Figure 12

The magnifier is a mouse feature that provides instant magnification of images or text.

to store or back up your files (for example, a USB thumb drive).

What other input devices are used with games? Game controllers such as joysticks, game pads, and steering wheels are also considered input devices because they send data to the computer. Game controllers, which are similar to the devices used on gaming consoles, such as the Xbox 360 and the PlayStation, are also available for use with computers. They have buttons and miniature pointing devices that provide input to the computer. Force-feedback joysticks and steering wheels deliver data in both directions. They translate your movements to the computer and translate its responses into forces on your hands, creating a richer simulated experience. Most game controls, such as those for Rock Band and the Wii system, are wireless to provide extra mobility.

Touchscreens

Figure 13

Tablet PCs use the finger or a stylus to input data and commands on a touchscreen display that twists and folds flat.

How else can I input data and commands? You've seen and used touch-sensitive screens in fast food restaurants, airport check-in kiosks, and ATM machines for quite some time. A **touchscreen** is a display screen that responds to commands initiated by a touch with a finger or a stylus. Touchscreens are becoming increasingly popular on many computing devices including desktops, notebooks, smartphones, and portable media players. A **tablet PC** is similar to a notebook PC but features a touch-sensitive screen that can

swivel and fold flat (see Figure 13). Users input data and commands on a tablet PC via a stylus or with their fingers. Although all tablet PCs have built-in keyboards that allow you to type text just as you would with a normal keyboard, the touchscreen functionality often makes it a better choice when inputting with a keyboard is impractical or unwieldy. Portable gaming devices such as the Nintendo DS also feature touch-sensitive screens that use a stylus (or finger) for input. Dell and Hewlett Packard have released all-in-one desktop PCs with touchscreen displays.

Tablet PCs, which were developed primarily because many people find it easier to write than to type input into a computer, are expensive compared to conventional notebooks. An alternative is a digital pen like the EPOS Digital Pen (see Figure 14). This pen works in conjunction with a flash drive (a portable electronic storage device that connects to a USB port on a computer). You can write with the pen on any conventional paper. The pen captures your writing and then wirelessly transmits and stores it in the flash drive. When the flash drive is connected to a computer, you can use software to translate your writing into digital text.

Image Input

How can I input digital images into my computer? Digital cameras,

EPOS

Figure 14

The EPOS Digital Pen captures writing and stores it in a flash drive for later transfer to a computer. No typing is required!

ACTIVE HELP-DESK

Using Input Devices

In this Active Helpdesk call, you'll play the role of a helpdesk staffer, fielding calls about different input devices, such as the different mice and keyboards on the market, what wireless input options are available, and how to best use these devices.

Ethics: What Is Ethical Computing?

If you were asked to cite an example of unethical behavior while using a computer, you could easily provide an answer. You've probably heard news stories about people using computers to commit such crimes as unleashing viruses or committing identity theft. You may also have read about students who were prosecuted for illegally sharing copyrighted material such as videos. All of these are examples of unethical behavior while using a computer. However, if you were asked what constitutes *ethical* behavior while using a computer, could you provide an answer just as quickly?

Loosely defined, *ethics* is a system of moral principles, rules, and accepted standards of conduct. So what are the accepted standards of conduct when using computers (see Figure 15)? The Computer Ethics Institute developed the Ten Commandments of Computer Ethics, which is widely cited as a benchmark for companies that are developing computer usage and compliance policies for employees. The ethical computing guidelines listed below are based on the Computer Ethics Institute's work.

Ethical Computing Guidelines

1. Avoid causing harm to others when using computers.
2. Do not interfere with other people's efforts at accomplishing work with computers.
3. Resist the temptation to snoop in other people's computer files.
4. Do not use computers to commit theft.
5. Agree not to use computers to promote lies.
6. Do not use software (or make illegal copies for others) without paying the creator for it.
7. Avoid using other people's computer resources without appropriate authorization or proper compensation.
8. Do not claim other people's intellectual output as your own.
9. Consider the social consequences of the products of your computer labor.
10. Only use computers in ways that show consideration and respect for others.

The United States has enacted laws that support some of these guidelines, such as Guideline 6, the breaking of which would violate copyright laws, and Guideline 4, which is enforceable under numerous federal and state larceny laws. Other guidelines, however, require more subtle interpretation as to what behavior is unethical because there are no laws designed to enforce them.

Bennet\The Christian Science Publishing Society

Figure 15

Make sure the work you claim as your intellectual output is the product of your intellect alone.

Consider Guideline 7, which covers unauthorized use of resources. The college you attend probably provides computer resources for you to use for coursework. But if the college gives you access to computers and the Internet, is it ethical for you to use those resources to run a business on eBay in between classes or on the weekends? Although it might not be technically illegal, you are tying up computer resources that could be used by other students for their intended purpose: learning and completing coursework. (This behavior also violates Guidelines 2 and 10.)

Keep these guidelines in mind as you study, and think about how they relate to the actions you take as you use computers in your life.

---

camcorders, and cell phones are common devices for capturing pictures and video, and all of them are considered input devices. Digital cameras and camcorders are usually used in remote settings (away from a computer) to capture images for later downloading to the computer. These devices either connect to a computer with a data cable or

SOUND
BYTE
Tablet and Notebook Tour

In this Sound Byte, you'll take a tour of a Tablet PC and a notebook computer, learning about the unique features and ports available on each.

Input Devices

Built-in webcam

Webcam

Fancy/Veer\Corbis RF

Figure 16

A webcam is either built into a notebook monitor or placed on top of a monitor.

transmit data wirelessly. Windows automatically recognizes these devices when they are connected to a computer and makes the input of the digital data to the computer simple and easy.

How do I capture live video from my computer? A webcam (see Figure 16) is a small camera that sits on top of a computer monitor (connected to the computer by a cable) or is built into a notebook computer. Although some webcams are able to capture still images, they are used mostly for transferring live video directly to a computer. Webcams make it possible to transmit live video over the Web. They are often used to facilitate videoconferencing or calls made with video phones. Videoconferencing technology allows a person sitting at a computer equipped with a webcam and a microphone to transmit video and audio across the Internet.

Sound Input

Why would I want to input sound to my computer? Equipping your computer to accept sound input opens up a variety of possibilities. You can conduct audio conferences with work colleagues, chat with friends or family over the Internet instead of using a phone, record podcasts,

and more. Inputting sound to your computer requires equipping it with a **microphone** or **mic**, a device that allows you to capture sound waves (such as your voice) and transfer them to digital format on your computer. Many notebook computers come with built-in microphones, and some desktop computers come with inexpensive microphones. If you don't have a microphone or you aren't getting the quality you need from your existing microphone, then you probably need to shop for one.

What types of microphones are available? There are several different types of microphones available for a variety of needs. Desktop microphones, which have an attached base that allows them to sit on a flat surface (see Figure 17), are convenient for recording podcasts or in other situations in which you might need your hands to be free. Unidirectional microphones pick up sound from only one direction. These are best used for recording podcasts with a single voice or making phone calls over the Internet with only one person on the sender's end of the call. Omnidirectional microphones pick up sounds from all directions at once. These mics are best for recording more than one voice, such as during a conference call when you need to pick up the voices of multiple speakers.

Blue Microphones

Figure 17

Professional-quality microphones such as the Snowball are essential for producing quality podcasts.

Clip-on microphones (also called *lavaliere microphones*) are useful in environments, such as presentations, where you need to keep your hands free for other activities (such as writing on a white board) or move around the room. Many of these microphones are wireless.

Close-talk microphones, which are usually attached to a headset, facilitate using speech-recognition software, videoconferencing, or making telephone calls. With a microphone attached to a headset, your hands are free to perform other tasks while you speak (such as making notes or referring to paper documents), and the headset allows you to listen as well (such as when making Internet phone calls).

What input devices are available for people with disabilities? Many people who have physical challenges use computers often, but they sometimes need special input devices to access them. For visually impaired users, voice recognition is an obvious option. For those users whose visual limitations are less severe, keyboards with larger keys are available. Keyboards that display on a touchscreen can make input easier for some individuals. These keyboards are displayed as graphics on the computer monitor. The user presses the keys with a pointing device or simply presses on the touchscreen monitor.

People with motor control issues may have difficulty with pointing devices. To aid such users, special trackballs are available that can easily be manipulated with one finger and can be attached to almost any surface, including a wheelchair. When arm motion is severely restrained, head-mounted pointing devices can be used. Generally, these involve a camera mounted on the computer monitor and a device attached to the head (often installed in a hat). When the user moves his or her head, the camera detects the movement, which controls the cursor on the screen. In this case, mouse clicks are controlled by a switch that can be manipulated by the user's hands or feet or even by using an instrument that fits into the mouth and senses the user blowing into it.

Output Devices

An **output device** enables you to send processed data out of your computer in the form of text, pictures (graphics), sounds

(audio), or video. One common output device is a **monitor** (sometimes referred to as a **display screen**), which displays text, graphics, and video as soft copies (copies you can see only on screen). Another common output device is the **printer**, which creates hard copies (copies you can touch) of text and graphics. Speakers and earphones (or earbuds) are the output devices for sound.

Monitors

What are the different types of monitors? There are two basic types of monitors: CRTs and LCDs. If your monitor is big and boxy, then it has a picture-tube device called a **cathode ray tube (CRT)** such as the one shown in Figure 18. If your monitor is flat, it's using **liquid crystal display (LCD)** technology (see Figure 18). An LCD monitor, also called a **flat-panel monitor**, is lighter and more energy efficient than a CRT monitor, making it perfect for portable computers such as notebooks. The sleek style of LCD monitors also makes them a favorite for users with small workspaces, and now they have become the standard type of display monitor, replacing the CRT. Today CRT monitors are difficult to find or buy because they are fast becoming **legacy technology**, or computing devices or peripherals that use techniques, parts, and methods from an earlier time that are no longer popular. Although legacy technology may still be functional, it is quickly being replaced by newer technological advances. This doesn't mean that if you have a CRT monitor that is functioning well you should replace it with an LCD monitor. However, when your CRT

Figure 18

(a) CRT monitors are big and bulky. (b) LCDs (flat-panel monitors) save precious desktop space and weigh considerably less than CRT monitors.

Rear glass

Colored light

Polarizer

Front glass

Unpolarized
white light
from backlight

Polarizer

Liquid crystals

Color filters

Figure 19

A magnification of a single pixel in an LCD monitor.

monitor fails, you will most likely only be able to replace it with an LCD monitor.

Why have LCD monitors replaced CRT monitors? LCD monitors are much smaller than CRT monitors are and therefore take up far less space on a work surface. They are also generally brighter than CRT monitors are and use different refresh methods for the tiny dots of color, which causes less eyestrain. Another advantage is that LCD monitors use significantly less energy and emit less electromagnetic radiation, making them more environmentally friendly. Finally, LCD monitors weigh less than CRT monitors, making them the obvious choice for mobile devices.

How do monitors work? Monitor screens are grids made up of millions of tiny dots, each of which is called a **pixel**. Illuminated pixels create the images you see on your monitor. Each pixel is actually comprised of three subpixels of the colors red, blue, and green. LCD monitors are made of two or more sheets of material filled with a liquid crystal solution (see Figure 19). A fluorescent panel at the back of the LCD monitor generates light waves. When electric current passes through the liquid crystal solution, the crystals move around and either block the fluorescent light or let the light shine through. This blocking or passing of light by the crystals causes images to form on the screen. The various combinations of red, blue, and green make up the components of color we see on our monitors.

What factors affect the quality of an LCD monitor? The most important factor to consider when choosing an LCD monitor is its **resolution**: the clearness or sharpness of the image. Resolution is controlled by the number of pixels displayed on the screen. The higher the resolution, the sharper and clearer the image will be. Monitor resolution is listed as a number of pixels. A high-end monitor may have a native (or maximum) resolution of 1,600 × 1,200, meaning it contains 1,600 vertical columns with 1,200 pixels in each column. Note that you can adjust a monitor's resolution either to make the image displayed on the screen larger (reducing the resolution) or to fit more on your screen (increasing the resolution). You cannot increase the resolution of an LCD monitor beyond its native (maximum) resolution. Generally, you should select a monitor with the highest resolution available for the screen size (measured in inches).

Other factors to consider when judging the quality of an LCD monitor include the following:

- **Viewing angle:** An LCD's viewing angle, which is measured in degrees, tells how far you can move to the side of (or above or below) the monitor before the image quality degrades to unacceptable levels. For monitors that measure 17 inches or more, a viewing angle of at least 150 degrees is usually recommended.

- **Contrast ratio:** This is a measure of the difference in light intensity between the brightest white and the darkest black that the monitor can produce. If the contrast ratio is too low, colors tend to fade when you adjust the brightness to a high or low setting. A contrast ratio between 400:1 and 600:1 is preferable.

- **Brightness:** Measured as candelas per square meter (cd/m2) or *nits*, brightness is a measure of the greatest amount of light showing when the monitor is displaying pure white. A brightness level of 250cd/m2 or greater is recommended.

- **Response time:** This is the measurement (in milliseconds) of the time it takes for a pixel to change color. A lower response time means faster transitions; therefore, moving images will appear less jerky on the monitor. A response time lower than 15 milliseconds is important when using a monitor to play a game or display full-motion video such as movies or television.

Is a bigger screen size always better?
The bigger the monitor, the more you can display, and depending on what you want to display, size may matter. In general, the larger the panel, the larger number of pixels it can display. For example, a 21-inch monitor will typically be able to display 1680 × 1050 pixels, while a 19-inch monitor may only be able to display 1440 × 900 or 1280 × 1024. If you watch many high-definition movies on your monitor, you will need a monitor with at least the 1920 × 1080 resolution required to display HD-DVDs and Blu-Ray movies. Larger screens can also allow you to view multiple documents or Web pages at the same time, creating the effect of using two separate monitors side by side. Again, be mindful of cost. Buying two smaller monitors might be cheaper than buying one large monitor. For either option—a big screen or two screens—you should check that your computer has a video card to support these devices.

Another size issue is whether you should get a wide screen or a standard 4:3 ratio screen. Wide-screen monitors are helpful if you work with multiple windows, use the sidebar gadgets included with the Windows 7 or Vista operating system, or watch movies often. The standard 4:3 ratio means that the monitor is 4 units wide and 3 units tall (in other words, the height is ¾ of the width). The monitor with a standard ratio is fine for basic computing needs.

What other features should I look for in an LCD monitor?
Some monitors, especially those on notebook computers, come with convenient built-in features such as speakers, webcams, and microphones. A built-in multiformat card reader is convenient to display images directly on the monitor or to download pictures quickly from a camera memory card to the PC. Another nice feature to look for in a desktop LCD monitor is a built-in USB hub. This will enable you to connect extra peripherals easily without reaching around the back of the PC.

If these features are important to you, you should look for a monitor that has them, but be careful that the price of buying a monitor with these additional features isn't more than what it would cost you to buy the monitor and extra peripherals separately.

BITS AND BYTES — Cleaning Your Monitor

Have you ever noticed how quickly your monitor attracts dust? It's important to keep your monitor clean because dust buildup can act like insulation, keeping heat in and causing the electronic components to wear out much faster. To clean your LCD monitor, follow these steps:

1. Turn off the monitor (or your notebook computer) and make sure it is unplugged from the electrical power outlet.
2. Use a 50/50 solution of rubbing alcohol and water on a soft cloth and wipe the screen surface gently. Never spray anything directly onto the monitor. (Check your monitor's user manual to see if there are cleaning products you should avoid using.)
3. In addition to wiping the screen, wipe away the dust from around the case.

Also, don't place anything on top of the monitor or pack anything closely around it. This may block air from cooling it. Finally, avoid placing magnets (including your speaker system's subwoofer) anywhere near the monitor because they can interfere with the mechanisms inside the monitor.

3M

PRNewsFoto/NEC Solutions (America) Inc.\AP Wide World Photos

Figure 20
Inexpensive projectors are showing up more frequently in business and the home to provide large images for movie viewing and gaming.

How do I show output to a large group of people?
Crowding large groups of people around your computer isn't practical. However, it is possible to use a **projector**, a device that can project images

from your computer onto a wall or viewing screen (see Figure 20). Projectors are commonly used in business and education settings such as conference rooms and classrooms. These projectors are small and lightweight, and some, like the 3M MPro 110, are small enough to fit into the palm of your hand! These portable projectors are ideal for businesspeople that have to make presentations at client locations. *Entertainment projectors,* such as the Wonderwall, include stereo speakers and an array of multimedia connectors, making them a good option for use in the home to display TV programs, DVDs, digital images, or video games in a large format.

Printers

What are the different types of printers? There are two primary categories of printers: impact and nonimpact. An **impact printer** has tiny hammer-like keys that strike the paper through an inked ribbon, making marks on the paper. The most common impact printer is the dot-matrix printer. In contrast, a **nonimpact printer** sprays ink or uses laser beams to transfer marks onto the paper. The most common nonimpact printers are inkjet printers and laser printers. Today, nonimpact printers have replaced impact printers almost entirely. They tend to be less expensive, quieter, and faster, and they offer better print quality. The only place you may see a dot-matrix printer is at a company that still uses them to print multipart forms. For most users, dot-matrix printers are truly legacy technology.

What are the advantages of inkjet printers? An **inkjet printer** (see Figure 21) is the standard type of printer found in most homes. Inkjet printers are popular because they are affordable and produce high-quality color printouts quickly and quietly.
Inkjet printers work by spraying tiny drops of ink onto paper and are great for printing black-and-white text as well as color images. In fact, when loaded with the right paper,

Canon U.S.A., Inc.

Figure 21

Inkjet printers are popular among home users, especially with the rise of digital photography. Many inkjet printers are optimized for printing photos from digital cameras.

higher-end inkjet printers can print images that look like professional-quality photos. One thing to consider when buying an inkjet printer is the type and cost of the ink cartridges the printer needs. Some printers use two cartridges: black and color. Other printers use four or more cartridges, typically black, magenta, cyan, and yellow. Often the cost of buying replacement cartridges is more than that of a brand-new printer! Depending on how frequently you print, you might want to consider a laser printer.

Why would I want a laser printer? Laser printers (see Figure 22) are most often used in office or classroom settings because they have a faster printing speed than inkjet printers and produce higher-quality printouts. A **laser printer** uses laser beams and static electricity to deliver toner (similar to ink) onto the correct areas of the page. Heat is used to fuse the toner to the page, making the image permanent. In the past, laser printers generally were not found in the home because of their high purchase price and because they did not produce great color images. Recently, however, the price and quality of color laser printers have fallen dramatically, making them highly price competitive with high-end inkjet printers. When you include the price of ink or toner in the overall cost, laser printers can be more economical than inkjets.

What kind of printer can I take with me? Although some inkjet printers

Figure 22

Courtesy Xerox Corporation

Laser printers print quickly and offer high-quality printouts.

are small enough to carry with you, you may want to consider a printer designed for portability for added mobility and flexibility (see Figure 23). Portable printers are often compact enough to fit in a briefcase, are lightweight, and sometimes run on battery power instead of AC current.

Are there wireless printers? One of the reasons you may have bought a notebook was to be able to use a computer without the restriction of wires. Wireless printing

offers you the same freedom. In addition, wireless printers allow several people to print to the same printer from different places. There are two different types of wireless printers: Wi-Fi and Bluetooth. Both Wi-Fi and Bluetooth printers have a range of up to approximately 300 feet. Wi-Fi, however, sends data more quickly than Bluetooth. If your printer is not Bluetooth enabled, you can add Bluetooth by plugging a Bluetooth adapter into a USB port. This lets you take advantage of a great printing solution for photos stored on your cell phone or any other Bluetooth-enabled portable device.

Are there any other types of specialty printers? An **all-in-one printer** is a device that combines the functions of a printer, scanner, copier, and fax into one machine. Popular for their space-saving convenience, all-in-one printers can use either inkjet or laser technology. A **plotter** is another type of printer. Plotters produce oversize pictures that require the drawing of precise and continuous lines, such as maps, detailed images (see Figure 24), and architectural plans. Plotters use a computer-controlled pen that provides a greater level of precision than the series of dots that laser or inkjet printers are capable of making.

A **thermal printer**, such as the one shown in Figure 25, is another kind of specialty printer. These printers work either by melting wax-based ink onto ordinary paper (a process called *thermal wax transfer printing*), or by burning dots onto specially coated paper (a process called *direct thermal printing*). They are used in stores to print receipts and in airports for electronic ticketing, among other places. Thermal printers are also emerging as a popular technology for mobile and portable printing in conjunction with smartphones and similar devices. Many models, such as the printers that car rental agencies use to give you an instant receipt when you drop off your rental car, feature

Canon U.S.A., Inc.

Figure 23

Modern portable printers feature Bluetooth connectivity, allowing them to be used with mobile devices.

Output Devices

69

Photo courtesy of XEROX Corporate Public Relations

Figure 24

Plotters are large printers used to print oversize images, maps, and architectural plans.

Figure 25

Thermal printers are used in many restaurants to print receipts.

Extech Instruments Corporation

wireless infrared technology for complete portability.

How do I select the best printer?

There is a printer for every printing need. First, you need to decide whether you want just a printer or a device that prints and scans, copies, or faxes (an all-in-one). In addition, you should decide whether you want an inkjet or laser printer. As we discussed previously, that decision is typically determined by price and by the type of printing you do. Once you have narrowed down the type of printer you want, the following criteria will help you determine the best model to meet your needs.

- **Speed:** A printer's speed determines how many pages it can print per minute. Print speed is expressed as *pages per minute* or *ppm*. The speed of inkjet printers has improved over the years, and many inkjet printers now print as fast as laser printers. Printing speeds vary by model and range from 8 ppm to 38 ppm for both laser and inkjet printers. Text documents printed in black and white print faster than documents printed in color.

- **Resolution:** A printer's resolution (printed image clarity) is measured in dots per inch (dpi), which is the number of dots of ink in a one-inch line. The higher the dpi, the greater the level of detail and quality of the image. You'll sometimes see dpi represented as a horizontal number multiplied by a vertical number, such as 600×600, but you may also see the same resolution simply stated as 600 dpi. For general-purpose printing, 300 dpi is sufficient. For printing photos, 1,200 dpi is better. The dpi for professional photo-quality printers is twice that.

- **Color output:** If you're using an inkjet printer to print color images, buy a four-color printer (cyan, magenta, yellow, and black) or a six-color one (four-color plus light cyan and light magenta) for the highest-quality output. While some printers come with a single ink cartridge for all colors and others have two ink cartridges (one for black and one for color), the best setup is to have an individual ink cartridge for each color so you can replace only the specific color cartridge that is empty. Color laser printers have four separate toner cartridges (black, cyan, magenta, and yellow), and the toner is blended in various quantities to produce the entire color spectrum.

- **Memory:** Printers need memory to print. Inkjet printers run slowly if they don't have enough memory. If you plan to print small text-only documents on an inkjet printer, then 1 to 2 MB of memory should be enough. You need approximately 4 MB of memory if you expect to print large text-only documents and 8 MB if you print graphics-heavy files. Unlike inkjet printers, laser printers won't print at all without sufficient memory. To ensure your laser printer meets your printing needs, buy one with at least 16 MB of memory. Some printers allow you to add more memory later.

- **Use and cost of the printer:** If you will be printing mostly black-and-white, text-based documents or will be sharing your printer with others, then a black-and-white laser printer is best because of its printing speed and overall economy for volume printing. If you're planning to print color photos and graphics, then an inkjet printer or color laser printer is a must, even though the cost per page will be higher.

- **Cost of consumables:** You should carefully investigate the cost of consumables (such as printer cartridges and paper) for any printer you are considering purchasing because the cost of inkjet cartridges often can exceed the cost of the actual printer when purchased on sale. Reviews in consumer magazines such as *PC World* and *Consumer Reports* can help you evaluate the overall cost of producing documents with a particular printer.

Sound Output

What are the output devices for sound? Most computers include inexpensive speakers. A **speaker** is an output device for sound. These speakers are sufficient to play the standard audio clips you find on the Web and usually enable you to participate in videoconferencing or phone calls made over the Internet. However, if you plan to digitally edit audio files or are particular about how your music sounds, you may want to upgrade to a more sophisticated speaker system, such as one that includes subwoofers (special speakers that produce only low bass sounds) and surround-sound speakers. A **surround-sound speaker** is part of a speaker system whose design makes the user feel surrounded by sound. Wireless speaker systems are available now to help you avoid cluttering up your rooms with speaker wire.

If you work in close proximity to other employees or travel with a notebook, you may need to use headphones or earbuds for your sound output to avoid distracting other people. Both devices will plug into the same jack on the computer that speakers connect to, so using them with a computer is easy. Studies of users of portable media players have shown that hearing might be damaged by excessive volume,

BITS AND BYTES — Does It Matter What Paper I Print On?

The quality of your printer is only part of what controls the quality of a printed image. The paper you use and the printer settings that control the amount of ink used are equally important. If you're printing text-only documents for personal use, then using low-cost paper is fine. You also may want to consider selecting draft mode in your printer settings to conserve ink. However, if you're printing more formal documents such as résumés, you may want to choose a higher-quality paper (determined by the paper's weight, whiteness, and brightness) and adjust your print setting to "normal" or "best."

The weight of paper is measured in pounds, with 20 pounds being standard. A heavier paper may be best for projects such as brochures, but be sure to check that your printer can handle the added thickness. The degree of paper whiteness is a matter of personal preference. Generally, the whiter the paper, the brighter colors appear. However, for more formal documents, such as résumés, you may want to use a creamier color. The brightness of paper usually varies from 85 to 94. The higher the number, the brighter the paper, and the easier it is to read printed text. Opacity is especially important if you're printing on both sides of the paper because it determines the amount of ink that shows through from the opposite side of the paper.

If you're printing photos, then paper quality can have a big impact on the results. Photo paper is more expensive than regular paper and comes in a variety of textures ranging from matte to high gloss. For a photo-lab look, high-gloss paper is the best choice. Semigloss (often referred to as *satin*) is good for portraits, while a matte surface is often used for black-and-white printing.

especially when using earbuds, because they fit into the ear canals. Therefore, you should exercise caution when using these devices.

Processing and Memory on the Motherboard

We just looked at the components of your computer that you use to input and output data. But where does the processing take place, and where is the data stored? The **motherboard** is the main circuit board that contains the central electronic components of the computer, including the computer's processor (its brain), its memory, and the many circuit boards that help the computer function. On a desktop, the motherboard is located inside the **system unit**, the metal or plastic case that also houses the power source and all the storage devices (CD/DVD drive and hard drive). With a notebook computer, the system unit is combined with the monitor and the keyboard into a single package.

Ever wonder how a printer knows what to print and how it puts ink in just the right places? Most inkjet printers use drop-on-demand technology, in which the ink is "demanded" and then "dropped" onto the paper. Two different processes use drop-on-demand technology: Thermal bubble is used by Hewlett-Packard and Canon, and piezoelectric is used by Epson. The difference between the two processes is how the ink is heated within the print cartridge reservoir (the chamber inside the printer that holds the ink).

In the thermal bubble process, the ink is heated in such a way that it expands (like a bubble) and leaves the cartridge reservoir through a small opening, or nozzle. Figure 26 shows the general process for thermal bubble.

In the piezoelectric process, each ink nozzle contains a crystal at the back of the ink reservoir that receives an electrical charge, causing the ink to vibrate and drop out of the nozzle.

Laser printers use a completely different process. Inside a laser printer is a big metal cylinder (also called a drum) that is charged with static electricity. When asked to print something, the printer sends signals to the laser in the laser printer, telling it to "uncharge" selected spots on the charged cylinder. These spots correspond to characters and images in the document you wish to print. Toner, a fine powder that is used in place of liquid ink, is only attracted to those areas on the drum that are not charged (the areas where the desired characters and images are to be printed). The toner is transferred to the paper as it feeds through the printer. Finally, the toner is melted onto the paper. All unused toner is swept back to the toner hopper before the next job starts the process all over again.

Inkjet Printer

Print cartridges

Print head

Nozzles

Inverted print cartridge

The print cartridge is positioned inside your inkjet printer so that the print head faces down toward the paper. The print head has 50 to several hundred nozzles, or small holes, through which ink droplets fall. These nozzles are narrower than a human hair. Inside the print head of color inkjet printers, there are three ink reservoirs that hold magenta (red), cyan (blue), and yellow ink. Depending on your printer, a fourth ink reservoir may be required to hold black ink, as well. (In non-color inkjet printers, there is only one ink reservoir for the black ink.)

(1) Ink, Resistor, Firing chamber, Nozzle

(2) Bubble forming, Ink forced out of the nozzle

(3) Ink drop

(4) Ink dot

STEP 1: Once the printer receives the command to print, electrical pulses flow through thin resistors in the print head to heat the ink.

STEP 2: The heated ink forms a bubble. The bubble continues to expand until it is forced out of the nozzle.

STEP 3: The ink drops onto the paper.

STEP 4: As the ink leaves the cartridge, the chamber begins to cool and contract, creating a vacuum to draw in the ink for the process to begin again.

Figure 26
How a thermal bubble inkjet printer works.

What's on the motherboard? The motherboard contains the set of chips that powers the system, including the central processing unit (CPU). The motherboard also houses the chips that provide the short-term memory for the computer and a set of slots for expansion cards (see Figure 27). The various circuit boards have specific functions that augment the computer's basic functions. A circuit board that provides additional functionality is usually referred to as an **expansion card** (or **adapter card**). Typical expansion cards found in the system unit are the sound and video cards. A **sound card** provides a connection for the speakers and microphone, whereas a **video card** provides a connection for the monitor. Many low-end computer models have video and sound capabilities integrated into their motherboards. High-end models still use expansion cards to provide video and sound capabilities. Other expansion cards provide a means for network and Internet connections. These include the **modem card**, which provides the computer with a connection to the Internet via a traditional phone line, and a **network interface card (NIC)**, which enables your computer to connect with other computers or to a cable modem to facilitate a high-speed Internet connection. Lastly, some expansion cards provide additional USB and FireWire ports.

BITS AND BYTES

Maintaining Your Printer

In general, printers require minimal maintenance. Occasionally, it's a good idea to wipe the case of the printer with a damp cloth to free it from accumulated dust. However, do not wipe away any ink residue that has accumulated inside the printer. If you are experiencing streaking or blank areas on your printed paper, then your print head nozzles may be clogged. To fix this, run the printer's cleaning cycle. (Check your printer's manual for instructions, because every printer is different.) If this doesn't work, you may want to use a cleaning sheet to brush the print head clean. These sheets often come with printers or with reams of photo paper. If you still have a problem, try a cleaning cartridge. Cleaning cartridges contain a special fluid that scrubs the print head. These cartridges can be found where most ink cartridges are sold. As with ink cartridges, make sure you buy one that is compatible with your printer.

processor can request the RAM's contents, which can be located, opened, and delivered to the CPU for processing in a few nanoseconds (billionths of a second). If you look at a motherboard, you'll see RAM as a series of small cards (called *memory cards* or *memory modules*) plugged into slots on the motherboard.

Because the entire contents of RAM are erased when you turn off the computer, RAM is a temporary or **volatile storage** location. To save data permanently, you need to save it to the hard drive or to another permanent storage device such as a

Figure 27

A motherboard contains the CPU, the memory (RAM) modules, and slots for expansion cards.

Memory

What exactly is RAM? Random access memory **(RAM)** is the place in a computer where the programs and data the computer is currently using are stored. Sometimes RAM is referred to as *primary storage*, but it should not be confused with other types of permanent storage devices such as the hard drive. RAM is much faster to read from and write to than the hard drive and other forms of storage. The

Memory modules (RAM)

CPU

Expansion cards

Expansion slot

Processing and Memory on the Motherboard

Single path vs. dual path processors for data

Single execution core

Path 2

Path 1

Single core processor

Dual execution cores

Path 2

Path 1

Dual core processor

Figure 28

Two are faster than one! With their dual core processors, Intel CPUs can work in parallel, processing two separate programs at the same time instead of switching back and forth between them.

CD or flash drive. You can think of RAM as the computer's short-term memory, and the hard drive as long-term memory.

Does the motherboard contain any other kinds of memory besides RAM? In addition to RAM, the motherboard also contains a form of memory called **read-only memory (ROM)**. ROM holds all the instructions the computer needs to start up when the computer is powered on. Unlike data stored in RAM, which is volatile storage, the instructions stored in ROM are permanent, making ROM a nonvolatile storage location. This means the data is not erased when the power is turned off.

Processing

What is the CPU? The **central processing unit** (**CPU**, or **processor**) is sometimes referred to as the "brains" of the computer because it controls all the functions performed by the computer's other components and processes all the commands issued to it by software instructions. Modern CPUs can perform as many as 6 billion tasks a second without error, making them extremely powerful components.

How is processor speed measured? Processor speed is measured in units of hertz (Hz). Hertz means "machine cycles per second." A machine cycle is the process of the CPU getting the data or instructions from RAM and decoding the instructions into something the computer can understand. Once the CPU has decoded the instructions, it executes them and stores the result back into system memory. Older machines ran at speeds measured in **megahertz (MHz)**, or millions of machine cycles per second, whereas current systems run at speeds measured in **gigahertz (GHz)**,

or billions of machine cycles per second. Therefore, a 3.8 GHz processor performs work at a rate of 3.8 billion machine cycles per second. It's important to realize, however, that CPU clock speed alone doesn't determine the performance of the CPU.

Is speed the only measure of processor performance? While speed is an important consideration when determining processor performance, CPU performance also is affected by other factors. One factor is the number of *cores*, or processing paths, a processor has. Until just a few years ago, processors only could handle one instruction at a time. Now, processors have been designed so that they can have two, four, and even eight different paths, allowing them to process more than one instruction at a time (see Figure 28). Applications such as virus protection software and the operating system, which are always running behind the scenes, can have their own processors, freeing up the other processor to run other applications such as a Web browser, Word, or iTunes more efficiently.

Besides the number of cores, are there other factors that determine processing power? In addition to the number of cores in a processor, other factors such as additional memory and how fast data is exchanged between the CPU and RAM should be considered. The "best" processor will depend on your particular needs and is not always the processor with the highest GHz and the greatest number of cores. Intel, one of the leading manufacturers of computer processor chips, has created a pictorial rating system for CPU chips. Instead of stars, Intel uses one to five brains to illustrate the relative computing power of each type of CPU within the Intel line of processors. It also provides an overall

SOUND BYTE

Virtual Computer Tour

In this Sound Byte, you'll take a video tour of the inside of a system unit. From opening the cover to locating the power supply, CPU, and memory, you'll become more familiar with what's inside your computer.

Figure 29

Intel uses a five-brain rating system to illustrate the power of its processors.

ranking of "smart," "smarter," and "genius" and an overview of each processor's key benefits (see Figure 29).

Storing Data and Information

Earlier we characterized RAM as temporary or volatile memory because the entire contents of RAM are erased when you turn off the computer. Thus, if you want to save the files you're working on permanently, as well as your music, digital images, and any software ap- plications you use, you need to store them in a different location than RAM. To save data permanently, you need to save it to the hard drive or to an- other permanent storage device such as a CD, DVD, or flash drive. Each of these permanent storage devices is located in your desk- top or notebook computer in a space called a **drive bay** (see Figure 30). There are two

kinds of drive bays—internal and external—as described below:

- Internal drive bays cannot be seen or accessed from outside the system unit. Generally, internal drive bays are reserved for internal hard drives. An **internal hard drive** usually holds all permanently stored pro- grams and data.

- External drive bays can be seen and accessed from outside the system unit. External drive bays house CD and DVD drives, for example. On desktop computers, sometimes there are empty external drive bays that can be used to install additional drives. These extra spaces are covered by a faceplate on the front panel. Notebook computers generally do not give you the ability to add additional drives. Such expansion is done by attaching an external drive to the computer through a USB port.

You may occasionally see a PC that still has a bay for a *floppy disk drive*, which reads and writes to easily transportable floppy disks that hold a limited amount of data (1.44 MB). Some computers also feature what's called a *Zip disk drive*, which resembles a floppy disk drive but has a slightly wider opening. Zip disks work just like standard floppy disks but can carry much more data (up to 750 MB). These storage devices are fast becoming legacy technologies and are not found on new computers.

Figure 30

Storage devices in desktop and notebook computers.

CD/DVD drive

Empty drive bay

Hard drive

Lenovo, Inc.

Courtesy of International Business Machines Corporation. Unauthorized use not permitted.

Photo courtesy of Iomega Corporation

D. Hurst\Alamy Images Royalty Free

Courtesy Western Digital Corporation

Figure 31

(a) Internal hard drives hold the data and instructions that the computer needs and are inaccessible from outside the system unit. (b) High-capacity external hard drives are often used to back up data on internal hard drives. (c) Smaller external hard drives enable you to take a significant amount of data and programs on the road with you.

Figure 32

Flash drives are a convenient means of portable storage, and come in many different shapes and sizes.

Hard Drives

Which storage device holds the most data? The **hard drive** (see Figure 31) is your computer's primary device for permanent storage of software and documents. The hard drive is a **nonvolatile storage** device, meaning it holds the data and instructions your computer needs permanently, even after the computer is turned off. Today's internal hard drives, with capacities of as much as 2 **terabyte (TB)**, can hold more data than would fit in the books in a school's library.

Are all hard drives located inside the system? Because the hard drive stores all of the computer's data and programs, special measures are taken to protect the hard drive from any possible damage. Unlike other storage devices on the computer, the hard drive is enclosed in a case and is not accessible from the outside of the

system unit. If you need a more portable solution, external hard drives are readily available. An **external hard drive** (see Figure 31) is essentially like an internal hard drive. However, it has been made portable by making it small and lightweight and enclosing it in a protective case. Some external hard drives, which are small enough to fit into your pocket, have storage capacities of 1 or 2 TB (or larger). An external hard drive is often used to back up (make a copy of) data that is contained on an internal hard drive in case a problem develops with the internal hard drive and data needs to be recovered. Other external hard drives have more limited storage capacity (up to 500 GB). These are even smaller and are designed for the ultimate portability of files between computers (see Figure 31).

Optical Storage

What other kinds of storage devices are available? Internal hard drives are used to store your data, files, and installed software programs. Hard drives store their data on magnetized platters. Also included on most desktop and notebook computers is at least one **optical drive** that can read from and maybe even write to CDs, DVDs, or Blu-ray discs. Data is saved to a **compact disc (CD)**, **digital video disc (DVD)**,

Rafael Angel Irusta Machin\Alamy Images Royalty Free

Handout/KRT\Newscom

Looking at Computers: Understanding the Parts

or **Blu-ray disc (BD)** as tiny pits that are burned into the disc by a high-speed laser. CDs were initially created to store audio files. DVDs are the same size and shape as CDs but can hold more than 25 times as much data. If you're looking for more storage capacity than CDs or DVDs, a double-layer DVD is the next step. These discs have up to 8.5 GB of storage. What if you want even more storage capacity? Blu-ray is the latest incarnation of optical storage to hit the market. Although a dual-layered DVD can store approximately 8.5 GB of information, this isn't enough to hold movies in the high-definition (HD) digital format that has become so popular. Blu-ray discs, which are similar in size and shape to CDs and DVDs, can hold as much as 50 GB of data. This is enough to hold approximately 4.5 hours of high-definition video. Many systems are now available with BD-ROM drives and even Blu-ray burners. External BD drives are another inexpensive way to add HD storage capacity to your system.

Flash Storage

A **flash drive**, sometimes referred to as a **jump drive**, **USB drive**, or **thumb drive**, is a newer way of storing portable data. Flash drives plug into USB ports. These devices originally were more or less the size of a thumb, but now they vary in size, and are often combined with other devices such as pens or pocketknives (see Figure 32). Despite their diminutive size, flash drives have significant storage capacity—currently as much as 64 GB.

Several manufacturers now also include slots on the front of the system unit in which you can insert a portable **flash memory card** such as a Memory Stick or CompactFlash card. Many notebooks also include slots for flash memory cards in the sides. Flash memory cards let you transfer digital data between your computer and devices such as digital cameras, PDAs, smartphones, video cameras, and printers. Although incredibly small—some are just the size of a postage stamp—these memory cards have capacities that exceed the capacity of a DVD.

Figure 33 shows the storage capacities of the various portable storage media used in your computer's drive bays.

Figure 33 | STORAGE MEDIA CAPACITIES

MEDIUM	IMAGE	CAPACITY
Hard drive		External: as much as 2 TB Internal: as much as 750 GB
Portable hard drive	Courtesy Western Digital Corporation	Up to 500 GB
Flash drive	Christophe Testi\Shutterstock	64 GB or more
Blu-ray (dual layer)	Sony Electronics, Inc\Newscom	50 GB
Flash memory card		Up to 32 GB
Blu-ray (BD)		25 GB
DVD DL (dual layer)	Olaf Jansen\Alamy Images	9.4 GB
DVD	Studio 101\Alamy Images Royalty Free	4.7 GB
CD	Studio 101\Alamy Images Royalty Free	700 MB

Storing Data and Information

77

Connecting Peripherals to the Computer

Throughout this chapter, we have discussed peripheral devices that input, store, and output data and information. A **port** is a place through which a peripheral device attaches to the computer so that data can be exchanged between it and the operating system. Many ports are located on the back of a notebook computer (see Figure 34) and the system unit of a desktop computer (see Figure 34). However, some commonly used ports are placed on the front and sides of many desktop and notebook computers for easier access when connecting devices such as flash drives or digital and video cameras.

High Speed and Data Transfer Ports

What is the most common way to connect devices to a computer? A **universal serial bus (USB) port** is now the most common port type used to connect input and output devices to the computer. This is mainly because of a USB port's ability to transfer data quickly. USB 2.0 ports (see Figure 35) are the current standard, and transfer data at 480 megabits per second (Mbps), approximately 40 times faster than the original USB ports did. USB ports can connect a wide variety of peripherals to the computer, including keyboards, printers, mice, smartphones, external hard drives, flash drives, and digital cameras.

A traditional **serial port** sends data one bit (piece of data) at a time. Serial ports were often used to connect modems (devices used to transmit data over telecommunications lines) to the computer. Sending data one bit at a time was a slow way to communicate. A **parallel port** could send data between devices in groups of bits at speeds of 500 Kbps and was much faster than traditional serial ports. Parallel ports were often used to connect printers to computers. The speed advantage offered by USB ports is quickly making serial and parallel ports legacy technology.

What are the fastest ports available? Interfaces such as **FireWire 400** (or **IEEE 1394**) and **FireWire 800** are the fastest ports available. The FireWire 400 interface moves data at 400 Mbps, while the newer FireWire 800 doubles the rate to 800 Mbps. Devices such as external hard drives, digital video cameras, portable music players, and digital media players all benefit from the speedy data transfer capabilities of FireWire. The USB 3.0 standard is currently under development. When this standard is ratified, it should

Figure 34

The same ports are on the back of many (a) notebook and (b) desktop computers.

sight and thereby increasing neck strain. The table in Figure 47 provides guidelines on preventing injuries when computing on the go.

So whether you're computing at your desk or on the road, consider the ergonomics of your work environment. Doing so will help you avoid injury and discomfort.

Figure 47 | PREVENTING INJURIES WHILE ON THE GO

	PDA/Smartphone RSIs	PMP Hearing Damage	Small-Screen Vision Issues	Lap Injuries	Back, Neck, and Shoulder Injuries
Malady	Repetitive strain injuries (such as DeQuervain's tendonitis) from constant typing of instant messages.	Hearing loss from high decibel sound levels in earbuds or headphones.	Blurriness and dryness caused by squinting to view tiny screens on mobile devices.	Burns on legs from heat generated by notebook.	Pain caused from carrying notebook (messenger) bag hung over your shoulder.
Preventative measures	Restrict length and frequency of messages, take breaks often, and perform other motions with your thumbs and fingers during breaks to relieve tension.	Turn down volume (you should be able to hear external noises such as people talking), use software programs that limit sound levels (not over 60 decibels), and use external, over-ear style headphones instead of earbuds.	Blink frequently or use eye drops to maintain moisture level in eyes, after 10 minutes take a break and focus your eyes on something at least 8 feet away for 5 minutes, use an adequate amount of light, increase the size of fonts.	Place a book, magazine, or notebook cooling pad between your legs and your notebook.	Use a conventional backpack with two shoulder straps, lighten the load by only carrying essential equipment, and consider buying a lightweight notebook.

Today, LCD monitors dominate the desktop PC and notebook markets. Lighter and less bulky than previous monitors, they can be easily moved and take up less space on a desk. LCD technology has improved significantly over the past several years, and now monitors are sporting increased viewing angles, higher resolutions, and faster pixel response time, which makes full-motion video (critical for gamers) appear extremely smooth.

LCD technology has also infiltrated the television market and, along with plasma technology, will make the boxy TV as obsolete as the CRT monitor. However, as good as LCD technology is, some technology that is beginning to hit the market is even better.

OLED Displays

Organic Light Emitting Diode (OLED) displays use organic compounds that produce light when exposed to an electric current. Unlike LCDs, OLEDs do not require a backlight to function, and therefore draw less power and have a much thinner display, sometimes as thin as 3mm. They are also brighter, cheaper to manufacture, and more environmentally friendly than plasma displays or LCDs. Because of their lower power needs, OLED displays run longer on a single battery charge than do LEDs, which is why OLED technology is currently being used in small screens of mobile devices such as cell phones, portable media players, and digital cameras.

More recently, OLED technology has been incorporated in some high-end televisions. The benefits of OLED technology may make LCD flat-panel displays quickly obsolete (see Figure 48). The pixels in OLED screens illuminate quickly, like light bulbs, and produce brighter images than does LCD technology. Because of the quick on–off illumination capacity of OLED pixels, the faster refresh rate enables these screens to display full-motion videos with life-like motion. Sony and Toshiba have already produced OLED televisions. Eventually, you might not even need a separate display device; it could very well be built into the walls of your house!

Flexible Screens

An offshoot of OLED technology is flexible OLEDs (FOLEDs). Unlike LCDs, which use rigid surfaces such as glass, FOLED screens use lightweight,

ROBYN BECK/AFP/Getty Images\Newscom

Figure 48

Because they do not need a backlight, OLED displays are much thinner than LEDs, making LCD screens seem bulky!

inexpensive, flexible material such as transparent plastics or metal foils. As shown in Figure 49, these flexible screens can play a full-motion video while being completely bent.

This 2.5-inch screen is playing a full-motion video while being bent into a semicircle.

Courtesy of Sony Electronics Inc.

Figure 49

FOLEDs would allow advertising to progress to a new dimension. Screens could be hung where posters hang now (such as on billboards). Wireless transmission of data to these screens would allow advertisers to display easily updatable full-motion images. Combining transparency and flexibility, these displays can be mounted on windshields and eyeglasses.

Wearable Screens

Who needs a computer screen when you can just wear one? With the rise of the iPod and other portable devices that play digital video, users are demanding larger viewing areas. Although a larger screen is often incompatible with the main design features of portable devices (light weight and long battery life), wearable virtual displays offer a solution. Personal media viewer displays such as the **myvu**, shown in Figure 50, are available now (**myvu.com**). Eventually, when the technology advances sufficiently, you might be able to purchase conventional eyeglasses with displays built right in. Wearable displays might eventually replace heavier screens on notebooks, desktops, and even PDAs.

"Bistable" Screens

Your computer screen constantly changes its images when you are surfing the Internet or playing a game. Because PDA and cell phone screens don't

Myvu Corporation

Figure 50

Personal media viewers allow you to have a big-screen experience with your mobile devices. The display is projected in front of your eyes, giving you an "in the action" experience.

necessarily change that often, something called a "bistable" display, which is currently used in retail stores for pricing signs and in Amazon's Kindle (a wireless reading device), may one day be used in these devices. A bistable display has the ability to retain its image even when the power is turned off. In addition, bistable displays are lighter than LCD displays and reduce overall power consumption, resulting in longer battery life—perhaps as much as 600 times longer, according to Motorola. Because the market for portable devices such as smartphones continues to explode, you can expect to see bistable technologies emerging in mobile computer screens.

1. What exactly is a computer, and what are its four main functions?

Computers are devices that process data. They help organize, sort, and categorize data to turn it into information. The computer's four major functions are (1) to gather data (or allow users to input data), (2) to process that data (perform calculations or some other manipulation of the data), (3) to output data or information (display information in a form suitable for the user), and (4) to store data and information for later use.

2. What is the difference between data and information?

Data is a representation of a fact or idea. The number 3 and the words *televisions* and *Sony* are pieces of data. Information is data that has been organized or presented in a meaningful fashion. An inventory list that indicates that "three Sony televisions" are in stock is processed information. It allows a retail clerk to answer a customer query about the availability of merchandise. Information is more powerful than raw data.

3. What are bits and bytes, and how are they measured?

To process data into information, computers need to work in a language they understand. This language, called binary language, consists of two numbers: 0 and 1. Each 0, and each 1, is a binary digit, or bit. Eight bits create one byte. In computers, each letter of the alphabet, each number, and each special character consists of a unique combination of eight bits (one byte)—a string of eight 0s and 1s. For describing large amounts of storage capacity, the terms *megabyte* (approximately 1 million bytes), *gigabyte* (approximately 1 billion bytes), and *terabyte* (approximately 1 trillion bytes) are used.

4. What devices do I use to get data into the computer?

An input device enables you to enter data (text, images, and sounds) and instructions (user responses and commands) into a computer. You use keyboards to enter typed data and commands, whereas you use the mouse to enter user responses and commands. Keyboards are distinguished by the layout of the keys as well as the special keys found on the keyboard. The most common keyboard is the QWERTY keyboard. Notebook keyboards are more compact, and generally have fewer keys, than standard keyboards. Consequently, many notebook keys have alternate functions so that you can get the same capabilities from their limited number of keys as you do from the special keys on standard keyboards.

Most desktop computers come with wired optical mice. Other options include trackball mice and wireless mice. An optical mouse uses an internal sensor or laser to control the mouse's movement. Wireless mice use batteries and send data to the computer via radio frequency or Bluetooth technology. Notebooks incorporate the mouse into the keyboard area. Notebook pointing devices include trackpoints and touchpads.

Touchscreens are display screens that respond to commands initiated by a touch with a finger or a stylus. Tablet PCs feature a touchscreen display that swivels and folds flat. Other devices that feature touchscreens are portable media players, cell phones, smartphones, and portable gaming devices.

Images are input into the computer with digital cameras, camcorders, and cell phones. Live video is captured with webcams and digital video recorders. Microphones capture sounds. There are many different types of microphones, including desktop, headset, and clip-on models.

5. What devices do I use to get information out of the computer?

Output devices enable you to send processed data out of your computer. It can take the form of text, pictures, sounds, or video. Monitors display soft copies of text, graphics, and video, while printers create hard copies of text and graphics. LCDs are the most popular type of monitor. Also called *flat-panel monitors*, they take up less space and are lighter and more energy efficient than older CRT monitors (which are big and boxy), making LCDs perfect for portable computers. Today's LCD monitors support high screen resolutions, have wide viewing angles, and feature fast pixel response times so that full-motion video appears smooth.

There are two primary categories of printers: impact and nonimpact. Impact printers have hammerlike keys that strike the paper through an inked ribbon. Nonimpact printers

Looking at Computers: Understanding the Parts

spray ink or use laser beams to transfer marks to the paper. The most common nonimpact printers are inkjet printers and laser printers. Specialty printers are also available. These include all-in-one printers, plotters, and thermal printers. When choosing a printer, you should be aware of factors such as speed, resolution, color output, memory, and cost.

Speakers are the output devices for sound. Most computers include speakers. However, you may want to upgrade to a more sophisticated speaker system, such as one that includes subwoofers and surround sound.

6. What's on the motherboard?

The motherboard, the main circuit board of the system, contains a computer's central processing unit (CPU), which coordinates the functions of all other devices on the computer. The performance of a CPU is affected by the speed of the processor (measured in gigahertz), the amount of cache memory, the speed of the front side bus (FSB), and the number of processing cores. RAM, the computer's volatile memory, is also located on the motherboard. RAM is where all the data and instructions are held while the computer is running. ROM, a permanent type of memory, is responsible for housing instructions to help start up a computer. The motherboard also houses a set of slots for expansion cards. The various circuit boards have specific functions that augment the computer's basic functions. They are usually referred to as expansion cards or adapter cards. Typical expansion cards found in the system unit are the sound and video cards.

7. Where are information and programs

To save programs and information permanently, you need to save them to the hard drive or to another permanent storage device such as a CD, DVD, or flash drive. The hard drive is your computer's primary device for permanent storage of software and files. The hard drive is a nonvolatile storage device, meaning it holds the data and instructions your computer needs permanently, even after the computer is turned off. External hard drives are essentially internal hard drives that have been made portable by enclosing them in a protective case and making them small and lightweight. Optical drives that can read from, and maybe even write to,

CD, DVD, or Blu-ray discs are another means of permanent, portable storage. Data is saved to compact discs (CDs), digital video discs (DVDs), and Blu-ray discs (BDs) as tiny pits that are burned into the disc by a high-speed laser. Flash drives are another portable means of storing data. These devices can hold 64 GB or more of data. Flash drives plug into USB ports. Flash memory cards let you transfer digital data between your computer and devices such as digital cameras, smartphones, video cameras, and printers.

8. How are devices connected to the computer?

There are a wide variety of ports that allow you to hook up peripheral devices (such as your monitor and keyboard) to your system. The most common type of port used to connect devices to a computer is the USB port. It has replaced serial ports and parallel ports, which are now considered legacy technology. FireWire ports provide even faster data transfer.

Connectivity ports give you access to networks and the Internet and enable your computer to function as a fax machine. Connectivity ports include Ethernet ports and modem ports. Multimedia ports include VGA, DVI, and S-video ports. They connect the computer to monitors and other multimedia devices. Audio ports are where you connect headphones, microphones, and speakers to the computer. HDMI ports connect monitors, TVs, and gaming consoles to the computer and work with both audio and video content.

9. How do I set up my computer to avoid strain and injury?

Ergonomics refers to how you arrange your computer and equipment to minimize your risk of injury or discomfort. This includes positioning your monitor correctly, buying an adjustable chair that ensures you have good posture while using the computer, assuming a proper position while typing, making sure the lighting is adequate, and not looking at the screen for long periods of time. Other good practices include taking frequent breaks and using other specially designed equipment such as ergonomic keyboards. Ergonomics is also important to consider when using mobile devices.

key terms

all-in-one computer
all-in-one printer
application software
binary digit (bit)
binary language
Blu-ray disc (BD)
Bluetooth
brightness
byte
cathode ray tube (CRT)
compact disc (CD)
central processing unit
  (CPU or processor)
cold boot
computer
connectivity port
contrast ratio
data
desktop computer
digital video disc (DVD)
digital video interface (DVI)
drive bay
embedded computer
ergonomics
Ethernet port
expansion card (adapter card)
external hard drive
FireWire 400 (IEEE 1394)
FireWire 800
flash drive (jump drive, USB drive,
  or thumb drive)
flash memory card
flat-panel monitor
gigabyte (GB)
gigahertz (GHz)
hard drive
hardware
Hibernate mode
impact printer
information
inkjet printer
input device
internal hard drive
keyboard
kilobyte (KB)
laser printer
legacy technology
liquid crystal display (LCD)
mainframe
megabyte (MB)
megahertz (MHz)

microphone (mic)
modem card
modem port
monitor (display screen)
motherboard
mouse
network interface card (NIC)
nonimpact printer
nonvolatile storage
notebook computer
operating system (OS)
optical drive
optical mouse
output device
parallel port
peripheral device
pixel
plotter
port
power supply
printer
processing
projector
QWERTY keyboard
random access memory (RAM)
read-only memory (ROM)
resolution
response time
S-video (super video)
serial port
Sleep mode
sound card
speaker
stylus
supercomputer
surround-sound speaker
system software
system unit
tablet PC
terabyte (TB)
thermal printer
touchscreen
touchpad
trackball mouse
trackpoint device
universal serial bus (USB) port
video card
video graphics array (VGA)
volatile storage
warm boot
webcam

Looking at Computers: Understanding the Parts

Word Bank

- CPU
- CRT
- DVI
- ergonomics
- external hard drive
- FireWire
- inkjet printer
- laser printer
- LCD
- microphone
- monitor
- mouse
- notebook
- optical mouse
- QWERTY
- RAM
- ROM
- speakers
- system unit
- USB
- webcam

Instructions: Fill in the blanks using the words from the Word Bank above.

Austin had been getting a sore back and stiff arms when he sat at his desk, so he redesigned the (1) _____ of his notebook setup. He placed the notebook in a stand so the (2) _____ was elevated to eye level and was 25 inches from his eyes. He decided to improve his equipment in other ways. His (3) _____ was old, so he replaced it with a(n) (4) _____ that didn't need a mouse pad. To plug in the mouse, he used a(n) (5) _____ port on the side of his (6) _____. He considered buying a larger (7) _____ keyboard with a number pad because it's not convenient to input numeric data with his current keyboard. Because he often printed flyers for his band, Austin decided to buy a printer that could print text-based pages quickly. Although he decided to keep his (8) _____ to print photos, he decided to buy a new (9) _____ to print his flyers faster. While looking at printers, Austin also noticed widescreen (10) _____ monitors that would provide a larger display than that on his notebook so he bought one on sale. He hooked up the monitor to the (11) _____ port on the back of the notebook. He also bought a(n) (12) _____ headset and a(n) (13) _____ so he could talk to his friends over the Internet. Austin also knew he had to buy a(n) (14) _____ to back up all his files. Finally, knowing his system could use more memory, Austin checked out prices for additional (15) _____.

becoming computer literate

Your parents live a day's drive from your school and have just called asking you for help in setting up their new computer.

Instructions: Because you can't help them in person, prepare a setup guide for your parents. Format it as either a Word document or a PowerPoint presentation. Your setup guide should illustrate and define all the components of a computer system. In addition, you should describe with illustrations and words the types of ports your parents will need to use to attach various peripheral devices to the system unit. You may use the Internet for information, device pictures, and illustrations, but remember to credit all sources at the end of your guide.

self-test

Instructions: Answer the multiple-choice and true–false questions below for more practice with key terms and concepts from this chapter.

Multiple Choice

1. Which of the following devices are considered input devices?
   a. Keyboard and mouse
   b. Monitor and inkjet printer
   c. Hard drive and speakers
   d. Laser printer and CD-ROM drive

2. Which of the following handles the processing for a computer?
   a. RAM   c. ROM
   b. CPU   d. USB

3. Which of the following is an output device?
   a. Mouse   c. Hard drive
   b. Monitor   d. Microphone

4. The resolution of a monitor is governed by the
   a. size of the screen.
   b. cost of the monitor.
   c. number of pixels on the screen.
   d. contrast of the pixels on the screen.

5. All of the following are important to consider when buying an LCD monitor EXCEPT
   a. brightness.
   b. pixel swap rate.
   c. viewing angle.
   d. resolution.

6. Restarting the system while the computer is running is called
   a. a warm boot.   c. hibernation.
   b. a standby start. d. a cold boot.

7. An Ethernet port is used for connecting your computer to a
   a. network.   c. monitor.
   b. printer.   d. digital camera.

8. Which of the following devices is considered volatile storage?
   a. ROM   c. RAM
   b. Optical disc   d. Flash drive

9. Which of the following statements about hard drives is false?
   a. Hard drives are not always installed inside the system unit of a computer.
   b. Hard drives are considered volatile storage devices.
   c. External hard drives are often used for backups.
   d. Hard drives are considered nonvolatile storage devices.

10. Which of the following is not a reason to have an ergonomically correct setup for your computer?
   a. It reduces eyestrain.
   b. It prevents repetitive strain injuries.
   c. It complies with federal laws.
   d. It saves businesses money.

True-False

_____ 1. Data is information that has been organized or presented in a meaningful fashion.

_____ 2. ROM is volatile storage that is located on the motherboard.

_____ 3. Bluetooth devices have a shorter range of functionality than Wi-Fi devices.

_____ 4. USB ports are the most common type of port used for connecting peripherals to a computer.

_____ 5. A computer needs a cold boot when it resumes activity after hibernation.

1. **Choosing the Best Keyboard**

   Once you become more familiar with software products such as Microsoft Office, you may want to migrate to a customized keyboard design. Although keyboards have similar setups, some keyboards provide special keys and buttons to support different users. For example, some keyboards are designed specifically for multimedia use, Internet use, and gaming use. Which one is best for you?

   a. Examine the various keyboard setups at the Microsoft Web site (**microsoft.com/hardware/mouseandkeyboard/default.mspx**). Which keyboard would best suit your needs and why? What features would be most useful to you? How would you evaluate the additional costs versus the benefits?

   b. When would you need a keyboard for a portable computing device, such as a smartphone? What is the current price for a portable folding keyboard? Would the virtual keyboard described in the chapter be a better choice for you? Explain your answers.

2. **Watching Device Demos**

   YouTube is a great resource for product demonstrations. Open your browser, navigate to the YouTube Web site (**youtube.com**), search on any type of computer peripheral discussed in this chapter, and see if you can find a demonstration of a cool product. How helpful are these demonstrations? Try making a demonstration and uploading it to YouTube.

3. **Communicating with the Computer**

   You want to start using Voice over Internet Protocol (VoIP) to chat over the Internet with your family and friends who live far away. You know you and your family members need speakers, a microphone, and a webcam. On the Web, investigate the following:

   a. How much does a good pair of headphones cost? Would having separate speakers and a microphone be just as effective? Why or why not?

   b. How much does a webcam cost? Which kind would you most likely purchase? Would you get the same kind for your parents? Why or why not?

4. **Exploring Scanners**

   Scanners are one type of input device that we did not discuss in the text. Conduct the following research on the Web to find out about scanners:

   a. What are the different kinds of scanners on the market?

   b. What qualities do good scanners have?

   c. How much do scanners cost?

   Create a table comparing the qualities, features, and costs of several different scanners. Highlight the scanner you would be most interested in purchasing.

5. **Green Computing**

   Reducing energy consumption and promoting the recycling of computer components are key aspects of businesses' "green" (environmentally friendly) initiatives. Using the Web, research the following:

   a. What are the key attributes of the Energy Star and EPEAT Gold green PC certifications? Does your PC have these certifications?

   b. What toxic components are contained in computers and monitors? Where can you recycle computers and monitors in your area?

   c. Check out **goodcleantech.com** and find out which companies are currently working toward better green technology. If your school had to replace computers in a lab, which environmentally friendly company would you recommend? Why?

making the transition to... the Workplace

1. **Desktop versus Notebook**

   There are two main types of computers in the workplace: desktop computers with separate system units and monitors, and notebook computers that are portable and have the monitor, keyboard, and the system unit within a single case. If you were being interviewed for a job, what types of questions would you need to ask your prospective boss about the job to determine whether you would be using a desktop or a notebook computer?

2. **What System Will You Use?**

   When you arrive at a new position for a company, you'll most likely be provided with a computer. Based on the career you are in now or are planning to pursue, answer the following questions:

   a. What kind of computer system would you most like to use—desktop, notebook, tablet PC, or something else?
   b. If you were required to use a type of computer you had never used before (such as a Mac instead of a PC), how would you go about learning to use the new computer?
   c. What kind of keyboard, mouse, monitor, and printer would you like to have?
   d. Would you need any additional input or output devices to perform your job?

3. **Going Wireless**

   Investigate the wireless options for mice, keyboards, printers, and monitors. What are the costs associated with these wireless devices? Are they more expensive than their wired counterparts are? What are the benefits of having wireless technology? What are the factors to take into consideration when buying and using wireless devices? Which devices would work best for you?

4. **Choosing the Best Printer**

   You are looking for a new printer for your home business. You have always had an inkjet printer, but now that the costs for color laser printers are dropping, you're considering buying a color laser printer.

   a. Using the Web, investigate the merits of different inkjet and color laser printers. Focus on one printer in each category and note the initial cost of each.
   b. Research the cost of ink or toner for each printer. Calculate the cost of ink or toner supplies for each printer, assuming you will print 5,000 color pages per year. How much will printing cost per page, not including the initial cost of the printer itself?
   c. Investigate all-in-one printers that have faxing, scanning, and copying capabilities. How much more expensive are they than traditional inkjet or laser printers? Are there any drawbacks to these multipurpose machines? Do they perform each function as well as their stand-alone counterparts do? Can you print in color on these machines?
   d. Based on your research, which printer would be the most economical?

5. **Office Ergonomics**

   Your boss has designated you as the "ergonomics coordinator" for the department. She has asked you to design a flyer to be posted around the office to inform your co-workers of the proper computer setup as well as the potential risks if such precautions are ignored. Create an ergonomics flyer, making sure it fits on an 8.5 × 11-inch piece of paper.

Looking at Computers: Understanding the Parts

Instructions: Albert Einstein used *Gedankenexperiments*, or critical thinking questions, to develop his theory of relativity. Some ideas are best understood by experimenting with them in our own minds. The following critical thinking questions are designed to demand your full attention but require only a comfortable chair—no technology.

1. Keyboard of the Future

What do you think the keyboard of the future will look like? What capabilities will it have that keyboards currently don't have? Will it have ports, cables, or special communication capabilities?

2. Touchscreen Technology

Touchscreen technology is quickly becoming part of digital devices. Examples include the iPhone, Blackberry Storm, iPod touch, and HP Touchsmart PC. How do you think touchscreen technology could improve other devices, such as cars or home appliances?

3. Storage Devices of the Future

How do you think storage devices will change in the future? Will increased storage capacity and decreased size affect the ways in which we use computers? Will we need storage devices in the future, or will we access all of our data via the Internet?

4. Computers Decreasing Productivity?

Can you think of any situations in which computers actually decrease productivity? Why? Should we always expect computers to increase our productivity? What do you think the impact of using computers would be:

a. in a third-grade classroom?
b. in a manager's office for a large chain supermarket?
c. for a retired couple who just purchased their first computer?

5. "Smart" Homes

The Smart Medical Home project of the University of Rochester's Center for Future Health is researching how to use technology to monitor many aspects of your health. The Smart Medical Home is the creation of a cross-disciplinary group of scientists and engineers from the college, the medical center, and the university's Center for Future Health. This particular "smart home" includes a sophisticated computer system that helps keep track of items such as eyeglasses or keys, and a kitchen equipped with a new kind of packaging to signal the presence of dangerous bacteria in food. Spaces between ordinary walls are stuffed with gadgetry, including banks of powerful computers.

a. What abilities should a smart home have to safeguard and improve the quality of your life?
b. Could a smart home have potential hazards?

6. Toy or Computer?

When do you think a toy becomes a computer? The Microsoft Xbox 360 has a hard drive, a processor with three cores, internal RAM, and wireless capability. Apple iPods also have hard drives (or flash memory and a processor). Are these devices computers or toys? What capabilities do you think next-generation gaming consoles and iPods should have?

Notebook versus Desktop: Which Is Best?

team time

Problem

You have joined a small business that is beginning to evaluate its technology setup. Because of the addition of several new sales representatives and other administrative employees, many new computers need to be purchased. You are trying to decide which would be better to purchase: notebook computers or desktops.

Task

Split your class into small groups, divide each group into two teams, and assign the following tasks:

Team A explores the benefits and downfalls of desktop computers.

Team B explores the benefits and downfalls of notebook computers.

Process

1. Form the groups and teams. Think about what the technology goals are for the company and what information and resources you need to tackle this project.
2. Research and then discuss the components of each system you are recommending. Are any components better suited for the particular needs of the various employees (sales representatives versus administrative staff)? Consider all the input, output, processing, and storage devices. Are any special devices or peripherals required?
3. Write a summary position paper. Support your system recommendation for

   Team A—purchase desktop computers

   Team B—purchase notebook computers

Conclusion

Desktop and notebook computers have their own merits as computing systems. Beyond portability, there are other things to think about. Being aware of the options in the marketplace and knowing how to analyze the trade-offs of different designs allows you to become a better consumer as well as a better computer user.

Looking at Computers: Understanding the Parts

In addition to the review materials presented here, you'll find additional materials featured with the Pearson IT Multimedia Library and the Companion Website (**pearsonhighered.com/techinaction**), which will help reinforce your understanding of the chapter content. These materials include the following:

Active Helpdesk

In Active Helpdesk calls, you'll assume the role of helpdesk operator, taking calls about the concepts you've learned in this chapter. You'll apply what you've learned and receive feedback from a supervisor to review and reinforce those concepts. The Active Helpdesk calls for this chapter are listed below and can be found on the Pearson IT Multimedia Library:

- Understanding Bits and Bytes
- Using Input Devices
- Using Output Devices
- Exploring Storage Devices and Ports

Sound Bytes

Sound Bytes are dynamic multimedia tutorials that help demystify even the most complex topics. You'll view video clips and animations that illustrate computer concepts and then apply what you've learned by reviewing with the Sound Byte Labs, which include quizzes and activities specifically tailored to each Sound Byte. The Sound Bytes for this chapter are listed below and can be found on the Pearson IT Multimedia Library:

- Binary Numbers Interactive
- Tablet and Notebook Tour
- Virtual Computer Tour?
- Port Tour: How Do I Hook It Up
- Healthy Computing

Companion Website

The *Technology in Action* Companion Website includes a variety of additional materials to help you review and learn more about the topics in this chapter. The resources available at **pearsonhighered.com/techinaction** include:

- **Online Study Guide.** This chapter features an online true–false and multiple-choice quiz. You can take these quizzes, automatically check the results, and e-mail the results to your instructor.
- **Web Research Projects.** This chapter features several Web research projects that ask you to search the Web for information on computer-related careers, milestones in computer history, important people and companies, emerging technologies, and the applications and implications of different technologies.

using the Internet:

making the most of the Web's resources

From Chapter 3 of *Technology in Action Complete*, Seventh Edition, Alan Evans, Kendall Martin, Mary Anne Poatsy. Copyright © 2011 by Pearson Education, Inc. Published by Pearson Prentice Hall. All rights reserved.

using the Internet:

making the most of the Web's resources

resources

Active Helpdesk

- Doing Business Online
- Getting Around the Web
- Using Subject Directories and Search Engines
- Connecting to the Internet

Sound Bytes

- Creating a Web-Based E-mail Account
- Blogging
- Welcome to the Web

- Finding Information on the Web
- Connecting to the Internet

Companion Website

The Companion Website includes a variety of additional materials to help you review and learn more about the topics in this chapter. Go to: *pearsonhighered.com/techinaction*

how cool is *this?*

Want to find out about the newest sites on the Web? Check out **Looqe.com!**

With so many **new applications** popping up on the Web daily, it's practically impossible to keep up with what's new and current. Looqe.com is a type of **directory** that lets you quickly preview all these new **Web apps**. When you click a category from the tag cloud, a group of thumbnail screenshots displays so you can easily see what each site looks like. Hover your mouse over a thumbnail for a brief description, or click on the thumbnail to be taken directly to the site.

The Looqe **tag cloud** has topics such as "Am bored" and "Have a few minutes to kill" that help you fill some empty minutes in your day. "Travel," "Hotels," and "Trips" help you plan your next vacation. Additionally, there are helpful educational topics such as "Questions and Answers," "Knowledge," and "Learning" in which you'll find great how-to, reference, and other **useful** Web sites.

Check out Looqe.com to discover how cool it really is.

ildogesto\Shutterstock

The Internet

It's hard to imagine life without the Internet. We use it to shop, to communicate, to research, to find places and get directions, and to entertain ourselves (see Figure 1). It's accessible from our computers, smartphones, and portable music players (PMPs), and we can get to it while at home, at work, at school—even at Starbucks. But what exactly is the Internet, and how did it begin?

Why was the Internet created?

The **Internet**, or "Net" as it is sometimes called, is the largest computer network in the world—actually, a network of networks—that connects

Apple Computer, Inc.

Figure 1

From buying guitars on eBay to getting directions on your cell phone to checking e-mail or the latest snow stats, the Internet makes it all possible.

billions of computer users. The concept of the Internet was developed while the United States was in the midst of the Cold War with the Soviet Union. At that time, the U.S. armed forces were becoming increasingly dependent on computers to coordinate and plan their activities. They needed a computer system that would operate efficiently and that was located in various parts of the country so that it could not be disrupted easily in the event of an attack.

At the same time, researchers hoped the Internet would address the problems involved with getting different computers to communicate with each other. Although

computers had been networked since the early 1960s, there was no reliable way to connect computers from different manufacturers because they used different proprietary designs and methods of communication. What was lacking was a common communications method that all computers could use. The Internet was created to respond to these two concerns: establishing a secure form of military communications and creating a means by which all computers could communicate.

Who invented the Internet?

The modern Internet evolved from an early U.S. government–funded "internetworking" project called the Advanced Research Projects Agency Network (ARPANET). ARPANET began as a four-node network involving UCLA, Stanford Research Institute, the University of California at Santa Barbara, and the University of Utah in Salt Lake City. The first real communication occurred in late 1969 between the computer at Stanford and the computer at UCLA. Although the system crashed after the third letter was transmitted, it was the beginning of a revolution. Many people participated in the creation of the ARPANET, but two men who worked on the project, Vinton Cerf and Robert Kahn, are generally acknowledged as the "fathers" of the Internet. They earned this honor because in the 1970s they were primarily responsible for developing the communications protocols (standards) that are still in use on the Internet today.

So are the Web and the Internet the same thing?

Because the **World Wide Web** (**WWW** or the **Web**) is what we use the most, we sometimes think of the

"Net" and the "Web" as being interchangeable. However, the Web is the means we use to access information over the Internet. What distinguishes the Web from the rest of the Internet is its use of

- common communication protocols that enable different computers to talk to each other and display information in compatible formats
- special links (called *hyperlinks*) that enable users to jump from one place to another on the Web.

Did the same people who invented the Internet invent the Web? The Web was invented many years after the original Internet. In 1989, Tim Berners-Lee, a physicist at the European Organization for Nuclear Research (CERN), wanted a method for linking his research documents so that other researchers could access them. In conjunction with Robert Cailliau, Berners-Lee developed the basic architecture of the Web and created the first Web browser (a software application that enables a user to display and interact with text and other media on the Web). The original browser could handle only text and was usable only on computers running the NeXT operating system, a commercially unsuccessful operating system (OS), which limited its usage. So Berners-Lee put out a call to the Internet community to assist with development of browsers for other platforms.

In 1993, the National Center for Supercomputing Applications released its Mosaic browser for use on the Macintosh and Windows operating systems. Mosaic could display graphics as well as text. The once-popular Netscape Navigator browser evolved from Mosaic and heralded the beginning of the Web's monumental growth.

How much has the Internet grown? The Internet experienced explosive growth in the early to mid-1990s. By 1997, nearly everyone in the world had access to an Internet connection.

Because of such global Internet availability and access, as well as the increasing capabilities of hardware and software, the number of Web sites (locations on the Internet) grew exponentially, as shown in Figure 2. In December 1990, the first Web site appeared on the Web. Four years later, approximately 10,000 sites were online; by June 1996, a whopping 252,000 Web sites were created.

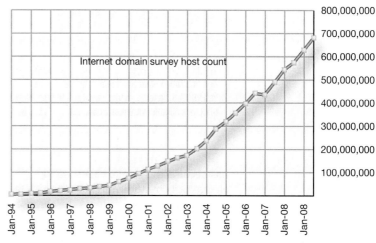

The Web experienced its greatest amount of growth in the year 2000—more than 160 percent in a single year. The growth of the Web has since begun to slow down, but is by no means complete. In January 2009, almost 700 million Web sites were online. The Web's growth is expected to continue, with more than 200 million Web sites anticipated by 2010.

Figure 2

The growth of the number of Web sites on the Internet has been explosive since the first Web site was hosted in 1990.

Source: **carolina-advertising. com/free-advertising/ internet-growth.gif/**

Communicating Through the Internet: E-Mail and Other Technologies

E-mail is fast becoming the main form of communication in the 21st century, and it is the primary use of the Web. However, e-mail is not the only type of Internet-based communication. You can use instant messaging, blogs, podcasts, social networks, chat rooms, newsgroups, and more for communicating via the Internet. (You can even talk over the phone through the Internet with Voice over Internet Protocol (VoIP). Like any other means of communication, you need to know how to use these tools efficiently to get the most out of them.

E-Mail

Why did e-mail catch on so quickly? **E-mail** (short for **electronic mail**) is a written message that is sent and received over the Internet. The messages can be formatted and enhanced with graphics and may also include other files as attachments. E-mail

SOUND BYTE

Creating a Web-Based E-mail Account

In this Sound Byte, you'll see a step-by-step demonstration that explains how to create a free Yahoo! Web-based e-mail account. You'll also learn the options available with such accounts.

has become the primary method of electronic communication because it's fast and convenient and reduces the costs of postage and long-distance phone calls. In addition, with e-mail, the sender and receiver don't have to be available at the same time in order to communicate. Because

controversial content in an e-mail. It could come back to haunt you. Finally, remember that even after you've deleted a message, it doesn't really vanish. Many Internet service providers and company e-mail servers archive e-mail, which can then be accessed or subpoenaed in the event of a lawsuit or investigation.

What do I need to send and receive e-mail? All you need to send and receive e-mail is a computer, an Internet connection, and an e-mail account. Each component, however, entails additional considerations. Although it's most common to send and receive e-mail from your computer, today many e-mail messages are exchanged wirelessly among smartphones and other portable devices.

Figure 3

You can organize your e-mail and assign messages to topic-specific folders.

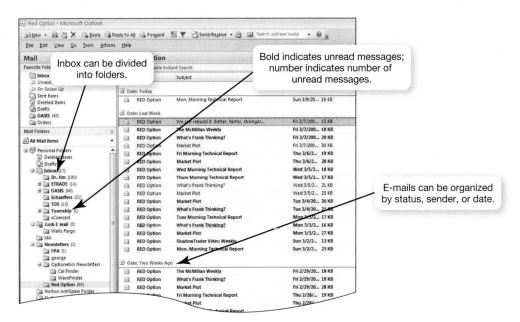

of these and other reasons, approximately 92 percent of Americans who access the Internet claim that their main online activity is sending and receiving e-mail.

Is e-mail private? E-mails are not private. In fact, the information in e-mail is no more private than a postcard. E-mails can be easily viewed by others, either by being printed out or forwarded, so you never know who eventually could read your e-mail. Also, because it is not encrypted, you shouldn't use e-mail to send personal or sensitive information such as bank account numbers or Social Security numbers, which could lead to identity theft. Employers have access to e-mail sent from the workplace, so use caution when putting negative or

Are there different types of e-mail accounts? To read, send, and organize your e-mail, you can use an e-mail client. **E-mail clients** such as Microsoft Outlook are software programs running on your computer that access your Internet service provider's (ISP's) server. However, with these e-mail clients, you are able to view your e-mail only from a computer on which the client program is installed, which can be less than convenient if you travel or want to view your e-mail when you're away from that computer.

Today, most broadband providers and ISPs offer the services of a Web-based e-mail client so that users can look at their e-mail directly from the Web. Web-based e-mail uses the Internet as the client; therefore, you can access a Web-based e-mail account from any computer that has access to the Web. No special client software is needed. Free e-mail accounts such as Yahoo! Mail, Hotmail, or Gmail are Web-based e-mail clients. Some e-mail providers—AOL, for example—offer both client-based and Web-based access to e-mail.

What are the advantages of a Web-based e-mail account? Unlike client-based e-mail, which is accessible only from a computer on which the client is installed, Web-based e-mail accounts make your e-mail accessible from any computer as long as you can access the Internet. Even if you use a client-based account, having a secondary Web-based e-mail account also provides you with a more permanent e-mail address. Your other e-mail accounts and addresses may change when you switch ISPs or change employers, so having a permanent e-mail address is important.

Why would I need a client-based e-mail program? Many people have more than one e-mail account. You may have a personal account, a work account, and an account you use when filling out forms on the Internet. One of the benefits of using a client-based e-mail program such as Microsoft Outlook is that you can download your e-mail from many different e-mail accounts so that it all can be accessed in one location. In addition, client e-mail programs offer several features to help you manage and organize your e-mail and coordinate e-mail with your calendar, tasks, and contact lists. As you can see in Figure 3, you can organize your e-mail by task, sender, or priority, or you can distribute your messages to designated folders within your inbox. Some Web-based e-mail systems such as Yahoo! feature many of the same organizational tools, but client-based programs are generally more fully featured.

Instant Messaging

How does instant messaging work?
Instant messaging (IM) services are programs that enable you to communicate in real time with others who are online (see Figure 4). Although IM is most often used for casual conversations between friends, many businesses use IM as a means of quick and instant communication between co-workers.

AOL's AIM is one of the most popular instant messaging services. ICQ, Yahoo!, Google, and Windows Live Messenger also host popular instant messaging services. These services are proprietary, meaning you can chat only with those who share the same IM service. But there are universal chat clients such as Trillian, Pidgin, and Zango Messenger that allow users of all the popular IMs to chat with each other regardless of the service they use. Meebo is a new Web-based universal chat service (no installation required) that lets you communicate with users on a variety of IM services from any computer anywhere. No software download is required.

How do I keep track of my IM contacts?
When you use IM, you set up a list of contacts, often called a buddy list. To communicate (or chat) with someone from your buddy list, that person must be online at the same time as you are. When someone wants to chat with you, a window pops open with his or her message. If it's not convenient to chat at that time, you can close or ignore the message. Some programs such as Yahoo! and AOL's AIM offer stealth

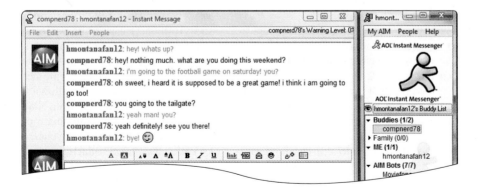

Figure 4

Instant messaging services such as AOL Instant Messenger enable you to have real-time online conversations with friends and family.

Figure 5

Google Groups is a convenient means to join a group or to create your own.

member posts messages and reads and replies to messages from other members of the newsgroup. Google Groups is a great source for various newsgroups. Google Groups (see Figure 5) allows you to join a group or create your own. A **listserv** is an electronic mailing list of e-mail addresses of people who are interested in a certain topic or an area of interest. Information and updates on shared topics of interest are exchanged between members through e-mail. Tile.net (**tile.net**) is a good source of discussion lists.

Social networking is another popular means of communicating with many people, which we will discuss in the Web 2.0 section later in this chapter.

Do dangers exist in group communications? When you use group communications, you generally need to register and sign in with a username and password. It's best not to disclose your identity but rather to "hide" behind a username, thus protecting your privacy. On the other hand, the people you are chatting with are also hiding their identities. Some chatters use this veil of privacy to cover dishonest intentions. You have probably heard of individuals, especially young teenagers, who were deceived (and sometimes harmed) by someone they met in a chat room. Several Web sites such as **chatdanger.com** try to protect vulnerable people, especially children, from malicious online users (see Figure 6).

Are there special ways to behave with group communication? General rules of etiquette, often referred to as **netiquette**, exist across chat rooms and other online forums, including obvious standards of behavior such as introducing yourself when you enter the room and specifically addressing the person to whom you are talking. Chat room users also are expected to refrain from swearing, name-calling, and using explicit or prejudiced language, and they are not allowed to harass other participants. In addition, chat room users cannot post the same text repeatedly with the intent to disrupt the chat, a behavior called *flooding*. Similarly, users shouldn't type in all capital letters, because this is interpreted as shouting.

settings so that you can appear offline to certain buddies.

If you want to chat with more than one person, you can hold simultaneous individual conversations, or if you all want to chat together, you can create custom IM chat rooms. Many IM services such as AIM and Live Messenger offer chat services so you can speak with your buddies if you have a microphone and speakers. A webcam allows you to see them as you chat.

Group Communication

What kinds of online group communication exist? You can interact with a wide variety of people online in many ways. Some forms are in real time, or synchronous; others are asynchronous. Some of the ways in which you can communicate and interact with a group of people online are through chat rooms, newsgroups, and listservs.

A **chat room**, such as those found at **icq.com/icqchat**, is a form of synchronous communication in which online conversations occur in real time and are visible to everyone in the chat room. Usually, chat rooms are organized around a specific theme or topic. Wireclub (**wireclub.com**) has a variety of chat rooms to suit every interest. A **newsgroup** is similar to a discussion group or forum in which people create threads (conversations). In a thread, a newsgroup

Figure 6

Childnet International works to make the Internet safe. The site **chatdanger.com** provides a lot of good safety advice for using chat rooms, mobile phones, e-mail, instant messaging programs, and games.

Web 2.0 Technologies: Collaborating and Communicating Through the Internet

Over time our use of the Internet has evolved from passively reading and using Web content created for us to actively creating, sharing, and collaborating on our own Web content. **Web 2.0** describes a new trend of Web interactions between people, software, and data. It can be classified as the social Web, in which the user is also a participant. Additionally, Web 2.0 describes a trend of new applications to combine the functionality of multiple applications. Hundreds of companies now exist to help us share, recommend, collaborate, create, and socialize (see Figure 7). The following discussions focus more on the social, collaborative, and communicative nature of Web 2.0 applications.

Weblogs (Blogs) and Video Logs (Vlogs)

What is a blog? A **weblog**, or **blog**, is a personal log or journal posted on the Web. The beauty of blogs is that they are simple to create, manage, and read. Anyone can create a blog, and there are millions of blogs available to read, follow, and comment on.

Several key characteristics define a blog. Blogs are generally written by a single author and are arranged as a listing of entries on a single page, with the most recent blog (entry) appearing at the top of the list. In addition, blogs are public. Blogs have searchable and organized content, making them user friendly. They are accessible from anywhere using a Web browser.

Are blogs just text? The traditional form of a blog is primarily text-based but may also include images and audio. A **video log** (**vlog** or **video blog**) is a personal journal that uses video as the primary content. It can also contain text, images, and audio. Vlogs quickly are becoming a highly popular means of personal expression, and

WEB 2.0 Landscape

Figure 7

Hundreds of companies and Web sites make up the Web 2.0 landscape, which helps us share, recommend, collaborate, create, and socialize.

Web 2.0 Technologies: Collaborating and Communicating Through the Internet

Figure 8

Video logs use video in addition to text, images, and audio. Blinkx is a video search engine that helps you sift through the increasing number of vlogs.

many can be found by searching the most popular video-sharing site today, YouTube (**youtube.com**). Software such as Vlog It! makes adding video content to your blog easy, although you can easily upload unedited video straight from your computer, video camera, or cell phone. Blinkx (**blinkx.com**) is a video search engine that helps you sift through all the video posted on the Web (see Figure 8). For a true video conversation, try Seesmic (**seesmic.com**), in which people post and reply to posts with videos.

What do people write in blogs?
Many people use blogs as a sort of personal scrapbook. Whenever the urge strikes, they just write a stream-of-consciousness flow of thoughts or a report of their daily activities. Many blogs, however, focus on a particular topic. For example, **themovieblog.com** is a blog that contains reviews and opinions about movies, and **engadget.com** (see Figure 9) is a blog that devotes itself to discussing techno-gadgets. Blogcatalog (**blogcatalog.com**) and Bloghub (**bloghub. com**) are two of many blog directories that can help you find blogs that best fit your interests.

How do I create a blog? It is easy to write and maintain a blog, and many Web sites provide the necessary tools for you to create your own. Two sites that offer free blog hosting are **blogger.com** and **livejournal.com**. You can add other features to your blog such as pictures or subpages. Another alternative is to host your blog yourself. Hosting your own blog requires that you have your own Web site and a URL so that people can access it.

Are there problems with blogs?
The popularity of blogs has brought about a new problem: spam blogs (splogs), which are artificially created blog sites filled with fake articles or stolen text (a tactic known as *blog scraping*). Spam blogs, which contain links to other sites associated with the splog's creator, have the intention of either increasing traffic to, or increasing search engine rankings for, these usually

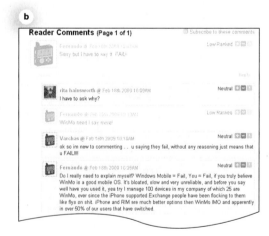

Figure 9

(a) Some blogs, like this one from **engadget.com**, are set up as online reviews organized by category. (b) Alternatively, they can appear as personal journals that record a blogger's thoughts, viewpoints, and feelings in reverse chronological order.

disreputable or useless Web sites. Although not terribly bad, splogs are another unwanted form of content that continues to grow like weeds on the Web.

Wikis

What are wikis?   Unlike traditional Web content, which the viewer of the site cannot change, a **wiki** is a type of Web site that allows users to change its content by adding, removing, or editing the content (see Figure 10). Wikis add the extra benefit of tracking revisions so that past versions can be easily accessed at any time by any reader. The popular collaborative online encyclopedia Wikipedia (**wikipedia.org**) uses wiki technology so that the content can be updated continually. Some Web-based document products, such as Google Docs (**docs.google.com**), have wiki-like features to promote online collaboration.

How accurate is Web content that anyone can change?   The idea behind publicly managed and edited content, such as that found in wikis, is that the public will keep the content valid. Those challenging the validity of publicly editable wikis argue that the content cannot be trusted because wikis are easily tampered with, whereas supporters argue that the community of users can quickly catch erroneous content and correct it.

In late 2005, Wikipedia content was measured for accuracy in its scientific content and was found to be as accurate as the *Encyclopedia Britannica*. Nonetheless, free and easy access to edit pages also can lead to improper manipulation, which results in tighter access controls. To thwart malicious editing of the wiki content, for example, users who want editing privileges are required to register. Citizendium (**citizendium.org**), another

Elijah provides initial text (in black)

Jordan includes additional text (in green)

Mackenzie-Jordan Law Associates has a significant number of celebrity clients. One of the most important aspects of our legal counsel to these individuals is to help protect the use of their images and likenesses.

Sometimes this is referred to as the right of publicity. This right is a valuable asset because there are endless licensing opportunities that can be quite lucrative. Some states have a publicity law that protects a celebrity's image and likeness for 100 years, but as yet that law has not been enacted in the state of Texas.

The merchandising of celebrity images has become a huge source of income for many celebrities as well as others. In recent years, legal disputes have resulted from artists and illustrators manipulating celebrity images.

In the past, courts have typically protected the First Amendment rights of artists in these cases. But recently there have been a few cases where celebrities have been allowed to sue creators of fictional works for the violation of the right of publicity.

The right of publicity is intended to prevent others from capitalizing on a celebrity's fame. Many people in the entertainment industry are fearful that unauthorized biographies, docudramas, and celebrity spoofs and satires will no longer be protected. Many entertainment lawyers say a celebrity's right to publicity is intended solely for ads and merchandise, not for literary works.

jeny\Shutterstock, Supri Suharjoto\Shutterstock, AVAVA\Shutterstock

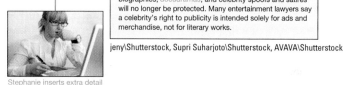
Stephanie inserts extra detail (in blue)

Figure 10

Rather than collaborating by exchanging e-mails and attachments—and potentially losing track of the most recent version of a document—different users can collaborate on a wiki page.

open wiki encyclopedia, requires contributors to provide real names and sign an ethics pledge, and all postings are monitored.

Are wikis used for anything other than encyclopedias and manuals? Wikis provide an excellent source for collaborative writing, both in and out of the classroom. Wiki technology is currently incorporated in Blackboard, a popular online course-management application, to encourage collaborative learning in online courses. Wikis are also becoming popular tools for business collaboration. Rather than passing documents back and forth via e-mail and losing track of which updated version is the most recent, wikis allow all who have access to the page to post their ideas and modify the content of just one document. A history of all changes is kept, so users can revert to earlier versions if desired.

These same collaborative efforts also extend to user manuals. One site, wikiHow (**wikihow.org**), is an online project that uses both wikis and the collaborative process to build a large, online how-to manual. Blender (**blender.org**), an open source software application for 3D modeling, uses MediaWiki, a more feature-rich wiki implementation product, to provide users with documentation, help with game development and 3D modeling, and tutorials for Blender software.

Like blogs, wikis also can be used to express thoughts and opinions about certain topics. Unlike blogs, wikis can be edited and therefore can present an emergent "common" opinion, rather than the individual opinion of the initial writer.

Podcasts and Webcasts

What is a podcast?   A podcast is a clip of audio or video content that is broadcast over the Internet using compressed audio and video files such as MP3s and MP4s. This content might include radio shows, audiobooks, magazines, and even educational programs. The word "podcast" is a combination of "broadcasting" and "iPod"—not because you have to use an iPod but because iPods are the most popular form of portable media player

(PMP) and because people download audio files to listen to on their iPods. However, you don't have to listen to podcasts on a portable media player. You can listen to podcasts on your computer or even on a smartphone as long as the device can play the content. To listen to a podcast on your computer, you'll need a media player such as iTunes, RealPlayer, or Windows Media Player. If you want to enjoy a video podcast on your PMP, you need to make sure your mobile device can play video as well as audio files.

So what makes podcasting different from just listening to an audio file on the computer or a PMP player?   The difference is that podcasts are files that come to you through syndication so you do not have to search for them. Perhaps you are used to getting your news from a certain Web site, but the only way you can determine that new content has been added is to go to the site and look for the newly added information. In contrast, if you subscribe to podcasts, when the content changes, it is brought to you. What's more, if you have several favorite Web sites, rather than individually checking the content, you can collect all the site updates in one place. Podcasts are possible because of RSS technology, which makes it more efficient for you to gather updates to your favorite content.

What Is RSS?   Really Simple Syndication (RSS) is an XML-based format that facilitates the delivery of frequent content updates on Web pages. Using RSS, Web content can be formatted in such a way that **aggregators** can find it and download only the new content to your computer. Aggregators are software programs that go out and grab the latest updates of Web material according to your specifications. They are

Figure 11

Podcasts are available in a wide variety of topics and content. Web sites such as **podcast.com** allow you to add your own podcast to their directories.

available for all major operating systems as well as some mobile devices such as smartphones. Some aggregators work with Atom, another specification, to distribute new Web content.

Where can I find podcasts? Podcasts can be found all over the Web. Most newspapers, TV news organizations, and radio sites offer podcasts of their programs. Although many podcasts are news related, many podcasts offer more entertaining and informative content. The television network ABC, for example, offers podcasts of some of its most popular TV shows, such as *Grey's Anatomy* and *Lost*. Sites such as Yoga Today offer extensive yoga classes. Many schools are beginning to recognize this format as a way to supply students with course content updates, and instructors create podcasts of their lectures.

iTunes (**itunes.com**), Podcast Alley (**podcastalley.com**), and Podcast.com (**podcast.com**) are aggregators as well as great directories of podcasts, organized by genre, to help you easily locate podcasts of most interest to you (see Figure 11). If there is a particular topic for which you'd like to hear a podcast, Podscope (**podscope.com**) is a podcast-specific search engine that searches podcasts for specific words or phrases and then displays the results with audio clips. YouTube is also becoming a popular source of RSS feeds for video content.

Can I create my own podcast? It is simple to create audio content that can be delivered to the Web and then listened to by people all over the world. In fact, you could become a radio broadcaster overnight. Although high-end equipment always will produce a more sophisticated output, you really need only the most basic equipment to make your own podcast.

To record the content, at the minimum you need a computer with a microphone. If you want to make a video podcast, you also need a Web camera (webcam) or video camera. Additional software may be needed to edit the digital audio and video content. After the podcast content has been recorded and edited, it needs to be exported to MP3 format. Sound editing software, such as the freeware program Audacity, can be used to record and edit audio files and then export them to MP3 format. The last steps involve creating an RSS feed and then uploading the content to the Web.

What's a webcast? A webcast is the broadcast of audio or video content over the Internet. Unlike podcasts that are prerecorded and made available for download, most webcasts are live or are a one-time event. Webcasts are not updated automatically, but some, such as Microsoft's On-Demand Webcasts, are RSS feeds. Webcasts use a special kind of media technology that continuously feeds the multimedia content, which facilitates the viewing and downloading process of large audio and video files. Webcasts can include noninteractive content such as simulcasts of radio or TV broadcasts. More recent webcasts invite interactive responses from the viewing or listening audience. For example, **ORLive.com** provides surgical webcasts that demonstrate the latest surgical innovations and techniques (see Figure 12). Many of these webcasts present live procedures and then allow time afterward for a panel of physicians to answer viewers' questions. Webcasts also are used in the corporate world to broadcast annual meetings and in the educational arena to transmit seminars.

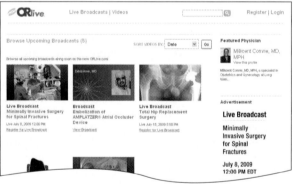

Figure 12

ORLive provides webcasts that demonstrate the latest surgical techniques.

Social Networking

What is social networking? Social networking is a means by which people use the Internet to communicate and share information among their immediate friends, and meet and connect with others through common interests, experiences, and friends

Computers in Society: Online Storage and Secure Backup for Your Valuable Digital Assets

The hard drive on most notebook or desktop computers sold today can hold more than 500 GB of data. Chances are you have a lot of important school files, personal and financial documents, e-mails, digital photos and videos of your friends and family, music files, and more. Although it's convenient to have all your information readily available, your precious data is extremely vulnerable.

Hard drive crashes, virus attacks, and physical damage (especially to dropped notebooks) can render the data stored on your hard drive useless. For this reason, many people choose to buy external hard drives as a simple, cost-effective alternative to store and back up

their digital assets, keeping them from being lost or damaged if their computer is harmed or stolen. However, even external hard drives are not immune to data loss. Your computer or external device could be destroyed by a fire, flood, or hurricane, or it could be stolen. If that happens, all those digital photographs, your music collection, and everything else will be lost. One alternative that helps avoid this problem is online storage or backup. Most likely you need both.

In essence, You can think of online storage as using the Internet as an alternative to a portable storage device such as a flash drive or external hard drive (see Figure 13). The beauty of online storage is that your data is available anywhere you are; you do not need to be at your computer or lug around your external hard drive to access the information. More importantly, because the information is stored online, it is in a secure, remote location, so data is much less vulnerable to all the potential disasters that could harm data stored in physical devices such as your desktop or notebook computer or external hard drive. Some services also offer sharing capabilities that allow you to share your photos and videos more easily with others. Several easy-to-use services offer free storage for a limited

Notebook

INTERNET

Online storage and backup

Home Computer

Figure 13

Online storage and backup uses the Internet as an alternative to external hard drives.

(see Figure 14). Social networking services such as Facebook (**facebook.com**) and MySpace (**myspace.com**) have become amazingly popular because they provide ways for members to communicate with their friends by voice, chat, instant message, videoconference, and blogs so that members don't need separate communication accounts. These services were first accepted broadly among the younger, nonprofessional population, but now many adults create their own social networking profiles on Facebook and MySpace. Ning (**ning.com**) is a social networking site that allows you to create your own network around your own common topic or join a social networking group that has already been formed.

Is social networking just for fun?
Networking has long been a means of creating links between you and your friends—and their friends and acquaintances. Traditionally, networking has been helpful in

the business community for the purposes of finding and filling open job positions. The Internet, with its speedy connections and instantaneous means of communicating, facilitates such business networking as well as promoting more socially based networks. In addition to the more social networks of Facebook and MySpace, the professional, business-oriented online networks such as LinkedIn (**linkedin.com**) are helpful for members seeking to find potential clients, business opportunities, jobs, or job candidates. Like a true business network, LinkedIn helps you meet other professionals through the people you know.

Are there precautions I should take with my social networking content?
When social networking sites first became popular, there was huge concern over privacy issues, especially for young teenagers who put personal information on their pages without considering the possibility of that information being misused by a stalker

amount of data. If you are taking advantage of one of these free online storage services, selectivity is the key. Although you might have hundreds of gigabytes of data sitting on your computer, perhaps you only need to store several gigabytes online so that they are always available.

Online storage may be a good solution for housing files that need "always available" access. But if you want to make a complete copy of your hard drive that will protect all your digital assets in case of a complete failure, you might also consider online backup. Plenty of services are available for these larger and more secure backup needs.

For the most protection, you should initially choose to image your hard drive, a process that copies all the files on your computer. In addition to your data files, *imaging* captures all the operating system files (such as Windows or OS X files) and application files (such as Microsoft Office). The idea of imaging is to make an exact copy of the setup of your computer so that in the event of a total hard drive failure, you could copy the image to a new hard drive and have your computer configured exactly the way it was before the crash.

Even with modest use, your files change. Therefore, it is important to back up the system periodically to capture the changes. You can do either an incremental or a total backup.

Incremental backups involve backing up only files that have changed or been created since the last backup was performed. Incremental backups won't make full copies of the stored data every time. Many of the key documents that you want to protect change only periodically: monthly banking statements, yearly tax returns, weekly employee payment records, or daily work documents. You should choose an online service that allows incremental backups. It will save a tremendous amount of time because backing up files that haven't changed is redundant.

A *total backup* means that all system, application, and data files are backed up, not just the files that have changed. While incremental backups are most efficient, you should still perform a total backup of your computer at least monthly to capture changes to application files, such as automatic software updates, that an incremental backup might not capture.

Another issue to consider when choosing online storage and backup services is security. Security might not be an issue if you're just using online storage for your family pictures. However, it is important to consider if you are backing up sensitive or essential files. Some services encrypt your data or scatter it among several servers. For the utmost in security, some services even offer you the option of being the only person to hold the decryption key. However, be forewarned that if you choose this option, there is no way you can restore your data should you forget your password!

All of these services are great, but only if you can retrieve your data should the original source become unavailable. That is the reason you go through a backup process, after all. Different services offer different features depending on whether you just want to restore the data on the original machine or whether you need to restore your data to a new computer (because the original computer was completely destroyed or stolen). Make sure your service can easily restore data to a different computer. Some popular online services include Carbonite Online PCBackup, HP Upline, IDrive, and MozyHome Online Backup.

Protecting our most important data is an often-forgotten step in our daily computing lives. Local backup or imaging to a DVD, external hard drive, or other local network storage device is still a viable option, especially with the cost of these local storage devices continuing to drop. However, if you really care about preserving and protecting your irreplaceable digital photos, documents, and other files, or want anytime-and-anywhere access, look into taking advantage of one of these online storage and backup services.

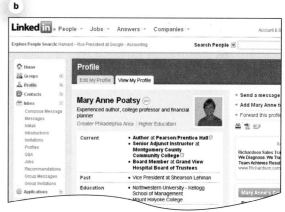

Figure 14

Social networking sites are popular places for people to keep up with friends and learn more about the people they meet.

What's Everyone Twittering About?

Twitter is a social networking and micro-blogging service that enables you to exchange short text messages with your friends or "followers" (see Figure 15). It also lets you specify which Twitter users you want to follow so you can read their messages in one place. All you need is a device (such as your computer or mobile device) connected to the Internet.

Twitter messages, called *tweets*, are limited to 140 characters, so comments exchanged in Twitter are short and simple. While Twitter works well among close-knit groups for messages such as "Joe and I are going to Murphy's Café. See you there," it can also be used to gain a sense of the "pulse" of what the general public is talking about within a broader community. Twitter received a lot of attention during the 2008 presidential campaigns when the masses were "twittering" their opinions about the various presidential candidates and positions. Your Twitter account tracks the number of "followers," or people who are paying attention to your tweets, and the number of "friends," or people you are following. So, "twitter" away to stay connected.

Figure 15

Twitter is a social networking and micro-blogging service for staying connected to "followers" in real time.

or identity thief. While those concerns still exist, many of the most popular social networking sites have improved their privacy policies, thereby reducing, but not eliminating, such concerns. Still, users must be cautious about the type of content they post on these sites. For example, think before you add information like "your mother's maiden name" or "your first pet's name" because these are often security questions that businesses use to verify your identity.

Social networking sites are a great way to exchange photos, but again, use caution when posting images. Although privacy settings may offer some comfort, some images may be available for view through search engines and may not require site registration to be viewed. Online images may become public property and subject to reproduction, and there might be some images that you don't want distributed. Additionally, many employers use social networks as another means of gaining information about a potential job candidate before granting an interview or extending a job offer. The responsibility for your content rests with you. Make sure your profile, images, and site content project an image that accurately represents you.

Web Entertainment: Multimedia and Beyond

Internet radio, MP3 music files, streaming video, and interactive gaming are all part of a growing entertainment world available over the Internet. What makes the Web appealing to many people is its rich multimedia content. **Multimedia** is anything that involves one or more forms of media in addition to text.

Many types of multimedia are used on the Web. Graphics (drawings, charts, and photos) are the most basic form of multimedia. Audio files are what give sound to the Web—the clips of music you hear when you visit certain Web sites, MP3 files that you download, or live broadcasts you can listen to through Internet radio. Video files on the Web range from the simple (such as short video clips) to the complex (such as hour-long live concerts). In addition to movies, you can watch live or prerecorded television broadcasts, movie trailers, and sporting events. **Hulu.com** is a great Web site where you can find popular TV shows and movies for free.

What are streaming audio and video? Because of the large file sizes of media content, watching video files such as movies or TV shows, listening to live audio broadcasting, and playing online games is possible because of streaming media. **Streaming audio** continuously feeds an audio file to your browser so you avoid having to wait for the entire file to download completely before listening to it. Likewise, **streaming video** continuously feeds a video file to your browser so that you can watch large files as they download instead of first having to download the files completely.

What kinds of games are played on the Web? Streaming audio and video helped to bring popularity to online user interactivity and online gaming. Many game Web sites, such as AddictingGames (**addictinggames.com**), offer thousands of free online games in arcade, puzzle, sports, shooting, word, and strategy categories. Simple multiplayer games such as backgammon, chess, and checkers became popular and offered users the chance to play the game with others from around the world.

In addition, there are many **multiplayer online games**, in which play occurs among hundreds or thousands of other players over the Internet in a persistent (or always-on) game environment. In these games, you can interact with other players around the world in a meaningful context by trading, chatting, or playing cooperative or combative mini-games. There are several types of massive multiplayer online games. Role-playing games such as World of Warcraft (**worldofwarcraft.com**) and Guild Wars (**guildwars.com**) are the best-known type of massive multiplayer games. Other types include first-person shooter (**battlegroundeurope.com**), sports (**footballsuperstars.com**), and racing (**needforspeed.com**). Second Life (**secondlife.com**) can also be considered a massive multiplayer online social game, but with its own well-established, in-world virtual economy, it has transcended into a much bigger concept and function.

Do I need anything besides a browser to view or hear multimedia on the Web? Without any additional software, most graphics on the Web will appear in your browser. However, to view and hear some multimedia files—for example, podcasts, videos on YouTube, and MP3 files—you might need a special software program called a **plug-in** (or **player**). Figure 16 lists the most popular plug-ins.

If you purchased your computer within the past several years, many plug-ins probably came preinstalled with your browser. If a Web site requires a plug-in you don't have, it usually displays a message on the screen that includes links to a site where you can download the plug-in free of charge. For example, to use streaming audio on a Web site, your browser might send you to adobe.com, where you can download Shockwave Player.

Do I need to update players and plug-ins? As with most technological resources, improvements and upgrades are available for players and plug-ins, and most will alert you to check for and download upgrades when they are available. It is best to keep the players and plug-ins as current as possible so that you get the full effects of the multimedia running with these players.

Figure 16 | POPULAR PLUG-INS AND PLAYERS AND THEIR USES

	Plug-In or Player Name	Where You Can Get It	What It Does
	Adobe Reader	**adobe.com**	Views and prints portable document format (PDF) files
	Authorware Web Player	**adobe.com**	Helps to deliver engaging e-learning applications
	Flash Player	**adobe.com**	Plays animation and other graphics files
	QuickTime Player	**apple.com**	Plays MP3 animation, music, musical instrument digital interface (MIDI), audio, and video files
	RealPlayer	**real.com**	Plays streaming audio, video, animations, and multimedia presentations
	Shockwave Player	**adobe.com**	Plays interactive games, multimedia, graphics, and streaming audio and video on the Web
	Windows Media Player	**microsoft.com**	Plays MP3 and WAV files, music files and live audio, and views movies and live video broadcasts on the Web

Web Entertainment: Multimedia and Beyond

Are there any risks with using plug-ins? When a browser requires a plug-in to display particular Web content, it usually automatically accesses the plug-in. Sometimes, depending on your settings, this access happens without asking you for consent to start the plug-in. Such automatic access can present security risks. To minimize such risks, update your plug-ins and browser software frequently so that you will have the most up-to-date remedies against identified security flaws.

Is there any way to get multimedia Web content to load faster? When you're on the Internet, your browser keeps track of the Web sites you've visited so that it can load them faster the next time you visit them. This *cache* (temporary storage place) of the text pages, images, and video files from recently visited Web sites can make your Internet surfing more efficient, but it also can congest your hard drive. To keep your system running efficiently, delete your temporary Internet cache periodically. All popular Web browsers have an option to clear the Internet cache manually, and most have a setting to allow you to clear the cache automatically every time you exit the browser.

BITS AND BYTES

Using PayPal for Safe Online Payments

Many people were not initially comfortable buying online from sites such as eBay because the sites required them to exchange personal financial information such as credit card numbers or banking information with complete strangers. PayPal (**paypal.com**) resolved that issue and is now a standard means of online payment exchanges. PayPal also offers buyer protection and dispute resolution services.

Here's how PayPal works (see Figure 17):

1. You provide your financial information to PayPal, which stores it on PayPal servers.
2. You provide only your PayPal e-mail address to the merchant.
3. The merchant receives payment from PayPal without seeing your financial information.

PayPal acts as a payment intermediary and allows anyone to pay with credit cards, bank accounts, or buyer credit without sharing financial information. PayPal is now owned by eBay, the online auction site.

PayPal is not without controversy, however. Many criticisms of the company focus on its poor customer service and freezing of accounts without explanation. So, diligence and care are still as important as they are with anyone who has access to your personal financial information.

Provide your information to PayPal

PayPal securely stores your information

Merchant receives payment from PayPal

Cecilia Lim H M\Shutterstock, Tatiana Popova \Shutterstock

Figure 17
PayPal is an online payment intermediary, allowing anyone to shop without sharing financial information with the seller.

Conducting Business over the Internet: E-Commerce

E-commerce, or **electronic commerce**, is the process of conducting business online, such as through advertising and selling products. A good example of an e-commerce business (also called an *e-business*) is Amazon.com. The company's online presence offers customers a convenient way to shop for almost anything. Its success is the result of creative marketing, an expanding product line, and reliable customer service and product delivery—all hallmarks of traditional businesses as well.

Are there different types of e-commerce businesses? Traditional stores with an online presence are referred to as *click-and-brick* businesses. These stores, such as Best Buy (**bestbuy.com**) and Target (**target.com**), provide a variety of services on their Web sites. Customers can visit their sites to check the availability of items or to get store locations and directions. Some click-and-bricks allow online purchases and in-store pickup and returns.

A significant portion of e-commerce consists of **business-to-consumer (B2C)** transactions—exchanges that take place between businesses and consumers—such as the purchases that consumers make at online stores. There is also a **business-to-business (B2B)** portion of e-commerce; this consists of businesses buying and selling goods and services to other businesses. An example is Omaha Paper Company (**omahapaper.com**), which distributes paper products to other companies. Finally, the **consumer-to-consumer (C2C)** portion of e-commerce consists of consumers selling to each other through online auction and exchange sites such as eBay (**ebay.com**) and Craigslist (**craigslist.com**).

What are the most popular e-commerce activities?

Approximately $100 billion each year is spent on goods purchased over the Internet, accounting for approximately 25 percent of all retail sales. So what is everyone buying online? Consumers buy books, music and videos, movie and event tickets, and toys and games more often online than in retail stores. Travel items such as plane tickets, hotel reservations, and rental car reservations are also frequently made online. With the advent of more lenient return policies, online retail sales of clothing and shoes also have increased. Sites such as eBay and Craigslist, together with payment exchange services such as PayPal and Google Checkout, are becoming the online equivalent of the weekend yard sale and have dramatically increased in popularity.

But e-commerce encompasses more than just shopping opportunities. Today, anything you can do inside your bank you can do online, and more than 50 percent of U.S. households do some form of online banking. Many people use online services to check their account balances, and checking stock and mutual fund performances is also popular. Credit card companies allow you to view, schedule, and pay your credit card bill; brokerage houses allow you to conduct investment activities online; and banks allow you to pay you bills online.

E-Commerce Safeguards

Just how safe are online transactions?

When you buy something online, you most likely use a credit card; therefore, the exchange of money is done directly between you and a bank. Because online shopping eliminates a salesclerk or other human intermediary from the transaction, it can actually be safer than traditional retail shopping. Still, because users are told to be wary of online transactions and because the integrity of online transactions is the backbone of e-commerce, businesses must have some

> **"Just how safe are online transactions?"**

ACTIVE HELP-DESK   Doing Business Online

In this Active Helpdesk call, you'll learn about e-commerce and what e-commerce safeguards protect you when you're.

form of security certification to give their customers a level of comfort. Businesses hire security companies such as VeriSign to certify that their online transactions are secure. Thus, if the Web site displays the VeriSign seal (see Figure 18), you can usually trust that the information you submit to the site is protected.

Another indication that a Web site is secure is the appearance of a small icon of a closed padlock (in both Microsoft's Internet Explorer and Mozilla's Firefox), as shown in Figure 18. In addition, the beginning of the URL of the site changes from "http://" to "https://"—with the "s" standing for *secure socket layer* (see Figure 18).

How else can I shop safely online?

To ensure that your online shopping experience is a safe one, follow these guidelines:

- **Shop at well-known, reputable sites.** If you aren't familiar with a site, then investigate it with the Better Business Bureau (**bbb.org**) or at **bizrate.com** or **webassured.com**. When you place an order, print a copy of the order and make sure you receive a confirmation number. Make sure the company has a phone number and street address in addition to a Web site.

- **Pay by credit card, not debit card.** Federal consumer credit laws protect credit card users, but debit card users do not have the same level of protection. If possible, reserve one credit card for Internet purchases only; even better, use a prepaid credit card that has a small credit limit.

- **Check the return policy.** Print a copy and save it. If the site disappears overnight, this information may help you in filing a dispute or reporting a problem to a site such as the Better Business Bureau.

Accessing the Web: Web Browsers

None of the activities for which we use the Web could happen without an important software application: a Web browser. A **Web browser**, or **browser**, is software installed on your computer system that allows you to locate, view, and navigate the Web. Most browsers in use today are graphical browsers, meaning they can display pictures (graphics) in addition to text and other forms of multimedia such as sound and video.

 Why Should You Run the Latest Version of Browser Software?

When new file formats are developed for the Web, browsers need new plug-ins to display content properly. Constantly downloading and installing plug-ins can be a tedious process. Although many Web sites provide links to sites that enable you to download plug-ins, not all do, resulting in frustration when you can't display the content you want. When new versions of browsers are released, they normally include the latest versions of popular plug-ins. Corrections of security breaches are typically included in these versions of browser software as well. Therefore, upgrading to the latest version of your browser software provides for safer, more convenient Web surfing. Fortunately, most updates are free, and you can set most of the popular Web browsers to notify you when updates are available or to download the updates automatically.

What are some common Web browsers?   Internet Explorer (IE) is the main browser from Microsoft and is included in the Windows operating system. It has been the most widely used browser since 1999, and still enjoys predominant market share, although its popularity has slipped over the years. Other browsers, discussed below, have become popular alternatives to Internet Explorer.

- **Firefox** is a popular open source browser from Mozilla (**mozilla.org**). Firefox continues to enjoy increasing popularity, capturing approximately 21.5 percent of the U.S. browser market. Add-ons are available to customize and increase the functionality of Firefox. Examples include the Video Download Helper that converts Web videos, like those found on YouTube, to savable files and a Facebook toolbar that integrates Facebook functionality into your browser. Other handy features found in Firefox are spell checking for e-mail, blogs, and other Web postings, as well as Session Restore, which brings back all your active Web pages if the system shuts down unexpectedly.
- **Safari** is a browser developed by Apple (**apple.com**). Although it was created as the default browser for Macintosh computers and is included with the Mac

OS, a Windows-based version is also available. Safari has quickly gained public acceptance, and it now has approximately an 8 percent share of the U.S. browser market.

- **Google Chrome** is the newest browser on the market, distributed by Google (**google.com**) (see Figure 19). The unique features offered by Chrome include thumbnail access to your most recently visited sites from the home page and shortcuts to Google applications.

What features do browsers offer?

Most browsers' toolbars provide convenient navigation and Web page management tools. The most recent features include tabbed browsing and quick tabs (see Figure 20). Quick tabs, in Internet Explorer 7 and higher, shows thumbnail images of all open Web pages in open tabs, and Google Chrome offers thumbnail images of most recently visited sites on the home page. Most of the popular Web browsers have tabbed browsing in which Web pages are loaded in "tabs" within the same browser window. Rather than having to switch among Web pages in several open windows, you can flip between the tabs in one window. You can even open several of your favorite Web sites from one folder and choose to display them as tabs. You may also save a group of tabs as a Favorites group, if there are several tabs you often open at the same time.

Most browsers also include a built-in search box in which you can designate your preferred default search engine and tools for printing, page formatting, and security settings.

Getting Around the Web: URLs, Hyperlinks, and Other Tools

You gain initial access to a particular **Web site**, or location on the Web, by typing its unique address, or **Uniform Resource Locator** (**URL**), pronounced "you-are-ell"),

Figure 19

Google Chrome includes thumbnails of most recently visited Web sites for easy access.

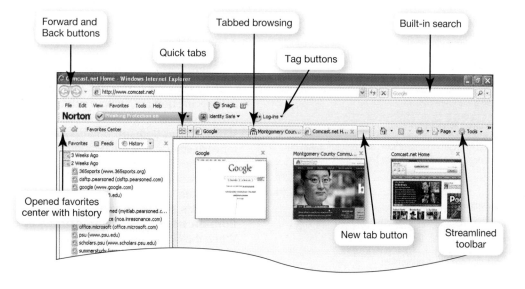

Figure 20

Internet Explorer 7 (IE7) includes tabbed browsing and quick tabs. IE7 has also reduced the display of navigation tools to a simple toolbar and built a Google search engine right into the browser.

Getting Around the Web: URLs, Hyperlinks, and Other Tools

Figure 21
The parts of a URL.

in your browser. For example, the URL of the Web site for *Popular Science* magazine is popsci.com. By typing this URL for *Popular Science* magazine, you connect to the **home page**, or main page, of the Web site. Once you are in the home page, you can move all around the site by clicking specially formatted pieces of text called *hyperlinks*. Let's look at these and other navigation tools in more detail.

URLs

What do all the parts of the URL mean?   As noted above, a URL is a Web site's address. Like a regular street address, a URL is composed of several parts that help identify the Web document for which it stands (see Figure 21). The first part of the URL indicates the *protocol* (set of rules) used to retrieve the specified document. The protocol is generally followed by a colon,

two forward slashes, *www* (indicating *World Wide Web*), and the **domain name**. (Sometimes the domain name is also thought to include the *www*.) The domain name is also referred to as the *host name*.

What's the protocol?   Most URLs begin with *http*, which is short for **hypertext transfer protocol (HTTP)**. HTTP is the protocol (or set of rules) that allows files to be transferred from a computer that hosts the Web site you are requesting (known as a *Web server*) so that you can see the Web site on your computer by using a browser.

Another common protocol used to transfer files over the Internet is **file transfer protocol (FTP)**. It is used to upload and download files from one computer to another. FTP files use an FTP file server, whereas HTTP files use a Web server. To connect to most FTP servers, you need a user ID and a password. FTP addresses, like e-mail addresses or URLs, identify one location on the Web. They can have several formats, such as ftp://ftp.microsoft.com or ftp://wuarchive.wustl.edu. To upload and download files from FTP sites, you can use a Web browser or file transfer software such as WS_FTP, Fetch, or CuteFTP.

What's in a domain name?   The domain name identifies the site's **host**. For example, **berkeley.edu** is the domain name for the University of California at Berkeley. Although using *www* is conventional, it is not necessary.

The suffix in the domain name after the dot (such as .com or .edu) is called the **top-level domain**. This suffix indicates the kind of organization to which the host belongs. Figure 22 lists the most frequently used top-level domains.

Each country has its own top-level domain. These are two-letter designations such as .za for South Africa and .us for the United States. A sampling of country codes is shown in Figure 23. Within a country-specific domain, further subdivisions can be made for regions or states. For instance, the .us domain contains subdomains for each state, using the two-letter abbreviation of the state. For example, the URL for Pennsylvania's Web site is state.pa.us.

What's the information after the domain name that I sometimes see? When the URL is only the domain name (such as nytimes.com), you are requesting a site's home page. However, sometimes a

Figure 22 | COMMON TOP-LEVEL DOMAINS AND THEIR AUTHORIZED USERS

Domain Name	Who Can Use It
.biz	Businesses
.com	Originally for commercial sites, but now can be used by anyone
.edu	Degree-granting institutions
.gov	United States government
.info	Information service providers
.int	Limited to organizations, offices, and programs that are sanctioned by a treaty between two or more nations
.mil	United States military
.name	Individuals
.net	Originally for networking organizations, but no longer restricted
.org	Organizations (often nonprofits)

Figure 23 | EXAMPLES OF COUNTRY CODES

Country Code	Country
.au	Australia
.ca	Canada
.uk	United Kingdom
.us	United States
.mx	Mexico

Note: For a full listing of country codes, refer to **norid.no/domenenavnbaser/domreg.html**.

forward slash and additional text follow the domain name, such as in nytimes.com/pages/cartoons. The information after the slash indicates a particular file or **path** (or **subdirectory**) within the Web site. In this example, you would connect to the cartoon pages on the *New York Times* site.

Hyperlinks and Beyond

What's the best way to get around in a Web site? Unlike text in a book or a Microsoft Word document, which is linear (meaning you read it from top to bottom, left to right, one page after another), the Web is anything but linear. As its name implies, the Web is a series of connected paths, or links, that connect you to different Web sites. You can jump from one location, or Web page, to another within the same Web site or navigate to another Web site altogether by clicking on a specially coded element called a **hyperlink**, as shown in Figure 24. Generally, text that operates as a hyperlink appears in a different color (often blue) and is underlined. Sometimes images also act as hyperlinks. When you pass your cursor over a hyperlinked image, for example, a cursor may change to a hand with a finger pointing upward. To access the hyperlink, you simply click the image.

How do I return to a Web page I've already visited? To retrace your steps, some sites also provide a **breadcrumb list**—a list of pages within a Web site you've visited. It usually appears at the top of a page. Figure 24 shows an example of a breadcrumb list. "Breadcrumbs" get their name from the fairy tale "Hansel and Gretel," in which the characters drop

breadcrumbs on the trail to find their way out of a forest. By clicking on earlier links in a breadcrumb list, you can retrace your steps back to the page on which you started.

To get back to your original location or visit a Web page you viewed previously, you use the browser's Back and Forward buttons (see Figure 24). To back up more than one page, click the down arrow next to the Back button to access a list of most recently visited Web sites. By selecting any one of these sites in the list, you can return directly to that page without having to navigate through other Web sites and Web pages you've visited.

The History list (see Figure 24) on your browser's toolbar is also a handy feature. The History list shows all the Web sites and pages that you've visited over a certain period of time. These Web sites are organized according to date and can go back as far as three weeks. To access the history list on IE7, click the down arrow next to the navigation arrows. On the Firefox toolbar, the history button is the alarm clock icon.

Favorites, Live Bookmarks, and Tagging

What's the best way to mark a site so I can return to it later? If you want an easy way to return to a specific Web page

Figure 24

When you click on a hyperlink, you jump from one location in a Web site to another. When you click on the links in a breadcrumb list, you can navigate your way back through a Web site.

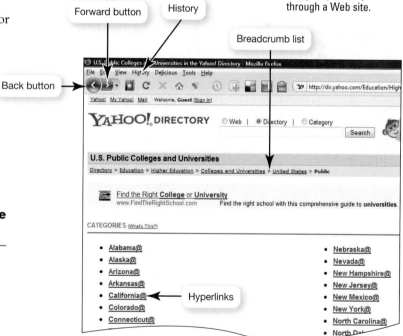

without having to remember to type in the address, you can use your browser's **Favorites** or **Bookmarks** feature. Internet Explorer and Safari call this feature Favorites; Firefox and Google Chrome call the same feature a Bookmark. This feature places a marker of the site's URL in an easily retrievable list in your browser's toolbar. To organize the sites into categories, most browsers offer tools to create folders. Most browsers also provide features to export the list of bookmarks to another computer or another browser.

Favorites and Bookmarks are great for quickly locating those sites you use the most, but they are accessible to you only when you are on your own computer. One way to access your Bookmarks and Favorites from any computer is to use MyBookmarks (**mybookmarks.com**), a free Internet service that stores your Bookmarks and Favorites online.

What are live bookmarks? The **live bookmark** feature of the Firefox browser adds the technology of RSS feeds to bookmarking. Because the Web is constantly changing, the site you bookmarked last week may subsequently change and add new content. Traditionally, you would notice the change only the next time you visited the site. With live bookmarks, the content comes to you. Instead of constantly checking your favorite Web pages for new content, a live bookmark delivers updates to you as soon as they become available. Live bookmarks are useful if you are interested in the most up-to-date news stories, sports scores, or stock prices.

What is social bookmarking? Social bookmarking, also known as *tagging,* lets you store, organize, and manage bookmarks (or tags) of Web pages. A **social bookmark** or **tag** is a keyword or term that is assigned to a piece of information such as a Web page, digital image, or video. A tag describes the item so that it can be found again by browsing or searching. Tags were

popularized by Web 2.0 Web sites such as YouTube and Flickr.

The social bookmarking Web site Delicious (**delicious.com**) gives you the ability to add tags as bookmarks to your favorite Web sites (see Figure 25). Digg (**digg.com**) and Newsvine (**newsvine.com**) offer similar systems for organizing news content. The tag can be something meaningful to you, or you can select one from a list of suggested tags. Later, you can go back to Delicious, conduct a search using your tag, and find bookmarks tagged with the same word from everyone in your network. You can also see how many other Web users tagged the same site.

Delicious offers convenient toolbars for your browsers, and many Web sites incorporate bookmarking icons for ease of use. Figure 26 lists several popular social bookmarking tag tools. StumbleUpon (**stumbleupon.com**) recommends Web sites based on your personal preferences, and the recommendations of people you know or the general surfing public.

Searching the Web Effectively

With its billions of Web pages, the Internet offers visitors access to masses of information on virtually any topic. To narrow down the quantity of Web information to something more useful, we use a search engine and a keyword query. A **search engine** is a set of programs that searches the Web for **keywords**—specific words you wish to look for (*query*)—and then returns a

Figure 25

Icons of some popular social bookmarking Web sites.

list of the Web sites on which those keywords are found. Popular search engines include Google, Yahoo!, and Ask.com.

For some searches you also can search the Web using a **subject directory**, which is a structured outline of Web sites organized by topics and subtopics. Librarians' Internet Index (**lii.org**) is a subject directory and some popular search engines such as Yahoo! also feature directories. If you can't decide which search engine is best, you may want to try a **metasearch engine**. Metasearch engines search other search engines rather than individual Web sites. Figure 27 lists search engines and subject directories that are alternatives to Google, Yahoo!, and Ask.com.

Search Engines

How do search engines work? Search engines have three parts. The first part is a program called a **spider**. The spider constantly collects data on the Web, following links in Web sites and reading Web pages. Spiders get their name because they crawl over the Web using multiple "legs" to visit many sites simultaneously. As the spider collects data, the second part of the search engine, an indexer program, organizes the data into a large database. When you use a search engine, you interact with the third part: the search engine software. This software searches the indexed

Figure 26

Tagging tools are incorporated into Web browsers and in some Web pages for easy access.

Figure 27 | POPULAR SEARCH ENGINES AND SUBJECT DIRECTORIES

Search Tools on the Internet		
AltaVista	**altavista.com**	Keyword search engine
Bing	**bing.com**	New search engine from Microsoft
Clusty	**clusty.com**	Keyword search engine that groups similar results into clusters
ChaCha	**chacha.com**	Don't like your search results? This site lets you chat with a real live professional guide who helps you search, and it's free of charge.
Complete-Planet	**completeplanet.com**	Deep Web directory that searches databases not normally searched by typical search engines
Dogpile	**dogpile.com**	Metasearch engine that searches Google, Yahoo!, MSN Search, and Ask
Excite	**excite.com**	Portal with keyword search capabilities
InfoMine	**infomine.com**	Subject directory of academic resources with keyword search engine capabilities
Rollyo	**rollyo.com**	Short for Roll Your Own Search Engine. Basically, this site lets you create your own search engine (searchroll) that searches just the sites you want it to search.
Open Directory Project	**dmoz.org**	Subject directory with keyword search capabilities
Stumbleupon	**stumbleupon.com**	Lets you rate pages "thumbs up" or "thumbs down." As it learns your preferences, your search results improve.
Technorati	**technorati.com**	A great search engine for blog content

Note: For a complete list of search engines, go to **searchengineguide.com**.

data, pulling out relevant information according to your search. The resulting list appears in your Web browser as a list of hits (sites that match your search).

Why don't I get the same results from all search engines? Each search engine uses a unique formula, or *algorithm*, to formulate the search and create the resulting index of related sites. In addition, search engines differ in how they rank the search results. Most search engines rank their results based on the frequency of the appearance of your queried keywords in Web sites as well as the location of those words in the sites. Thus, sites that include the keywords in their URL or site name most likely appear at the top of the hit list. After that, results vary because of differences in each engine's proprietary formula.

In addition, search engines differ as to which sites they search. For instance, Google and Ask.com search nearly the entire Web, whereas specialty search engines search only sites that are relevant to a particular subject. Specialty search engines exist for almost every industry or interest. For example, **dailystocks.com** is a search engine used primarily by investors that searches for corporate information to help them make educated decisions. Search Engine Watch (**searchenginewatch.com**) has a list of

many specialty search engines organized by industry.

Can I use a search engine to search for images and videos? With the increasing popularity of multimedia, search engines such as Google, Ask.com, and Yahoo! have capabilities to search the Web for digital images and audio and video files. YouTube (**youtube.com**) is one of many sites that has gained recent popularity because of its wealth of video content. In addition to the amusing videos that are captured in popular news, YouTube contains instructional and informational videos.

How can I refine my searches for better results? When you conduct a Web search, you may receive a list of hits that includes thousands—even millions—of Web pages that have no relevance to the topic you're trying to search. Initially Boolean operators were needed to help refine a search. **Boolean operators** are words such as AND, NOT, and OR that describe the relationships between keywords in a search.

Today, most search engines offer an advanced search page that provides the same types of strategies in a well-organized form (see Figure 28). Using the advanced search form can make your Internet research a lot more efficient. With the simple addition of a few words or constraints, you can narrow your search results to a more manageable and more meaningful list.

Are there other helpful search strategies? Instead of using the advanced search form, you can use other strategies to help refine your searches when entering your search phrases.

- **Search for a phrase.** To search for an exact phrase, place quotation marks around your keywords. The search engine will look for only those Web sites that contain the words in that exact order. For example, if you want information on the movie *Lord of the*

Web 1.0

Producer → Web Page → Consumer

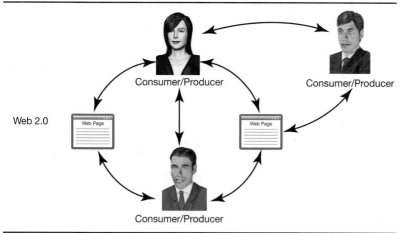

Web 2.0

Consumer/Producer

Consumer/Producer

Consumer/Producer

Consumer/Producer

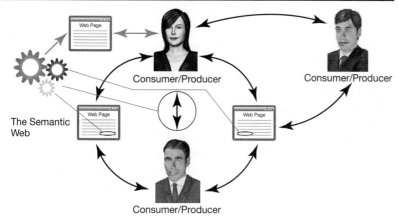

The Semantic Web

Consumer/Producer

Consumer/Producer

Consumer/Producer

Consumer/Producer

Although some of the Semantic Web functionalities are beginning to emerge in Web 2.0 technologies, the majority of the functionality and implementation of the Semantic Web is still in development. The World Wide Web Consortium (W3C), led by Tim Berners-Lee, is the primary organization leading the charge. The greatest challenge is recoding all the information currently available on the Web into the type of metadata that computers could recognize. The very grandeur of that task means that we will not see a fully functional Semantic Web until sometime in the distant future. In the meantime, we can continue to benefit from each small step toward that goal.

Figure 33

Web 2.0 technologies enable us to become creators and users of Internet content. The Semantic Web enables the computer to add context to Web content, providing meaning to information from different sources.

contains multimedia, which is the norm for most Web pages today. Similarly, if you visit many Web sites at the same time, or receive or send large files through e-mail, you'll find that a dial-up connection is especially slow. Another disadvantage of dial-up is that when you're on the Internet, you tie up your phone line if you don't have a separate line.

Choosing the Right Internet Connection Option

How do I choose which Internet connection option is best for me? In 2007, approximately half of all U.S. households connected to the Internet used some form of broadband connection. Depending on the area in which you live, you might not have a choice as to the type of broadband connection that is available. Check with your local cable TV provider, phone company, and satellite TV provider(s) to determine what broadband options are available where you live and what the transfer rates are in your area. It might also be good to check with your neighbors to see what kind of broadband connections they use. Speeds vary by neighborhood, sometimes exceeding advertised rates, so it's always good to check actual experiences.

Figure 34 | COMPARING CABLE, DSL, AND FIBER-OPTIC INTERNET CONNECTION OPTIONS

	DSL	Cable	Fiber-Optic
Maximum upload speeds	Average speeds of 1.5 Mbps, with a maximum of 6 + Mbps	Average speeds of 3 Mbps, with a maximum of 12 + Mbps	Average speeds of 20 Mbps, with a maximum speed of 30 Mbps
Pros	Lets you surf the Net and talk on the same phone line simultaneously.	Speeds are not dependent on distance from central office.	Increased speeds. Service is not shared or dependent on distance from central office.
Cons	Speed drops as you get farther from phone company's central office. Not every phone line will work; no easy way exists to find out if yours will.	Line is shared with others in neighborhood; speeds may vary. May require professional installation if cable not already present.	Cost, although this is a diminishing concern as the technology continues to be deployed and accepted. Not available in all areas.

Note: The data transfer rates listed in this table are approximations. As technologies improve, so do data transfer rates.

One factor to consider in choosing the right Internet connection is speed. **Data transfer rate** is the measurement of how fast data travels between computers. It is also informally referred to as *connection speed*. For example, dial-up modems have a maximum data transfer rate of 56 Kbps. This speed is usually referred to as *56K*. A kilobit is 1,000 bits and is normally used to represent the amount of data that is transferred in 1 second between two telecommunication points. Satellite Internet is faster than dial-up but is still slower than DSL and cable. Although DSL is catching up, cable wins out over DSL for speed. However, the availability of fiber-optic service through DSL providers can increase download rates to as high as 30 Mbps.

Finally, you may also need to consider which other services you want bundled into your payment, such as phone or TV. The table in Figure 34 compares several features of cable, DSL, and fiber-optic service to help you with your decision.

The Future of the Internet

The Internet of the future will have more bandwidth and offer increased services. Because of the prevalence of wireless technologies, the Internet will be more accessible, and we will become more dependent on it. However, because commerce and communication activities are increasingly dominating the Internet, the concern is that there will be no bandwidth left for one of the Internet's original purposes: exchange of scientific and academic research. Two major projects currently under way in the United States to develop advanced technologies for the Internet are the large scale networking (LSN) program and Internet2.

What are the large scale networking and Internet2 programs? Out of a project titled the Next Generation Internet (which ended in 2002), the U.S. government created the **large scale networking (LSN)** program. Large scale networking's aim is to fund the research and development of cutting-edge networking and wireless technologies and to increase the speed of networks.

The Internet2 is a research and development consortium of more than two hundred universities (supported by government and industry partners) that seeks to expand the possibilities of the Internet by developing new Internet technologies and disseminating them as rapidly as possible to the rest of the Internet community. Many of the current technologies of the commercial Internet are possible because of the research done by the Internet2 consortium. The Internet2 backbone supports extremely high-speed communications—up to 9.6 gigabits per second (Gbps)—and provides an excellent testing area for new data transmission technologies.

How else will the Internet become a more integral part of our lives? As this chapter explained, the Internet is already an integral part of our lives. It is the way we communicate, shop, research, entertain, and express ourselves. Many of the tools on the Web that have been described in this chapter—social networking sites, wikis, podcasts, and user content databases such as YouTube (for videos) and Flickr (for photos)—are part of a wave of Web-based services that emphasize online collaboration and sharing among users. The future Internet will continue to evolve with more Web-based applications driven by user input, interaction, and content.

In the future, you can expect to use the Internet to assist you with many day-to-day tasks that you now do manually. No longer will PCs and mobile devices be our primary access to the Internet. We can already see the convergence of the Internet with telephony, television, and gaming devices.

As other less obvious Internet-enabled devices become popular and more accessible to the common consumer, our lives will become more Internet dependent. For example, Internet-enabled appliances and household systems are now available that allow your home virtually to run itself. Today, there are refrigerators that can monitor their contents and go online to order more diet soda when they detect that the supply is getting low. Meanwhile, Internet heating and cooling systems can monitor weather forecasts and order fuel deliveries when supplies run low or bad weather is expected. These appliances will become more widespread as the price of equipment drops.

The uses of the Internet are limited only by our imaginations and the current constraints of technology. At some point, the Internet will no longer be a place we "go" to, but an integral part of our lives.

The Future of the Internet

summary

1. **What is the origin of the Internet?**

   The Internet is the largest computer network in the world, connecting millions of computers. Government and military officials developed the Internet as a reliable way to communicate in the event of war. Eventually, scientists and educators used the Internet to exchange research. Today, we use the Internet and the Web (which is a part of the Internet) to shop, research, communicate, and entertain ourselves.

2. **How can I communicate through the Internet?**

   Communication was one of the reasons the Internet was developed and is one of the primary uses of the Internet today. E-mail allows users to communicate electronically without the parties involved being available at the same time, whereas instant messaging services are programs that enable you to communicate in real time with others who are online at the same time. Voice over Internet Protocol (VoIP) is a form of voice-based Internet communication that turns a standard Internet connection into a way to place phone calls. Other forms of group communication include chat rooms, newsgroups, and listservs.

3. **How can I communicate and collaborate using Web 2.0 technologies?**

   Web 2.0 is a new trend of Web interactions among people, software, and data. Examples of these technologies include blogs, wikis, and more. Blogs are journal entries posted to the Web that are generally organized by a topic or area of interest and are publicly available. Generally, one person writes the blog, and others can comment on the journal entries. Video logs are personal journals that use video as the primary content in addition to text, images, and audio. Wikis are a type of Web site that allows users to change content by adding, removing, or editing it. A wiki is designed to allow many users to collaborate on the content. Podcasts are audio or video content that is broadcast over the Internet. Users subscribe to receive updates to podcasts. Social networking sites enable users to communicate and share information with existing friends as well as to meet and connect with others through common interests, experiences, or friends.

4. **What are the various kinds of multimedia files found on the Web, and what software do I need to use them?**

   The Web is appealing because of its enriched multimedia content. Multimedia is anything that involves one or more forms of media in addition to text, such as graphics, audio, and video clips. Sometimes you need a special software program called a plug-in (or player) to view and hear multimedia files. Plug-ins are often installed in new computers or are offered free of charge at manufacturers' Web sites.

5. **What is e-commerce, and what e-commerce safeguards protect me when I'm online?**

   E-commerce is the business of conducting business online. E-commerce includes transactions between businesses (B2B), between consumers (C2C), and between businesses and consumers (B2C). Because more business than ever before is conducted online, numerous safeguards have been put in place to ensure that transactions are protected.

6. **What is a Web browser?**

   Once you're connected to the Internet, in order to locate, navigate to, and view Web pages, you need to install special software called a Web browser on your system. The most common Web browsers are Microsoft Internet Explorer, Mozilla, Firefox, and Safari. Google Chrome is the newest browser on the market.

7. **What is a URL, and what are its parts?**

   You gain access to a Web site by typing in its address, called a Uniform Resource Locator (URL). A URL is composed of several parts, including the protocol, the domain, the top-level domain, and, occasionally, paths (or subdirectories).

Using the Internet

8. How can I use hyperlinks and other tools to get around the Web?

One unique aspect of the Web is that you can jump from place to place by clicking on specially formatted pieces of text or images called *hyperlinks.* You can also use tools such as Back and Forward buttons, History lists, breadcrumb lists, and Favorites or Bookmarks to navigate the Web. Favorites, live bookmarks, and tagging help you return to specific Web pages without having to type in the URL and help you organize the Web content that is most important to you.

9. How do I search the Internet effectively?

A search engine is a set of programs that searches the Web using specific keywords you wish to query and then returns a list of the Web sites on which those keywords are found. Search engines can be used to search for images, podcasts, and videos in addition to traditional text-based Web content. A subject directory is a structured outline of Web sites organized by topic and subtopic. Metasearch engines search other search engines.

10. How do I evaluate a Web site?

Not all Web sites are equal, and some are better sources for research than others are. To evaluate whether it is appropriate to use a Web site as a resource, determine whether the author of the site is reputable and whether the site is intended for your particular needs. In addition, make sure that the site content is not biased, the information in the site is current, and all the links on the site are available and appropriate.

11. How does data travel on the Internet?

A computer connected to the Internet acts as either a client (a computer that asks for information) or a server (a computer that receives the request and returns the information to the client). Data travels between clients and servers along a system of communication lines or pathways. The largest and fastest of these pathways is the Internet backbone. To ensure that data is sent to the correct computer along the pathways, IP addresses (unique ID numbers) are assigned to all computers connected to the Internet.

12. What are my options for connecting to the Internet?

Home users have many options for connecting to the Internet. A dial-up connection, in which you connect to the Internet using a standard phone line, was at one time the standard way to connect to the Internet. Today's broadband connections are faster and have made dial-up a legacy connection technology. Broadband connections include cable, DSL, and fiber-optic. Satellite is a connection option for those who do not have access to faster broadband technologies. Wi-Fi allows users to connect to the Internet wirelessly.

13. What will the Internet of the future look like?

The Internet of the future will have faster connections and will be able to provide additional services as a result of projects such as the large-scale networking program and Internet2. The Internet will become more integrated into our daily lives as Internet-enabled appliances and household systems provide more remote-control features for our homes.

key terms

aggregator
aircard
blog (weblog)
Bookmarks
Boolean operator
breadcrumb list
broadband
business-to-business (B2B)
business-to-consumer (B2C)
cable
chat room
client
client/server network
consumer-to-consumer (C2C)
data transfer rate
dial-up connection
dial-up modem
digital subscriber line (DSL)
domain name
e-commerce (electronic commerce)
e-mail (electronic mail)
e-mail client
Favorites
fiber-optic service (FiOS)
file transfer protocol (FTP)
home page
host
hyperlink
HyperText Transfer Protocol (HTTP)
instant messaging (IM)
Internet
Internet backbone
Internet Protocol address (IP address)
keyword

large scale networking (LSN)
listserv
live bookmark
metasearch engine
modem
multimedia
multiplayer online game
netiquette
network interface card (NIC)
newsgroup
path (subdirectory)
PC card (PCMCIA card)
plug-in (player)
podcast
Really Simple Syndication (RSS)
satellite Internet
search engine
server
social bookmark (tag)
social networking
spider
streaming audio
streaming video
subject directory
tag (social bookmark)
top-level domain
Uniform Resource Locator (URL)
video log (vlog or video blog)
Web 2.0
Web browser (browser)
Web site
webcast
wiki
World Wide Web (WWW or the Web)

buzzwords

Word Bank

- blogs (weblogs)
- Bookmarks
- broadband
- DSL
- fiber-optic service (FiOS)
- hyperlink
- instant messaging (IM)
- keyword
- search engine
- social bookmarking
- social networking
- tag
- Uniform Resource Locators (URLs)
- Voice over Internet Protocol (VoIP)
- Web 2.0
- Web browser
- Wi-Fi
- wiki

Instructions: Fill in the blanks using the words from the Word Bank above.

Juan rests his new notebook on his lap and powers it up while waiting for his next class to begin. Using the (1) _____ access provided by his college, Juan is able to connect to the Internet wirelessly. Although the school's wireless access to the Internet is fast, it's not as fast as the (2) _____ connection at home, because his parents just switched to (3) _____, which transfers data at the speed of light.

Knowing he has only a few minutes before class, Juan launches Internet Explorer, the (4) _____ software from Microsoft that allows him to connect to the Internet. He quickly goes to Facebook, the (5) _____ site, to catch up on the activities of his friends. He also reads a few of the updates to the online journal Engadget.com, one of his favorite (6) _____. He's glad that the new (7) _____ technologies make such collaboration possible. Just before class begins, Juan's friend Marie, who is using her (8) _____ service, sees that Juan is available on her buddy list. She sends him a quick, real-time note to let him know she'll catch up with him after class.

At home Juan types in a (9) _____ in Google, the (10) _____, to find Web sites for a research paper. One of the first sites listed is Wikipedia, the online encyclopedia that takes advantage of the collaborative nature of (11) _____ technology. Because anyone can add, change, or edit content on Wikipedia, Juan knows that he can't rely completely on this information but finds that it is usually a pretty good starting point for his research. Juan clicks on a (12) _____, the specially coded text at the bottom of the Wikipedia article, which links him to another Web site. He adds a (13) _____ with a meaningful keyword in the (14) _____ site Delicious so he can return to it later. Finally, before going to bed, Juan uses (15) _____ technology to speak to his friend across the country with his Skype service.

becoming computer literate

Using key terms from the chapter, write a letter to the owners of your local coffee shop explaining why they should make it a Wi-Fi hot spot. Include in your letter the advantages Wi-Fi would bring to the customers and identify some security considerations that customers need to be aware of.

self-test

Instructions: Answer the multiple-choice and true–false questions below for more practice with key terms and concepts from this chapter.

Multiple Choice

1. Which of the following statements is NOT true about instant messaging?
a. It is a popular form of communication.
b. You communicate in real time.
c. More than two people can IM at the same time.
d. Unlike e-mail, IM is good for private conversations.

2. When you are shopping online, which of the following does NOT indicate that you have a secure connection?
a. A closed padlock icon in the status bar
b. A URL that begins with *https*
c. The word "secure" in the title bar
d. The VeriSign seal on the Web page

3. With a podcast, you can
a. subscribe to video and audio content.
b. have the most recent content "delivered" automatically.
c. play the video and audio content on a portable media player.
d. All of the above.

4. A Web page that enables online collaboration is
a. a podcast.   c. a blog.
b. a wiki.   d. an IM chat.

5. When searching the Internet, which of the following is true?
a. All search engines provide the same results.
b. A metasearch engine delivers the most specific results.
c. Using advanced search pages broadens your results.
d. Using words surrounded by quotation marks searches for those words in that exact order.

6. In the Web address **http://www.irs. gov**, which part is considered the top-level domain?
a. www   c. http
b. .gov   d. www.irs.gov

7. Which of the following broadband Internet connections transmits data at the speed of light?
a. Cable   c. FiOS
b. DSL   d. Satellite

8. Which is an advantage to Web-based e-mail clients?
a. They require you to download specific software to your computer.
b. They offer more functionality than client-based software.
c. They are accessible from any computer with an Internet connection.
d. All of the above.

9. In evaluating Web sites as appropriate sources for research, which criteria you should consider?
a. Authority, relevancy, bias, audience
b. Authority, Web design, audience, links
c. Relevancy, bias, Web design, audience
d. Relevancy, Web design, audience, links

10. Which accurately defines an IP address?
a. The means by which computers are identified on the Internet
b. A set of four groups of numbers separated by dots
c. A unique identification number assigned to a computer when it connects to the Internet
d. All of the above

True–False

_____ 1. *Web* and *Internet* are interchangeable terms.

_____ 2. Social bookmarking is also known as *tagging*.

_____ 3. Because Google generates the most search results of any of the search engines, it is called a metasearch engine.

_____ 4. DSL, cable, and FiOS are all considered broadband Internet connections.

_____ 5. You cannot connect to the Internet wirelessly unless you're in a Wi-Fi hot spot.

Using the Internet

1. Online Support Facilities

Your school most likely has many online support facilities. Do you know what they are? Go to your school's Web site and search for online support.

a. Is online tutoring available?
b. Can you reserve a book from the library online?
c. Can you register for classes online?
d. Can you take classes online?
e. Can you buy books online?

2. Plagiarism Policies

Does your school have a plagiarism policy?

a. Search your school's Web site to find the school's plagiarism policy. What does it say?
b. How well do you paraphrase? Find some Web sites that help test or evaluate your paraphrasing skills.

3. Searching Beyond Google

While Google is probably your first choice among search engines, there are many other very good search engines that are good to know about. Conduct searches for inexpensive travel deals for spring break by using the following search engines. Record your results and a summary of the differences among search engines. Would you choose to use any of these search engines again? Why or why not?

a. Clusty.com
b. Dogpile.com
c. Rollyo.com

4. Free Speech Online

Jeanne was suspended from school for several days because her posts on MySpace about her teacher and a few of her classmates were "vulgar" and "derogatory." Tom was expelled from his school because the picture he posted of himself was in violation of his school's code of conduct. Similarly, Bill, a local employer, changed his mind about a job offer to a recent graduate after seeing questionable content on the candidate's Facebook page.

a. Should a person be penalized for his or her content on any Web site?
b. Is the issue denial of free speech or prudent reactions to improper behavior?

5. Using Web 2.0 in Education

Social networking sites, blogs, and wikis are commonly referred to as Web 2.0 technologies. Sites that use Web 2.0 offer opportunities for collaboration, creativity, and enterprise. Describe how Web 2.0 sites such as Wikipedia, YouTube, Delicious, and Digg might change how you learn and manage information.

1. Online Résumé Resources

Using a search engine, locate several Web resources that offer assistance in writing a résumé. For example, the University of Minnesota (**umn.edu/ohr/careerdev/resources/ resume**) has a résumé tutor that guides you as you write your résumé.

a. What other Web sites can you find that help you write a résumé?

b. Do these sites all offer the same services and have the same features?

2. Online Cover Letter Resources

Your résumé will need to be accompanied by a cover letter. Research Web sites that offer advice for writing cover letters and samples of good ones.

a. Which Web sites do you feel offer the best advice on how to write a cover letter? Which style cover letter works best for you?

b. What do the Web sites say you should include in your cover letter, and why?

3. Evaluating Web Content

You have noticed that your co-workers are using the Internet to conduct research. However, they are not careful about checking the validity of the Web sites they find before using the information.

a. Search the Internet for Web site evaluation guidelines. Print out your sources and findings.

b. Using the material from step (a), create a scorecard or set of guidelines that will help others determine whether a Web site is reliable.

4. Internet Connection Option

Now that you've graduated, you are planning to move into your first apartment and leave behind the comforts of broadband access at the residence halls. Evaluate the Internet options available in your area.

a. Create a table that includes information on broadband services in your area. The table should include the name of the provider, the cost of the service, information on bundled services (TV, Internet, phone), and the cost of bundled services.

b. Based on the table you create, write a brief paragraph describing which service you would choose, and why.

5. Internet Connection Speed

You would like to know how fast your Internet connection speed is. Your co-worker in the information technology (IT) department recommended that you check out **bandwidthplace.com** and **pcpitstop.com**.

a. Choose one of the recommended sites and test your connection speed. How is the test conducted? What is used to measure the connection speed?

b. List reasons why you would be interested in measuring your Internet connection speed.

6. E-Mail Privacy

Take a moment to think about this statement: An e-mail is no more private than a postcard.

a. Search the Web for resources that support and oppose the preceding statement. Print out sources for both sides of the argument.

b. Write a paragraph that summarizes your position.

Using the Internet

Instructions: Albert Einstein used *Gedankenexperiments*, or critical thinking questions, to develop his theory of relativity. Some ideas are best understood by experimenting with them in our own minds. The following critical thinking questions are designed to demand your full attention but require only a comfortable chair—no technology.

1. Internet and Society

The Internet was initially created in part to enable scientists and educators to share information quickly and efficiently. The advantages Internet access brings to our lives are evident, but does Internet access also cause problems?

a. What advantages and disadvantages does the Internet bring to your life?

b. What positive and negative effects has the Internet had on our society as a whole?

c. Some people argue that conducting searches on the Internet provides answers but does not inspire thoughtful research. What do you think?

d. Should use of the Internet be banned, or at least limited, for research projects in schools? Why or why not?

2. File Swapping Ethics

Downloading free music, movies, and other electronic media from the Internet, although illegal, still occurs on sites such as Limewire and Bit Torrents.

a. Do you think you should have the ability to download free music files of your choice? Do you think the musicians who oppose online music sharing have made valid points?

b. Discuss the differences you see between sharing music files online and sharing CDs with your friends.

c. The current price to buy a song online is about $1. Is this a fair price? If not, what price would you consider to be fair?

3. The Power of Google

Google is the largest and most popular search engine on the Internet today. Because of its size and popularity, some people claim that Google has enormous power to influence a Web user's search experience solely by its Web site ranking processes. What do you think about this potential power? How could it be used in negative or harmful ways?

a. Some Web sites pay search engines to list them near the top of the results pages. These sponsors therefore get priority placement. What do you think of this policy?

b. What effect (if any) do you think that Google has on Web site development? For example, do you think Web site developers intentionally include frequently searched words in their pages so that they will appear in more hits lists?

c. When you "google" someone, you type their name in the Google search box to see what comes up. What privacy concerns do you think such "googling" could present? Have you ever "googled" yourself or your friends?

4. Charging for E-Mail?

Should there be a charge for sending e-mail or having IM conversations? What would be an appropriate charge? If a fee were charged for e-mail and IM conversations, what would happen to their use?

5. Internet and Politics

What role has the Internet played in political campaigns? What role will it play in the future? Do you see the day when voting will happen through the Internet? Why or why not?

Comparing Internet Search Methods

Problem

With millions of sites on the Internet, finding useful information can be a daunting—and at times, impossible—task. However, there are methods to make searching easier, some of which have been discussed in this chapter. In this Team Time, each team will search for specific items or pieces of information on the Internet and compare search methodologies.

Process

Split your group into three or more teams, depending on class size. Each group will create a team wiki using free wiki software such as that found at **pbwiki.com**. To appreciate the benefits of wiki collaboration fully, each team should have at least five or six members.

1. Each team should come up with a theme for their wiki. Some suggestions include the following:

   Best computer technology Web sites

   Coolest new technology gadgets

   All-time greatest rock n' rollers

   All-time greatest athletes

   Best places to visit in the United States

   Best beaches in the United States

   Best skiing areas in the United States

2. Each student should pick one example to research and must design a wiki page highlighting that subject. For example, if the team chose all-time greatest rock n' rollers, one student could select Bruce Springsteen and create a wiki page on Bruce Springsteen. The wiki page should contain links to other Web sites and, if possible, images and videos.

3. After the team wikis are created, teams should make their wikis available to the other teams for comments.

Conclusion

After all the team wikis have been completed and shared, discuss the following with your class. What is the benefit of using wiki technology to create team pages? How did wikis help or hinder the team process? What other conclusions can the class draw about using wiki technology?

multimedia

In addition to the review materials presented here, you'll find additional materials on the Pearson IT Multimedia Library and the Companion Website (**pearsonhighered.com/ techinaction**), which will help reinforce your understanding of the chapter content. These materials include the following:

Active Helpdesk

In Active Helpdesk calls, you'll assume the role of helpdesk operator, taking calls about the concepts you've learned in this chapter. You'll apply what you've learned and receive feedback from a supervisor to review and reinforce those concepts. The Active Helpdesk calls for this chapter are listed below and can be found on the Pearson IT Multimedia Library:

- Doing Business Online
- Getting Around the Web
- Using Subject Directories and Search Engines
- Connecting to the Internet

Sound Bytes

Sound Bytes are dynamic multimedia tutorials that help demystify even the most complex topics. You'll view video clips and animations that illustrate computer concepts and then apply what you've learned by reviewing with the Sound Byte Labs, which include quizzes and activities specifically tailored to each Sound Byte. The Sound Bytes for this chapter are listed below and can be found on the Pearson IT Multimedia Library:

- Creating a Web-Based E-mail Account
- Blogging
- Welcome to the Web
- Finding Information on the Web
- Connecting to the Internet

Companion Website

The *Technology in Action* Companion Website includes a variety of additional materials to help you review and learn more about the topics in this chapter. The resources available at **pearsonhighered.com/techinaction/** include:

- **Online Study Guide.** This chapter features an online true–false and multiple-choice quiz. You can take these quizzes, automatically check the results, and e-mail the results to your instructor.
- **Web Research Projects.** This chapter features several Web research projects that ask you to search the Web for information on computer-related careers, milestones in computer history, important people and companies, emerging technologies, and the applications and implications of different technologies.

application software:

programs that let you work and play

From Chapter 4 of *Technology in Action Complete*, Seventh Edition, Alan Evans, Kendall Martin, Mary Anne
Poatsy. Copyright © 2011 by Pearson Education, Inc. Published by Pearson Prentice Hall. All rights reserved.

application software:

programs that let you work and play

objectives

Objectives

After reading this chapter, you should be able to answer the following questions:

1. What's the difference between application software and system software?
2. What kinds of applications are included in productivity software?
3. What are the different types of multimedia software?
4. What are the different types of entertainment software?
5. What are the different types of drawing software?
6. What kinds of software do small and large businesses use?
7. What kind of software is available online?
8. Where can I go for help when I have a problem with my software?
9. How can I purchase software or get it for free?
10. How do I install, uninstall, and start software?

resources

resources

 Active Helpdesk

- Choosing Software
- Buying and Installing Software

 Sound Bytes

- Creating Web Queries in Excel 2007
- Using Speech-Recognition Software
- Enhancing Photos with Image Editing Software

 Companion Website

The Companion Website includes a variety of additional materials to help you review and learn more about the topics in this chapter. Go to: ***pearsonhighered.com/techinaction***

how cool is *this?*

There are millions of applications, and new ones are developed and released every day. How can you **find** the right application to meet your needs? What are the **cool new applications**, or the ones that just don't work? The editors and analysts at *PC Magazine* have put together AppScout (**appscout.com**), which provides **reviews** of the best software, Web sites, and Web applications. **AppScout** might be a good place to check first when you are in need of a new application.

Tatiana Popova\Shutterstock

The Nuts and Bolts of Software

A computer without software is like a sandwich without filling. Although a computer's hardware is critical, a computer system does nothing without software.

What is software? Technically speaking, the term **software** refers to a set of instructions that tells the computer what to do. An instruction set, also called a **program**, provides a means for us to interact with and use the computer, even if we lack specialized programming skills. Your computer has two basic types of software: system software and application software.

- **System software** includes software such as Windows Vista and Mac OS X, which help run the computer and coordinate instructions between application software and the computer's hardware devices. System software includes the operating system and utility programs (programs in the operating system that help manage system resources).
- **Application software** is the software you use to do tasks at home, school, and work. You can do a multitude of things with application software, such as writing letters, sending e-mail, paying taxes, creating presentations, editing photos, and taking an online course, to name a few.

Figure 1 shows the various types of application software available. In this chapter, we look at each of these types in detail, starting with productivity software.

More Productivity at Home

One reason to have a computer is to make it easier to tackle the tasks you have in your daily life. Productivity software is all about helping you do that, making it easier to keep your budget, send letters, or keep track of the kids' school events. It's safe to say you regularly use some form of productivity software already. **Productivity software** includes programs that enable you to perform various tasks required at home, school, and business. This category includes word processing, spreadsheet, presentation, database, and personal information manager (PIM) programs.

Word Processing Software

What is the best software to use to create general documents? Most students use **word processing software** to create and edit documents such as research papers, letters, and résumés. Microsoft Word and Corel WordPerfect are popular word processing programs. Writer, a word processing program from the OpenOffice suite

Figure 1

Application software enables computer users to do a variety of tasks.

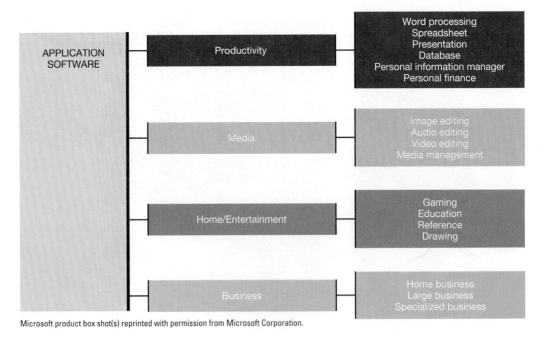

Microsoft product box shot(s) reprinted with permission from Microsoft Corporation.

Application Software: Programs That Let You Work and Play

(**openoffice.org**), and AbiWord (**abiword. com**) are gaining in popularity because they are available as free downloads from the Internet. Both AbiWord and Writer have many of the same features as their higher-priced Word and WordPerfect competitors, making either a great choice for cost-conscious consumers.

Also gaining in popularity are several word processing programs that are Web-based, such as those found in Google Docs (**docs.google.com**), which can be accessed from any computer that has an Internet connection. Web-based applications are great for collaborating and coordinating input from a variety of users on a single document.

Because of its general usefulness, word processing software is the most widely used application. Word processing software has a key advantage over its ancestral counterpart, the typewriter: you can make revisions and corrections without having to retype an entire document. Instead, you can quickly and easily insert, delete, and move pieces of text, as well as move and insert text from one document into another seamlessly.

How do I control the way my documents look? Another advantage of word processing software is that you can easily format, or change the appearance of, your document. As a result, you can produce professional-looking documents without having to send them to a professional. With formatting options, you can change fonts, font styles, and sizes; add colors to text; adjust margins; add borders to portions of text or entire pages; insert bulleted and numbered lists; and organize your text into columns. You also can insert pictures from your own files or from a gallery of images and graphics, such as clip art and SmartArt, which are included with the software. You also can enhance the look of your document by creating an interesting background or by adding a "theme" of coordinated colors and styles throughout your document. Figure 2 shows some of the formatting options found in many word processing applications. However, many of the open source and Web-based applications are not as fully featured as the proprietary applications.

Keep one thing in mind when you choose a free or Web-based software product: support. Unlike Microsoft Office and other proprietary applications, these applications offer no formal support. Instead, open source and Web-based applications are supported from their community of users across Web sites and newsgroups.

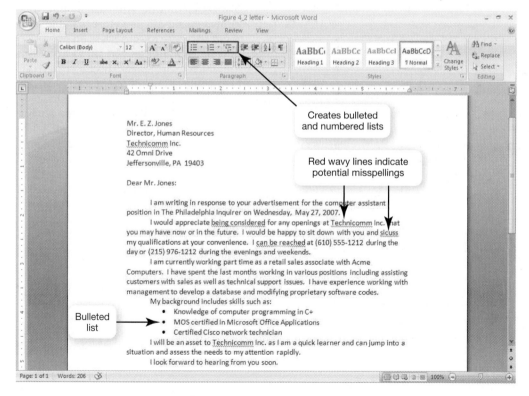

Figure 2

Nearly every word processing application has basic features to help you make your document look professionally formatted and to ensure that words are spelled correctly and used grammatically.

Word Processing Software

Looking for a Free or More Affordable Productivity Suite?

If you're looking for a more affordable alternative to proprietary software such as Microsoft Office, you may want to consider downloading a free open source productivity suite. **Open source software** is program code that is publicly available with few restrictions. The code can be copied, distributed, or changed without the stringent copyright protections of software products you purchase. OpenOffice is a popular open source software suite. In addition, some Web-based products are available free of charge. These Web-based applications, such as Google Docs and the Zoho suite, are accessible from wherever you are and are easily shared, so they are perfect for virtual workgroups.

Compared to Microsoft Office, you won't find all the features you're used to seeing, but OpenOffice offers most of the features required by the average user. And if you use OpenOffice, you can easily read, write, and edit files created in other applications, although you may lose some formatting when migrating or transferring files to OpenOffice. Similarly, users of other productivity suites can open files created in OpenOffice.

What special tools do word processing programs have? You're probably familiar with the basic tools of word processing software. Most applications come with some form of spelling and grammar checker and a thesaurus, for example. Another popular tool is the search-and-replace tool that allows you to search for text in your document and automatically replace it with other text.

The average user is unaware of many interesting word processing software tools. For example, did you know that you could translate words or phrases to another language or automatically correct your spelling as you type? You also can automatically summarize key points in a text document. Writer, the word processing program in the OpenOffice suite, has many of the same tools you're used to seeing in Microsoft Word and Corel WordPerfect, as well as some unique ones (see Figure 3).

Spreadsheet Software

Why would I need to use spreadsheet software? **Spreadsheet software**—for example, Microsoft Excel and Open Office Calc—enables you to do calculations and numerical analyses easily. You can use spreadsheet software to track your expenses and create a simple budget. You also can use it to determine how much you should be paying on your student loans, car loan, or credit card bills each month. You know you should pay more than the minimum payment to spend less on interest, but how much more can you afford to pay, and for which loan? Spreadsheet software can help you evaluate different scenarios, such as planning the best payment strategy.

How do I use spreadsheet software? The basic element in a spreadsheet program is the worksheet, which is a grid consisting of columns and rows. As shown in Figure 4, the columns and rows form individual boxes called *cells*. Each cell can be identified according to its column and row position. For example, a cell in column A, row 1 is referred to as "cell A1." You can enter several types of data into a cell.

- **Text:** Any combination of letters, numbers, symbols, and spaces. Text is often used as labels to identify the contents of a worksheet or chart.

- **Values:** Numerical data that represent a quantity or an amount and are often the basis for calculations.

Designs and other visual effects

Bibliography tool organizes sources

Figure 3

Writer, the word processing program in the OpenOffice suite, has many of the same features as Word and WordPerfect as well as some unique ones.

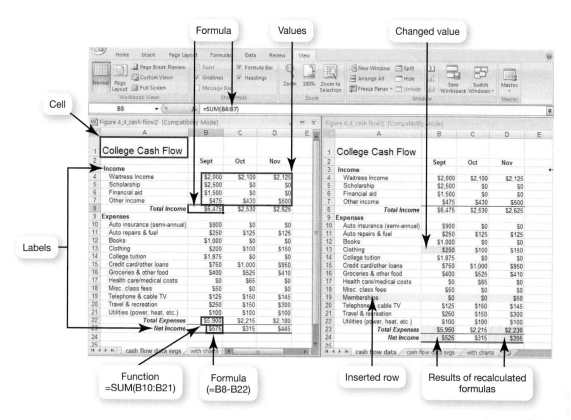

Figure 4

Spreadsheet software enables you to calculate and manipulate numerical data easily with the use of built-in formulas.

- **Formulas:** Equations that you build yourself using addition, subtraction, multiplication, and division, as well as values and cell references. For example, in Figure 4, you would type the formula "=B8-B22" to calculate net income for September.

- **Functions:** Formulas that are preprogrammed into the spreadsheet software. Functions help you with calculations ranging from the simple (such as adding groups of numbers) to the complex (such as determining monthly loan payments), without your needing to know the exact formula. Therefore, in Figure 4, to calculate your average earned income in September, you could use the built-in AVERAGE function, which would look like this: =AVERAGE(B4:B7).

The primary benefit of spreadsheet software is its ability to recalculate all functions and formulas in the spreadsheet automatically when values for some of the inputs change. For example, as shown on the spreadsheet on the right side of Figure 4, you can insert an additional row (Memberships), change a value (September clothing expense), and then recalculate the results for Total Expenses and Net Income without having to redo the worksheet from scratch.

Because automatic recalculation enables you to see immediately the effects that different options have on your spreadsheet, you can quickly test different assumptions in the same analysis. This is called a *what-if analysis*. Look again at Figure 4 and ask, "What if I add $50 to my clothing budget? What impact will such an increase have on my budget?"

What kinds of graphs and charts can I create with spreadsheet software? Sometimes it's easier to see the meaning of numbers when they are shown in a graphical format such as a chart. As shown in Figure 5, most spreadsheet applications allow you to create a variety of charts, including basic column charts, pie charts, and line charts, with or without three-dimensional (3D) effects. In addition

SOUND BYTE

Creating Web Queries in Excel 2007

In this Sound Byte, you'll learn what Excel Web queries are, as well as how to use them effectively.

Word Processing Software

153

to these basic charts, you can use stock charts (for investment analysis) and scatter charts (for statistical analysis), or create custom charts.

Are spreadsheets used for anything besides financial analysis? There are so many powerful mathematical functions built into spreadsheet programs that they can be used for serious numerical analyses or simulations. For example, an Excel spreadsheet could be designed to compute the output voltage at a point in an electrical circuit or to simulate customer arrival and wait times. In these settings, spreadsheet programs can often solve problems that formerly required custom programming. Many spreadsheet applications also have database capabilities and can sort, filter, and group data.

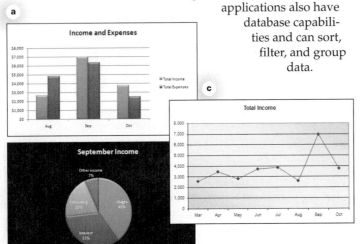

Figure 5

(a) Column charts show comparisons. (b) Pie charts show how parts contribute to the whole. (c) Line charts show trends over time.

Presentation Software

What software do I use to create presentations? You've probably sat through presentations during which the speaker's topic was displayed in slides projected on a screen. These presentations can be the most basic of outlines, containing only a few words and simple graphics, or elaborate multimedia presentations with animated text, graphic objects, and colorful backgrounds. You use **presentation software** such as Microsoft PowerPoint, OpenOffice Impress, or Zoho Show (shown in Figure 6) to create these types of dynamic slide shows. Because these applications are simple to use, you can produce high-quality presentations without a lot of training.

How do I create a presentation? Using the basic features included in

presentation software, creating a slide show is simple. To arrange text and graphics on your slides, you can choose from a variety of slide layouts. These layouts give you the option of using a single or double column of bulleted text, various combinations of bulleted text, and other content such as clip art, graphs, photos, and even video clips.

You also can lend a theme to your presentation by choosing from different design templates. You can use animation effects to control how and when text and other objects enter and exit each slide. Slide transitions add different effects as you move from one slide to the next during the presentation.

Database Software

How can I use database software? **Database software** such as Oracle, MySQL, and Microsoft Access is basically a complex electronic filing system. As mentioned earlier, spreadsheet applications include many database features and are easy to use for simple database tasks such as sorting, filtering, and organizing data. However, you need to use a more robust, fully featured database application to manage larger and more complicated groups of data that contain more than one table; to group, sort, and retrieve data; and to generate reports.

Traditional databases are organized into fields, records, and tables, as shown in Figure 7. A field is a data category such as "First Name," "Last Name," or "Street Address." A record is a collection of related fields such as "Douglas Seaver, Printing Solutions, 7700 First Avenue, Topeka, KS, (888) 968-2678." A table groups related records such as "Sales Contacts."

How do you benefit when businesses use database software? FedEx, UPS, and other shipping companies let customers search their online databases for tracking numbers, allowing customers to get instant information on the status of their packages. Other businesses use databases to keep track of clients, invoices, and personnel information. Often that information is available to a home computer user. For example, at Amazon.com you can use the company's Web site to access the entire history of all the purchases you have ever made.

Are there software programs to help students be more productive? Popular programs are available to help students take notes during lectures and

Figure 6

Several programs allow you to create presentation materials: (a) Microsoft Office PowerPoint 2007, (b) OpenOffice Impress, and (c) Zoho's Show.

organize and maintain their lecture notes and the recordings they create from lectures. For example, Microsoft OneNote allows students who have Tablet PCs to write their notes directly onto the tablet, using it as an electronic notebook. Pieces of text can be easily moved around the page. With one click, Web links can be quickly integrated and audio or video recordings of lectures can be added. Students can search for a term across the full set of notebooks they have created during the term, helping them to find connecting ideas among their courses.

Personal Information Manager (PIM) Software

Which applications should I use to manage my time, contact lists, and tasks? Most productivity suites contain some form of **personal information manager (PIM) software** such as

Microsoft Outlook or Lotus Organizer. Chandler (**chandlerproject.org**) is another PIM program that is open source and, therefore, free. These programs strive to replace the management tools found on a traditional desk—a calendar, address book, notepad, and to-do list, for example.

Table

ID	FirstName	LastName	Company	Street	City	State	ZipCode	Business
1	Susan	Scantosi	eWidget Plus	363 Rogue Street	St. Louis	MO	63136	(612) 444
2	Thomas	Mazeman	BooksRUs	2165 Piscotti Avenue	Springfield	IL	62702	(888) 234
3	Douglas	Seaver	Printing Solutions	7700 First Avenue	Topeka	KS	66603	(888) 968
4	Amir	Raviv	TechStands	1436 Riverfront Road	St. Louis	MO	63136	(877) 867
5	Franklin	Scott	WorksSuite	8789 Ploughman Ave	Tulsa	OK	74101	(800) 864
6	Ronald	Komeika	Creekside Financial	1264 Pond Hill Road	Toledo	OH	43601	(343) 332
7	Barbara	Mitchell	Market Tenders	9823 Bridge Street	La Porte	IN	46350	(888) 283
*	(New)							

SalesContacts

Field

Record

Figure 7

In databases, information is organized into tables, fields, and records.

Word Processing Software

155

Task reminder   New messages

E-mail inbox

Figure 8

The Outlook Today feature in Microsoft Outlook includes common PIM features such as a summary of appointments, a list of tasks, and the number of new e-mail messages.

Some PIMs contain e-mail management features so that you not only can receive and send e-mail messages but also organize them into various folders, prioritize them, and coordinate them with other activities in your calendar (see Figure 8).

If you share a network at home or at work and are using the same PIM software as others on the network, you can use a PIM program to check people's availability before scheduling meeting times. Whether coordinating a team project or a family event, you can create and electronically assign tasks to group members by using a PIM. You can even track each person's progress to ensure that the tasks are finished on time.

Are there Web-based PIM programs? Many Web-based e-mail clients such as Yahoo!, Google, and AOL have developed coordinating calendar and contacts programs similar to Microsoft Outlook. Yahoo! includes Notepad for jotting down notes and tasks. Google's calendar and contacts sync with Outlook so that you can access your Outlook calendar information by logging into Google, giving you access to your schedule anywhere you have access to a computer and an Internet connection. AOL's Instant Messenger, AIM, has coordinated e-mail, calendar, and contact functions.

Productivity Software Features

What tools can help me work more efficiently with productivity software? Whether you are working on a word processing document, spreadsheet, database, or slide presentation, you can make use of several tools to increase your efficiency:

- A **wizard** is a systematic guide that walks you through the steps necessary to complete a complicated task. At each step, the wizard asks you questions. Based on your responses, the wizard helps you complete that portion of the task. When you install software, you are often guided by a wizard.

- A **template** is a predesigned form. Templates are included in many productivity applications. They provide the basic structure for a particular kind of document, spreadsheet, or presentation. Templates can include specific page layout designs, formatting and styles relevant to that particular document, and automated tasks (macros). Typical templates allow you to lay out a professional-looking résumé, structure a home budget, or communicate the results of a project in a presentation.

- A **macro** is a small program that groups a series of commands so they will run as a single command. Macros are best used to automate a routine task or a complex series of commands that must be run frequently. For example, a teacher may write a macro to sort the grades in her grade book automatically in descending order

---

BITS AND BYTES   **Productivity Software Tips and Tricks**

Looking for tips on how to make better use of your productivity software? Many Web sites send subscribers daily e-mails. Most of these services are free, although some require that you subscribe to an ancillary product full of tips, tricks, and shortcuts to their favorite software programs. Nerdy Books (**nerdybooks.com**), for example, sends a free tip each day to the e-mail accounts of its subscribers. (Note that it does not provide tips for Office 2007 users). Nerdy Books also publishes Bob's Blog, containing software tips, and podcasts for those tips that can't be written in just a few sentences. Dummies eTips (**etips.dummies.com**), based on the *For Dummies* series of help books, offers subscribers tips on a variety of topics, including using productivity applications.

Apple Computer, Inc.

and to highlight those grades that add up to less than a C average. Every time she adds the results of an assignment or test, she can set up the macro to run through that series of steps automatically.

Integrated Software Applications

What's an integrated software application? An **integrated software application** is a single software program that incorporates the most commonly used tools of many productivity software programs into a single integrated program. Note that integrated software applications are not substitutes for the full suite of applications they replace. Generally, because they don't include many of the more complex features of the individual productivity software applications, they can be thought of as "software lite." To have access to the full functionality of word processing and spreadsheet software, for example, you should get the individual applications or a suite that includes each of these applications.

Microsoft Works 9 is an example of an integrated software application. This integrated software application includes word processing, spreadsheet, and database functionality as well as templates, a calendar, a dictionary, and map features. iWork '09 is an integrated software application from Apple that includes word processing (Pages), presentation (Keynote), and spreadsheet (Numbers) functionality. Figure 9 shows the multifunctionality of Apple iWork. The Task Launcher is the first window that opens when you launch iWork.

Why would I use an integrated software application instead of individual stand-alone programs? Integrated software applications are perfect if you don't need the more advanced features found in the individual full versions of each program. Like stand-alone applications, integrated software programs provide templates for frequently developed documents such as résumés and invoices. An integrated software program is also less expensive than its individual, fully featured alternatives. If you find your needs go beyond the limited capabilities of an integrated program, you might want to consider buying the individual programs that meet your particular requirements or a software suite.

Software Suites

What's a software suite? A **software suite** is a group of software programs that have been bundled as a package. You can buy software suites for many different categories of applications, including productivity, graphics, and virus protection (see Figure 10). There are three primary developers of productivity software suites: Microsoft, Corel, and Lotus. Microsoft and Corel offer different packages with different combinations of applications, whereas Lotus (owned by IBM) offers only SmartSuite.

Which applications do productivity software suites contain? Most productivity software suites contain similar basic components, such as word processing, spreadsheet, presentation, and PIM software. However, depending on the version and

Figure 9

Although an integrated software application such as Apple iWork is one program, it contains the most commonly used features of several individual productivity applications.

Word Processing Software

Figure 10

Software suites provide users with a cheaper method of obtaining all of the software they want to buy in one bundle.

toolbars, and menus. For example, when using applications in the Microsoft Office suite, you can seamlessly create a spreadsheet in Excel, import it into Access, and then link a query created in Access to a Word document. It would be much harder to do the same thing using different applications from a variety of software developers.

Personal Financial Software

What software can I use to prepare my taxes?

Everyone has to deal with taxes, and having the right computer software can make this burden much simpler and keep it completely under your control. **Tax preparation software** such as Intuit TurboTax and H&R Block TaxCut enable you to prepare your state and federal taxes on your own instead of hiring a professional. Both programs offer a complete set of tax forms and instructions, as well as videos that contain expert advice on how to complete each form. In addition, error-checking features are built into the programs to catch mistakes. TurboTax also can run a check for audit alerts, file your return electronically, and offer financial planning guidance to help you effectively plan and manage your financial resources in the following year (see Figure 12). Remember, however, that the tax code changes annually, so you must obtain an updated version of the software each year.

manufacturer, they may also include other types of applications, such as database programs and desktop publishing software. When you are shopping for software, it can be difficult to figure out which bundle is the right one for your needs. For example, Microsoft Office 2007 is bundled in eight different ways; four of these are described in the table in Figure 11. Be sure to research carefully the bundling options for software you are buying.

Why would I buy a software suite instead of individual programs?

Most people buy software suites because doing so is cheaper than buying each program individually. In addition, because the programs bundled in a software suite come from the same company, they work well together (that is, they provide for better integration) and share common features,

Figure 11 | A SAMPLING OF MICROSOFT OFFICE 2007 SUITES

Application	Function	Home and Student 2007	Standard 2007	Professional 2007	Ultimate 2007
Word	Word processing	X	X	X	X
Excel	Spreadsheet	X	X	X	X
PowerPoint	Presentation	X	X	X	X
Access	Database			X	X
Outlook	PIM		X	X	X
Publisher	Desktop publishing			X	X
OneNote	Note taking	X			X
InfoPath, Groove	Collaboration				X

Which software can I use to help keep track of my personal finances?
Financial planning software helps you manage your daily finances. Intuit Quicken and Microsoft Money are popular examples. Financial planning programs include electronic checkbook registers and automatic bill payment tools. With these features, you can print checks from your computer or pay recurring monthly payments, such as rent or student loans, with automatically scheduled online payments. The software records all transactions, including online payments, in your checkbook register. In addition, you can assign categories to each transaction and then use these categories to analyze your spending patterns. You even can set up a budget and review your spending habits.

Web-based programs such as Mint (**mint. com**) and Wesabe (**wesabe.com**) are rapidly gaining in popularity (see Figure 13). Although they do not offer bill-paying services or help track your investment portfolio like Quicken and Money do, they are great at analyzing your spending habits and offering advice on how to manage your spending better. Because they are Web-based, you can monitor and update your finances from any computer in a private and secure setting. Users also have access to a network of other users with whom to exchange tips and advice.

Financial planning applications also coordinate with tax preparation software. Quicken, for example, integrates seamlessly with TurboTax, so you never have to go through your checkbook and bills to find tax deductions, tax-related income, or expenses. Many banks and credit card companies also offer online services that download a detailed monthly statement into Quicken or Money. Quicken even offers a credit card. All of your purchases are organized into categories and are downloaded automatically to your Quicken file to streamline your financial planning and recordkeeping. You can also purchase Pocket Quicken to install on your smartphone so that your financial records are always at your fingertips.

More Media at Home

From movies and television to music and photography, the entertainment world is becoming digital. Your computer can help you create, organize, and modify digital images, songs, and movies, if you have the

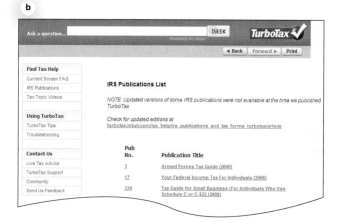

Figure 12

Tax preparation software, such as Intuit TurboTax, enables you to prepare and file your taxes using a guided, systematic process.

Figure 13

Wesabe.com is an online financial management tool. An extensive online community provides helpful tips and discussions with other people in similar situations.

More Media at Home

159

Dragon NaturallySpeaking is a leading **speech-recognition software** (or **voice-recognition software**) that translates your spoken words into typed text. With this software, you can dictate documents and e-mail messages, use voice commands to start and switch between applications, control the operating system, and even surf or fill out forms on the Web. Speech-recognition software is available in different language versions, including Dutch, French, German, Italian, and Spanish, as well as English. Accuracy levels of 95 percent to 99 percent can be achieved in quiet environments with a quality microphone.

Microsoft has incorporated a powerful speech-recognition system into Windows Vista. After starting speech recognition (from the Start menu, type "speech" in the search box and click on "Windows Speech Recognition"), the speech-recognition toolbar appears and indicates whether or not the computer is "listening" for voice input. Just click the microphone icon to make the computer listen to or ignore voice input. Figure 14 shows how you can use Vista's speech recognition functionality to instruct the software to run commands within an application. If you aren't sure which speech commands are available, just say, "What can I say?" to display the speech reference card.

Speech-recognition software is complicated. As you speak, the software divides each second of your speech into 100 individual *samples* (sounds). It then compares these individual sounds with a database

Figure 14

(a) Speech-recognition software allows you to create documents using simple voice commands.
(b) Speaking "What can I say?" brings up the speech reference card.

right software. **Multimedia software** includes image, video, and audio editing software; animation software; and other specialty software required to produce computer games, animations, and movies. In this section, we look at several popular types of multimedia software, as shown in Figure 15.

Digital Image Editing Software

What can I do with a digital image that I can't do with a photograph?
Once the image information is in a digital format (taken with a digital camera or scanned), you can use it easily with all your other software. For example, you can store a

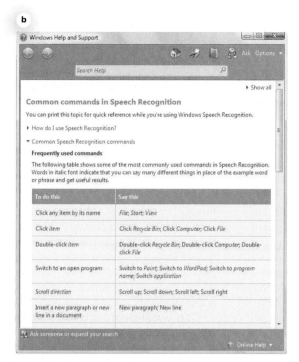

b

Figure 14 (Continued)

on separately; the phonemes are then chained together to form words that are contained in the word list. Because a variety of sounds can be put together to form many different words, the software analyzes all the possible values and picks the one value that it determines has the best probability of correctly matching your spoken word. The word is then displayed on the screen or is acted upon by the computer as a command.

However, there are problems with speech-recognition software. We don't always speak every word the same way, and accents and regional dialects produce great variation in pronunciations. Therefore, speech recognition is not perfect and requires training. Training entails getting the computer to recognize your particular way of speaking by reading prepared text into the computer so the phoneme database can be adjusted to your specific speech patterns.

Another approach to improve speech inconsistencies is to restrict the word list to a few keywords or phrases, and then have the computer guess the probability that a certain phrase is being said. This is how cell phones that respond to voice commands work. The phone doesn't really figure out that you said "call home" by breaking down the phonemes. It just determines how likely it is that you said "call home" as opposed to "call office." This reduces the processing power needed as well as the chance of mistakes. However, it also restricts the words you can use to achieve the desired results.

Though not perfect, speech-recognition software programs can be invaluable to individuals who don't type well or who have physical limitations that prevent them from using a keyboard or mouse. For those whose careers require a lot of typing, using speech-recognition software reduces their chances of incurring debilitating repetitive-strain injuries. In addition, because most people can speak faster than they can write or type, speech-recognition software can help individuals work more efficiently. Doctors are incorporating speech-recognition software into their practices to create a summary of the visit before the patient leaves the room. This eliminates the need for a dictated summary to be transcribed by a separate service, and increases the physician's in-office efficiency.

Speech-recognition software also can help you to be productive during generally nonproductive times. For example, you can dictate into a digital recording device while doing other things, such as driving, then download the digital file to your computer and let the program type up your words for you. Recently, voice recognition technologies have been incorporated into in-car communication and entertainment systems, such as Ford SYNC, which allows drivers to control mobile phones and digital music players with voice commands.

Speech recognition should continue to be incorporated into our daily lives. Aside from the obvious benefits to persons with disabilities, it will provide continued efficiencies to many others as well.

(called a *codebook*) that contains samples of every sound a human being can make. When it finds a match, it gives your voice sound a number that corresponds to the number of the similar sound in the database.

After your voice sounds are assigned values, these values are matched with another database containing phonemes for the language being spoken. A *phoneme* is the smallest phonetic unit that distinguishes one word from another. For example, "b" and "m" are both phonemes that distinguish the words *bad* and *mad* from each other in the English language. Many languages, including English, are made up of thousands of different phonemes. Moreover, because of differences in pronunciation, some phonemes may actually have several different corresponding matching sounds.

Once all the sounds are assigned to phonemes, word and phrase construction can begin. The phonemes are matched against a word list that contains transcriptions of all known words in a particular language. Because pronunciation can vary (for example, the word *the* can be pronounced so that it rhymes with either *duh* or *see*), the word list must contain alternative pronunciations for many words. Each phoneme is worked

digital picture of each person in your Outlook contacts list or add a digital image you captured into a newsletter you are writing.

Products such as Microsoft Photo Story and Google Picasa, which are both free downloads, make it easy for you to use your collection of digital images in new ways. In Photo Story, you can add text, music, and camera movement to create a fully featured slide show with your images. Using Picasa, you can create a poster or several different styles of collages from your images.

What software can I use to edit my photos? As its name implies, **image editing software** (sometimes called **photo editing software**) enables you to edit

Figure 15

There are many varieties of graphics and multimedia software.

Figure 16

With some image editing software, you can take two individual pictures and combine them into one picture.

photographs and other images. Image editing software includes tools for basic modifications to digital images such as removing red-eye; modifying contrast, sharpness, and color casts; or removing scratches or rips from scanned images of old photos. Many of these software packages now also include an extensive set of painting tools such as brushes, pens, and artistic media (such as paints, pastels, and oils) that allow you to create realistic-looking images. Often graphic designers use digital photos and images as a basis for their design and then modify these images within image editing software to create their final products.

Adobe Photoshop and Corel Paint Shop Pro Photo are fully featured image editing applications. They each offer sophisticated tools for tasks like layering images (placing pictures on top of each other) and masking images (hiding parts of layers to create effects such as collages). As shown in Figure 16, these image editing applications offer sophisticated tools. Designers use these more sophisticated tools to create the enhanced digital images used commercially in logos, advertisements, and on book and CD covers.

Can a nonprofessional use image editing software? Image editing programs such as Adobe Photoshop Elements and Roxio PhotoSuite are geared toward the casual home user. Adobe also offers Adobe Photoshop Album Starter Edition, which is a free download. With these applications, you can perform the most common image editing tasks, such as taking out red-eye and cropping and resizing pictures. These programs enable you to add creative effects such as borders and frames. Some include templates so you can insert your favorite pictures into preformatted calendar pages or greeting cards. They may also have photo fantasy images that let you paste a face from your digital image onto the body of a professional athlete or other famous person.

If you want to use a program that offers more than basic features but is still easy to use, try Adobe Photoshop Elements (see Figure 17). With this program, you can improve the color balance of an image, touch up an image (by removing red-eye, for example), add creative effects to an image, or group images together to create montages. If you later decide to upgrade to the professional version of Adobe Photoshop, you will already be familiar with the user interface.

Digital Audio Software

Why would I have digital audio files on my computer? Best-selling novels, newspapers, and radio shows all can be purchased as audio files from sellers such as

Audible, Inc. (**audible.com**). Huge numbers of free audio files are also available through the phenomenon of *podcasting*, the distribution of audio files such as radio shows and music videos over the Internet. Offered by subscription, these audio files are delivered to your machine free with the release of each edition. You may also choose to extract (*rip*) your CD collection to store on your computer. In addition, with programs such as Magix Music Maker or Apple Garage-Band, you can compose your own songs or soundtracks with virtual instruments, voice recorders, synthesizers, and special audio effects. You may quickly have several gigabytes of audio files on your hard drive before you even know it!

Why are MP3 files so popular?
MP3 is a type of audio compression format that reduces the file size of traditional digital audio files so that they will take up less storage capacity. For example, a typical CD stores between 10 and 15 songs in uncompressed format, but with files in MP3 format, the same CD can store between 100 and 180. The smaller file size not only lets you store and play music in less space, but also allows quick and easy distribution over the Internet. You can find hundreds of digital audio applications that allow you to copy, play, edit, and organize MP3 files, and record and distribute your own music online. Most digital audio software programs support one of the following

functions. Others, such as iTunes, incorporate many of these capabilities into one multifunctional program:

- **MP3 recording** allows you to record directly from streaming audio and other software or microphone sources to MP3 format.
- **CD ripping** allows you to copy or extract CDs and encode to the MP3 format.
- **CD burning** allows you to create your own CDs from your MP3 collection.
- **Encoding and decoding** is done by *encoders*, programs that convert files to MP3 format at varying levels of quality. Most ripping software has encoders built in to convert the files directly into MP3 format.
- **Format conversion** programs allow you to convert MP3 files to other digital audio formats such as WAV (short for Waveform audio format), WMA (Windows Media Audio), and AIFF (Audio Interchange File Format).

Figure 17

Image editing software such as Adobe Photoshop Elements makes it easy to create (a) calendars, (b) greeting cards and postcards, (c) slide shows, and (d) more from your digital photos.

More Media at Home

Figure 18

Video editing programs such as Apple iMovie make it easy to create and edit movies.

Video clips in clips pane

Window used to view or edit movie clips

Movie clips display in clip viewer

Trans icon controls transition effects between clips

Apple Computer, Inc.

MacBook

Can I edit audio files? Audio editing software in-

cludes tools that make editing your audio files as easy as editing your text files. Software such as the open source Audacity (**audacity.sourceforge.net**) and Sony Sound Forge Audio Studio (**sonycreativesoftware. com**) enables you to perform such basic editing tasks as cutting dead air space from the beginning or end of the song or cutting a portion from the middle. You also can add special sound effects, such as echo or bass boost, and remove static or hiss from your MP3 files. Both of these applications support recording sound files from a microphone or any source you can connect through the input line of a sound card.

Digital Video Editing Software

What kind of software do I need to edit my digital videos? With the boom of digital camcorders and the improved graphics capabilities on home computers, many people are experimenting with **digital video editing software**. Several video editing applications are available at a wide range of prices and capabilities. Although the most expensive products (such as Adobe Premiere Pro) offer the widest range of special effects and tools, some moderately priced video editing

programs have enough features to keep the casual user happy. Microsoft Movie Maker and Apple iMovie HD have intuitive drag-and-drop features that make it simple to create professional-quality movies with little or no training (see Figure 18). Microsoft Movie Maker is included with Windows XP and Vista. Other software developers offer free trial versions so that you can decide whether their product meets your needs before purchasing it.

Does video editing software support all kinds of video files? Video files come in a number of formats. Many of the affordable video editing software packages support only a few types of video files. For example, one application may support Windows Media Player video files, whereas another may support Apple QuickTime or RealPlayer video files instead. Fortunately, software packaging lists which types of video files are supported by the software. You should buy the least expensive application that supports the greatest number of supported file formats.

In what format are the videos I watch on my portable media player? Videos that can be watched on portable media players, such as the fifth-generation iPod and iPod Touch, are in the MP4 (MPEG-4) video format. This format stores digital audio and digital video streams, as well as other items, such as text for subtitles

Application Software: Programs That Let You Work and Play

164

and still images. Similar to the MP3 format, MP4 compresses the audio and video content into a more manageable file size. Most MP4 files have the file extension .mp4. However, Apple has created other MPEG-4 extensions to identify specific content such as .m4b, which is often used to identify audiobook and podcast files, and .m4r, which is used to identify ringtone files for the iPhone.

Media Management Software

How do I manage the audio, video, and image files on my system?

Many people add hundreds or even thousands of files to their systems by purchasing music and downloading images and video. Your hard drive is a convenient place to store all your music and images, but only if you can find what you're looking for!

Software such as Windows Media Player, Nullsoft Winamp, and Apple iTunes allows you to organize audio and video files so that you can sort, filter, and search your music collection by artist, album, or category (see Figure 19). Using these programs, you can manage individual tracks, generate playlists, and even export the files to a database or spreadsheet application for further manipulation. Then you can burn the songs to a CD, and the program will print liner notes that you can place inside the CD case.

Are there Web-based programs available to edit, share, and store my photos? One great advantage of taking digital images is that you can easily share the images via the Internet. Initially, we had to send images as attachments—and our exuberance in sending several images at the same time often clogged someone's inbox. Several online photo sharing and photo storing sites, such as Snapfish (**snapfish. com**), Kodak (**kodak.com**), and Shutterfly (**shutterfly.com**), enable you to upload your digital images from your computer, create photo albums, and share them with friends and family. These sites offer printing services as well.

Flickr (**flickr.com**) is probably one of the best of these online photo management and photo sharing applications. It lets you organize your images and then share them publicly with millions of users, or just with your closest friends and family. Discussion boards are available so that groups can exchange comments about the images, just as you would if you were passing them around the dinner table. In addition, taking advantage of online mapping technologies, Flickr enables you to link your images to a map so that you can show exactly where you took the images or see where others took theirs.

Google Picasa (**picasa.google.com**) is another popular application in the online photo editing, storing, and sharing field.

Figure 19

Software programs such as iTunes help you manage all the MP3 files on your computer. You can sort, filter, and search your collection by artist, album, or category, and you can create playlists.

Album covers flow by in a smooth display

Smart playlists select song lists based on criteria you specify

More Media at Home

165

Picasa helps you send images to your friends, your mobile devices, or your blog by automatically resizing a huge 5-megapixel image to a more manageable size for electronic transmission. With Picasa, you can then attach the image to an outgoing e-mail message, or transfer the image directly to your blog or to a mobile device such as an iPod or smartphone.

More Fun at Home

As the term implies, **entertainment software** is designed to provide users with thrills, chills, and all-out fun! Computer games make up the vast majority of entertainment software. These digital games began with Pong, Pac-Man, and Donkey Kong, and have evolved to include many different categories, including action, driving, puzzles, role-playing, card-playing, sports, strategy, and simulation games. Entertainment software also includes other types of computer applications, such as **virtual reality programs** that turn artificial environments into a realistic experience.

Figure 20

PhotoEdit Inc.

Computer controllers can be specialized. *Rock Band* controllers include a guitar, a drum set, and a microphone.

Gaming Software

Do I need special equipment to run entertainment software? As with any software, you need to make sure your system has enough processing power, memory (RAM), and hard drive capacity to run the program. Because games often push the limit of sound and video quality, be sure your system has the appropriate sound cards, video cards, speakers, monitor, and CD or DVD drives.

Some gaming software may require a special controller. Some games, such as *Steel Battalion, Rock Band*, and many games in the Nintendo Wii system, are sold with their own specialized controllers (see Figure 20). These controllers also can be adapted to your computer. Complex simulation programs can benefit from configurable wireless controllers such as the Cyborg Evo.

How do I tell what computer games are appropriate for a certain user? The **Entertainment Software Rating Board (ESRB)** is a self-regulatory body established in 1994 by the Entertainment Software Association (**esrb.org**). The ESRB's rating system helps consumers choose the computer and video games that are right for their families by providing information about game content so they can make informed purchasing decisions. ESRB ratings have two parts: rating symbols that suggest age appropriateness, and content descriptors that indicate elements in a game that may have triggered a particular rating or be of interest or concern. It's important to check both the rating symbol (on the front of the game box) and the content descriptors (on the back of the game box). The rating symbols currently in use by the ESRB include E (Everyone), T (Teens), M (Mature), and AO (Adult Only).

Can I make video games? Now that video games represent an industry with revenue of more than $10 billion each year, designing and creating video games is emerging as a desirable career opportunity. Professionally created video games involve artistic storytelling and design, as well as sophisticated programming. Major production houses such as Electronic Arts use applications that are not easily available to the casual home enthusiast. However, you can use the editors and game engines available for games such as *EverQuest, Oblivion*, and *Unreal Tournament* to create custom levels and characters or to extend the game.

If you want to try your hand at creating your own video games, multimedia applications such as Adobe Flash CS4 and RPG Maker VX provide the tools you need to explore game design and creation. The program GameMaker (**yoyogames.com**) is a free product that allows you to build a game with no programming at all; key elements of the new game creation are dragged and dropped into place. Alice (**alice.org**) is another free environment to check out. It lets you easily create 3D animations and simple games and will soon include the actual Sims characters!

Educational Software

What kinds of educational applications are there? Although a multitude of educational software products are geared toward the younger set, software developers have by no means ignored adult markets. In addition to all the products relating to the younger audience, there are software products that teach users new skills such as typing, languages, cooking, and playing the guitar. Preparation software for students who will be taking the SAT, GMAT, LSAT, and MCAT exams is also popular. In addition, there are many computer and online brain training games and programs designed to improve the health and function of our brains. Lumosity (**luminosity. com**) is one such site that has a specific "workout" program. Brain Age (**brainage.com**) has software for the Nintendo DS and is designed for players of all ages.

What types of programs are available to train you to use software or special machines? Many programs provide tutorials for popular computer applications. These programs use illustrated systematic instructions to guide users through unfamiliar skills. Some training programs, known as **simulation programs**, allow users to experience or control the software as if it were the actual software or an actual event. Such simulation programs include commercial and military flight training, surgical instrument training, and machine operation training. Often these simulators can be delivered locally on CD or DVD or over the Internet.

One benefit of these simulated training programs is that they safely allow users to experience potentially dangerous situations such as flying a helicopter during high winds. Consequently, users of these training programs are more likely to take risks and learn from their mistakes—something they could not afford to do in real life. Simulated training programs also help prevent costly errors. Should something go awry, the only cost of the error is restarting the simulation program.

Do I need special software to take courses online? As long as you have a compatible Web browser, online classes will be accessible to you. Depending on the content and course materials, however, you may need a password or special plug-ins to view certain videos or demos.

Taking classes over the Internet is rapidly becoming a popular method of learning because it offers greater schedule flexibility for busy students. Although some courses are run from an individually developed Web site, many online courses are run using **course management software** such as Blackboard, Moodle, and Angel. These programs provide traditional classroom tools such as calendars and grade books over the Internet (see Figure 21). Special areas are available for students and professors to

Figure 21

Course management software such as Blackboard provides a method for doing traditional classroom tasks, such as participating in discussions and taking tests, in an online environment.

exchange ideas and information through the use of chat rooms, discussion forums, and e-mail. Other areas are available for posting assignments, lectures, and other pertinent class information.

Reference Software

How can I use software to research information? Encyclopedias are no longer those massive sets of books in the library. Now you can find full sets of encyclopedias such as World Book, Britannica, and Grolier on CDs and DVDs. In addition to containing all the information found in traditional paper encyclopedias, electronic encyclopedias include multimedia content such as interactive maps and video and audio clips. When researching famous sports figures, for example, not only can you read about Jackie Robinson, but you can also view a video of him in action.

Can I find reference information online? In addition to the traditional atlases, dictionaries, and thesauri available on CD and DVD, many other types of reference software are available online. Many traditional encyclopedias have online components. In addition, most of us are familiar with wiki-based online "encyclopedias" like Wikipedia (**wikipedia.org**) and Citizendium (**citizendium.org**). Other types of reference information are also available online. The American Sign Language dictionary, for example, is available online and includes video clips that show finger spelling and the modeling of each gesture. WebMD (**webmd.com**) offers medical information, and FindLaw (**findlaw.com**) provides basic legal information and forms that you previously would have had to pay a professional to obtain.

Drawing Software

What kind of software should I use for simple illustrations? Drawing software (or **illustration software**) lets you create or edit two-dimensional, line-based drawings. You can use drawing software to create technical diagrams or original nonphotographic drawings, animations, and illustrations using standard drawing and painting tools such as pens, pencils, and paintbrushes. You also can drag geometric objects from a toolbar onto the canvas area to create images and use paint bucket, eyedropper, and spray can tools to add color and special effects to the drawings.

Are there different types of drawing software? Drawing software is used in both creative and technical drawings. Applications such as Adobe Illustrator CS4 include tools that let you create professional-quality creative and technical illustrations. Illustrator's tools help you create complex designs, such as muscle structures in the human body, and use special effects, such as charcoal sketches. Its warping tool allows you to bend, stretch, and twist portions of your image or text. Because of its many tools and features, Illustrator is one of the preferred drawing software programs of most graphic artists.

There are many software packages to help plan the layout of rooms, homes, and landscapes, such as those offered by Broderbund. Microsoft Visio is a program used to create technical drawings, maps, basic block diagrams, networking and engineering flowcharts, and project schedules, but it can also be used by the more casual designer. Visio uses project-related templates with special objects that you drag onto a canvas. For example, by using the Visio floor template and dragging furniture and other interior objects onto it, you can create an interior design like the one shown in Figure 22. Visio also provides mindmapping templates to help you organize your thoughts and ideas.

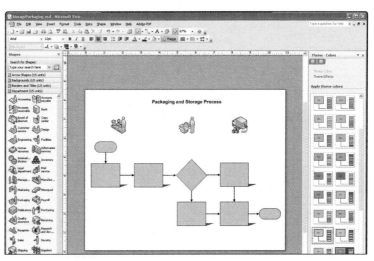

Figure 22

The drawing program Visio lets you create different types of diagrams easily with drag-and-drop options.

Business Software

With the amount of power available in a typical home computer, you have more opportunities than ever to run a business from your home. No matter what service or product you provide, there are common types of software you'll want to consider. Accounting software will help manage the flow of money, and desktop publishing and Web page creation tools will help you market and develop your new enterprise. A number of software packages are designed to organize and help with the daily operations of a typical business. If you ever plan to run a business from your own home, or even if you are just a user of large business products and services, it is helpful to know what functions business software can perform.

Home Business Software

Which programs are good for people with small businesses? If you have a small business or a hobby that produces income, then you know the importance of keeping good records and tracking your expenses and income. **Accounting software** helps small-business owners manage their finances more efficiently by providing tools for tracking accounts receivable and accounts payable. In addition, these applications offer inventory management, payroll, and billing tools. Examples of accounting applications are Intuit QuickBooks and Peachtree by Sage. Both programs include templates for invoices, statements, and financial reports so that

small-business owners can create common forms and reports.

What software can I use to lay out and design newsletters and other publications? Desktop publishing (DTP) software allows you to incorporate and arrange graphics and text in your documents in creative ways. Although many word processing applications allow you to use some of the features that are hallmarks of desktop publishing, specialized desktop publishing software such as QuarkXPress and Adobe InDesign allows professionals to design books and other publications that require complex layouts (see Figure 23).

What tools do desktop publishing programs include? Desktop publishing programs offer a variety of tools with which you can format text and graphics. With text formatting tools, you easily can change the font, size, and style of your text and arrange text on the page in different columns, shapes, and patterns. You also can import files into your documents from other sources, including elements from other software programs (such as a chart from Excel or text from Word) and image files. You can readily manipulate graphics with tools that crop, flip, or rotate images or modify the image's color, shape, and size. Desktop publishing programs also include features that allow you to publish to the Web.

What software do I use to create a Web page? Web page authoring software allows even the novice to design interesting and interactive Web pages, without knowing any HyperText Markup Language (HTML) code. Web page authoring applications often include wizards, templates, and

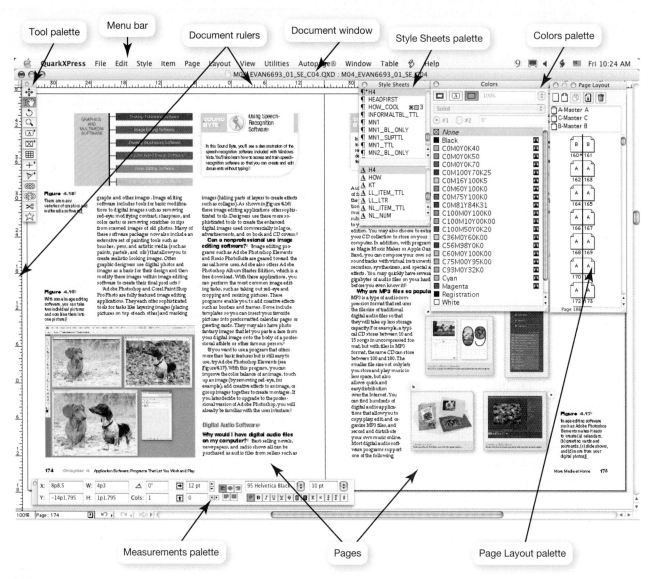

Figure 23

Major publishing houses use professional publishing programs such as QuarkXPress to lay out the pages of textbooks.

reference materials to help you easily complete most Web page authoring tasks. More experienced users can take advantage of these applications' advanced features, such as features that enable you to add headlines and weather information, stock tickers, and maps to make your Web content current, interactive, and interesting. Microsoft Expression Web and Adobe Dreamweaver are two of the programs to which both professionals and casual page designers turn.

Are there other ways to create Web pages? If you need to produce only the occasional Web page and do not need a separate page authoring program, you'll find that many applications include features

that enable you to convert your document into a Web page. For example, in some Microsoft Office applications, if you choose to save a file as a Web page, the application will automatically convert the file to a Web-compatible format.

Large Business Software

There is an application for almost every aspect of business. There are specialized programs for marketing and sales, finance, point of sale, general productivity, project management, security, networking, data management, e-commerce, and human resources, to name just a few. In the following sections, we discuss this seemingly endless list.

What software do businesses use for planning and management? Planning is a big part of running a successful business. Software programs such as Palo Alto Software's Business Plan Pro and Marketing Plan Pro help users write strategic and development plans for general business and marketing needs. Another category of business planning software is **project management software**, such as Microsoft Project. This type of software helps project managers create and modify scheduling charts like the one shown in Figure 24, which help them plan and track specific tasks and coordinate personnel resources.

Customer relationship management (CRM) software stores sales and client contact information in one central database. Sales professionals use CRM programs to get in touch with and follow up with their clients. These programs also include tools that enable businesses to assign quotas and create reports and charts that document and analyze actual and projected sales data. Customer relationship programs coordinate well with PIM software such as Outlook and can be set up to work with smartphones. Gold-Mine from FrontRange Solutions is one example of a CRM program.

An **enterprise resource planning (ERP) system** lets a business consolidate multiple systems into one and improve coordination of these business areas across multiple departments. ERP systems are used to control many "back office" operations and processing functions such as billing, production, inventory management, and human resources management. These systems are implemented by third-party vendors and matched directly to the specific needs of a company. Oracle and SAP are well-known companies that sell ERP software.

What software helps business travelers? **Mapping programs** such as DeLorme Street Atlas USA and Microsoft Streets & Trips are perfect for businesses that require employees to travel frequently. These programs provide street maps and written directions to locations nationwide, and users can customize maps to include landmarks and other handy traveling sites such as airports, hotels, and restaurants. More users now turn to an **online mapping service** such as MapQuest, Yahoo! Maps,

Google Maps, or Google Earth than to a more traditional mapping software program because the online services are easily accessible with any Internet connection and are updated more frequently than offline ones. Mapping programs, which can work in conjunction with a global positioning system (GPS), are available in versions for smartphones and for cars. Such programs help you navigate unfamiliar territory and are essential for sales representatives or delivery-intensive businesses. They are useful for nonprofessionals traveling to unfamiliar locations.

Is mapping software just used to assist with travel? Travel is only one of several applications that use mapping

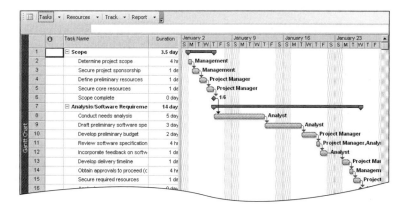

Figure 24

A Gantt chart in Microsoft Project gives project managers a visual tool for assigning personnel and scheduling and managing tasks.

Need a Way to Share Files? Try PDF

Say you've created a file in Microsoft Excel, but the person to whom you want to send it doesn't have Excel, or any spreadsheet software, installed on his computer. Further, you do not want the contents of the original file to be changed. What do you do in these situations? One solution is to create a PDF file. Portable Document Format (PDF) is a file format you can create with Adobe Acrobat or Cutepdf Writer, a freeware program available from **cutepdf.com**. These programs transform any file, regardless of its application or platform, into a document that can be shared, viewed, and printed by anyone who has Adobe Reader. If you are using Microsoft Office 2007, OpenOffice, or Corel WordPerfect Office, you can create PDF files easily with a built-in feature. Adobe Reader (available from **adobe.com**.), the program you need to read all PDF files, is a free download.

Many graphics, animation, video, and gaming systems use applications from Autodesk called Autodesk 3ds Max and Autodesk Maya to create 3D models with complex textures and lighting models. Autodesk 3ds Max and Autodesk Maya are complex and rich programs. A slightly simpler package is the open source program Blender (**blender.org**.), which is available free of charge. A simple, Web-based, and fairly full-featured free 3D modeling application is Google's SketchUp. SketchUp designs coordinate well with other Google applications so, for example, you could easily import a 3D image of a deck you created in SketchUp into a Google Earth image of your home.

Large Business Software

Digital elevation

Streets

Land use and cover

Topographic map

Digital line graph of rivers

Real world

Figure 25

A geographic information system (GIS) applies geographic data to provide solutions to complex business situations.

technologies to assist businesses in making complex decisions and managing complex systems. Many companies use a geographic information system (GIS) to assist with managing, analyzing, and displaying data, most often in spatial or map form (see Figure 25).

These maps are used by power companies to manage electric grids, by water distribution companies to manage water distribution, by shipping and transportation companies to determine the most efficient routes, and even by school districts to manage the flow of students to the appropriate schools. Many of these systems are complex, proprietary ones such as those produced by ESRI. Google Earth and interactive maps like Google Maps are simple and free examples of basic forms of a GIS.

What software is used with e-commerce? It seems that every business has an online presence to display company information or products, handle online sales, or offer customer service and support. Depending on the size of the company and its specific needs, it may use products such as IBM's WebSphere, goEmerchant from William Bryan Company, and ProStores Business from ProStores (an eBay company). These products offer bundled Web site creation and hosting services, shopping cart setup, and credit card processing services. For larger businesses, specialized software to handle each aspect of e-commerce is available; alternatively, a large business might develop proprietary software tailored to its specific needs.

Specialized Business Software

Some applications are tailored to the needs of a particular company or industry. Software designed for a specific industry is called **vertical market software**. For example, the construction industry uses software such as Sage Master Builder, which features estimating tools to help construction companies bid on jobs. It also integrates project management functions and accounting systems that are unique to the construction industry.

Other examples of vertical market software include property management software for real estate professionals; ambulance scheduling and dispatching software for emergency assistance organizations; and library automation software that combines cataloging, circulation, inventory, online catalog searching, and custom report printing.

In addition to these specific business applications, which companies can buy off the shelf, programs often are custom developed to address a company's specific needs. These custom applications are referred to as **proprietary software** because they are owned and controlled by the company that uses them.

What software is used to make 3D models? Computer-aided design (CAD) programs are a form of 3D modeling that engineers use to create automated designs, technical drawings, and model visualizations. Specialized CAD software such as Autodesk's AutoCAD is used in areas such as architecture, the automotive industry, aerospace, and medical engineering.

With CAD software, architects can build virtual models of their plans and readily visualize all aspects of design before actual construction. Engineers use CAD software to design everything from factory components to bridges. The 3D nature of these programs allows engineers to rotate their models and make adjustments to their designs where necessary, thus eliminating costly building errors.

CAD software also is being used in conjunction with GPS devices for accurate placement of fiber-optic networks around the country. The medical engineering community uses CAD to create anatomically accurate solid models of the human anatomy, allowing them to develop medical implants quickly and accurately. The list of CAD applications keeps growing as more and more industries realize the benefits CAD can bring to their product development and manufacturing processes.

Software can take us beyond what is familiar to us and into alternate realities. Virtual reality uses software to allow people to interact in a simulated three-dimensional environment that users can manipulate and explore as if they were in that world. Beyond video games, the applications of virtual reality are almost endless. Three-dimensional environments created by computers are getting better and better at helping people experience new things or experience familiar things in new ways.

Virtual environments are used in military training programs, the space program, and in the medical field. Studies show that soldiers who have gone through virtual reality (VR) training are just as effective as those who have trained in traditional combat situations. Flight simulators are used by airlines to prepare commercial pilots to fly in a wide range of flight conditions; the military and NASA also use them. The obvious benefit of simulators and VR is that there is little machine or human expense when a mistake is made in virtual conditions—but there would be in "live" conditions.

Engineers and designers are also using virtual reality technologies. Car manufacturers build virtual prototypes of new vehicles, test them, and make alterations in design before producing a single physical part. Architects create virtual models of building plans so that clients or potential buyers can "walk through" and get a more realistic idea of what the completed building will be like.

Second Life, a virtual world launched in 2003 by Linden Research, Inc., has gained worldwide popularity. Users create avatars, or virtual representations of themselves, with which they interact in the virtual world. Second Life has its own economy, where users have created "in-world" businesses and residents can legally trade in the world's own currency, called Linden dollars.

Second Life has also begun to permeate the outside world. "Outside world" businesses now assist and advise "in-world" businesses. For example, real-world programmers build complex in-world projects for clients such as Dartmouth College, Major League Baseball, and Lego. Real-world accountants offer services to advise "in-world" businesses on finance, strategic planning, or budget forecasting. There is fertile ground for innovative and entrepreneurial thinkers both inside and outside Second Life.

Finally, businesses and educational institutions also recognize the marketing potential in Second Life, and they use the virtual world to test new ideas. Educational institutions such as Harvard, Princeton, and Ohio University have built virtual campuses with the intention of offering "virtual tours" to prospective students. At these "campuses," current students can take courses (see Figure 26), participate in student organizations, or meet and collaborate online just as they would if they met in the real-world student center.

Virtual worlds such as Second Life are innovative ways to hold distance learning classes. Online classes held in a virtual world environment give students the online convenience of not having to travel to class, while providing a more enjoyable and perhaps even more effective experience. In a virtual world, students are able to convene in traditional classrooms, on sandy Malibu beaches, or in open-air venues—environments limited only by the imagination of the instructor and the students. Given such enjoyable choices, students might be more inclined to make time to attend classes, thus increasing their productivity and the interactivity of the online classroom.

Virtual classroom environments may add an additional layer of experience that students may be able to bring into their professional lives. Seton Hall University, for example, uses Second Life in an emergency preparedness course that allows students to work in simulated catastrophic situations, which would otherwise be difficult to experience in the real world.

Just as in the real world, the virtual world has its problems. However, it is likely that virtual reality and virtual environments will continue to find uses in entertainment, education, distance learning, design, and manufacturing.

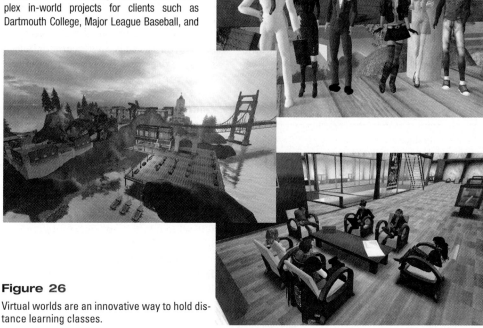

Figure 26

Virtual worlds are an innovative way to hold distance learning classes.

Getting Help with Software

If you need help while you are working with software, you can access several different resources to find answers to your questions. For general help or information about a product, many manufacturers' Web sites offer answers to **frequently asked questions (FAQs)**.

Where can I find help while I'm working in an application? Some programs offer online help and support. Online help may consist of documentation comparable to a user's manual. However, many applications' online help allows you to chat over the Internet with an online support team member. Some applications are context sensitive and offer task-specific help or screen tips to explain where your cursor is resting.

In Microsoft Office applications, you will see a question mark icon on the far top right of the program screen. This icon takes you to the main Help interface. **Integrated help** means that the documentation for the product is built directly into the software so you don't need to keep track of bulky manuals. You can type your question, search for a term, or browse the Help topics (see Figure 27). Like many software packages, Microsoft Office offers help documentation, which is installed locally on your machine, and online help resources, which are updated continually.

Finally, the Help menu, found on the menu bar of most applications, lets you choose to search an index or content outline to find out the nature of almost any Microsoft application feature.

Figure 27

Microsoft Office gives you tips on tasks you're working on and answers specific questions you have about using online and offline resources.

Where do I go for tutorials and training on an application? If you need help learning how to use a product, the product's developer may offer online tutorials or program tours that show you how to use the software features. Often you can find good tutorials by searching the Internet. MalekTips (**malektips.com**), for example, includes a vast array of multimedia help files; you can find podcasts for applications such as Excel and Photoshop in iTunes; and even YouTube has some helpful videos.

Buying Software

These days, you no longer need to go to a computer supply store to buy software. You can find software in almost any retail environment. In addition, you can purchase software online, through catalogs, and at auctions.

Software Licenses

Don't I own the software I buy? Most people don't understand that, unlike other items they purchase, the software they buy doesn't belong to them. The only thing they're actually purchasing is a license that gives them the right to use the software for their own purposes as the *only* user of that copy. The application is not theirs to lend or copy for installation on another computer, even if it's another of their own machines.

What is a software license? A **software license** is an agreement between you, the user, and the software company. You accept this agreement before installing the software on your machine. It is a legal contract that outlines the acceptable uses of the program and any actions that violate the agreement. Generally, the agreement will state who the ultimate owner of the software is, under what circumstances copies of the software can be made, and whether the software can be installed on any other machine. Finally, the license agreement will state what, if any, warranty comes with the software.

Do you always buy just one license? Most individuals buy single licenses to cover their specific use. These licenses cannot be shared and you cannot "extend" the license to install the software on more than one of your computers.

However, Apple also offers a "family license" that permits a user to install some of its software legally on as many as five computers, and some versions of Microsoft Office come with three licenses. Businesses and educational institutions often buy multiuser licenses that allow more than one person to use the software. Some multiuser licenses are per-seat and limit the number of users overall, while others, called *concurrent licenses*, limit the number of users accessing the software at any given time.

Preinstalled Software

What application software comes with my computer? Virtually every new computer comes with some form of application software, although the particular applications depend on the hardware manufacturer and computer model. You usually can count on your computer having some form of productivity software preinstalled, such as Microsoft Works or Corel WordPerfect Office.

Multimedia-enriched computers also may offer graphics software or a productivity suite that includes page authoring software. Many new computers also include some software that is of interest to home users, such as image editing or financial planning software.

Can I get the manufacturer to install software before shipping? If you know you'll need a particular type of software not offered as standard on your new computer, you may want to see if the computer manufacturer has a special offer that will allow you to add that particular software at a reduced price. Sometimes, initially buying software through the hardware manufacturer is less expensive than buying software on the retail market. This is not always the case, so do some comparative pricing before you buy.

Web-Based Application Software

Does all application software require installation on my computer? Most application software you acquire, whether by purchasing a CD or DVD at a retail store or by downloading the software from a Web site, must be installed on your computer before use. However, Web-based software is

BITS AND BYTES — Applications on the Go

More and more of us carry some kind of mobile digital device that enables us to use software on the go. We can install productivity, entertainment, communication, and navigation software on our iPhones, Blackberries, iPods, and other mobile devices. The newest version of Microsoft Office is expected have modestly featured Web-based Word, Excel, and PowerPoint applications, so you'll have access to your productivity documents without having to worry about transferring files from one machine to another. Although mobile applications have been available for smartphones for a while, they have been limited in scope and content, in addition to being slightly pricey. One of the features that makes the iPhone and iPod Touch so popular is their ability to run small applications. Many of these applications are fun and free (such as the flashlight and Sudoku applications), while others (such as the Tip Calculator, the Remember the Milk list, or a connection to your online banking files) help you be more productive. The full list of available applications for the iPhone and iPod Touch is available on the iTunes music store Web site.

growing in popularity. **Web-based application software** is a program hosted on a Web site that does not require installation on your computer. In most cases, a Web-based application will not occupy space on your hard drive, but sometimes a small plug-in or control software module may need to be downloaded.

Is all Web-based software free? Web-based applications are run from software stored completely on a Web server instead of your hard drive. Web-based applications are a reflection of a movement toward a new software distribution model.

Although most Web-based software programs are free, some Web sites charge a fee for their online products. TurboTax Online (**turbotax.com**) is a version of the popular tax preparation software that you can access online to prepare your tax returns. In addition to saving you the hassle of software installation, TurboTax Online stores your information in a secure location so that you can retrieve it anytime.

More and more of your software needs might be met by some of the emerging Web-based providers. Many Web sites offer free Web-based applications, such as the mapping software Mapquest (**mapquest.com**) and Yahoo! Maps (**maps.yahoo.com**), which allow you to generate driving directions from point to point. Sites such as Zoho (**zoho.com**, see Figure 28), ThinkFree (**thinkfree.com**), and Google (**docs.google.com**) offer Web-based applications that cover a range of word processing,

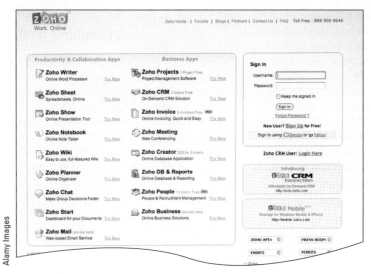

Figure 28

Zoho.com is one of the many emerging Web sites that offers free Web-based productivity software.

presentation, project management, and spreadsheet needs.

The features of these programs are generally a subset of what the installed versions offer, but they do offer other advantages. Google Docs, for example, is a free application with word processing, spreadsheet, and presentation capabilities. You can invite people to share your files and work together in real time, watching as others make changes to the document. As long as you have a Web browser, you can access your files, which are stored securely online. Although these free applications are not as fully featured as the products from Microsoft, they can read and export to many different file formats and be used with other software packages. Microsoft, in their newest release of Office, will provide Web-based Word, Excel, and PowerPoint applications that have limited functionality compared with the fully featured traditional version of the applications. It is expected that these will not be free, but will come as a part of the Office suite.

There is also a relatively new trend of on-demand software deployment, referred to as **Software as a Service (SaaS),** that many businesses are taking advantage of. Instead of the traditional model that requires software to be purchased and installed on individual machines or network servers, with the SaaS delivery model the application is hosted by the vendor and made available

to the customer over the Internet. Some examples include Intuit's Quick-Books online, Salesforce.com, and Citrix Online.

Discounted Software

Is it possible to buy software at a discount? Software manufacturers understand that students and educators often need to use software for short periods of time because of specific classes or projects. In addition, they want to encourage you to learn with their product, hoping you'll become a long-term user of their software. Therefore, if you're a student or an educator, you can purchase software that is no different from regularly priced software at prices that are sometimes substantially less than general consumer prices.

Campus computer stores and college bookstores sometimes offer discounted prices to students and faculty who possess a valid ID. Online software suppliers such as Journey Education Marketing (**journeyed.com**), CampusTech, Inc. (**campustech.com**), and Academic Superstore (**academicsuperstore.com**) also offer popular software to students at reduced prices.

Can I buy used software? Often you can buy software through online auction sites such as eBay. If you do so, be sure that you are buying licensed (legal) copies. Computer shows that display state-of-the-art computer equipment are generally good sources for software. However, here, too, you must exert a bit of caution to make sure you are buying licensed copies and not pirated versions.

Can I buy software directly from the Internet? As with many other retail products, you can buy and download software directly from many companies and retail Web sites such as Microsoft.com and Amazon.com. You also can use the Internet to buy software that is custom developed for your specific needs. Companies such as Ascentix Corporation (**ascentix.com**) act as intermediaries between you (the software user) and a software developer, who tweaks open source software code to meet your particular needs.

When buying software from the Internet, you should also request that the software be sent to you on CD or DVD, if this is available. Without a physical copy of the software, it is much more difficult to reinstall the software if you change computers or if your hard drive crashes. If a physical copy is not available, make sure you create a backup and keep it in a safe place.

The Microsoft .NET program (**microsoft. com/net**) offers software over the Internet for all devices—not just computers—that have a connection to the Internet. Therefore, you can download software specifically for your smartphone by using .NET. In addition, if you have a Microsoft .NET account (available free of charge at the Microsoft Web site), you can connect to any other .NET-connected device.

Freeware and Shareware

Can I get software for free legally?

Freeware is any copyrighted software that you can use for free. Plenty of freeware exists on the Web, ranging from games and screen savers to business, educational, graphics, home and hobby, and system utility software programs. To find free software, type "freeware" in your search engine. One good source of a large variety of freeware programs is Freeware Home (**freewarehome.com**).

Although they do not charge a fee, some developers release free software and request that you mail them a postcard or send them an e-mail message to thank them for their time in developing the software and to give them your opinion of it. Such programs are called *postcardware* and *e-mailware*, respectively.

Another option is to search for an open source program to fit your needs. Open source programs are free to use on the condition that any changes you make to improve the source code also must be distributed for free. SourceForge.net (**sourceforge.net**) is an excellent site to begin your hunt for a group that may already have built a solution that will work for you!

While many legitimate freeware exists, some unscrupulous people use freeware to distribute viruses and malware. Be cautious

BITS AND BYTES

Software 911

If your software problem is a technical one—the kind that might generate an error message—many resources are available on the Web. Most software manufacturers have support on their Web sites that include FAQs, discussion boards monitored by employees of the company, and collections of tutorials and troubleshooting advice. For example, to resolve problems with Microsoft products, check the Help and Support database located at **support.microsoft.com,** a collection of more than 250,000 articles written by Microsoft support professionals reflecting their resolution of customer issues and problems. To search Microsoft's Help and Support most effectively, use a search engine such as Google. To do so, go to Google (**google.com**) and select the Advanced Search option. Specify "support.microsoft.com" as the domain to be searched and then type your search terms. Technical communities, such as those from Microsoft (**microsoft.com/communities**) in the form of blogs, newsgroups, webcasts, and forums are also available on the Web and provide opportunities for you to interact with employees, experts, and peers.

when installing such programs, especially if you are unsure of the provider's legitimacy.

Can I try new software before it is really released? Some software developers offer beta versions of their software free of charge. A **beta version** is an application that is still under development. By distributing free beta versions, developers hope users will report errors or bugs they find in their programs. Many beta versions are available for a limited trial period, and are used to help the developers correct any errors before they launch the software on the market at retail prices.

Is it still freeware if I'm asked to pay for the program after using it for a while? One model for distributing software is to allow users to test software first by running it for a limited time, free of charge. Large corporations do this by offering free trial software products. These are fully functional packages, but they expire if not purchased within a certain timeframe. Small software developers also use this kind of distribution. This is referred to as **shareware**. Shareware software is distributed free, but with certain conditions. Sometimes the software is released on a trial basis only and must be registered after a certain period of time; in other cases, no support is available unless the software is registered. In some cases, direct payment to the author is required. Shareware is not freeware. If you use the software after the initial trial period is over, then you are breaking the software license agreement.

Software developers put out shareware programs to get their products into users' hands without the added expense and hassle of marketing and advertising. Therefore, quite a few great programs are available as shareware, and they can compete handily with programs on retail shelves. For example, TechSmith Corporation (**techsmith.com**) offers screen capture and desktop recording applications as shareware, including SnagIt Screen Capture and Camtasia Studio, a screen recording and presentation application. You can try these products for free for a 30-day period, after which time you must purchase the software to continue using it. For a listing of other shareware programs, visit the CNET site Tucows (**tucows.com**), as shown in Figure 29, or the CNET site Shareware.com (**shareware.com**).

Can shareware programmers make me pay for their shareware once I have it? The whole concept of shareware assumes that users will behave ethically and abide by the license agreement. However, to protect themselves, many developers have incorporated code into the program to stop it from working completely or to alter the output slightly after the trial period expires.

Are there risks associated with installing beta versions, freeware, and shareware or downloading them from the Internet? Not all files available as shareware and freeware will work on your computer. You easily can crash your system, and may even need to reinstall your operating system as a result of loading a freeware or shareware program that was not written for your computer's operating system.

Of course, by their very nature, beta products are unlikely to be bug free, so you always run the risk of something going awry with your system. Unless you're willing to deal with potential problems, it may be best to wait until the last beta version is released. By that time, most of the serious bugs will have been worked out.

As a matter of precaution, you should be comfortable with the reliability of the source before downloading a freeware, shareware, or beta version of software. If it's a reliable developer whose software you are already familiar with, you can be more certain that a serious bug or virus is not hiding in the software. However, downloading software from an unknown source could potentially put your system at risk of contracting a virus.

A good practice to establish before installing any software on your system is to use the Windows Vista operating system's Restore feature and create a *restore point*. That way, if anything goes wrong during installation, you can restore your system to the way it was before you started. Also, make sure that your virus protection software is up-to-date.

Figure 29

Tucows is a useful site for finding freeware applications. The site provides product reviews, hardware requirements, and details about the limitations of free versions of software.

Software Versions and System Requirements

What do the numbers after software names indicate? Software companies change their programs to repair problems (or bugs) or add new or upgraded features. Generally, they keep the software program's name but add a number to it to indicate that it is a different version. Originally, developers used numbers only to indicate different software versions (major upgrades) and releases (minor upgrades). Today, however, they also use years (such as Microsoft Office 2007) and letters (such as WordPerfect Office X3) to represent version upgrades.

When is it worth buying a newer version? Although software developers suggest otherwise, there is no need to rush out and buy the latest version of a software program every time one is available. Depending on the software, some upgrades may not be sufficiently different from the previous version to make it cost-effective for you to buy the newest version. Unless the upgrade adds features that are important to you, you may be better off waiting to upgrade every other release. You also should consider whether you use the software frequently enough to justify an upgrade and whether your current system can handle the new system requirements of the upgraded version.

If I have an older version of software and someone sends me files from a newer version, can I still open them? Software vendors recognize that people work on different versions of the same software. Vendors, therefore, make new versions backward compatible, meaning that they can recognize (open) files created with older versions. However, many software programs are not forward compatible, so older versions cannot recognize files created on newer versions of the same software. For example, when Microsoft came out with Office 2007, users of earlier versions of Microsoft Office could not read files created in Office 2007. Microsoft provided free conversion programs so users with earlier versions could read Office 2007 files. In addition, Microsoft incorporated a feature within Office 2007 that allows Office 2007 users to save documents so that they can be read by users of earlier versions.

How do I know whether the software I buy will work on my computer? Every software program has a set of **system requirements** that specify the minimum recommended standards for the operating system, processor, primary memory (RAM), and hard drive capacity. Sometimes there are other specifications for the video card, monitor, CD drive, and other peripherals. These requirements generally are printed on the software packaging or are available at the manufacturer's Web site. Before installing software on your computer, ensure that your system setup meets the minimum requirements by having sufficient storage, memory capacity, and processing capabilities.

Installing, Uninstalling, and Starting Software

Before you use your software, you must permanently place it, or install it, on your system. The installation process will differ slightly depending on whether you've

Figure 30
Part of the installation process in Windows Vista is a security check to confirm that the software is from a reliable source.

purchased the software from a retail outlet and have an installation CD or are downloading it from the Internet. Deleting or uninstalling software from your system requires that you take certain precautions to ensure you remove all associated programs as well.

How do I install software? When you purchase software, the program files may come on a CD or a DVD. For most programs created for installation on a PC, an installation wizard automatically opens when you insert the disc, as shown in Figure 30. By following the steps indicated by the wizard, you can install the application on your system. If the wizard doesn't open automatically for some reason, the best way to install the software is to go to the Programs and Features icon, located on the Control Panel on the Start menu. This feature locates and launches the installation wizard.

How is the installation process different for software I download from the Web? When you download software from the Web, you typically do not get an installation disc. Instead, everything you need to install and run the downloaded program is contained in one file that has been compressed (or zipped) to make the downloading process quicker. For the most part, these downloaded files unzip or decompress themselves and automatically start or launch the setup program. During the installation and setup process, these

programs select or create the folder on your computer's hard drive in which most of the program files will be saved. Usually, you can select a different location if you desire. Either way, note the name and location of the files, because you may need to access them later.

What do I do if the downloaded program doesn't install by itself? Some programs you download do not automatically install and run on your computer. Although the compressed files may unzip automatically as part of the download process, the setup program may not run without some help from you. In this case, you need to locate the files on the hard drive (this is why you must remember the location of the files) and find the program that is controlling the installation (sometimes named *setup.exe* or *install.exe*). Files ending with the .exe extension are executable files or applications. All the other files in the folder are support, help, and data files. Once the setup program begins, you will be prompted to take the actions necessary to complete the installation.

What's the difference between a custom installation and a full installation? One of the first steps in the installation wizard asks you to decide between a full installation and a custom installation. A **full installation** will copy all the files and programs from the distribution disc to the computer's hard drive. By selecting **custom installation**, you can decide which features you want installed on the hard drive. Installing only the features you know you want allows you to save space on your hard drive.

Can I just delete a program to uninstall it? An application contains many different files—library files, help files, and other text files—in addition to the main file you use to run the program. By deleting only the main file, or only the icon on your desktop, you are not ridding your system of all the pieces of the program. In addition, some applications make changes to a variety of settings, and none of these will be restored if you just delete the desktop icon or remove the main file from your programs list.

Some programs place an Uninstall Program icon in the main program folder on the Start menu. Using this icon runs the proper cleanup routine to clear out all of the files associated with the application, and also restores any settings that have been changed. If you can't locate the uninstall program for a particular application, click the Start menu, click Control Panel, and then click Programs and Features. This will give you a list of applications installed on your system; from this list, you can choose which application you would like to uninstall.

Is there a best way to start an application? The simplest way to start an application is by clicking its icon in the All Programs list found on the Start menu. Every program that you install on your system is listed on the Start menu. However, if you find you use only a few programs often, you can place a shortcut to those programs either on the Quick Launch toolbar on the taskbar or on your desktop. To place a program in the Quick Launch toolbar on the taskbar, right-click the program icon on your desktop or right-click the program name on the Start menu. From the shortcut menu that is displayed, select Add to Quick Launch. This places an icon for this program on the Quick Launch toolbar (see Figure 31a).

To create a shortcut on the desktop, right-click the icon of the desired program, click Send To, and select Desktop (see Figure 31b). This places the shortcut icon directly on the Desktop. You can identify a shortcut icon by the arrow in its lower left corner, as shown in Figure 31a.

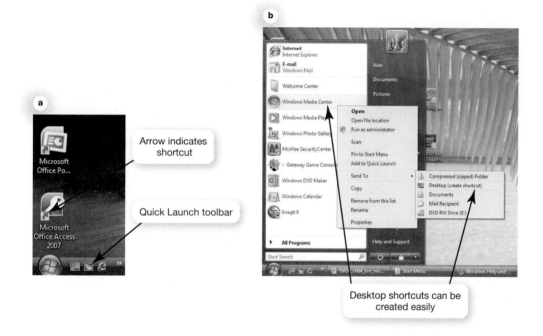

Figure 31

For quick access to an application you use often, you can place a shortcut in (a) the Quick Launch toolbar or (b) on your desktop.

A computer user who copies an application onto more than one computer is participating in **software piracy**, unless his or her license specifically provides for multiple distribution. What many software users do not realize, or do not think about, is that when they purchase software, they are actually purchasing a license to use it, rather than purchasing the actual software. That license is what tells you how many times you can install the software, so it is important to read it. If you make more copies of the software than the license permits, you are pirating. Historically, the most common way software has been pirated among computer users has been by supplementing each other's software library by borrowing installation CDs and installing the software on their own computers. Larger-scale illegal duplication and distribution by counterfeiters is quite common as well. In addition, the Internet provides various ways to copy and distribute pirated software illegally.

Is it really a big deal to copy a program or two? As reported by the Business Software Alliance, 40 percent of all software is pirated. Not only is pirating software unethical and illegal, but the practice has financial impacts on all software consumers. The dollars manufacturers lose when software is pirated decreases the amount of money available for further software research and development, while increasing the up-front costs to legitimate consumers.

To determine whether you have a pirated copy of software installed on your computer at work or at home, you can download a free copy of GASP (a suite of programs designed to help identify and track licensed and unlicensed software and other files) from the Business Software Alliance Web site (**bsa.org/usa**). A similar program is available at the Microsoft Web site (**microsoft.com/piracy**). These programs check the serial numbers of the software installed on your computer against software manufacturer databases of official licensed copies and known fraudulent copies. Any suspicious software installations are flagged for your attention.

As of yet, there's no such thing as an official software police force, but software piracy is so rampant that the U.S. government is taking steps to stop piracy worldwide. Efforts to stop groups that reproduce, modify, and distribute counterfeit software over the Internet are in full force. Software manufacturers also are becoming more aggressive in programming mechanisms into software to prevent repeated installations. For instance, with many Microsoft products, installation requires you to activate the serial number of your software with a database maintained at Microsoft. This is different from the traditional "registration" that enrolled you voluntarily and allowed you to be notified of product updates, for example. Activation is required, and failure to activate your serial number or attempting to activate a serial number that has been used previously results in the software going into a "reduced functionality mode" after the 50th time you use it. Therefore, without activation, you would not be able to save documents in Office—a strong motivator to let Microsoft watch how many times you install the software you purchased!

Installing, Uninstalling, and Starting Software

183

summary

1. What's the difference between application software and system software?

System software is the software that helps run the computer and coordinates instructions between application software and the computer's hardware devices. System software includes the operating system and utility programs. Application software is the software you use to do everyday tasks at home, school, and work. Application software includes productivity software, such as word processing and finance programs; media software, such as applications used for image editing; home and entertainment software, such as games or educational programs; and business software.

2. What kinds of applications are included in productivity software?

Productivity software programs include word processing, spreadsheet, presentation, personal information manager (PIM), and database programs. You use word processing software to create and edit written documents. Spreadsheet software enables you to do calculations and numerical and what-if analyses easily. Presentation software enables you to create slide presentations. Personal information manager (PIM) software helps keep you organized by putting a calendar, address book, notepad, and to-do lists within your computer. Database programs are electronic filing systems that allow you to filter, sort, and retrieve data easily. Individuals can also use software to help with business-like tasks such as preparing taxes and managing personal finances.

3. What are the different types of multimedia software?

Multimedia software includes digital image, video, and audio editing software; animation software; and other specialty software required to produce computer games. Many software programs are available for playing, copying, recording, editing, and organizing multimedia files. Because modern users have so many audio, video, and image files, many software solutions are available for organizing and distributing these types of files.

4. What are the different types of entertainment software?

Beyond the games that most of us are familiar with, entertainment software includes virtual reality programs that use special equipment to make users feel as though they are actually experiencing the program in a realistic 3D environment.

5. What are the different types of drawing software?

Drawing software includes a wide range of software programs that help you create and edit simple line-based drawings or create more complex designs for both imaginative and technical illustrations. Floor plans, animations, and mind maps are some of the types of images that can be created.

6. What kinds of software do small and large businesses use?

Many businesses, including home businesses, use software to help them with finance, accounting, strategic planning, marketing, and Web-based tasks common to most businesses. In addition, businesses may use specialized business software (or vertical market software) that is designed for their specific industry.

7. What kind of software is available online?

Web-based software refers to programs that are hosted on a Web site and do not require installation on your computer. Many applications are available as Web-based software, including productivity, tax preparation, and financial planning software. Digital photos and videos can be manipulated, saved, and stored online. The features of many Web-based applications are not as robust as those of their downloadable counterparts, but this is likely to change.

Application Software: Programs That Let You Work and Play

8. Where can I go for help when I have a problem with software?

Most software programs have a Help menu built into the program with which you can search through an index or subject directory to find answers. Some programs group the most commonly asked questions into a single "frequently asked questions" (FAQ) document. In addition, many free and fee-based help and training resources are available on the Internet and through booksellers.

9. How can I purchase software or get it for free?

Almost every new computer system comes with some form of software to help you accomplish basic tasks. You must purchase all other software unless it is freeware or open source code, which you can download from the Web for free. You can also find special software called shareware you can run free of charge for a test period. Although you can find software in many stores, as a student you can purchase the same software at a reduced price with an academic discount.

10. How do I install, uninstall, and start software?

When installing and uninstalling software, it's best to use the specific Add or Remove Program feature that comes with the operating system. Most programs are installed using an installation wizard that walks you through the installation. Other software programs may require you to activate the setup program, which then will begin the installation wizard. Using the Add or Remove Programs feature when uninstalling a program will help you ensure that all ancillary program files are removed from your computer.

key terms

accounting software

application software

audio editing software

beta version

computer-aided design (CAD)

course management software

custom installation

customer relationship management (CRM)
  software

database software

desktop publishing (DTP) software

digital video editing software

drawing software (illustration software)

enterprise resource planning (ERP) system

entertainment software

Entertainment Software Rating
  Board (ESRB)

financial planning software

freeware

frequently asked questions (FAQs)

full installation

image editing software
  (photo editing software)

integrated help

integrated software application

macro

mapping program

multimedia software

online mapping service

open source software

personal information
  manager (PIM) software

presentation software

productivity software

program

project management software

proprietary software

shareware

simulation program

software

Software as a Service (SaaS)

software license

software piracy

software suite

speech-recognition software
  (voice-recognition software)

spreadsheet software

system requirements

system software

tax preparation software

template

vertical market software

virtual reality program

Web-based application software

Web page authoring software

wizard

word processing software

Word Bank

- application software
- beta version
- freeware
- illustration software
- image editing software
- integrated help
- integrated software
- productivity software
- shareware
- software piracy
- software suite
- spreadsheet
- system requirements
- system software
- templates
- Web-based applications
- wizards
- word processing

Instructions: Fill in the blanks using the words from the Word Bank above.

Roxanne is so pumped! Her aunt is upgrading to a newer computer and is giving Roxanne her old one. Roxanne has just enrolled in college and knows she's going to need at least (1) a(n) _____ program to help her write papers and (2) a(n) _____ program to help her keep track of expenses while she is at school. Because both of these applications are part of a larger group of applications called (3) _____ , she knows she can buy them as a group. She's been told that it's cheaper to buy them as (4) a(n) _____ than to buy them individually. Because she knows she'll need the stable, tested versions of the software, she cannot get by using (5) a(n) _____ of the program. Roxanne is also aware of many interesting (6) _____ that are available from the Internet and that she can access any-where she has an Internet connection.

As a graduation present, Roxanne received a new digital camera. She needs to install the (7) _____ that came with her camera to edit and manage her digital pictures. Although she's used the software a couple of times on her parents' computer, she is still glad for the (8) _____ feature to assist her with specific feature-related questions and the (9) _____ that provide systematic guides to help her do things.

Roxanne especially likes the decorative preformatted (10) _____ she can use to insert pictures and make them seem professional. She also knows of some (11) _____ games she can download without cost from the Internet and other (12) _____ programs that she could try but eventually pay for. She found some really useful utility programs under the category of (13) _____ programs, which she can download for no charge and would like to install and try out. It's tempting for her to borrow software from her friends, but she knows that it's considered (14) _____ . She also knows that before installing any of the programs she must check the (15) _____ to determine if the software is compati-ble with her system as well as whether the system has enough resources to support the software.

becoming computer literate

Using key terms from this chapter, write a letter to one of your friends or relatives about which applications he or she may need to be able to work more productively. Also, include which application(s) that individual may need to modify, review, and store the pictures taken with a digital camera he or she just purchased.

Instructions: Answer the multiple-choice and true–false questions below for more practice with key terms and concepts from this chapter.

Multiple Choice

1. Application software
   a. is another name for system software.
   b. helps maintain the resources of the computer.
   c. includes products such as Microsoft Office, tax software, and editing packages.
   d. Both A and C.

2. Which of the following is an example of a software suite?
   a. Microsoft Word
   b. Google Docs
   c. WordPerfect Office X3
   d. None of the above

3. A Web-based software program is
   a. a stand-alone program developed to work exclusively for one company.
   b. an application designed specifically for a Web-based business or industry.
   c. a program that helps you design Web pages.
   d. an application that does not need to be installed but is run directly from the Web.

4. An integrated software application such as Microsoft Works is
   a. an individual program.
   b. meant only for business purposes.
   c. sold in specific collections, which reduces the price.
   d. only available in open source format.

5. The type of software you would use to help you coordinate many people on a single task is
   a. project management.
   b. spreadsheet.
   c. database.
   d. system.

6. What software is the best for creating a newsletter?
   a. Word processing software
   b. Desktop publishing software
   c. Computer-aided design software
   d. Media management software

7. Which is NOT true about Web-based applications?
   a. They are accessible from any computer that has an Internet connection.
   b. They are great for collaboration.
   c. They are typically more expensive than traditional applications.
   d. They are used to coordinate input from a variety of users on a single document.

8. Which of the following is true?
   a. MP4 files contain audio and video data.
   b. MP3 files are the only recognized format for digital audio.
   c. Windows Media player is able to organize large collections of audio files.
   d. Only A and C are true.

9. Where can you find help on how to use software and solve specific software problems?
   a. An index or subject directory found in the Help menu
   b. Documents containing frequently asked questions
   c. Resources on the Web
   d. All of the above

10. Which of the following best describes open source software?
    a. It is free and is as fully featured as similar proprietary applications.
    b. It is available from the Internet and can be virus ridden.
    c. It is freely available from the Internet, but has limited functionality when compared with proprietary products.
    d. It is freely available, but can only be used for a limited amount of time.

True–False

_____ 1. Software can be installed only from a CD or DVD.

_____ 2. Open source software such as Audacity is used to organize video files.

_____ 3. The best way to delete a program from your system is to delete the shortcut on the desktop.

_____ 4. When you buy software, it's yours to do whatever you'd like with, including making a copy for a friend.

_____ 5. Web-based application software will run from any computer without the need for any installation.

Application Software: Programs That Let You Work and Play

1. Installing Software

You have just spent $285 on a software package. You have a desktop computer that you use at home and a notebook that you use only at work.

a. Are you allowed to install the software on both computers? Should you be allowed to do that?

b. What if you wanted to install the software on two computers that you own and use exclusively at home?

c. Can you install the software on two computers if you use only one computer at a time?

d. Are you allowed to install the software package on your computer and also on a friend's computer if she is interested in buying her own copy but wants to test it first?

2. Software Training

You are most likely familiar with many applications, and you probably will use many more applications before your coursework is done. Make two lists. In one list, itemize by category the applications you are already familiar with. In the other list, identify at least three other applications you think you may need or would want to try in the future. Research the types of on-campus or online training or help features that may be offered for those programs you put on your second list.

3. Upgrading Software

You are trying to decide whether to upgrade some software that you used this past semester. How do the following items weigh into your decision to upgrade the software or not?

a. The cost of the upgrade

b. The length of time the upgrade has been available

c. Hardware requirements

d. Features of the upgrade versus the stability of your current system

4. Choices, Choices

There are many word processing software options. Describe the decision process you would use to choose among a free Web-based word processing application, an open source word processing application, and a standard packaged application if you are

a. traveling abroad for a semester, visiting 15 different cities, and not carrying a notebook with you.

b. staying at home for the term and compiling a capstone report using several hundred researched sources of information.

c. working with three people from other colleges on a joint paper that will be presented at a conference at the end of the term.

5. Choosing the Best Software

This past semester you spent a lot of time doodling, and created a comic strip character that all your friends love. You've decided to start a small newsletter, including some articles and a few comics each week. Which applications would be the best fit for the following tasks?

a. Designing and laying out the newsletter

b. Creating the text articles

c. Creating the comic strip

After the first five issues, the newsletter is clearly a smash. You decide to expand it into an Internet-delivered magazine. Which applications will you use now for the same tasks?

1. Surveying the Competition

You are asked to develop a departmental report that analyzes the key competitors in your market. You will need to take the following steps:

a. Identify the major competitors in your market.
b. Gather information on their companies, their sales, and the features of their products.
c. Organize your data so it can be easily sorted and filtered.
d. Analyze the trends in the marketplace and predict future direction of growth.
e. Create a final report and presentation to deliver to the department heads.

Identify what software products you would use to complete each of these tasks. How would you use them, and how would they work together to support your efforts?

2. Integrating Applications

Some applications work well together and some do not. Certainly, all of the applications within a given suite, such as Microsoft Office, are well integrated. Give an example of a business office need that would benefit from the following:

a. Integrating Excel with Word
b. Integrating Access with Excel
c. Integrating Access with Word

3. Choosing the Best Software for the Job

For each of the following positions, describe the set of applications you would expect to encounter if you were:

a. a photographer opening a new business to sell your own photography.
b. an administrative assistant to a college president.
c. a graphic designer at a large publishing house.
d. the publicity director of a new summer camp for children.
e. a presenter giving a program to elementary school students about a year spent living abroad.
f. a Web page designer for a small nonprofit organization.
g. a construction site manager.
h. a person in the career you are pursuing.

4. The Right Productivity Suite

You are asked to research the cost and use of productivity software for your small company. Until now, the company has been using Microsoft Works, but the need to expand to a full-fledged productivity suite is evident. Research the major productivity suites on the market. Look at cost, the ability to exchange files with customers and other employees easily (for example, does file type make a difference?), and the various features within each version of the software. Explore the major developers' products as well as the open source option OpenOffice and a set of Web-based packages. Which productivity suite would you recommend, and why? Be specific in your recommendation.

Application Software: Programs That Let You Work and Play

190

Instructions: Albert Einstein used *Gedankenexperiments* (critical thinking questions) to develop his theory of relativity. Some ideas are best understood by experimenting with them in our own minds. The following critical thinking questions are designed to demand your full attention but require only a comfortable chair—no technology.

1. Software Ethics 1

The cost of new software can be prohibitively high. You need to do a project for school that requires the use of an application you don't own, but your roommate has a copy that her dad gave her. He brought it home from his workplace, and she is letting you install it on your machine.

a. Is it okay for you to borrow this software?
b. Would it be okay if you uninstalled the application after you finished using it?
c. Would it be okay if the software was on the school's network and you could copy it from there?

2. Software Ethics 2

Currently, there is no accurate way to check for illegal installations of software programs. What kind of program or system do you think could be developed to do this type of checking? Who would pay to develop, run, and maintain the program: the developers or the software users?

3. Media Management

Less than a decade ago, home users had no media files on their computer systems. Today, many users have a library of music, a collection of digitized movies, personal photo collections, and even a large set of recorded television shows. Examine three different software packages on the market today for managing these materials. What features do they need to make the PC the primary entertainment device for a home? What would make users move their PC from the office into the living room?

4. Software and Microcredit

The 2006 Nobel Peace Prize was awarded to Muhammad Yunus, who created the Grameen Bank. This bank makes quite small loans to the poor of Bangladesh, without requiring collateral. Often these loans are smaller than $200, but they allow women to begin small businesses and climb out of poverty. How has software made the Grameen Bank productive and able to serve almost 7 million borrowers? What other ways could software make a difference to the struggling peoples of the world?

5. Software for the Hearing and Visually Impaired

The World Wide Web Consortium (W3C) currently has an initiative to ensure that all Web pages are accessible to everyone, including those with vision and hearing impairments. The W3C site has a list of currently available commercial and free Web accessibility evaluation tools (**w3.org/WAI/ER/tools**) that Web site developers can use to ensure their Web sites conform to the disability standards.

a. Pick a favorite Web site and see how it checks out by using one of the freeware programs on the W3C list. What changes would be necessary for that Web site to conform to W3C standards?
b. Can you think of other ways in which software might make the world a better place for those with vision and hearing impairments?
c. How might recommendations made by the W3C also benefit people without physical limitations?

Assessing Software Needs

Problem

Gizmos, Inc. is a start-up company in the business of designing, building, and selling the latest gizmos. You have been hired as director of information systems. As such, one of your responsibilities is to ensure that all necessary applications are purchased and installed on the company's server.

Task

Split your class into as many groups of four or five as possible. Each group is to perform the same activity. The groups will present and compare results with each other at the end of the project.

Process

1. Identify a team leader who will coordinate the project and record and present results.
2. Each team is to identify the various kinds of software that Gizmos, Inc. needs. Ensure that all activities and departments of the company have software to meet their needs. Consider software that employees will need for several tasks: software they can use to design the gizmos, productivity software they may need, and software the sales reps will need to help keep track of their clients. Also, consider software that human resources personnel can use to keep track of employee data, and that software product managers can use to track projects. Finally, think of other software that might be useful to Gizmos, Inc.
3. Create a detailed and organized list of required software applications. If possible, include licensing fees. Assume that the company has 50 users.

Conclusion

Software helps us do both the simplest and the most complex tasks every day. It's important to understand how dependent we are becoming on computers and technology. Compare your results with those of other team members. Were there applications that you didn't think about, but that other members did? How expensive is it to ensure that even the smallest company has all the software required to carry out daily activities?

In addition to the review materials presented here, you'll find additional materials featured with the Pearson IT Multimedia Library and the Companion Website (**pearsonhighered. com/techinaction**), which will help reinforce your understanding of the chapter content. These materials include the following:

Active Helpdesk

In Active Helpdesk calls, you'll assume the role of helpdesk operator, taking calls about the concepts you've learned in this chapter. You'll apply what you've learned and receive feedback from a supervisor to review and reinforce those concepts. The Active Helpdesk calls for this chapter are listed below and can be found on the Pearson IT Multimedia Library.

- Choosing Software
- Buying and Installing Software

Sound Bytes

Sound Bytes are dynamic multimedia tutorials that help demystify even the most complex topics. You'll view video clips and animations that illustrate computer concepts and then apply what you've learned by reviewing it with the Sound Byte Labs, which include quizzes and activities specifically tailored to each Sound Byte. The Sound Bytes for this chapter are listed below and can be found on the Pearson IT Multimedia Library.

- Creating Web Queries in Excel 2007
- Using Speech-Recognition Software
- Enhancing Photos with Image Editing Software

Companion WebSite

The *Technology in Action* Companion Website includes a variety of additional materials to help you review and learn more about the topics in this chapter. The resources available at **pearsonhighered.com/techinaction** include:

- **Online Study Guide.** This chapter features an online true–false and multiple-choice quiz. You can take these quizzes, automatically check the results, and e-mail the results to your instructor.
- **Web Research Projects.** This chapter features several Web research projects that ask you to search the Web for information on computer-related careers, milestones in computer history, important people and companies, emerging technologies, and the applications and implications of different technologies.

using system software:

the operating system, utility programs, and file management

From Chapter 5 of *Technology in Action Complete*, Seventh Edition, Alan Evans, Kendall Martin, Mary Anne Poatsy. Copyright © 2011 by Pearson Education, Inc. Published by Pearson Prentice Hall. All rights reserved.

using system software:

the operating system, utility programs, and file management

objectives

After reading this chapter, you should be able to answer the following questions:

1. What software is included in system software?

2. What are the different kinds of operating systems?

3. What are the most common operating systems?

4. How does the operating system provide a means for users to interact with the computer?

5. How does the operating system help manage resources such as the processor, memory, storage, hardware, and peripheral devices?

6. How does the operating system interact with application software?

7. How does the operating system help the computer start up?

8. What are the main desktop and window features?

9. How does the operating system help me keep my computer organized?

10. What utility programs are included in system software, and what do they do?

resources

 Active Helpdesk

- Managing Hardware and Peripheral Devices: The OS
- Starting the Computer: The Boot Process
- Organizing Your Computer: File Management
- Using Utility Programs

 Sound Bytes

- Customizing Windows
- File Management
- File Compression
- Hard Disk Anatomy Interactive
- Letting Your Computer Clean Up After Itself

 Companion Website

The Companion Website includes a variety of additional materials to help you review and learn more about the topics in this chapter. Go to: *pearsonhighered.com/techinaction*

how cool is *this?*

Have you ever wanted to capture what appears on your **desktop**? You can use the PrtScr (print screen) key on your keyboard, but that captures the entire screen, and only onto the clipboard. You then need to crop and save the file for that **screen capture** to be useful. There are also screen capture software programs that you can purchase. However, Windows Vista and Windows 7 include a **Snipping Tool** to capture an entire screen image, or to take a freeform or rectangular "snip" of any window or object on the screen. Once snipped, you can **annotate**, save, or **share** the object. You can find the Snipping Tool by clicking the Start button, selecting All Programs, and then opening the Accessories folder. **Jing** (**jingproject.com**), a freeware tool from TechSmith, not only captures still screen shots, but also records video of on-screen action. You can share Jing files over the Web, or via instant messaging or e-mail.

Alex White/Shutterstock

197

System Software Basics

There are two basic types of software on your computer: application software and system software. **Application software** is the software you use to do everyday tasks at home and at work. **System software** is the set of programs that help run the computer and coordinate instructions between application software and the computer's hardware devices. From the moment you turn on your computer to the time you shut it down, you are interacting with system software. System software consists of two primary types of programs: the operating system and utility programs.

What does an operating system do? The **operating system (OS)** is a group of programs that controls how your computer system functions. The OS manages the computer's hardware, including the processor (also called the central processing unit, or CPU), memory, and storage devices, as well as peripheral devices such as the monitor and printer. The OS also provides a consistent means for software applications to work with the CPU, and is responsible for the management, scheduling, and coordination of tasks as well as system maintenance. Your first interaction with the OS is the user interface—the features of the program that allow the user to communicate with the computer system.

System software also includes utility programs. A **utility program** is a small program that performs many of the general housekeeping tasks for the computer, such as system maintenance and file compression.

Do all computers have operating systems? Every computer, from the smallest notebook to the largest supercomputer, has an operating system. Even cell phones, game consoles, and some appliances have operating systems. The role of the OS is critical; the computer cannot operate without it. As explained more fully in the section of this chapter titled "What the Operating System Does," the operating system coordinates the flow of data and information through the computer system by coordinating the hardware, software, user interface, processor, and system memory.

> "Every computer has an operating system."

Are all operating systems alike? Although most computer users can name only a few operating systems, many types exist. Some operating systems, such as those found in household appliances and car engines, don't require any user intervention at all. Some are proprietary systems developed specifically for the devices they manage. Some operating systems are available for personal and business use, and other operating systems coordinate resources for many users on a network. These operating systems were traditionally classified into categories, depending on the number of users they served (single user or multiple user) and the tasks they performed (single task or multitask). However, as devices begin to converge in their functionalities, and the operating systems continue to become more powerful, the distinction in the traditional categorization of operating systems begins to blur (see Figure 1).

For example, personal computers were at one time run by single-task, single-user operating systems such as the **Microsoft Disk Operating System (MS-DOS).** MS-DOS (or DOS) was the first widely installed operating system in personal computers. Compared to the operating systems we are familiar with today, DOS was a highly user-unfriendly OS. To use it, you needed to type specific commands, and didn't have the option to click on icons or choose from menus.

Eventually, single-user, multitasking operating systems, such as Apple's Mac OS and the Microsoft Windows operating systems, replaced DOS. These systems enabled the computer user to multitask (perform two or more tasks simultaneously). Then, networking capabilities were added to these personal computer operating systems to facilitate sharing peripheral devices and Internet access among multiple computers at home. These systems, while still traditionally used as single-user, multitask operating systems, technically became multiuser, multitask operating systems. Similar transitions are happening with mobile devices, as cell phones and PDAs converge and incorporate the functionalities of cameras and personal media players. Although these were initially single-task devices with combined functionalities, the newer devices are beginning to add multitasking capabilities.

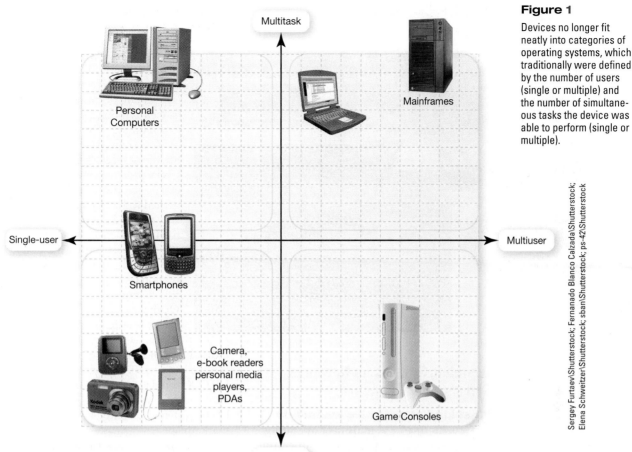

Sergey Furtaev\Shutterstock; Fernanado Blanco Calzada\Shutterstock; Elena Schweitzer\Shutterstock; sban\Shutterstock; ps-42\Shutterstock

Figure 1

Devices no longer fit neatly into categories of operating systems, which traditionally were defined by the number of users (single or multiple) and the number of simultaneous tasks the device was able to perform (single or multiple).

In the next section, we will look at different types of operating systems that work with a variety of computers.

Types of Operating Systems

Operating systems can be categorized by the type of device in which they are installed, such as robots and specialized equipment, mainframes and network computers, mobile devices, and personal computers.

Real-Time Operating Systems

Why do machines with built-in computers need an operating system? Machinery that is required to perform a repetitive series of specific tasks in an exact amount of time requires a **real-time operating system (RTOS)**. Real-time operating systems require minimal user interaction. The programs are written specifically for the needs of the devices and their functions. Therefore, there are no commercially available standard RTOS software programs.

This type of operating system is a program with a specific purpose, and it must guarantee certain response times for particular computing tasks; otherwise, the machine is useless. Devices that must perform regimented tasks or record precise results—such as measurement instruments found in the scientific, defense, and aerospace industries—require real-time operating systems. Examples include digital storage oscilloscopes and the Mars Reconnaissance Orbiter.

Where else are RTOSs in use today? You also encounter real-time operating systems in everyday life. They are in devices such as fuel-injection systems in car engines, inkjet printers, VoIP phones, and some medical devices (see Figure 2). Real-time operating systems are also found in many types of robotic equipment. Television stations use robotic cameras with real-time operating systems that glide across a suspended cable system to record sports events from many angles.

Figure 2

Devices such as some cars, radiography devices, VoIP phones, and inkjet printers use real-time operating systems.

one at a time. Examples of network operating systems include Linux and UNIX.

What is UNIX? UNIX is a multiuser, multitask operating system used as a network operating system, primarily with mainframes, although it is also often found on PCs. Developed in 1969 by Ken Thompson and Dennis Ritchie of AT&T's Bell Labs, the UNIX code was initially not proprietary—in other words, no company owned it. Rather, any programmer was allowed to use the code and modify it to meet his or her needs. Later, AT&T licensed the UNIX source code to the Santa Cruz Operation Group. UNIX is a brand that belongs to the company The Open Group, but any vendor that meets testing requirements and pays a fee can use the UNIX name. Individual vendors then modify the UNIX code to run specifically on their hardware. HP/UX from Hewlett-Packard, Solaris from Sun, and AIX from IBM are some of the UNIX systems currently available in the marketplace.

What other kinds of computers require a multiuser operating system? Large corporations with hundreds or thousands of employees often use powerful computers known as mainframes. A **mainframe** is responsible for storing, managing, and simultaneously processing data from all users. Mainframe operating systems fall into the multiuser category. Examples include UNIX and IBM's i5/OS and z/OS.

Supercomputers also use multiuser operating systems. Scientists and engineers use supercomputers to solve complex problems or to perform massive computations. Some supercomputers are single computers with multiple processors, whereas others consist of multiple computers that work together.

Operating Systems for Networks, Servers, and Mainframes

What kind of operating system do networks use? A **multiuser operating system** (also known as a **network operating system**) enables more than one user to access the computer system at one time by efficiently handling and prioritizing requests from multiple users. Networks (groups of computers connected to each other for the purposes of communicating and sharing resources) require a multiuser operating system because many users simultaneously access the **server**, which is the computer on a network that manages network resources such as printers.

The latest versions of Microsoft Windows and Mac OS X can be considered network operating systems, and enable users to set up networks in the home and for small businesses. (A more complete discussion of Microsoft Windows and Mac OS can be found in the "Operating Systems for Personal Computers" section.) In larger networks, a network operating system is installed on the server and manages all user requests, ensuring they do not interfere with each other. For example, on a network where users share a printer, the printer can produce only one document at a time. The OS is therefore responsible for managing all the printer requests and making sure they are processed

Operating Systems for Mobile Devices

What kind of operating system controls a PDA or simple cell phone? A computer on which one user is performing just one task at a time requires a **single-user, single-task operating system**. In the days when cell phones and PDAs (personal digital assistants) were separate, single-function devices, they only required operating systems that could perform one task at a time. Cell phones had their own proprietary embedded operating systems, and PDAs were powered by operating systems such as Palm OS and Windows Mobile (see Figure 3). These operating systems were designed to look similar to desktop operating systems and included basic applications for personal information management, such as calendars, contact lists, and note pads. Microsoft's Windows Mobile also bundled application software, including versions of Word, Excel, PowerPoint, Outlook, Internet Explorer, and Windows Media Player. When PDAs began to include cell phone functionality (and became known as smartphones), these operating systems were expanded to have modest multitasking capabilities, so users can handle a phone call while accessing the calendar or contacts at the same time.

What kind of operating system do smartphones use? When cell phones and PDAs first came out, they were single-task devices. However, over the past several years, a convergence between the two devices has created the smartphone. A **smartphone** does more than let the user make and answer phone calls. It also has productivity features traditionally found on PDAs, in addition to features found on personal media players and cameras. The most current smartphones have the ability to connect to the Web. Examples of smartphones include BlackBerry devices and the iPhone. Initially, although multifunctional, smartphones were still primarily single-task devices and only capable of doing one task at a time. Now, most modern smartphones

Figure 3

SONDA DAWES\The Image Works

Some PDAs, like this older Palm V, used the Palm OS operating system, with which one user could perform only one task at a time. The OS was designed to look similar to that of a traditional desktop operating system.

have modest multitasking capabilities. The most common operating systems that can be found on smartphones include the Symbian OS, RIM's BlackBerry operating system, Windows Mobile, and the iPhone OS. Google's Android and Palm's webOS are the newest entries into this expanding market. The newest version of the iPhone and the Palm Pre have more multitasking capabilities, which let the user run more than one application concurrently.

Do gaming consoles and personal media players require an operating system? Gaming systems, like Microsoft's Xbox 360, the Nintendo Wii, and the Sony PlayStation, as well as personal media players like Microsoft's Zune, Apple's iPod, and SanDisk's Sansa, all require some form of customized system software that is developed specifically for the particular device. The system software includes system programs—also known as **firmware**—that control the device, as well as other programs that come with the personal media player or the gaming device. For example, the programs included with most portable media players allow users to manage music files on the player and to rip audio CDs. The operating systems on gaming consoles support Web browsing and file storage of media and photos as well as playing DVDs and games.

Operating Systems for Personal Computers

What type of operating system controls my personal computer?

Because personal computers—desktops, notebooks, and even tablet PCs—can

Types of Operating Systems

201

handle only one person working on them at a time but can perform a variety of tasks simultaneously, one might think that they would use a **single-user, multitask operating system**. Indeed, the early versions of the Microsoft Windows and Macintosh operating systems were single-user, multitask operating systems. However, the newer versions, such as Mac OS X Snow Leopard and Windows 7, have networking capabilities, so technically they are considered multiuser operating systems.

Does it matter what operating system is on my computer? The type of processor in the computer determines which operating system a particular desktop computer uses. The combination of operating system and processor is referred to as a computer's **platform**. For example, Microsoft Windows operating systems are designed to coordinate with a series of processors from Intel Corporation and Advanced Micro Devices (AMD) that share the same or similar sets of instructions. Until a few years ago, Apple Macintosh operating systems worked primarily with processors from the Motorola Corporation and IBM that were designed specifically for Apple computers. Now Intel also makes processors for Apple computers.

Yet the two operating systems (Windows and Mac OS) are not interchangeable, even if both machines have Intel processors. If you attempted to load a Windows OS on a Mac computer, for example, the processor in the Mac would not understand the Windows operating system and would not function properly. Most application software is also platform dependent. For example, there are special Mac versions of Microsoft Office, Adobe Photoshop Elements, Intuit Quicken, and other "traditional" PC software applications.

Despite their inability to run the same software applications as PCs, Mac computers can be networked with PCs. Mac OS X Snow Leopard provides a variety of features and technologies that enable Macs and PCs running Windows to work seamlessly together. A utility called Boot Camp, available with OS X Snow Leopard, allows you to run Windows on a Mac while also running OS X. In addition, Macs and PCs can easily share files and even peripherals, such as printers, scanners, and cameras.

SOUND BYTE — Customizing Windows

In this Sound Byte, you'll find out how to customize your desktop. You'll learn how to configure the desktop, set up a screen saver, change pointer options, customize the Start menu, and manage user accounts.

Microsoft Windows

What is the Microsoft Windows operating system? Microsoft Windows began as an operating environment that worked with MS-DOS and incorporated a graphical user interface like the one that was first introduced with the Mac OS. In 1995, Microsoft released Windows 95, a comprehensive update that made changes to the user interface and incorporated multitasking capabilities. Windows XP was the next major update; it provided networking capabilities in its consumer editions. The new **Windows 7** operating system builds upon the security and user interface upgrades that the Windows Vista release provided, and gives users with touch-screen monitors the ability to use touch commands to scroll, resize windows, pan, and zoom. What was once only a single-user, single-task operating system is now a powerful multiuser, multitask operating system. Over time, Windows improvements have concentrated on increasing user functionality and friendliness, improving Internet capabilities, and enhancing file privacy and security.

What is the difference between the various editions of Windows 7 operating systems? With each new version of its operating system, Microsoft continues to make improvements. However, it's still not a "one size fits all" operating system. Windows 7, the newest version, comes in a number of editions to accommodate different users: home users (Starter, Home Basic, Home Premium), business users (Professional and Enterprise), and combination users (Ultimate). Figure 4 outlines the features and benefits of each edition of Windows 7.

Mac OS

What is the Mac Operating System? In 1984, **Mac OS** became the first commercially available operating system to incorporate a graphical user interface (GUI) with user-friendly point-and-click technology into an affordable computer. Mac OS X Snow Leopard, the most recent version of the OS, is based on the UNIX operating system. Macs have long been recognized for their superior graphics display and processing capabilities. Users also attest to Mac's greater system reliability and superior file backup utilities. Despite these advantages, fewer software applications are available for the Mac platform than for Windows, and Mac systems tend to be more expensive than Windows-based PCs.

How do the Mac and Windows operating systems compare?

Although the Apple Mac OS and the Windows operating system are not compatible, they are extremely similar in terms of functionality.

Both Windows and Mac operating systems have similar window-like work areas on the desktop that house individual applications and support users working in more than one application at a time. They both also have a streamlined user interface. Macs feature a Dock for the most commonly used programs and a Dashboard with widgets (a **widget** is a mini-application). These features enable quick access to frequently used tools and activities (such as stock prices, to-do lists, and games). The latest version of Windows has followed suit with a revised taskbar that has Dock-like capabilities and *gadgets* that provide functionality similar to that of the Mac widgets (see Figure 5). Despite their similarities, there are many subtle and not-so-subtle differences that have created loyal fans for each operating system.

Figure 4 | WINDOWS 7 EDITIONS

Edition	Description
Windows 7 Starter	This edition is designed to run on small netbooks, and is for those users who have basic computing requirements. The user is limited to running three applications concurrently.
Windows 7 Home Basic	This edition is for users in emerging markets. It is not being distributed in the United States and Canada.
Windows 7 Home Premium	This edition incorporates multimedia functions as core components. No extra software is needed to run DVDs, and other audio and video files. Networking as well as file and peripheral sharing across PCs are included.
Windows 7 Professional	As its name implies, this edition is aimed at the business market, but is also appropriate for the advanced home user. This edition builds on Windows 7 Home Premium and features advanced networking capabilities.
Windows 7 Enterprise	This edition is geared to the large enterprise user and is available only through volume licensing.
Windows 7 Ultimate	This is the "ultimate" operating system for high-end PC users, gamers, multimedia professionals, and PC enthusiasts.

Linux

What is Linux?   Linux is an open source operating system designed for use on personal computers and as a network operating system. Open source software is freely available for developers to use or modify as they wish. The Linux operating system is based on the central programming code of an operating system, and the rest of the code is from the GNU (pronounced

Figure 5

Although not compatible with each other, the Windows OS and the Mac OS have many similar features.

Widgets (Mac)/
Gadgets (Windows)

Files

Icons

Windows

Access to
applications

Types of Operating Systems

Emerging Technologies: Open Source Software—Why Isn't Everyone Using Linux?

Proprietary software such as Microsoft Windows and Mac OS is developed by corporations and sold for profit. This means that the **source code**, the actual lines of instructional code that make the program work, is not accessible to the general public. Without being able to access the source code, it's difficult for a user to modify the software or see exactly how the program author constructed various parts of the system.

Restricting access to the source code protects companies from having their programming ideas stolen, and prevents customers from using modified versions of the software. However, in the late 1980s, computer specialists became concerned that large software companies (such as Microsoft) were controlling a large portion of market share and driving out competitors. They also felt that proprietary software was too expensive and contained too many bugs (errors).

These people felt that software should be developed without a profit motive and distributed with its source code free for all to see. The theory was that if many computer specialists examined, improved, and changed the source code, a more full-featured, bug-free product would result. Hence, the open source movement was born.

Open source software is freely distributed (no royalties accrue to the creators), contains the source code, and can in turn be redistributed freely to others. Most open source products are created by teams of programmers and are modified (updated) by hundreds of other programmers around the world. You can download open source products for free from the Internet. Linux is probably the most widely recognized name in open source software, but other products such as MySQL (a database program) and OpenOffice.org (a suite of productivity applications) are also gaining in popularity.

So, if an operating system such as Linux is free, why does Windows (which users must pay for) have such a huge market share (nearly 90 percent), and why does Linux have less than 1 percent of the desktop market? One reason is that corporations and individuals have grown accustomed to one thing that proprietary software makers can provide: technical support. It is almost impossible to provide technical support for open source software because anyone can freely modify it; thus, there is no specific developer to take responsibility for technical support (see Figure 6). Similarly, corporations have been reluctant to install open source software extensively because of the cost of the internal staff of programmers that must support it.

Companies such as Red Hat have been combating this problem. Red Hat offers a free, open source operating system called Fedora. In addition, Red Hat has modified the original Linux source code and markets a version, Red Hat Enterprise Linux, as a proprietary program. Fedora is the testing ground for what eventually goes into this proprietary program. Red Hat Enterprise Linux 5 is the current system on the market, and comes in versions for servers and desktops. Purchasers of Red Hat Enterprise Linux receive a warranty and technical support. Packaging open source software in this manner has made its use much more attractive to businesses. As a result, many Web servers are hosted on computers running Linux.

When will free versions of Linux (or another open source operating system) be the dominant OSs on home computers? The answer is, maybe never. Most casual computer users won't feel comfortable without technical support; therefore, any open source products for home use will need to be marketed the way Red Hat markets Enterprise Linux. In addition, many open source products are not easy to maintain.

However, some companies are making easy-to-use visual interfaces, such as GNOME and KDE, which work with the Linux operating system. If one of these companies can develop an easy-to-use product and has the marketing power to challenge Microsoft, you may see more open source OSs deployed in the home computer market in the future.

Figure 6

Companies like Ubuntu and Xandros provide free (or low-cost) Linux software, but users must purchase technical support.

"g-noo") Project and other sources. Linux began in 1991 as a part-time project of Finnish university student Linus Torvalds, who wanted to create a free OS to run on his home computer. He posted his OS code to the Web for others to use and modify. It has since been tweaked by scores of programmers as part of the Free Software Foundation GNU Project (**gnu.org**).

Linux is gaining a reputation as a stable OS that is not subject to crashes or failures.

Because the code is open and available to anyone, Linux can be tweaked quickly to meet virtually any new operating system need. For example, when the Palm PDA emerged, the Linux OS was promptly modified to run on this new device. Similarly, only a few weeks were necessary to get the Linux OS ready for the Intel Xeon processor, a feat unheard of in proprietary OS development. Some Linux-based operating systems have been modified to run on iPods and gaming systems. Linux is also gaining popularity among computer manufacturers, which have begun to ship it with some of their latest PCs. Android, the new operating system developed by Google, is Linux-based. Because the overall size of Android is much smaller than that of Windows, many netbook users choose to use it in place of the factory-installed Windows operating system.

Where can I get Linux? You can download open source versions of Linux for free from the Internet. These free, open source Linux distributors include Mandriva, Ubuntu, Fedora, Suse, Debian GNU/Linux, and Gentoo Linux. However, several versions of Linux are more proprietary in nature and must be purchased. These versions come with support and other features that are not generally associated with the open source Linux. Red Hat has been packaging and selling versions of Linux since 1994 and is probably the best-known Linux distributor. For a full listing and explanation of all Linux distributors, visit Distrowatch (**distrowatch.com**).

What the Operating System Does

As shown in Figure 7, the operating system is like a traffic cop. It coordinates the flow of data and information through the computer system. In doing so, the OS performs several specific functions:

- It provides a way for the user to interact with the computer.
- It manages the processor, or CPU.
- It manages the memory and storage.
- It manages the computer system's hardware and peripheral devices.
- It provides a consistent means for software applications to work with the CPU.

In this section, we look at each of these functions in detail.

Figure 7

The operating system is the traffic cop of your computer, coordinating its many activities and devices.

Manages computer hardware and peripherals devices

Provides user interface

The Operating System

Manages memory and storage

Manages processor

Provides a consistent interaction between applications and CPU

What the Operating System Does

Now that broadband Internet access is becoming commonplace, the concept of a more universal operating system, called a *Web-based OS*, is being discussed and some prototype sites are in their infancy. So what is a Web-based operating system? Actually, the terms *Web-based operating environment* or *portable desktop* might be more accurate. The concept behind this movement is to make the Web the primary application interface through which users can view content, manage data, and use various services (calendars, e-mail, and picture sharing and storage) on their local machine and on the Web without noticing any difference between interfaces.

Currently, most applications we use have been installed on a specific computer and can be used only on that computer. A Web-based operating environment would allow users access to applications and content via the Web, regardless of the machine they are using. This means business travelers would not need to lug their notebooks everywhere they went. Instead, they would only need to find a computer that had Internet access to be able to work on documents, see their calendar, read their e-mail, and so on. All of their settings and preferences (even a customized desktop image), as well as working documents, could be stored in an individual Web-based account for them to access anywhere and on any machine at any time. Google is the closest to having a complete Web-based system. Its Google Docs application and Chrome browser are the initial components of a completely Web-based operating environment, which is expected to come out by 2011. Because security measures have not been completely worked out, it's advisable that Web-based accounts not be used to store or manipulate personal or proprietary data and information. For more information, or to open your own account, check out the Web sites of the current Web-based OS innovators, including Google, eyeOS (**eyeos.org**), and GoGUI (**gogui.com**).

The User Interface

How does the operating system control how I interact with my computer?
The operating system provides a **user interface** that enables you to interact with the computer. As noted earlier, the first

personal computers had a DOS operating system with a command-driven interface, as shown in Figure 8. A **command-driven interface** is one in which you enter commands to communicate with the computer system. The DOS commands were not always easy to understand; as a result, the interface proved to be too complicated for the average user. Therefore, PCs were used primarily in business and by professional computer operators.

The command-driven interface was later improved by incorporating a menu-driven interface, as shown in Figure 8. A **menu-driven interface** is one in which you choose commands from menus displayed on the screen. Menu-driven interfaces eliminated the need for users to know every command because they could select most of the commonly used commands from a menu. However, they were still not easy enough for most people to use.

What kind of interface do operating systems use today?
Current personal computer operating systems such as Microsoft Windows and Mac OS use a **graphical user interface**, or **GUI** (pronounced "gooey"). Unlike the command- and menu-driven interfaces used earlier, GUIs display graphics and use the point-and-click technology of the mouse and cursor, making them much more user-friendly. As illustrated in Figure 9, a GUI uses **windows** (rectangular boxes that contain programs displayed on the screen), **menus** (lists of commands that appear on the screen), and **icons** (pictures that represent an object such as a software application or a file or folder).

Unlike Windows or Mac OS, Linux does not have a single default GUI interface. Instead, users are free to choose among many commercially available and free interfaces, such as GNOME and KDE, each of which provides a different look and feel. For example, GNOME (pronounced "gah-NOHM")

Figure 8

(a) A command-driven interface. (b) A menu-driven interface.

actually allows you to select which desktop appearance (Windows or Mac) you'd like your system to have. This means that if you're using Linux for the first time, you don't have to learn a new interface; you just use the one you're most comfortable with already.

Processor Management

Why does the operating system need to manage the processor? When you use your computer, you are usually asking the CPU to perform several tasks at once. For example, you might be printing a Word document, waiting for a file to download from the Internet, listening to a CD on your CD drive, and working on a PowerPoint presentation—all at the same time, or at least what appears to be at the same time. Although the processor is the powerful brain of the computer, processing all of its instructions and performing all of its calculations, it needs the OS to arrange for the execution of all these activities in a systematic way, creating the appearance that everything is happening simultaneously.

To do so, the operating system assigns a slice of its time to each activity that requires the processor's attention. The OS must then switch among different processes thousands of times a second to make it appear that everything is happening seamlessly. Otherwise, you wouldn't be able to listen to a CD and print at the same time without experiencing delays in the process. When the OS allows you to perform more than one task at a time, it is said to be **multitasking**.

How exactly does the operating system coordinate all the activities? When you create and print a document in Word while also listening to a CD, for example, many different devices in the computer system are involved, including your keyboard, mouse, CD drive, and printer. Every keystroke, every mouse click, and each signal to the printer and from the CD drive creates an action, or **event**, in the respective device (keyboard, mouse, CD drive, or printer) to which the operating system responds.

Sometimes these events occur sequentially (such as when you type characters one at a time), but other events involve two or more devices working concurrently (such as the printer printing while you continue to type and listen to a CD). Although it looks as though the keyboard, CD drive, and printer are working at the same time, in fact, the OS switches back and forth among processes, controlling the timing of events the processor works on.

For example, assume you are typing and want to print a document. When you tell your computer to print your document, the printer generates a unique signal called an **interrupt** that tells the operating system that it is in need of immediate attention. Every device has its own type of interrupt, which is associated with an **interrupt handler**, a special numerical code that prioritizes the requests. These requests are placed in the interrupt table in the computer's primary memory (random access memory, or RAM). The operating system processes the task assigned a higher priority before processing a task that has been assigned a lower priority. This is called **preemptive multitasking**.

In our example, when it receives the interrupt from the printer, the operating system pauses the CPU from its typing activity and from the CD activity, and puts a "memo" in a special location in RAM called a *stack*. The memo is a reminder of what the CPU was doing before it started to work on the printer request. The CPU then retrieves the printer request from the interrupt table and begins to process it. On completion of the printer request, the CPU

Windows

Menu

Icons

Gadgets

Figure 9
Today's operating systems coordinate a user's experience through a graphical user interface.

Ethics: Sugar—The Sweet OS for Every Child

The Internet is a fantastic tool, but only if you can access it. In an effort to give children in developing countries a better opportunity to "learn, share, and create," the One Laptop per Child (OLPC) initiative was founded by Nicholas Negroponte and other faculty from MIT Media Lab, in conjunction with partners such as Google, AMD, and News Corporation. The mission of OLPC (**laptop.org**) is to ensure that all school-age children in lesser-developed communities receive their own personal computers so that they are no longer excluded from the educational, economic, and entertainment benefits that computers can provide. Laptops have been distributed to children in areas and countries such as the South Pacific, Uruguay, Mongolia, Nigeria, Ethiopia, and Rwanda.

This ambitious project to develop and distribute a low cost notebook computer (currently, the cost is $199) would provide access to electronic textbooks and other learning aids—and eventually the Internet. The project has expanded to include a wide variety of professionals from academia, business, the arts, and technology. The main thrust of the project is to overcome the so-called digital divide (the gap between people who have access to computers and those who don't) and provide computing resources to everyone regardless of their financial means.

fuseproject

Figure 10

The revolutionary design of the XO-1 notebook is rugged yet child-friendly. The XO-1 can be easily converted from a traditional notebook to an e-book. It is extremely power-efficient but can also be self-powered.

The notebook itself is revolutionary in design (see Figure 10). Called the XO-1, the notebook is small and has a comfortable, child-sized, built-in handle. It also has a tablet-like monitor that can twist to turn the notebook into an electronic book (e-book) reader, which is critical in areas where books are hard to come by. The outside of the notebook is rugged and child-friendly. In addition, it is power efficient, running on less than one-tenth the power a standard notebook requires. Because access to electricity is minimal in many of the project's target areas, the notebook is self-powered by an easy-to-use pull-string.

At the core of the project is Sugar, the operating system. It is based on open source code components from Red Hat's Fedora Core 6 version of the Linux operating system, but has a user interface that is completely different from Windows, Mac OS, or Linux. Credit goes to the developers, who really thought about how the users of the notebook would interact with the device. The OLPC notebooks will most likely be the first computer that many of these children use. Because children have no idea of what to do with the machine and may not have anyone to tell them, the user interface was designed to be as intuitive as possible.

The operating system focuses on activities rather than applications. When the machine powers up, the first image is that of the XO man (an O on top of an X) in the

---

goes back to the stack, retrieves the memo it placed about the keystroke or CD activity, and returns to that task until it is interrupted again.

What happens if there is more than one document waiting to be printed? The operating system also coordinates multiple activities for peripheral devices such as printers. When the processor receives a request to send information to the printer, it first checks with the operating system to ensure that the printer is not already in use. If it is, the OS puts the request in another temporary storage area in RAM, called the *buffer*. The request then waits in the buffer until the **spooler**, a program that helps

coordinate all print jobs currently being sent to the printer, indicates the printer is available. If more than one print job is waiting, a line (or *queue*) is formed so that the printer can process the requests in order.

Memory and Storage Management

Why does the operating system have to manage the computer's memory? As the operating system coordinates the activities of the processor, it uses RAM as a temporary storage area for instructions and data the processor needs. The processor then accesses these instructions and data from RAM when it is ready to process them. The middle of a circle. It is surrounded by icons that represent home, friends, and neighborhood. The computer includes a built-in microphone and webcam for children to create their own multimedia. For example, the multimedia tool allows children to add music to their drawings. Other activities include browsing the Internet, chatting, text editing, and playing games. At the core of each activity is the ability to collaborate, which facilitates the community learning experience. To enhance collaboration, the notebooks are all interconnected in a wireless mesh network, providing the potential for every activity to be a networked activity. Browsing, for example, would no longer be an isolated, individual activity; it could also be a collaborative group experience (see Figure 11). Wireless capabilities also help extend the community beyond its physical borders. These computers make it possible for a child in Africa, for example, to connect with another child in Europe.

In addition, the operating system uses a journaling technique for file management (see Figure 11). The file system records what the child has done (rather than just what the student has saved), working as a scrapbook of the student's interactions with the computer as well as with peers. The journal can be tagged, searched, and sorted in a variety of ways.

Another general concept behind the operating system is that children learn through doing, so the software puts an emphasis on tools for exploration and expression, as well as encouraging students to learn by helping each other. Because Sugar is built on an open source platform, it also encourages students to explore how it works and to modify the code to meet their individual preferences.

The OLPC is not the only organization interested in increasing the reach of technology to those in less-developed nations. Intel has gone forward with its own program and produced the Classmate PC. Although the Classmate PC is more closely aligned with the traditional Windows-based PC model—it runs on either Windows or the open source OS Mandriva Discovery 2007 (a version of Linux)—it offers some of the same user-friendly hardware features as the XO-1 machine does. Some reviewers and

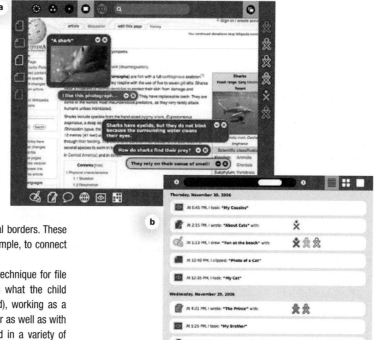

Figure 11

(a) One student shares a browsing experience with several others. (b) The journaling file management system chronicles what the student saves as well as the student's interaction with the machine and with others.

followers of both projects have offered the opinion that the Classmate PC is better suited for the older student user, whereas the XO-1 laptop is geared toward a younger, less sophisticated user. With so many children waiting to be exposed to technology and to a more fun and intuitive learning process, there is most likely room in the market for both machines.

OS is therefore responsible for coordinating the space allocations in RAM to ensure that there is enough space for all of the pending instructions and data. It then clears the items from RAM when the processor no longer needs them.

Does the amount of RAM on a system control the type of OS I get? Until recently, the maximum amount of RAM found on most personal computers was 4 GB. That was considered a lot! Now, many personal computer systems that are reasonably priced provide for 8 GB or more of RAM. Systems that offer 4 GB or more of RAM will feature a 64-bit version of Windows. Compared to the more traditional 32-bit systems, a 64-bit operating system provides the added responsiveness required by users who are running several applications at the same time, and are switching among them frequently. At the moment, the problem is that not all applications and devices are compatible with 64-bit systems. If you purchase a 64-bit system, you will need to make sure that all your hardware and software programs are updated to work well with the 64-bit version of your operating system. To assist you in this process, Microsoft has created the Windows 7 Upgrade Advisor. This downloadable free program checks to determine whether your computer is compatible in all respects with Windows 7, including the 64-bit compatibility.

Can my system ever run out of RAM? RAM has limited capacity. Like most users, over time you will expand how you use your computer by adding new software and new peripherals. Most computers sold for home use have between 1 and 4 GB of RAM. A system with 1 or 2 GB of RAM is usually sufficient if you're running several applications at the same time. If you're running Windows 7, however, the minimum requirement for the operating system using minimal capabilities is 1 GB of RAM. If you want to incorporate the translucent Aero user interface themes that are available in some versions of Windows 7, your system should have at least 2 GB of RAM and a video card with at least 128 MB of RAM. Systems that run Windows 7 may be challenged if they have only 1GB of RAM, especially if you run graphic-intensive programs such as Adobe Photoshop, many gaming applications, or even the latest version of Microsoft Office. As you add and upgrade software and increase your usage of the computer system, you will likely find that the amount of RAM you once found to be sufficient is no longer enough.

What happens if my computer runs out of RAM? When there isn't enough RAM for the operating system to store the required data and instructions, the operating system borrows room from the more spacious hard drive. This process of optimizing RAM storage by borrowing hard drive space is called **virtual memory**. As shown in Figure 12, when more RAM is needed, the operating system swaps out from RAM the data or instructions that have not been recently used and moves them to a temporary storage area on the hard drive called the **swap file** (or **page file**). If the data or instructions in the swap file are needed later,

the operating system swaps them back into active RAM and replaces them in the hard drive's swap file with less active data or instructions. This process of swapping is known as **paging**.

Can I ever run out of virtual memory? Only a portion of the hard drive is allocated to virtual memory. You can manually change this setting to increase the amount of hard drive space allocated, but eventually your computer system will become sluggish as it is forced to page more and more often. This condition of excessive paging is called **thrashing**. The solution to this problem is to increase the amount of RAM in your system so that it will not be necessary for it to send data and instructions to virtual memory.

How does the operating system manage storage? If it weren't for the operating system, the files and applications you save to the hard drive and other storage locations would be an unorganized mess. Fortunately, the OS has a file management system that keeps track of the name and location of each file you save and the programs you install. We will talk more about file management later in the chapter.

Hardware and Peripheral Device Management

How does the operating system manage the hardware and peripheral devices? Each device attached to your computer comes with a special program called a **device driver** that facilitates communication between the hardware device and the operating system. Because the OS must be able to communicate with every device in the computer system, the device driver translates the device's specialized commands into commands that the operating system can understand, and vice versa. Devices would not function without the proper device drivers because the OS would not know how to communicate with them.

Do I always need a driver? Today, most devices, such as flash drives, mice,

Figure 12

Virtual memory borrows excess storage capacity from the hard drive when there is not enough capacity in RAM.

RAM

Data and instructions not recently used

OS

Windows 7 Home Premium

Data and instructions needed now

Hard drive's swap file

keyboards, and many digital cameras, come with the driver already installed in Windows. The devices whose drivers are included in Windows are called Plug and Play devices. **Plug and Play (PnP)** is a software and hardware standard that Microsoft created with the Windows 95 OS. PnP is designed to facilitate the installation of new hardware in PCs by including in the OS the drivers these devices need in order to run. Because the OS includes this software, incorporating a new device into your computer system seems automatic. Plug and Play enables users to plug a new device into a port on the system unit, turn on the computer, and immediately play (use) the device. The OS automatically recognizes the device and its driver without any further user manipulations of the system.

What happens if the device is not Plug and Play? Some current devices, such as many types of printers and many older devices are not Plug and Play. When you install a non–PnP device, you will be prompted to insert the driver that was provided with the device. If you obtain a non–PnP device secondhand and do not receive the device driver, or if you are required to update the device driver, you can often download the necessary driver from the manufacturer's Web site. You can also go to Web sites such as DriverZone.com (**driverzone.com**) or Driver Guide (**driverguide.com**) to locate drivers.

Can I damage my system by installing a device driver? Occasionally, when you install a driver, your system may become unstable (that is, programs may stop responding, certain actions may cause a crash, or the device or the entire system may stop working). Although this is uncommon, it can happen. Fortunately, Windows has a Roll Back Driver feature that removes a newly installed driver, and replaces it with the last one that worked, to remedy the problem (see Figure 13). Roll Back Driver is found by accessing the Device Manager dialog box under System and Maintenance in the Control Panel.

Software Application Coordination

How does the operating system help application software run on the computer? Application software feeds

What Do I Do When My Computer Freezes?

At some point in time, we have all experienced our computers freezing up—nothing seems to respond to a mouse click or a tap on any keyboard key. What should you do? Try following these steps:

1. Press Ctrl + Alt and then the Delete key to access the Task Manager. On the Applications tab, close the application that is listed as not responding by clicking on the application and then clicking the End Task button.

2. If the non-responding application will not close from the Task Manager, press Ctrl + Alt and then Delete again to restart the computer. Restarting the computer is called a "soft" or "warm" boot. You might also try using the Start menu and choosing Restart.

3. If the computer will not restart from the Task Manager or from the Start menu, then press the power button one time to try to restart the computer. (Older computers may have a separate Restart button.)

4. If the computer still won't restart, press and hold down the Power button until the power turns completely off. You may have to hold down the power button for several seconds.

5. Leave the computer turned off for a minute or so to allow all the internal components to shut down completely. Then turn the computer on again. (Powering the computer on from an off position is called a "cold" or "hard" boot.)

the CPU the instructions it needs to process data. These instructions take the form of computer code. Every computer program, no matter what its type or manufacturer, needs to interact with the CPU. For programs to work with the CPU, they must contain code that the CPU recognizes. Rather than having the same blocks of code for similar procedures in each program, the operating system includes the blocks of code—each called an **application programming interface (API)**—that application software needs in order to interact with the

Figure 13

The Roll Back Driver feature in Windows removes a newly installed driver and replaces it with the last one that worked.

>To access Device Manager, click the **Start** button, **Control Panel**, **Hardware** and **Sound Group**; then click the **Device Manager** link.

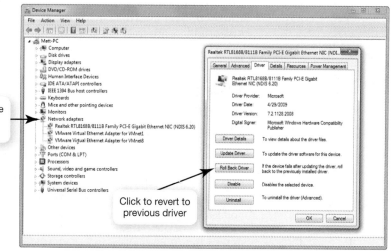

Locate drive in device list and click for device properties

Click to revert to previous driver

OS. Microsoft DirectX, for example, is a group of multimedia APIs built into the Windows operating system that improves graphics and sounds when you're playing games or watching video on your PC.

What are the advantages of using APIs? To create applications that can communicate with the operating system, software programmers need only refer to the API code blocks when they write an application. They don't need to include the entire code sequence in the application. APIs not only prevent redundancies in software code, but also make it easier for software developers to respond to changes in the operating system.

Large software developers such as Microsoft have many applications under their corporate umbrella and use the same APIs in all or most of their applications. Because APIs coordinate with the operating system, all applications that have incorporated these APIs have similar interface features, such as toolbars and menus. Therefore, many features of the applications have the same look. An added benefit to this system is that applications sharing these formats can easily exchange data with each other. As such, it's easy to create a chart in Microsoft Excel from data in Microsoft Access and incorporate the finished chart into a Microsoft Word document.

The Boot Process: Starting Your Computer

Although it only takes a minute or two, many things happen quickly between the time you turn on the computer and the time when it is ready for you to start using it. As you learned earlier, all data and instructions (including the operating system) are stored in RAM while your computer is on. When you turn off your computer, RAM is wiped clean of all its data (including the OS). How does the computer know what to do when you turn it on if there is nothing in RAM? It runs through a special **boot process** (or start-up process) to load the operating system into RAM. The term *boot*, from *bootstrap loader* (a small program used to start a larger program), alludes to the straps of leather, called *bootstraps*, that men used in former times to help them pull on their boots. This is the source of the expression "pull oneself up by the bootstraps."

What are the steps involved in the boot process? As illustrated in Figure 14, the boot process consists of four basic steps:

1. The basic input/output system (BIOS) is activated by powering on the CPU.

2. The BIOS checks that all attached devices are in place (called a **power-on self-test** or **POST**).

3. The operating system is loaded into RAM.

4. Configuration and customization settings are checked.

How can I tell if my computer is entering the boot process? As the computer goes through the boot process in a Windows operating system, indicator lights on the keyboard and disk drives may illuminate, and the system may emit various beeps. If you have a version of Windows earlier than XP, text will scroll down the screen as well. When you boot up on a PC with Windows or on a Mac, you won't hear any beeps or see any keyboard lights illuminate, but you will most likely see the Windows or Mac OS logo display on the monitor, indicating the progress of the start-up process. Once the boot process has completed these steps, it is ready to accept commands and data. Let's look at each of these steps in more detail.

Step 1: Activating BIOS

What's the first thing that happens after I turn on my computer? In the first step of the boot process, the CPU activates the **basic input/output system (BIOS)**. BIOS (pronounced "bye-OSE") is a program that manages the exchange of data between the operating system and all the

Side by Side." When you want to undo the arrangement, right-click the taskbar again and select "Undo Show Stacked" (or "Side by Side"). To bring a window back to its full size, click the Restore button in the top right corner of the window.

Windows Vista and 7 offer two more ways to navigate through open windows. To see live thumbnail images of open windows, press Alt + Tab to access Windows Flip. Pressing the Windows key + Tab initiates the Windows Flip 3D feature. You can then "flip" through open windows in a stack by using the scroll wheel on your mouse or the arrow keys on your keyboard. The open windows appear in a three-dimensional configuration as shown in Figure 18.

Can I move or resize the windows once they are tiled? Regardless of whether the windows are tiled, you can resize them and move them around the desktop. You can reposition windows on the desktop by using the mouse to point to the title bar at the top of the window and, while holding down the left mouse button, drag the window to a different location. To resize a window, place your mouse pointer over any side or corner of a window until it changes to a double-headed arrow [↕]. You can then left-click and drag the window to the new desired size.

Organizing Your Computer: File Management

So far you have learned that the operating system is responsible for managing the processor, memory, storage, and devices, and that it provides a mechanism whereby applications and users can interact with the computer system. An additional function of an operating system is to enable **file management**, which entails providing organizational structure to the computer's contents. The OS allows you to organize the contents of your computer in a hierarchical **directory** structure that includes files, folders, libraries, and drives. In this section, we discuss how you can use this hierarchical structure to make your computer more organized and efficient.

Organizing Your Files

What exactly is a file? Technically, a **file** is a collection of related pieces of information stored together for easy reference. A file in an operating system is a collection of program instructions or data that is stored and treated as a single unit. Files can be generated from an application such as a Word document or an Excel workbook. In addition, files can represent an entire

Figure 18
The Windows Flip 3D feature gives you the ability to move through live images of open windows.

  Upgrading Your Operating System

At some point, a new version of the operating system you are using will be released. You are then faced with the decision of whether to upgrade to the new version (such as going from Windows XP or Vista to Windows 7). Here are a few key things to consider before taking the plunge:

- **Are there significant features in the new version that will make your life easier?** If the only features the new version offers are ones you don't need, why bother upgrading?

- **Will your hardware work with the new OS?** Check the minimum operating requirements (required RAM, processor speed, hard drive space, etc.) of the new version to ensure that your computer can handle the workload of the new software. You will also need to make sure drivers for the new OS are available for all your hardware devices and peripherals to ensure they will work properly with the new OS.

- **Is your application software compatible with the new version of the OS?** Usually, application software works fine with a new version of an OS. Sometimes it doesn't. Check with the software vendors regarding compatibility.

- **Is your current operating system still supported?** When it deploys new versions of operating systems, the company may stop supporting older versions. If your version will not be supported, it's best to upgrade to a newer version.

Before starting the upgrade, you should back up all your data files. Upgrades are usually designed not to disturb data files, but upgrades do not always go smoothly. Make sure you have current backups of all your data files so you won't lose anything accidentally during the upgrading process.

application, a Web page, a set of sounds, or an image. Files are stored on the hard drive, a flash drive, or another permanent storage medium. As the number of files you save increases, it becomes more important to keep them organized in folders and libraries. A **folder** is a collection of files. Windows 7 introduces the concept of libraries. A **library** is a folder that gathers files from different locations and displays them as if they were all saved in a single folder, regardless of where they are actually physically stored.

How does the operating system organize files? Windows organizes the contents of your computer in a hierarchical structure comprising drives, folders, subfolders, and files. The hard drive, represented as the C drive, is where you permanently store most of your files. Other storage devices on your computer are also represented by letters. The A drive has traditionally been reserved for a floppy drive, which you may or may not have installed on your computer. Any additional drives (such as flash, CD, or DVD drives) found on your computer are represented by other letters (D, E, F, and so on).

How is the hard drive organized? The C drive, or hard drive, is like a large filing cabinet in which all files are stored. As such, the C drive is the top of the filing structure of the computer system and is referred to as the **root directory**. All other libraries, folders, and files are organized within the root directory. There are areas in the root directory that the operating system has filled with files and folders holding special OS files. The programs within these files help run the computer and generally

shouldn't be touched. The Windows operating system creates special folders, such as Documents, Pictures, Music, and Videos, where you may begin to store and organize your text, image, audio, and video files, respectively. However, users do not always carefully save their files in these special folders. Files are often stored all over the PC in various folders. For example, picture files may not just be stored in the Pictures folder, but might also be stored in the temporary folder, in a separate folder within the Documents folder, or even in remote storage, making finding all picture files difficult. Windows 7 tries to remedy this situation with the use of libraries. Recall, libraries gather files from different locations and display the files as if they were all saved in a single folder, regardless of where they are actually physically stored. Some libraries are created already in Windows, and Windows has defined specific folders to include in each standard library, but users can create other libraries to meet their special needs, or can modify the standard libraries, adding or deleting folders to meet their needs.

How can I easily locate and see the contents of my computer? If you use a Windows PC, **Windows Explorer** is the main tool for finding, viewing, and managing the contents of your computer. It shows the location and contents of every drive, folder, and file. As illustrated in Figure 19, Windows Explorer is divided into two panes, or sections.

The navigation pane on the left shows the contents of your computer in a traditional hierarchical tree structure. It displays all the drives of the system, as well as other commonly accessed areas such as the Desktop, Libraries, and Documents, Music, Pictures, and Video folders.

How should I organize my files? Creating folders is the key to organizing your files because folders keep related documents together. Again, think of your computer as a big filing cabinet that is filled with many folders. Those folders have the capacity to hold individual files, or even other folders that contain individual files. For example, you might create one folder called

Figure 19

Windows Explorer lets you see the contents of your computer.

>Click the **Windows Explorer** icon on the taskbar.

Navigation pane

File path

Libraries

Music folder

Files and folders in MGT 111

Opened MGT 111 folder

Classes to hold all of your class work. Inside the Classes folder, you could create folders for each of your classes (such as CIS 110, MGT 111, and HIS 112). Inside each of those folders, you could create subfolders for each class's assignments, completed homework, research, notes, and so on.

Grouping related files into folders makes it easier for you to identify and find files. Which would be easier—going to the MGT 111 folder to find a file or searching through the 143 individual files in Documents hoping to find the right one? Grouping files in a folder also allows you to move them more efficiently, so you can quickly transfer critical files needing frequent backup, for instance. Sometimes, it's not always possible to put all similar files into one folder. For example, you might have PowerPoint files stored in separate folders that correspond to each particular class. If you want to always have quick access to your PowerPoint files, you could create a PowerPoint Library and specify the folders where the PowerPoint files are located. The PowerPoint Library would then gather the PowerPoint files from the different locations and display them as if they were all saved in a single folder.

Viewing and Sorting Files and Folders

Are there different ways I can view and sort my files and folders? When you open any folder in Windows, the toolbar at the top displays a Views button. Clicking on the Views button offers you different ways to view the folders and files, which are discussed in more detail below. In some views, the folders are displayed as Live Icons, which is a feature that began in Windows Vista. Live Icons allows you to preview the actual contents of a specific file or folder without actually opening the file. Live Icons can be displayed in a variety of views.

- **Tiles view:** Displays files and folders as icons in list form. Each icon represents the application associated with the file, and also includes the file name and the file size, though the display information is customizable to include other data. The Tiles view also displays picture

Sort files and folders by clicking the headers

Figure 20

Details view enables you to sort and list your files in a variety of ways to enable quick access to the correct file.

dimensions, a handy feature for Web page developers.

- **Details view:** The most interactive view. Files and folders are displayed in list form, and the additional file information is displayed in columns alongside the file name. You can sort and display the contents of the folder by any of the column headings, so you can sort the contents alphabetically by file name or type, or hierarchically by date last modified or by file size (see Figure 20).

- **List view:** Another display of icons and file names that are even smaller than in Tiles view. This is a good view if you have a lot of content in the folder and need to see most or all of it at once.

- **Small and Medium Icons views:** These views also display files and folders as icons in list form, but the icons are either small- or medium-sized, respectively. Additional file information displays in a ScreenTip (the text that appears when you place your cursor over the file icon).

- **Large and Extra Large Icons views:** Large Icons view (see Figure 21) shows

Figure 21

The Large Icons view is an especially good way to display the contents of files and folders. The preview pane on the right enables you to see the first page of your document without first opening it.

>To access Large Icons view, from the command bar in any folder dialog box, click the **Views arrow**, and then select **Large Icons** view. To access the Preview Pane, click **Organize**, select **Layout**, and then **Preview Pane**.

Folders with live preview of contents

Preview pane allows viewing without opening file

Live preview of Excel and PowerPoint files

the contents of folders as small images. There is also Extra Large Icons view, which shows folder contents and other icons as even larger images. Large Icons and Extra Large Icons views are the best to use if your folder contains picture files, or for PowerPoint presentations, because the title slide of the presentation will display, making it easier for you to distinguish among presentations. You may use the scale feature to adjust the size of the icons further. Additionally, a preview pane is available in this view. It allows you to view the first page of the selected document without having to open it completely (see Figure 21).

For those folders that contain collections of MP3 files, you can download the cover of the CD or an image of the artist to display on any folder to identify that collection further.

What's the best way to search for a file? You've no doubt saved a file and forgotten where you saved it, or have downloaded a file from the Internet and then were not sure where it was saved. What's the quickest way to find a file? Looking through every file stored on your computer could take hours, even with a well-organized file management system. Fortunately, the newer

SOUND BYTE File Management

In this Sound Byte, you'll examine the features of file management and maintenance. You'll learn the various methods of creating folders, how to turn a group of unorganized files into an organized system of folders, and how to maintain your file system.

versions of Windows include Instant Search, a search feature, found on the Start menu, which searches through your hard drive or other storage device (CD or flash drive) to locate files that match criteria you provide. Your search can be based on a part of the file name or just a word or phrase in the file. You can also narrow your search by providing information about the type of file, which application was used to create the file, or even how long ago the file was saved. (Mac OS Snow Leopard has a similar feature called Spotlight, known as Sherlock in earlier versions.) Instant Search can also find e-mails based on your criteria. Instant Search is found in Windows Explorer, too, and is used to search the contents of current folders.

Figure 22 | COMMON FILE NAME EXTENSIONS

Extension	Type of Document	Application
.doc	Word processing document	Microsoft Word 2003
.docx	Word processing document	Microsoft Word 2007
.wpd	Word processing document	Corel WordPerfect
.xlsx	Spreadsheet	Microsoft Excel 2007
.accdb	Database	Microsoft Access 2007
.pptx	PowerPoint presentation	Microsoft PowerPoint 2007
.pdf	Portable Document Format	Adobe Acrobat or Adobe Reader
.rtf	Text (Rich Text Format)	Any program that can read text documents
.txt	Text	Any program that can read text documents
.htm or .html	HyperText Markup Language for a Web page	Any program that can read HTML
.jpg	Joint Photographic Experts Group (JPEG) image	Most programs capable of displaying images
.gif	Graphics Interchange Format (GIF) image	Most programs capable of displaying images
.bmp	Bitmap image	Windows
.zip	Compressed file	WinZip

Select desired file format

Type file name

Change file type

Check to maintain compatibility with previous versions

Figure 23

When you save a file in Microsoft Word 2007, you can first (a) select in what format you would like the file to be saved, and then (b) type the file name in the Save As dialog box.

>The Save As features are displayed by selecting the Office button and then selecting **Save As**.

Naming Files

Are there special rules I have to follow when I name files? Files have names just like people. The first part of a file, or the **file name**, is similar to your first name, and is generally the name you assign to the file when you save it. For example, "bioreport" may be the name you assign a report you have completed for a biology class.

In a Windows application, an **extension**, or **file type**, follows the file name and a period or dot (.). Like a last name, this extension identifies what kind of family of files the file belongs to, or which application should be used to read the file. For example, if "bioreport" is a document created in Microsoft Works, it has a .wks extension and its name is "bioreport.wks." If the bioreport file is a Word 2007 document, then it has a .docx extension and its name is "bioreport.docx." Figure 22 lists some common file extensions and the types of documents they indicate.

Do I need to know the extension of a file to save it? As shown in Figure 23, when you save a file created in most applications running under the Windows operating system, you do not need to add the extension to the file name; it is added automatically for you. Mac and Linux operating systems do not require file extensions. This is because the information as to the type of application the computer should use to open the file is stored inside the file itself. However, if you're using these operating systems and will be sending files to Windows users, you should add an extension to your file name so that Windows can more easily open your files. To ease the frustration

of users of previous versions of Office, when using any Office 2007 application, you can choose to save the file in either a 2007 format or a 2003 or earlier format.

Are there things I shouldn't do when naming my files? Each operating system has its own naming conventions, or rules, which are listed in Figure 24. Beyond those conventions, it's important that you name your files so that you can easily identify them. A file name such as "research.docx" may be descriptive to you if you're only working on one research paper. However, if you create other research reports later and need to identify the contents of these files quickly, you'll soon wish

Figure 24 | FILE NAMING CONVENTIONS

	Mac OS	Windows
File and folder name length	As many as 255 characters*	As many as 255 characters
Case sensitive?	Yes	No
Forbidden characters	Colon (:)	" / \ * ? <<>	:
File extensions needed?	No	Yes
Path separator	Colon (:)	\

*Note: Although Mac OS X supports file names with as many as 255 characters, many applications running on OS X still support only file names with a maximum of 31 characters.

you had been more descriptive. Giving your files names that are more descriptive, such as bioresearch.docx or, better yet, bio101research.docx, is a good idea.

Keep in mind, however, that all files must be uniquely identified, unless they are saved in different folders or in different locations. Therefore, although files may share the same file name (such as "bioreport.docx" or "bioreport.xlsx") or share the same extension ("bioreport.xlsx" or "budget.xlsx"), no two files stored on the same device and folder can share *both* the same file name and the same extension.

How can I tell where my files are saved? When you save a file for the first time, you give the file a name and designate where you want to save it. For easy reference, the operating system includes default folders where files are saved unless you specify otherwise. In Windows, the default folders are "Documents" for files, "Downloads" for files downloaded from the Internet, "Music" for audio files, "Pictures" for graphic files, and "Videos" for video files. Although you can create your own folders, these default folders are the beginning of a well-organized system.

You can determine the location of a file by its **file path**. The file path starts with the drive in which the file is located and includes all folders, subfolders (if any), the file name, and the extension. For example, if you were saving a picture of Emily Brontë for a term paper for an English composition course, the file path might be C:\Users\Username\Documents\Spring 2010\English Comp\Term Paper\Illustrations\EBronte.jpg.

As shown in Figure 25, C is the drive on which the file is stored (in this case, the hard drive), and Documents is the file's primary folder. Spring 2010, English Comp, Term Paper, and Illustrations are successive subfolders within the Documents main folder. Last is the file name, EBronte, separated from the file extension (in this case, jpg) by a period. Notice that there are backslash characters (\) in between the drive, primary folder, subfolders, and file name. This backslash character, used by Windows and DOS,

is referred to as a **path separator**. Mac files use a colon (:), whereas UNIX and Linux files use the forward slash (/) as the path separator.

Working with Files

How can I move and copy files? Once you've located your file with Windows Explorer, you can perform many other file-management actions such as opening, copying, moving, renaming, and deleting files. You open a file by double-clicking the file from its storage location. Based on the file extension, the operating system then determines which application needs to be started to open the requested file and opens the file within the correct application automatically. You can copy a file to another location using the Copy command. When you copy a file, a duplicate file is created and the original file remains in its original location. To move a file from one location to another, use the Move command. When you move a file, the original file is deleted from its original location.

Where do deleted files go? The **Recycle Bin** is a folder on the desktop where files deleted from the hard drive reside until you permanently purge them from your system. Unfortunately, files deleted from other drives (such as a CD/DVD drive, flash drive, external hard drive, or network drive) do not go to the Recycle Bin but are deleted from the system immediately. (Mac systems have something similar to the Recycle Bin, called Trash, which is represented by a wastebasket icon. To delete files on a Mac, drag the files to Trash on the Dock.)

Figure 25

Understanding file paths.

How do I permanently delete files from my system? Files in the Recycle Bin or Trash are held only until they are permanently deleted. To delete your files from the Recycle Bin permanently, select Empty the Recycle Bin after right-clicking the desktop icon. On Macs, select Empty Trash from the Finder menu in OS X.

Utility Programs

You have learned that the operating system is the single most essential piece of software in your computer system because it coordinates all the system's activities and provides a means by which other software applications and users can interact with the system. However, there is another set of programs included in system software. Utility programs are small applications that perform special functions. Some utility programs help manage system resources (such as disk defragmenter utilities, or *defrag* utilities); others (such as screen savers) help make your time and work on the computer more pleasant; and still others (such as file compression utilities) improve efficiency.

Some of these utility programs are incorporated into the operating system. For example, Windows has its own firewall and file-compression utilities. Other utility programs, such as antivirus and security programs, are so large and require such frequent updating that they are sold as standalone programs or as Web-based services available for an annual fee. Sometimes utility programs, such as Norton SystemWorks, are offered as software suites, bundled with other useful maintenance and performance-boosting utilities. Still other utilities, like Lavasoft's Ad-Aware, are offered as freeware or shareware programs and are available as downloads from the Web.

Figure 27 illustrates some of the various types of utility programs available within the Windows operating system as well as those for sale as stand-alone programs. In general, the basic utilities designed to manage and tune the computer hardware are incorporated in the operating system. The stand-alone utility programs typically offer more features or an easier user interface for backup, security, diagnostic, or recovery functions.

In this section, we explore many of the utility programs you'll find installed on a

BITS AND BYTES — A File Type for Everyone

Imagine you are sending an e-mail to a diverse group of individuals. You are not sure what word processing software each of them uses, but you assume that there will be a mix of people who use Word, WordPerfect, and even Writer. How can you be sure that all users will be able to open the attachment regardless of the program installed on their computers? Save the file in Rich Text Format (.rtf), Portable Document Format (.pdf), or Text (.txt) format. Rich Text and Text files can be read by any modern word processing program, although some formatting may be lost when a document is saved in Text (.txt) format. Anyone can read a PDF file by downloading the Acrobat Reader from the Adobe Web site (**adobe.com**). To save files as RTF, PDF, or TXT files, simply change the file type when saving your file. In Microsoft Word, for example, you can select the file type in the Save As menu shown in Figure 26.

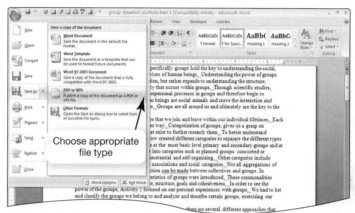

Figure 26

By changing a word processing file's type to PDF, RTF, or TXT (plain text), you can ensure that everyone can read your file, no matter which word processing program they are using.

Windows 7 operating system. Unless otherwise noted, you can find these utilities in the Control Panel or on the Start menu by selecting All Programs, Accessories, and then System Tools. (We also take a brief look at some Mac utilities.)

Display Utilities

How can I change the appearance of my desktop? The Personalization icon, found in Appearance and Personalization on the Control Panel, has all the features you need to change the appearance of your desktop. It provides different options for the desktop background, screen savers, and window colors. Although Windows

Windows Utility Program	Stand-Alone Windows Utility Program	Function
File Management		
Programs and Features		Properly installs and uninstalls software
Windows Explorer File Compression	WinZip	Reduces file size
Windows System Maintenance and Diagnostics		
Backup	Acronis True Image, Norton Ghost	Backs up important information
Disk Cleanup	CCleaner, McAfee Quick Clean	Removes unnecessary files from hard drive
Disk Defragmenter	Norton SystemWorks, Diskeeper	Arranges files on hard drive in sequential order
Error-checking (previously ScanDisk)		Checks hard drive for unnecessary or damaged files
System Restore	FarStone RestoreIT!, Norton Ghost	Restores system to a previous, stable state
Task Manager		Displays performance measures for processes; provides information on programs and processes running on computer
Task Scheduler		Schedules programs to run automatically at prescribed times

comes with many different background themes and screen saver options preinstalled, hundreds of downloadable options are available on the Web. Just search for "backgrounds" or "screen savers" on your favorite search engine to customize your desktop. Another way to access the background and screen saver options is to right-click an empty space on your desktop and choose Personalize from the shortcut menu.

Do I really need to use a screen saver? A **screen saver** is an animated image that appears on a computer monitor when no user activity has been sensed for a certain time. Originally, screen savers were used to prevent burn-in, the result of an image being burned into the phosphor inside the monitor's cathode ray tube when the same image was left on the monitor for long periods of time. Screen savers are now used almost exclusively for decoration.

You can control how long your computer sits idle before the screen saver starts. For example, if you don't want people looking at what's on your screen when you leave your computer unexpectedly for a time, you may want to program your screen saver to run after only a minute or two of inactivity. (Right-click on the Windows desktop, click Personalize, and then click Screen Saver on the bottom right of the personalization window.) However, if you find that you tend to let your computer sit inactive for a while but need to look at the screen image—while you study or read a document or spreadsheet, for example—you may want to extend the period of inactivity.

The Programs and Features Utility

What is the correct way to add new programs to the system? These days, when you install a new program, the program automatically runs a wizard (a step-by-step guide) that walks you through the installation process. If a wizard does not start automatically, you should go to the Programs and Features utility found in the Programs folder in the Control Panel. This prompts the operating system to look for the setup program of the new software and starts the installation wizard.

What is the correct way to remove unwanted programs from my system? Some people think that deleting a program from the Program Files folder on the C drive is the best way to remove a program from the system. However, most programs include support files such as a help file, dictionaries, and graphics files that are not located in the main program folder found in Program Files. Depending on the supporting file's function, support files can be scattered throughout various folders within the system. You would normally miss these files by deleting only the main program file from the system. By selecting the Windows uninstaller utility, Programs and Features (found in the Control Panel), you delete not only the main program file but also all supporting files and most registry entries.

File Compression Utilities

What is file compression? A file **compression utility** is a program that takes out redundancies in a file to reduce the file size. File compression is helpful

because it makes a large file more compact, making it easier and faster to send over the Internet, upload to a Web page, or save onto a disc. As shown in Figure 28, Windows has built-in compression (or zip) file support. There are also several stand-alone freeware and shareware programs, such as WinZip (for Windows) and StuffIt (for Windows or Mac), that you can obtain to compress your files.

How does file compression work? Most compression programs look for repeated patterns of letters and replace these patterns with a shorter placeholder. The repeated patterns and the associated placeholder are cataloged and stored temporarily in a separate file called the *dictionary*. For example, in the following sentence, you can easily see the repeated patterns of letters.

The rain **in Sp**ain **falls m**ain**ly on the pl**ain**.**

Although this example contains obvious repeated patterns (**ain** and **the**), in a large document the repeated patterns may be more complex. The compression program's algorithm (a set of instructions designed to complete a solution in a step-by-step manner) therefore runs through the file several times to determine the optimal repeated patterns to use to obtain the greatest compression.

How effective are file compression programs? The effectiveness of file compression—that is, how much a file's size is reduced—depends on several factors, including the type and size of the individual

Figure 28

(a) File compression is a built-in utility of the Windows operating system. (b) Compressing the PowerPoint document reduced the file size from 1,935 KB to 1,453 KB.

>To access the Windows file compression utility, right-click the file or folder that is to be compressed, select **Send to** from the shortcut menu, and then select **Compressed (zipped) Folder**.

Compression reduces file size from 1935 KB to 1453 KB

Utility Programs

STEP 1: Right-click zipped folder.

STEP 2: Select Extract All...

STEP 3: Browse to storage location.

STEP 4: Extracted file displays in selected location.

Figure 29

The Extraction Wizard in Windows makes unzipping compressed folders and files easy.

file and the compression method used. Current compression programs can reduce text files by as much as 50 percent. However, some files, such as PDF files, already contain a form of compression, so they do not need to be compressed further. Other file types, especially some graphics and audio formats, have gone through a compression process that reduces file size by permanently discarding data. For example, image files such as Joint Photographic Experts Group (JPEG), Graphics Interchange Format (GIF), and Portable Network Graphics (PNG) files discard small variations in color that the human eye may not pick up. Likewise, MP3 files permanently discard sounds that the human ear cannot hear. These graphic and audio files do not need further compression.

How do I decompress a file I've compressed? When you want to restore the file to its original state, you need to decompress the file so that the pieces of file that the compression process temporarily removed are restored to the document. Generally, the program you used to compress the file has the capability to decompress the file as well (see Figure 29).

System Maintenance Utilities

Are there any utilities that make my system work faster? Disk Cleanup is a Windows utility that cleans, or removes, unnecessary files from your hard drive. These include files that have accumulated in

the Recycle Bin as well as temporary files, which are files created by Windows to store data temporarily when a program is running. Windows usually deletes these temporary files when you exit the program, but sometimes it forgets to do this, or doesn't have time because your system freezes up or incurs a problem that prevents you from properly exiting a program. Disk Cleanup, found by clicking the Start button, then selecting All Programs, Accessories folder, and then the System Tools folder, also removes temporary Internet files (Web pages stored on your hard drive for quick viewing) as well as offline Web pages (pages stored on your computer so you can view them without being connected to the Internet). If not deleted periodically, these unnecessary files can hinder efficient operating performance.

How can I control which files Disk Cleanup deletes? When you run Disk Cleanup, the program scans your hard drive to determine which folders have files that can be deleted and calculates the amount of hard drive space that would be freed by doing so. You check off which type of files you would like to delete, as shown in Figure 30.

What else can I do if my system runs slowly? Over time, as you add and delete information in a file, the file pieces are saved in scattered locations on the hard drive. Locating all the pieces of the file takes extra time, making the operating system less efficient. Windows **Disk Defragmenter** regroups related pieces of files on the hard drive, thereby allowing the OS to work more efficiently. You can find the Windows Disk Defragmenter utility by clicking the Start menu, then All Programs, Accessories, and then System Tools. Using the Windows Disk Defragmenter Analyzer feature, you should check several times a year to determine whether your drive needs to be defragmented. Unfortunately, Macs do not have a defrag utility built into the system because developers thought that the file system used by Mac OS X was so efficient that defragging the hard drive would be unnecessary. Those users who feel the need to defrag their Mac can use iDefrag, an external program that can be purchased from Coriolis Systems.

Total space to be freed

Space freed with the selections

Description of folder contents

Figure 30

Using Disk Cleanup will help free space on your hard drive.

>Disk Cleanup is accessed by clicking **Start**, **All Programs**, **Accessories**, and then **System Tools**.

How do I diagnose potential errors or damage on my storage devices? Error-checking, once known as ScanDisk, is a Windows utility that checks for lost files and fragments as well as physical errors on your hard drive. Lost files and fragments of files occur as you save, resave, move, delete, and copy files on your hard drive. Sometimes the system becomes confused, leaving references on the **file allocation table** or **FAT** (an index of all sector numbers in a table) to files that no longer exist or have been moved. Physical errors on the hard drive occur when the mechanism that reads the hard drive's data (which is stored as 1s or 0s) can no longer determine whether the area holds a 1 or a 0. These areas are called *bad sectors*. Sometimes Error-checking can recover the lost data, but more often, it deletes the files that are unnecessarily taking up space. Error-checking also makes a note of any bad sectors so that the system will not use them again to store data.

Where can I find Error-checking? Starting with Windows XP, the Error-checking utility is located in Disk Properties. To locate Error-checking, after clicking Computer from the Start menu, right-click the disk you

want to diagnose, select Properties, and select Tools. In earlier versions of the Windows operating system, Error-checking, known as ScanDisk, was located in System Tools. On Macs, you can use the Disk Utility to test and repair disks. You will find Disk Utility in the Utilities folder in the Applications folder on your hard drive.

How can I check on a program that has stopped running? If a program has stopped working, you can use the Windows **Task Manager utility** to check on the program or to exit the nonresponsive program. Although you can access Task Manager from the Control Panel, it is more easily accessible by pressing Ctrl + Alt and then the Delete key or by right-clicking an empty space on the taskbar at the bottom of your screen. The Applications tab of Task Manager lists all programs that you are using and indicates whether they are working properly (running) or have stopped improperly (not responding). You can terminate programs that are not responding by clicking the End Task button in the dialog box.

If you need outside assistance because of a program error, Dr. Watson for Windows, a tool that is included in Microsoft Windows XP, and Problem Reports and Solutions, a tool in Windows Vista and Windows 7, gather information about the computer when there is a program error. When an error occurs, these tools automatically create and save a text log. The log can then be viewed, printed, or delivered electronically to any technical support professional, who can then use this information to help diagnose the problem.

ACTIVE HELP-DESK Using Utility Programs

In this Active Helpdesk call, you'll play the role of a helpdesk staffer, fielding calls about the utility programs included in system software and what these programs do.

Utility Programs

227

To understand how disk defragmenter utilities work, you must first understand the basics of how a hard disk drive stores files. A hard disk drive is composed of several *platters*, or round, thin plates of metal, that are covered with a special magnetic coating that records the data. The platters are about 3.5 inches in diameter and are stacked onto a spindle. There are usually two or three platters in any hard disk drive, with data stored on one or both sides. Data is recorded on hard disks in concentric circles called tracks. Each **track** is further broken down into pie-shaped wedges, each called a **sector** (see Figure 31). The data is further identified by *clusters*, which are the smallest segments within the sectors.

When you want to save (or write) a file, the bits that make up your file are recorded onto one or more clusters of the drive. To keep track of which clusters hold which files, the drive also stores an index of all sector numbers in a table. To save a file, the computer will look in the table for clusters that are not already being used. It will then record the file information on those clusters. When you open (or read) a file, the computer searches through the table for the clusters that hold the desired file and reads that file. Similarly, when you delete a file, you are actually not deleting the file itself, but rather the reference in the table to the file.

How does a disk become fragmented? When only part of an older file is deleted, the deleted section of the file creates a gap in the sector of the disk where the data was originally stored. In the same way, when new information is added to an older file, there may not be space to save the new information sequentially near where the file was originally saved. In that case, the system writes the added part of the file to the next available location on the disk, and a reference is made in the table as to the location of this file fragment. Over time, as files are saved, deleted, and modified, the bits of information for various files fall out of sequential order and the disk becomes fragmented.

Disk fragmentation is a problem because the operating system is not as efficient when a disk is fragmented. It takes longer to locate a whole file because more of the disk must be searched for the various pieces, greatly slowing down the performance of your computer.

How can you make the files line up more efficiently on the disk? At this stage, the disk defragmenter utility enters the picture. The defragmenter tool takes the hard drive through a defragmentation process in which pieces of files that are scattered over the disk are placed together and arranged sequentially on the hard disk. Also, any unused portions of clusters that were too small to save data in before are grouped, increasing the available storage space on the disk. Figure 32 shows before and after shots of a fragmented disk that has gone through the defragmentation process.

For more about hard disks and defragmenting, be sure to check out the Sound Byte "Hard Disk Anatomy Interactive."

Fragmented files on disk

Defragmented files on disk

Figure 31

On a hard disk platter, data is recorded onto tracks, which are further broken down into sectors and clusters.

Track

Sector

Cluster

Figure 32

Defragmenting the hard drive arranges file fragments so that they are located next to each other. This makes the hard drive run more efficiently.

System Restore and Backup Utilities

Is there an undo command for the system? Say you have just installed a new software program and your computer freezes. After rebooting the computer, when you try to start the application, the system freezes once again. You uninstall the new program, but your computer continues to freeze after rebooting. What can you do now?

The most recent versions of Windows have a utility called **System Restore** that lets you roll your system settings back to a specific date when everything was working properly. A System Restore point is made every day you use your computer. You also can create a custom restore point if needed, such as before installing new software or hardware. Should problems occur, if the computer was running just fine before you installed new software or a hardware device, you could restore your computer to the settings that were in effect before the software or hardware installation. System Restore does not affect your personal data files (such as Microsoft Word documents, browsing history, or e-mail), so you won't lose changes made to these files when you use System Restore. You can find System Restore by clicking Start, All Programs, Accessories, and then System Tools.

How does the computer remember its previous settings? Every time you start your computer or install a new application or driver, Windows automatically creates a snapshot of your entire system's settings. This snapshot is called a **restore point**. You also can create and name your own restore points at any time. Creating a restore point is a good idea before making changes to your computer such as installing hardware or software. If something goes wrong with the installation process, Windows can reset your system to the restore point. As shown in Figure 33, Windows includes a Restore Point Wizard that walks you through the process of setting restore points.

SOUND BYTE

Hard Disk Anatomy Interactive

In this Sound Byte, you'll watch a series of animations that show various aspects of a hard drive, including the anatomy of a hard drive, how a computer reads and writes data to a hard drive, and the fragmenting and defragmenting of a hard drive.

How can I protect my data in the event something malfunctions in my system? When you use the Windows **Backup and Restore utility** (found in the Control Panel), you can create a duplicate copy of all the data on your hard drive (or just the folders and files you specify) and copy it to another storage device, such as a DVD or external hard drive. A backup copy protects your data in the event your hard drive fails or files are accidentally erased. Although you may not need to back up every file on your computer, you should back up the files that are most important to you and keep the backup copy in a safe location. Mac OS X Snow Leopard includes a backup utility called Time Machine that will automatically back up your files to a specified location. Apple also offers backup hardware called Time Capsules, which are wireless devices designed to work with Time Machine and record your backup data.

The Task Scheduler Utility

How can I remember to perform all these maintenance procedures? To keep your computer system in top shape, it is important to run some of the utilities

Figure 33

Setting a restore point is good practice before installing any hardware or software.

>The Restore Point Wizard is found by clicking **Start**, **All Programs**, **Accessories**, **System Tools**. In the System Tools folder, click **System Restore**. The System Restore wizard appears, with Restore Point shown on the first page of the Wizard.

Utility Programs

229

described previously on a routine basis. Depending on your usage, you may want to defrag your hard drive or clean out temporary Internet files periodically. However, many computer users forget to initiate these tasks. Luckily, the Windows **Task Scheduler utility**, shown in Figure 34, allows you to schedule tasks to run automatically at predetermined times, with no additional action necessary on your part.

SOUND BYTE

Letting Your Computer Clean Up After Itself

In this Sound Byte, you'll learn how to use the various maintenance utilities within the operating system. In addition, you'll learn how to use Task Scheduler to clean up your hard drive automatically. You'll also learn the best times of the day to schedule these maintenance tasks, and why they should be done on a routine basis to make your system more efficient.

Accessibility Utilities

Are there utilities designed for users with special needs? Microsoft Windows includes an Ease of Access Center, which is a centralized location for assistive technology and tools to adjust accessibility settings. In the Ease of Access Center, you can find tools to help you adjust the screen contrast, magnify the screen image, have screen contents read to you, and display an on-screen keyboard, as more fully explained in the following list. If you're not sure where to start or what settings might help, a questionnaire asks you about routine tasks and provides a personalized recommendation for settings that will help you use your computer (see Figure 35). Some of these features are described below.

- **High Contrast:** Allows you to select a color scheme setting in which you can control the contrast between text and background. Because some visually impaired individuals find it easier to see white text on a dark background, there are color schemes that invert screen colors.

- **Magnifier:** A utility that creates a separate window that displays a magnified portion of the screen. This feature makes the screen more readable for users who have impaired vision.

Figure 34

To keep your machine running in top shape, use Task Scheduler to schedule maintenance programs to run automatically at selected times and days.

>Task Scheduler is found by clicking **Start**, **All Programs**, **Accessories**, and then **System Tools**.

Word Bank

- Disk Defragmenter
- Error-checking
- file compression
- file management
- files
- folders
- Linux
- Mac OS
- platform
- system files
- system software
- Task Manager
- Task Scheduler
- tracks
- utility programs
- Windows
- Windows Explorer
- Windows 7

Instructions: Fill in the blanks using the words from the Word Bank above.

Veena was looking into buying a new computer and was trying to decide what (1) _____ to buy—a PC or a Mac. She had used PCs all her life, so she was more familiar with the (2) _____ operating system. Still, she liked the way the (3) _____ looked and was considering switching. Her brother didn't like either operating system, so he used (4) _____, a free operating system instead.

After a little research, Veena decided to buy a PC. With it, she got the most recent version of Windows, (5) _____. She vowed that with this computer, she'd practice better (6) _____ because she often had a hard time finding files on her old computer. To view all of the folders on her computer, she opened (7) _____. She made sure that she gave descriptive names to her (8) _____ and placed them in organized (9) _____ and libraries.

Veena also decided that with her new computer, she'd pay more attention to the (10) _____, those little special-function programs that help with maintenance and repairs. These special-function programs, in addition to the OS, make up the (11) _____. Veena looked into some of the more frequently used utilities. She thought it would be a good idea to run the (12) _____ on her hard drive regularly so that all the files lined up in sequentially ordered (13) _____ and so that it was more efficient. She also looked into (14) _____ utilities, which would help her reduce the size of her files when she sent them to others over the Internet. Finally, she decided to use the Windows (15) _____ utility to schedule tasks automatically so that she wouldn't forget.

becoming computer literate

Using key terms from the chapter, write a letter to your 70-year-old aunt who just received her first computer, explaining the benefits of simple computer maintenance. First, explain any symptoms her computer may be experiencing (such as a sluggish Internet connection); then include a set of steps she can follow in setting up a regimen to remedy each problem. Make sure you explain some of the system utilities described in this chapter, including but not limited to Disk Defragmenter, Disk Cleanup, and Task Scheduler. Include any other utilities she might need, and explain why she should have them.

self-test

Instructions: Answer the multiple-choice and true–false questions below for more practice with key terms and concepts from this chapter.

Multiple Choice

1. Smartphones use which category of operating system?
   a. Single-user, single-task
   b. Multiuser, multitask
   c. Single-user, multitask
   d. Real-time

2. Which best describes Gadgets and widgets?
   a. Smaller versions of traditional peripheral devices
   b. Mini programs that display on the desktop
   c. The most commonly used programs displayed at the bottom of the desktop
   d. Other names for icons and shortcuts

3. Virtual memory is
   a. unlimited in capacity.
   b. borrowed space on the hard drive.
   c. another name for RAM.
   d. synonymous with cache memory.

4. Plug and Play devices
   a. don't require drivers.
   b. have drivers included in the Windows OS.
   c. must be installed using Add or Remove Programs.
   d. None of the above.

5. Which is not a function of the operating system?
   a. Providing a means for the user to interact with the computer
   b. Enabling the processor to handle multiple operations, seemingly at the same time
   c. Carefully shutting the system down when RAM limits have been reached
   d. Facilitating installation of peripheral devices with the inclusion of drivers

6. The term that defines the condition that occurs when your system is running out of virtual memory is
   a. thrashing.   c. caching.
   b. multitasking.   d. paging.

7. Which view option would be best to sort picture or presentation files?
   a. Details   c. Large Icons
   b. Tiles   d. All of the above

8. Which of the following file names indicates a file created by a word processing program in the Office 2007 suite?
   a. bioreport.xls
   b. bioreport.docx
   c. bioreport.jpg
   d. All of the above

9. Which utility would you use to help manage your files and folders?
   a. System Restore
   b. Disk Defragmenter
   c. Windows Explorer
   d. Disk Cleanup

10. Which utility is NOT an accessibility utility?
    a. Magnifier
    b. Narrator
    c. Windows Speech Recognition
    d. File Compression

True–False

_____ 1. All computing devices need some form of operating system software.

_____ 2. Symbian OS is a common OS for smartphones.

_____ 3. Linux is not a common OS because it's more expensive than Windows or Mac OS.

_____ 4. Because of virtual memory, it is not possible for a computer to run out of memory.

_____ 5. Files deleted from a flash drive end up in the Recycle Bin.

Using System Software: The Operating System, Utility Programs, and File Management

1. Organizing Files and Folders

It's the beginning of a new semester and you promise yourself that you are going to keep all files related to your schoolwork more organized this semester. Develop a plan that outlines how you'll set up libraries, folders, and subfolders for each subject. Identify at least three different folders for each class. If time and schedule permit, discuss your organization scheme with your instructor.

2. OS Compatibility Issues

Your school requires that you purchase a notebook computer. All your other family members, as well as your school, use computers with Windows operating system. However, you really want a Mac notebook.

a. Research the compatibility issues between Mac and Windows computers.
b. How does a smartphone using Symbian OS fit into the equation?
c. Can you synchronize the smartphone with either or both machines?
d. Explore the application called Boot Camp. What does it do? Would it be helpful in this situation?

3. Understanding Safe Mode

It is the night before the major term paper for your philosophy class is due. Your best friend comes screaming down the hall, begging for help. His only copy of his draft paper is on his notebook, and the computer is suddenly booting up with the words "Safe Mode" in the corners of the screen. What would be the most useful questions to ask him? What steps would you take to debug the problem? If you cannot get the computer to come out of Safe mode, is there a way to retrieve the draft? How many times will you say, "Make backups!" that evening?

4. Software Requirements

This semester you upgraded to the most recent operating system and productivity software on your notebook to match what your college is using. You know which courses you'll be taking next semester, and you realize they will require the installation of more applications. A friend who is in a similar position tells you she's not worried about putting that much software on her computer because she has a really big hard drive.

a. Is hard drive storage your only concern? Should you also worry more about having sufficient RAM? How will your use of the software on your computer affect your answer?
b. Does virtual memory management by your operating system allow you to ignore RAM requirements?

5. Connecting Peripherals

You are considering upgrading to the latest version of Windows. Your current notebook computer is approximately three years old.

a. What concerns would you have about upgrading?
b. How would you determine if your peripheral devices would work with the new OS?
c. Would you consider switching to Linux instead? What are the pros and cons of this decision?

1. Organizing Files and Folders

You have started a new job and have a new computer. You never kept your files and folders organized on the computer you used when in college, but now you are determined to do a better job at keeping your files organized. You know you need folders for the several clients with whom you will be working. For each client, you'll need to have folders for billing information, client documents, and account information. In addition, you need folders for the MP3 files and video files you will listen to and watch when you're not working, as well as a folder for the digital pictures you'll take for personal and company reasons. Finally, you're working toward an advanced degree and will be taking business finance and introductory marketing courses at night, so you'll need folders for all the homework assignments for both courses.

Determine the file structure you would need to create to accommodate your needs. Start with the C drive and use the default Libraries in addition to using Documents, Pictures, Video, and Music as the default folders for documents, pictures, video, and music files, respectively. Also create any new libraries that you feel are necessary to further organize your data, and include references to whatever folders should be included in each library.

2. Using Mac Utility Programs

Your company has been having trouble with some of its Mac computers, which are running inefficiently. Your boss asks you to research the utility programs your company could use on its Macs to make them run more efficiently. In particular, your boss would like you to determine what utilities are available in the Mac OS and then determine what utilities the company may need to purchase. In addition, your boss wants to ensure the availability of a disk defragmenting utility, a file compression utility, and a diagnostic utility you could run to check the hard drive for errors. Using the Internet for your research, what utilities are already in the Mac OS, and what stand-alone utilities can you purchase? Will they run on all versions of the Mac OS?

3. Monitoring Activities with the OS

The company that you work for has just announced a new internal accounting structure. From now on, each department will be charged individually for the costs associated with computer usage, such as backup storage space and Internet usage.

a. Research how the operating system may be set up to monitor such activity by department.
b. What other activities do you think the operating system can be set up to monitor?

4. Choosing the Best OS

Your new boss is considering moving some of the department operations away from Windows-based computer systems. He asks you to research the advantages and disadvantages of moving to Linux or Mac OS X. How would these choices affect his department in the following areas?

a. Budget for technical support for the systems
b. Choice and budget for hardware for the systems
c. Costs of implementation
d. Possibility for future upgrades

Using System Software: The Operating System, Utility Programs, and File Management

Instructions: Albert Einstein used *Gedankenexperiments* or critical thinking questions, to develop his theory of relativity. Some ideas are best understood by experimenting with them in our own minds. The following critical thinking questions are designed to demand your full attention but require only a comfortable chair—no technology.

1. Open Source Pros and Cons

Open source programming embraces a philosophy that states programmers should make their code available to everyone rather than keeping it proprietary. The Linux operating system has had much success as an open source code. The chapter mentions some of the advantages of open source code, such as quicker code updates in response to technological advances and changes.

a. What are other advantages of open source code?
b. Can you think of disadvantages to open source code?
c. Why do you think that companies such as Microsoft maintain proprietary restrictions on their code?
d. Are there disadvantages to maintaining proprietary code?

2. The OS of the Future

Operating system interfaces have evolved from a text-based console format to the current graphical user interface. What direction do you think they will move toward next? How could operating systems be organized and used in a manner that is more responsive to humans and better suited to how we think? Are there alternatives to hierarchical file structures for storage? Can you think of ways in which operating systems could adapt and customize themselves based on your usage?

3. Which OS Would You Choose?

Suppose you are building a computer system from scratch and have complete discretion as to your choice of operating system. Which one would you install, and why?

4. The OS: With or Without Utilities?

Which do you think is better for consumers: to have companies develop smaller, more inexpensive operating systems and then allow competing companies to develop and market utility programs, or to have companies develop extremely large, full-featured operating systems that include most utilities as operating system features? Do you think that including utility programs with an operating system makes the cost of the operating system higher?

Choosing the Best OS

Problem

You have been hired to help set up the technology requirements for a small advertising company. The company is holding off on buying anything until it makes a decision as to the platform on which the computers should run. Obviously, one of the critical decisions is the choice of operating system.

Task

Recommend the appropriate operating system for the company.

Process

1. Break up into three teams. Each team will examine one of the three primary operating systems today: Windows, Mac, and Linux.
2. As a team, research the pros and cons of your operating system. What features does it have that would benefit your company? What features does it not have that your company would need? Why (or why not) would your operating system be the appropriate choice? Why is your OS better (or worse) than either of the other two options?
3. Develop a presentation that states your position with regard to your operating system. Your presentation should have a recommendation and include facts to back it up.
4. As a class, decide which operating system would be the best choice for the company.

Conclusion

Because the operating system is the most critical piece of software in the computer system, the selection should not be taken lightly. The OS that is best for an advertising agency may not be best for an accounting firm. It is important to make sure you consider all aspects of the work environment and the type of work that is being done to ensure a good fit.

Using System Software: The Operating System, Utility Programs, and File Management

In addition to the review materials presented here, you'll find additional materials featured with the Pearson IT Multimedia Library and the Companion Website (**pearsonhighered.com/techinaction**), which will help reinforce your understanding of the chapter content. These materials include the following:

Active Helpdesk

In Active Helpdesk calls, you'll assume the role of helpdesk operator, taking calls about the concepts you've learned in this chapter. You'll apply what you've learned and receive feedback from a supervisor to review and reinforce those concepts. The Active Helpdesk calls for this chapter are listed below and can be found on the Pearson IT Multimedia Library:

- Managing Hardware and Peripheral Devices: The OS
- Starting the Computer: The Boot Process
- Organizing Your Computer: File Management
- Using Utility Programs

Sound Bytes

Sound Bytes are dynamic multimedia tutorials that help demystify even the most complex topics. You'll view video clips and animations that illustrate computer concepts and then apply what you've learned by reviewing with the Sound Byte Labs, which include quizzes and activities specifically tailored to each Sound Byte. The Sound Bytes for this chapter are listed below and can be found on the Pearson IT Multimedia Library:

- Customizing Windows
- File Management
- File Compression
- Hard Disk Anatomy Interactive
- Letting Your Computer Clean Up After Itself

Companion Website

The *Technology in Action* Companion Website includes a variety of additional materials to help you review and learn more about the topics in this chapter. The resources available at **pearsonhighered.com/techinaction** include:

- **Online Study Guide.** This chapter features an online true–false and multiple-choice quiz. You can take these quizzes, automatically check the results, and e-mail the results to your instructor.
- **Web Research Projects.** This chapter features several Web research projects that ask you to search the Web for information on computer-related careers, milestones in computer history, important people and companies, emerging technologies, and the applications and implications of different technologies.

Technology in Focus:

Computing Alternatives

HomeStudio\Shutterstock

Computing|Alternatives

You may think that there are no viable alternatives to buying computers that run Microsoft Windows and use Microsoft Office applications such as Word and Excel. In this Technology in Focus feature, we explore software and hardware alternatives to Microsoft products, many of which may provide you with less expensive and more flexible options. Let's get started by looking at alternatives to Microsoft Office products.

Application Software Alternatives

Proprietary (or commercial) software is developed by corporations such as Microsoft and Apple to be sold for a profit. Opponents of proprietary software contend that software should be developed without profit motive and that the source code (the actual lines of instructional code that make the program work) should be made available so that others may modify or improve the software.

Open source software is freely distributed (no royalties accrue to the creators), contains the source code, and can in turn be distributed to others. Therefore, you can download open source software for free from various Web sites, install it on as many computers as you wish, make changes to the source code if you know how to do this, and redistribute it to anyone you wish (as long as you don't charge for distributing it). In this section, we look at some open source software that you can download and use on your computer. For a list of open source resources available on the Web, visit **sourceforge.net**.

PRODUCTIVITY SOFTWARE ALTERNATIVES: OPENOFFICE

The OpenOffice.org suite (which we'll refer to as OpenOffice) is a free suite of productivity software programs that provides functionality similar to that of Microsoft Office. Versions of OpenOffice are available for a variety of operating systems, including Windows, Linux, and Mac. It currently offers support in more than 100 languages besides English, with more being added all the time by the development community. You can download the installation file you'll need to run OpenOffice at **openoffice.org**. The minimum system requirements for installing OpenOffice 3 in a Windows environment are less than those required for Microsoft Office.

The main components of OpenOffice are word processing (Writer), spreadsheet (Calc), presentation (Impress), and database (Base) programs. These provide functionality similar to that of the Word, Excel, PowerPoint, and Access applications you might be familiar with in Microsoft Office.

The OpenOffice 3 suite also includes additional programs. Draw provides the most common tools needed to communicate using graphics and diagrams, and Math creates equations and formulas for your documents.

The great advantage of OpenOffice is its compatibility with most programs. This means that if your friend uses Microsoft Office and you send her an OpenOffice file, she can still read it, and you can read all of her Microsoft Office files, too. OpenOffice 3 is able to open Microsoft Office 2007 or 2010 files without the need for a conversion program. Although the individual applications in OpenOffice are not as fully featured as those in Microsoft Office, and do not have the ribbon interface found in the newest versions of the Office applications, it is still a powerful productivity software suite, and the price is right.

When you launch OpenOffice via the **Quickstarter** icon (see Figure 1), you can choose a file type from the list displayed in the Templates and Documents dialog box. Once you select the appropriate file type (such as spreadsheet, presentation, or text) and click Open, the appropriate application and a new, blank document will open so that you can begin working.

FIGURE 1

Clicking the OpenOffice Quickstarter icon (in the system tray on the bottom right) displays a list of file types from which you can choose to begin working on your project.

Writer

Writer, the OpenOffice word processing application, is extremely similar in look and feel to Microsoft Word 2003 (see Figure 2). As is the case in Word, you can easily change text appearance in Writer by altering font type, style, alignment, and color. You can also easily insert graphics (pictures or clip art), tables, and hyperlinks into documents. Writer's wizards provide you with several templates you can use to create standard documents such as faxes, agendas, and letters. Special tools in Writer also allow you to create bibliographic references, indexes, and tables of contents.

When saving a document in Writer, the default file format has an .odt extension. By using the Save As command, you can save files in other formats, such as various versions of Word (.doc and .docx), Pocket Word (.psw) for mobile devices, Rich Text Format (.rtf), Text (.txt), and HTML Document (.htm). The handy Export Directly as PDF icon in Writer allows you to save documents as PDF files.

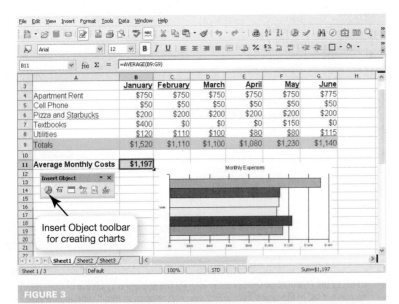

FIGURE 2

Writer provides similar functionality and icons to Microsoft Word.

Callouts in figure: Click to save as PDF — Formatting tasks and icons similar to Word

FIGURE 3

Calc offers many of the same features as Microsoft Excel.

Callout in figure: Insert Object toolbar for creating charts

Calc

Once you open a Calc spreadsheet, you enter text, numbers, and formulas into the appropriate cells, just as you would in Microsoft Excel. You also can apply a full range of formatting options (font size, color, style, and so on) to the cells, making it easy to create files such as the monthly budget spreadsheet shown in Figure 3. Built-in formulas and functions simplify the job of creating spreadsheets, and Calc's Function Wizard guides you through the wide range of available functions, providing suggestions as to which function to use.

When saving a document in Calc, the default file format has an .ods extension. You can also save files in other formats, such as Excel (.xls and .xlsx) and Pocket Excel (.pxl) for use on mobile devices. The handy Export Directly as PDF icon is also available in Calc.

Impress

When you select Presentation from the OpenOffice start-up interface, a wizard is displayed that offers you the option of creating a blank Impress presentation or building one from supplied templates. Compared to the vast array of stunning templates in Microsoft PowerPoint, the templates supplied with Impress are less than impressive. Still, it is easy to construct attractive slides and save them as templates. You can also "Google" the words "OpenOffice.org Impress Templates." You'll find a wide variety of templates for Impress that others have created and that you can download free of charge. To help you in the search, OpenOffice installation includes the option of installing the Google search bar (Web or Desktop), which will appear in the taskbar, making it easy to access while you are working in any of the OpenOffice applications.

Web-Based Alternatives

Open source alternatives to Microsoft Office applications are attractive because they are free, and they are also convenient because of their availability. Like most other applications, though, you can only use these programs with the computer on which they were installed. For ultimate accessibility and transferability, consider using Web-based Office software alternatives. With only a computer and an Internet connection, you can be productive almost anywhere because you access these programs from the Internet without having to install the software on your computer. Moreover, with Web-based applications you can collaborate on a document online with others, thus avoiding the coordination mess that generally occurs when transferring documents among colleagues or classmates via e-mail. Google Docs includes Web-based word processing, spreadsheet, and presentation applications. These applications, while useful for sharing and creating basic documents, lack many of the more robust features that Microsoft Office and other proprietary programs have.

Zoho (**zoho.com**) is another great Web-based productivity suite that features project management software, customer relationship management software, and other business solutions in addition to the traditional productivity applications. ThinkFree Office Live (**thinkfree.com**) is an online productivity suite comprising word processing (ThinkFree Write), spreadsheets (ThinkFree Calc), and presentations (ThinkFree Show). ThinkFree also offers ThinkFree Office for desktops and ThinkFree Mobile for smartphones and other mobile devices. Many of the features are available to you without your having to register and create an account, and Web services are supported in English and many Asian languages. Like Google and Zoho, ThinkFree applications are fully compatible with Microsoft Office—including the latest formats—and run on Mac, Windows, and Linux platforms.

Base

If you want to create or just manipulate databases, Base enables you to create and modify tables, forms, queries, and reports by using wizards, design views, and SQL views. Base is similar to Microsoft Access and SQL Server, and works seamlessly with files created in most database applications, although you will need a separate converter to work with Microsoft Access 2007.

DATABASE SOFTWARE ALTERNATIVES: MYSQL

While Base, the OpenOffice database program described above, is perfectly functional, if you're interested in getting your hands on a free high-end SQL database application, the most popular open source option is MySQL (**mysql.com**). Sporting many of the features contained in SQL Server and Oracle Database 11g, MySQL is a powerful database program you can use to develop serious database applications. The two main components you should download and install with MySQL are the Database Server and the Query Browser (see Figure 4). You

use the Database Server to create tables for your database and enter your data. The Query Browser provides a visual interface for the database to display the results of queries you create.

FIGURE 4

MySQL is a free open source database alternative to Microsoft Access.

Although it is more difficult to learn and use than Microsoft Access, many books and online tutorials are available to help you get MySQL up and running.

E-MAIL CLIENT ALTERNATIVES: THUNDERBIRD AND EUDORA

If you are exploring other choices for Microsoft Office productivity applications, don't overlook other e-mail clients as alternatives to Microsoft Outlook. Mozilla Thunderbird is an open source e-mail client that has many enhancements that allow you to organize e-mail with tagging, folders, search, and saved search features. The latest version, Mozilla Thunderbird 2, has increased security and privacy measures so that messages received and sent remain safe. Plenty of add-ons, including a blog editor, calendar, calculator, and multimedia tools, are available from the Mozilla Web site (**mozilla.org**). Thunderbird can run on Windows, Mac, and Linux platforms. Eudora, another popular e-mail client, is currently being retrofitted by Qualcomm and other contributors into an open source application. Eudora8 is in beta testing at the time of this writing and is based on the same technology as Mozilla Thunderbird.

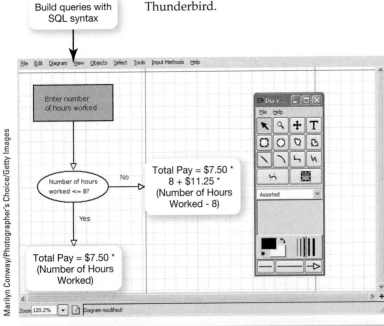

FIGURE 5

With Dia, you can create simple flowcharts, which a computer programmer might use in developing algorithms.

DRAWING SOFTWARE ALTERNATIVES: DRAW AND DIA

Microsoft Visio is a popular program for creating flowcharts and diagrams. However, Visio is not inexpensive. As mentioned previously, OpenOffice includes a program called Draw that allows you to create simple graphs, charts, and diagrams. Another option is Dia, a free program that allows you to create Visio-like diagrams and charts (see Figure 5). You can download a Windows-compatible version of Dia from **live.gnome.org/Dia**. The Web site also offers a tutorial to get you up and running.

Google offers yet another charting option. SketchUp (**sketchup.google. com**) is a full-featured 3D modeling software application. SketchUp comes in two versions. SketchUp7 is a free program that you can use to create, modify, and share 3D models. SketchUp Pro 7 is more fully featured and is available for less than $500.

WEB PAGE AUTHORING SOFTWARE ALTERNATIVES: SEAMONKEY

Although Microsoft Word and OpenOffice Writer can save documents as HTML files, sometimes you need a more versatile tool for creating Web pages, especially for larger sites with many linked pages. Adobe Dreamweaver is a popular commercial package for building Web sites, and Expression Web is a Web authoring application that is complementary to the Microsoft Office 2007 suite. Both of those solutions are proprietary applications that you must purchase. If you are looking for an open source alternative, SeaMonkey Composer, part of the SeaMonkey all-in-one Internet application suite (**seamonkey-project.org**), is a free, open source WYSIWYG ("what you see is what you get") Web authoring application that is compatible with the Windows, Mac, and Linux platforms. SeaMonkey Composer (see Figure 6) supports cascading style sheets, positioned layers, and dynamic image and table resizing. The SeaMonkey suite also includes a Web browser, e-mail and newsgroup client, and IRC chat.

IMAGE EDITING SOFTWARE ALTERNATIVES: GIMP

Do you need to create or edit some digital art but can't afford a high-end package such as Adobe Photoshop, or even a consumer package such as Adobe Photoshop Elements? Download a free copy of GIMP (short for GNU Image Manipulation Program) at **gimp.org** and you'll find a set of tools almost as powerful as Photoshop. GIMP is available for systems running Windows, Mac, Linux, and UNIX. Many good tutorials, available at **gimp.org/ tutorials**, can turn you into an accomplished user in no time.

Here are some handy things you can do with GIMP in five minutes or less:

- Crop or change the size of an image (see Figure 7).
- Reduce the file size of an image by decreasing its quality.
- Flip an image or rotate an image 90 degrees.

GIMP also enables you to use advanced techniques such as applying image filters, creating textures and gradients, drawing digital art, creating animated images through layer manipulation, and changing a photo into a painting or sketch.

Operating System Alternatives

Installing open source application software such as OpenOffice on a Windows machine is simple. Changing your OS from Windows to an open source OS such as Linux is a bit more complex. Why would you want to switch to Linux if you already own Windows?

Before Windows XP, many people felt Windows was not stable. Citing lockups and forced reboots, many users searched for an OS that would not crash as often. Starting with Windows XP, Microsoft has done a great deal to address stability issues.

Because Windows is the most widely used OS, with 90 percent of the market share, it's a prime target for viruses and other annoyances. From a virus creator or hacker's perspective, nuisances that spread via Windows have the greatest chance of causing the most aggravation. A lot of spyware, computer viruses, and other hacker

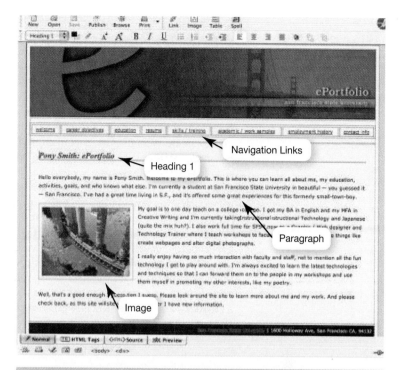

FIGURE 6

SeaMonkey Composer is an open source Web page authoring program that contains many features similar to those of leading commercial packages and is available at no cost.

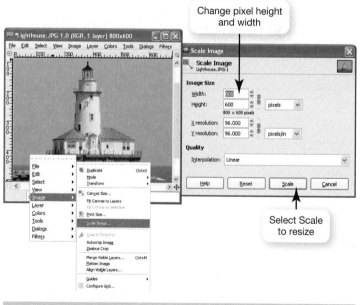

FIGURE 7

GIMP is a freely available software application for image editing.

Photo Management Software Alternatives: JAlbum

If you're like many people, you have gigabytes of digital photos on your hard drive. How can you easily organize photos for display on a Web site so that you can share them with friends and family? An open source option is JAlbum (**jalbum.net**), a program that allows you to create Web albums of your digital images easily using drag-and-drop tools. JAlbum is available for the Windows, Mac, Linux, and UNIX operating systems, and supports 30 languages.

JAlbum provides significant advantages over some commercial photo management systems because it provides a high degree of control over the look and feel of the album you create. It offers many templates if you don't have the time, energy, or artistic flair to create your own. You also can use JAlbum to create index and slideshow pages. The software even uploads your album to the Internet. Best of all, your friends and family don't need any software other than a current Web browser to view your album. (You can also choose to burn your album onto a CD for sharing.)

nuisances are designed to take advantage of security flaws in Windows. An open source OS alternative, such as Linux, that is not as widely used as Windows is less of a target for these annoyances.

Another reason to install an open source OS is portability. Depending on which version of Linux you use, you may be able to take it with you on a CD or flash drive and use it on almost any computer. This portability feature appeals to people who use many different computers (such as lab computers at school). Instead of getting used to a new configuration every time you're away from your home computer, wouldn't it be nice to have the same environment you're used to everywhere you go? Such portability also offers an additional level of protection for users of public computers. Using an open source OS that's installed on a portable flash drive helps reduce your risk of picking up viruses and malware from public computers. In addition, it enhances privacy, because temporary Internet files are stored on the portable device on which the OS is installed, rather than on the hard drive of the public computer you are using. Lastly, many users of netbooks, the lightest, smallest category of notebook computers, have opted to install Linux because it takes up less space on the hard drive and runs faster than the proprietary software that was installed originally

by the manufacturer. In the next section, we explore the different varieties of Linux and explain how to install them.

WHICH LINUX TO USE

Linux is available for download in various packages known as **distributions**, or **distros**. Think of distros as being like different makes and models of cars. Distros include the underlying Linux kernel (the code that provides Linux's basic functionality) and special modifications to the OS, and may also include additional open source software (such as OpenOffice). Which distro is right for you?

A good place to start researching distros is **distrowatch.com**. This site tracks Linux distros and provides helpful tips for beginners on choosing one. Figure 8 lists some popular Linux distros and their home pages.

Before you can decide which distro is right for you, there are a few things to consider. The overall requirements to run Linux are relatively modest:

- A 1.2 GHz processor
- 384 MB of RAM (text mode) and 192 MB RAM (graphical mode)
- 8 GB of hard drive space
- VGA graphics card capable of 640 × 480 resolution

Just like any other software program, however, Linux performs better with a faster processor and more memory. Depending on how much additional software is deployed in the distro you choose to use, your system requirements may be higher, and you may need more hard drive space. Check the specific recommendations for the distro you're considering on that distro's Web site.

EXPERIMENTING WITH LINUX

Some Linux distros (such as Ubuntu and PCLinuxOS) are designed to run from a CD or DVD. This eliminates the need to install files on the computer's hard drive. Therefore, you can boot up from a DVD on an existing Windows PC and run Linux without disturbing the existing Windows installation. If you're looking to do this with a public computer, please note that some public computers do not allow access to the CD or DVD drive. Additionally, depending on the distro you use, you may not have full access to the files on your Windows hard drive.

Booting your existing computer from a CD- or DVD-based version of Linux is a low-risk way to experiment with Linux and see how well you like it. Ubuntu, for example, uses an extremely familiar-looking, Windows-like desktop. When you access Ubuntu, you get the Firefox browser as well as GIMP, OpenOffice, and many other software packages, including utilities and games. The minimum system requirements to run Ubuntu are:

- An Intel-compatible CPU (including 64-bit PCs and Intel-based Macs)
- At least 4 GB of hard drive space (if you are installing Ubuntu and not just running it from a CD or DVD)
- 256 MB of RAM for the alternative installation CD, or 384 MB to use the live, CD-based installer
- A bootable CD/DVD-ROM drive
- A standard graphics card

Figure 9 shows Ubuntu in action. After you connect to the Internet from your home network via a high-speed connection, the computer boots from the Ubuntu disc when it detects it in the optical disc drive. As part of the installation sequence, Ubuntu automatically detects components of the computer (such as the network card) and

FIGURE 8	Linux Distributions
Distro	**Home Page**
Debian GNU/Linux	**debian.org**
Fedora Core (Red Hat)	**fedoraproject.org**
Gentoo Linux	**gentoo.org**
Mandriva Linux	**mandriva.com**
PCLinuxOS	**pclinuxos.com**
Slackware Linux	**slackware.com**
Ubuntu	**ubuntu.com**

configures Linux to recognize them. You will have no trouble browsing the Internet because Firefox, a Web browser, is included with the Ubuntu distro. You can also save any files you create with the included OpenOffice suite to a flash drive.

Mandriva Linux offers several versions of its OS. Mandriva Linux One 2009 Spring is the company's most recent and most basic product. It is free, remains true to the original open source principles, and is installable. Alternatively, you can try Mandriva in the "live" mode, which doesn't require installation. Other versions with more features are available for a fee, including PowerPack 2009 Spring, which offers a more complete package that includes added multimedia and gaming software. In addition, for a small fee, you can get Mandriva Flash. Flash is Mandriva's portable OS option, and is installed on a convenient 8 GB flash drive.

FIGURE 9

The Ubuntu user interface resembles the Windows desktop.

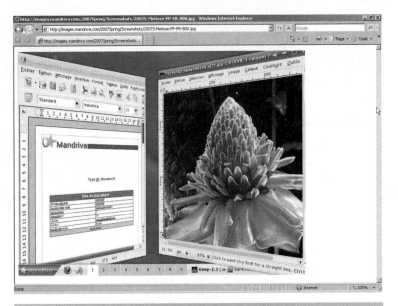

The Mandriva operating system has an innovative 3D desktop environment.

This portable version does not make changes on the host computer, so you can bring your computer environment anywhere you go. Mandriva Flash takes up one-quarter of the flash drive, leaving the remaining 6 GB free so you can conveniently store and take with you all your office work and Internet and multimedia files Mandriva also offers Metisse, an innovative 3D desktop environment (see Figure 10).

When you install the Mandriva OS, you also get other open source applications, such as OpenOffice, the Firefox browser, and the KMail e-mail manager, as well as several multimedia programs including applications for managing photo albums and digital music collections.

In addition to all this, Mandriva includes security features. The OS divides security levels into five rankings that range from "Poor" to "Paranoid." Your choice depends on how you're using the system. (Select "Paranoid" if you're running business transactions through your computer.) You also can set up a simple-to-configure firewall called Shorewall to prevent unauthorized Internet users from accessing your personal network.

If you don't like Mandriva Linux or Ubuntu, head out to distrowatch.com and find another free Linux distro to install. With hundreds of distros available, you're sure to find one that fits your needs.

Hardware Alternatives

Tired of your Windows-based PC? Is your old computer too slow for your current needs and not worth upgrading? If so, you may be in the market for some new hardware. Before you head off to the store to buy another Windows-based computer, why not consider two alternatives: (1) moving to an Apple platform or (2) building your own computer.

APPLE COMPUTERS

The best way to decide whether a Mac is right for you is to get your hands on one and take it for a test drive. Chances are that someone you know has a Mac. Alternatively, your school might have a Mac lab or have Macs in the library. If not, then Apple has retail stores chock full of employees who are very happy to let you test out the equipment. You also can test Macs at Best Buy. Be sure to check out the entry-level Macs (see Figure 11). The MacBook Air is Apple's thinnest notebook. It weighs less than three pounds, and includes a 13-inch screen and a full-sized keyboard. The MacBook weighs in at five pounds and features the Intel Core 2 Duo processor and a

(a) The MacBook Air. (b) The MacBook. (c) The iMac.

13-inch screen. The iMac line features sleek, space-saving desktop units sporting fast Intel Core 2 Duo processors.

Some people are switching to Macs because they love their iPods so much. Apple is leveraging the popularity of these digital devices by designing software to let its computers work seamlessly with the iPods. In addition, many Apple fans think Macs are more user-friendly and stylish than their PC competitors. Professionals such as digital artists and graphic designers who create or edit computer images change to Macs because the applications these users rely on deliver superior features on the Apple platform.

Mac OS X Snow Leopard

Many Mac users have switched from Windows because of the operating system, Mac OS X. The latest version, Snow Leopard, has many slick and innovative features that are tempting to even the most loyal Windows users. If you've been using Windows for a while, you shouldn't have any problem making the transition to Snow Leopard. You'll notice immediately that the Mac OS uses the same desktop metaphors as Windows, including icons for folders and a Trash Can (similar to a Recycle Bin) to delete documents. It also includes a window-based interface like the one you're already accustomed to using in Windows.

Like earlier versions of Mac OS, Snow Leopard is based on the UNIX OS, which is exceptionally stable and reliable. Aside from stability, security and safety are great reasons to switch to the Mac OS because it does not seem as vulnerable as Windows is to the exploitation of security flaws by hackers. This doesn't necessarily mean that the Mac OS is better constructed than Windows; it could just be that because Windows has a lead in market share, it is a more attractive target for hackers. Regardless of the reason, you're probably somewhat less likely to be inconvenienced by viruses, hacking, and spyware if you're running Mac OS. Of course, you won't have any better protection from spam, phishing, or other Internet scams than you would with Internet Explorer, so you still need to stay alert. Snow Leopard offers a 3D desktop environment as well as an automated backup utility called Time Machine (see Figure 12).

When you boot up a Mac, a program called the Finder automatically starts. This program is like Windows Explorer and

FIGURE 12

Time Machine, an automated backup and restore utility, is one of the features in Mac OS X.

controls the desktop and the windows with which you interact. It's always running when the Mac is on. With the Quick Look feature, it is possible for you to view the contents of a file without ever opening it. This allows you to flip through multipage documents, watch videos, and view an entire presentation with just a single click of the mouse. Spaces is the name of another feature, which helps to keep order when projects pile up. With Spaces, you can group your application windows.

Snow Leopard has kept other features from previous versions, such as Spotlight, a desktop search feature that allows you to find anything on your computer from one spot. The Dashboard and widgets enable you to have easy access to many mini-applications that allow you to perform common tasks and get quick access to real-time information such as weather, stock prices, and sports updates.

At the top of the desktop is the menu bar. The options on the menu bar change according to which program is "active" (that is, foremost on your screen) at the moment. When you click the Apple icon in the upper left corner, a drop-down menu displays, from which you can select several options. The Dock is similar to the Taskbar in Windows and includes a strip of icons that displays across the bottom of the desktop.

Each Finder window has an area on the left known as the Sidebar (see Figure 13).

FIGURE 13

The Sidebar holds any folders you specify (such as the PageOneEditing folder shown here).

>To access the Sidebar, double-click the hard drive icon on the desktop.

The Sidebar holds any folders you specify (even though the icons don't look like folders). This makes navigation easier and faster. You can choose to view the contents of files and folders in three different views: icon view, list view, and column view. As shown in Figure 13, the sidebar shows that the PageOneEditing folder is selected. The files

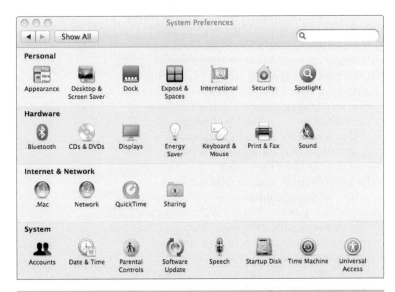

FIGURE 14

Much like the Control Panel in Windows, the System Preferences window allows you to customize and configure Mac OS X.

>To get to System Preferences, click the **Apple** menu icon in the top left corner of the screen and choose **System Preferences**.

and subfolders in the PageOneEditing folder display in the next two columns. A display window shows a thumbnail preview of the selected file. Navigating around a Finder window and copying and moving files work almost exactly the same way as they do in Windows.

Configuring a Mac

In Windows, you make changes to settings and preferences through the Control Panel. In Mac OS X Snow Leopard, you use System Preferences, which is an option on the Apple menu. Selecting System Preferences from the Apple menu displays the window shown in Figure 14.

Protecting Your Mac

Although Macs tend to be attacked less frequently by viruses and other hacker nuisances than PCs running Windows are, you can still be vulnerable if you don't take precautions. Snow Leopard comes with a firewall, but you should take the necessary steps to configure it properly before connecting to the Internet for the first time, because the firewall is set, by default, to allow all incoming connections. As shown in Figure 15, to block all connections except those that are critical to your computer's operation, select "Allow only essential services." If you'd rather set up your firewall on a per-application basis, select the Access for specific services and applications option.

In addition, hackers may be creating viruses and other nuisances to exploit security holes in the Mac OS. Mac users, like Windows users, should keep their software up to date with the latest fixes and software patches by setting their system to check automatically for software updates on a periodic basis. On Macs, this feature is available through the System Preferences window. Figure 16 shows the options you should choose to keep the Mac OS up to date. The Check Now button enables you to check for immediate updates, which is a great thing to do when you first set up your computer. Then, you can choose to have your computer check for updates regularly by scheduling software updates to run automatically at a time convenient to you. Make sure you choose to have the updates downloaded automatically. This feature alerts you when updates are ready to be connectivity options. AMD features notebook processors like the Turion 64 Mobile and the Mobile AMD Sempron. Desktop processors include Intel's Core i7, Core 2 Extreme, Quad, and Duo, and AMD's Athlon, Phenom, and Sempron.

What CPU does my current computer have? You can easily identify the type of CPU in your current system by accessing the system properties. As shown in Figure 8, you can view basic information about your computer, including which CPU is installed in your system as well as its speed. More detailed information, like the FSB speed and the amount of cache memory, is not shown in this screen. You can find those values by checking the manufacturer's Web site for the specific model number of CPU shown. For example, the CPU illustrated here is the Intel Core2 Duo, version E8400.

How can I tell whether my CPU is meeting my needs? As shown in Figure 9, several factors determine whether your CPU is meeting your needs. Although speed determines how fast your CPU is capable of performing operations, you also need to determine if that speed is capable of handling the tasks you need to perform. Even though your CPU meets the minimum requirements specified for a particular software application, if you're running other software (in addition to the operating system, which is always running), you'll need to check to see how well the CPU is handling the entire load. You can tell whether your CPU speed is limiting your system performance if you periodically watch how busy it is as you work on your computer. Keep in mind that the workload your CPU experiences will vary considerably depending on what you're doing. Even though it might run Word just fine, it may not be able to

handle running Word, a Web browser, iTunes, and IM at the same time. The percentage of time that your CPU is working is referred to as **CPU usage**.

A utility that measures information such as CPU usage and RAM usage is incredibly useful, both for considering whether you should upgrade and for investigating if your computer's performance suddenly seems to drop off for no apparent reason. On Windows systems, a program called Task Manager gives you easy access to all this data. Mac OS X has a utility similar to Task Manager called Activity Monitor, which is located in the Utilities folder in your Applications folder.

To view information on CPU usage, right-click an empty area of the taskbar, select Start Task Manager, and click the Performance tab, as shown in Figure 10. The CPU Usage graph records your CPU usage for the past several seconds. Of course, there will be periodic peaks of high CPU usage, but if you see that your CPU usage levels are greater than 90 percent during most of your work session, a faster CPU will contribute a great deal to your system's performance. If you are using the Windows Sidebar, there is a CPU Meter gadget you can add to track

Figure 8

The System Properties window identifies which CPU you have, as well as its speed.

>Click the **Start** button and then click **Computer** on the right panel of the **Start** menu. On the top toolbar, click **System Properties**.

Figure 9 | DO YOU NEED TO UPGRADE YOUR CPU?

	Current System	My Ideal System
What is my computer's CPU speed?		
How much cache memory is on the CPU*?		
What is the FSB speed*?		
What kind of multilevel processing does the CPU have—quad core, dual core, hyperthreaded, etc.?		
Is the CPU usage value below 90% during most of my daily tasks?		
*You can find these by checking the manufacturer's specifications for your model of CPU.		

both CPU and RAM usage. To see exactly how to use the Task Manager and the Sidebar gadget, watch the Sound Byte "Using Windows 7 to Evaluate CPU Performance."

Will improving the performance of the CPU be enough to improve my computer's performance? You may think that if you have the best processor, you will have a system with the best performance. However, upgrading your CPU will affect only the processing portion of the system performance, not how quickly data can move to or from the CPU. Your system's overall performance depends on many other factors, including the amount of RAM installed as well as hard drive speed. Therefore, your selection of a CPU may not offer significant improvements to your system's performance if there is a bottleneck in processing because of insufficient RAM or hard drive capacity.

Figure 10

The Performance tab of the Windows Task Manager utility shows you how busy your CPU actually is.

>In an empty area of the taskbar, right-click, select **Start Task Manager**, and click the **Performance** tab.

Current CPU usage level

CPU usage over time

Total RAM installed

Percentage of RAM in use

Evaluating RAM: The Memory Subsystem

Random access memory (RAM) is your computer's temporary storage space. Although we refer to RAM as a form of storage, it really is the computer's short-term memory. As such, it remembers everything that the computer needs to process the data into information, such as data that has been entered and software instructions, but only when the computer is on. RAM is an example of **volatile storage**. When the power is off, the data stored in RAM is cleared out. This is why, in addition to RAM, systems always include **nonvolatile storage** devices for permanent storage of instructions and data when the computer is powered off. ROM memory, for example, holds the critical startup instructions. Hard drives provide the greatest nonvolatile storage capacity in the computer system.

Why not use a hard drive to store the data and instructions? It's about one million times faster for the CPU to retrieve a piece of data from RAM than from a hard drive. The time it takes the CPU to retrieve data from RAM is measured in nanoseconds (billionths of seconds), whereas retrieving data from a fast hard drive takes an average of 10 milliseconds (ms), or thousandths of seconds. Figure 11 shows the various types of memory and storage that are distributed throughout your system: CPU registers, cache, RAM, and hard drive. Each of these has its own tradeoff of speed vs. price. Because the fastest memory is so much more expensive, systems are designed with much less of it. This principle is influential in the design of a balanced computer system and can have a tremendous impact on system performance.

Are there different types of RAM? Like most computer components, RAM has gone through a series of transitions. In current systems, the RAM used most often

Figure 11

A computer system's memory has many different levels, ranging from the small amounts in the CPU to the much slower but more plentiful storage of a hard drive.

Fast access but very little storage

CPU Registers

Level 1 cache

Level 2 cache

Level 3 cache

Physical RAM

Virtual Memory

Optical Disk Drives   Hard Drive

Huge amounts of storage but slow speeds

Hard drive

RAM

CPU registers and L1, L2 cache

comes in the form of double data rate 2 (DDR2) memory modules. Double data rate 3 memory (DDR3), which has an even faster data transfer rate, is seen in high-performance systems. In older systems, other types of RAM may have been used, including DRAM, static RAM (SRAM), and synchronous DRAM (SDRAM). RAM appears in the system on **memory modules** (or **memory cards**), small circuit boards that hold a series of RAM chips and fit into special slots on the motherboard (see Figure 12). Most memory modules in today's systems are called *dual inline memory modules (DIMMs)*.

Types of RAM are slightly different from each other in how they function and in the speed at which they access memory. On high-end systems, manufacturers may offer an option to purchase Corsair Dominator DDR3 modules. These are tested to high levels to guarantee optimum performance. A special heat exchanger is designed into the RAM module to help it operate at a lower temperature, making it more stable and more reliable. All of these factors boost the performance of the memory and make it popular with demanding video gamers.

If you're adding RAM to any system, you must determine what type your system needs. Consult your user's manual or the manufacturer's Web site. In addition, many online RAM resellers, such as Crucial (**crucial.com**), can help you determine the type of RAM that is compatible with your

Figure 12

Memory modules hold a series of RAM chips and fit into special slots on the motherboard.

system based on the model number and brand of your computer.

How can I tell how much RAM is installed in my computer? The amount of RAM that is actually sitting on memory modules in your computer is your computer's **physical memory**. The easiest way to see how much RAM you have is to look in the System Properties window. (On the Mac, choose About This Mac from the Apple menu.) This is the same tab you looked in to determine your system's CPU type and speed, and is shown in Figure 8. RAM capacity is measured in gigabytes (GB), and most machines sold today, especially those running Windows, have at least 2 GB of RAM. The computer in Figure 10 has 4094 MB (or 4.00 GB) of RAM installed.

More detailed information on physical memory is displayed in the Physical Memory table in the Performance tab of Windows Task Manager, shown in Figure 13. The Physical Memory table shows the total amount of physical memory you have installed as well as the available physical memory you have. If you are used to using Windows XP, when you have only a couple of applications running, you might expect to see lots of available memory. When using Windows Vista or Windows 7, even with just one application running, it will appear

SOUND BYTE — Memory Hierarchy Interactive

In this Sound Byte, you'll learn about the different types of memory used in a computer system.

that you have little available memory, because these versions of Windows manage memory differently from previous versions of the Windows OS. Windows now uses a memory-management technique known as SuperFetch. SuperFetch monitors which applications you use the most and preloads these into your system memory so they'll be ready.

Because RAM is so much faster to access than the hard drive that you have in your computer, it would be helpful to have as much information as possible about the programs you are currently using in RAM so your computer will respond faster. Windows 7 manages memory by anticipating what information you will need next and storing it in RAM instead of in cache memory or on your hard drive. For example, if you have Word running, Windows 7 stores as much of the information related to Word in RAM as it can, thereby almost filling up your RAM. Don't worry, because as other needs arise (if you start Excel, for instance), the operating system reallocates the contents of RAM to account for your use of multiple programs.

Figure 13

The Performance tab of the Windows Task Manager shows you how much physical memory is installed in your system, as well as how much is currently being used and how much is available.

>In the **Taskbar** area, right-click. Select **Start Task Manager**. Click the **Performance** tab.

Memory required to run the operating system

How much memory does the operating system need to run? The memory that your operating system uses is referred to as **kernel memory**. This memory is listed in a separate Kernel Memory table in the Performance tab. In Figure 13, the Kernel Memory table tells you that approximately 555 MB (total kernel memory) of the total 4 GB of RAM is being used to run the operating system.

The operating system is the main software application that runs the computer. Without it, the computer does not work. At a minimum, the system needs enough RAM to run the operating system. Therefore, the amount of kernel memory that the system is using is the absolute minimum amount of RAM that your computer can run on. However, because you run additional applications, you need to have more RAM than the minimum.

How much RAM do I need?
Because RAM is the temporary holding space for all the data and instructions that the computer uses while it's on, most computer users need quite a bit of RAM. In fact, systems running all the new features of Windows 7 should have a minimum of 1 GB of RAM, but for peak performance, systems are recommended to have at least 2 GB of RAM. Ultimately, the amount of RAM your system needs depends on how you use it. At a minimum, you need enough RAM to run the operating system (as explained earlier), plus whatever other software applications you're using, and then a bit of additional RAM to hold the data you're inputting.

To determine how much RAM you need, list all the software applications you might be running at one time. Figure 14 shows an example of RAM requirements. In this example, if you are running your operating system, word processing and spreadsheet programs, a Web browser, a music player, and photo editing software simultaneously, then you will need a minimum of 2.15 GB of RAM. It's always best to check the system requirements of any software program before you buy it to make sure your system can handle it. System requirements can be found on the software packaging or on the manufacturer's Web site.

It's a good idea to have more than the minimum amount of RAM you need now, so you can use more programs in the future. Remember, too, that these are the minimum values recommended by the manufacturers,

Figure 14 | SAMPLE RAM REQUIREMENTS

Application	Minimum RAM Required
Windows 7	1,000 MB
Microsoft Office Professional 2007	256 MB
Internet Explorer 8	128 MB
iTunes	256 MB
Adobe Photoshop Elements	512 MB
Total RAM required to run all programs simultaneously	2,152 MB (2.15 GB)

SOUND BYTE — Installing RAM

In this Sound Byte, you'll learn how to select the appropriate type of memory to purchase, how to order memory online, and how to install it yourself. As you'll discover, the procedure is a simple one and can add great performance benefits to your system.

and having more RAM often helps programs run more efficiently. When upgrading RAM, the rule of thumb is to buy as much as you can afford but no more than your system will handle.

Virtual Memory

Would adding more RAM improve my system performance? You should consider several factors when determining if your system needs more RAM. When there's not enough RAM installed in your system, it will become sluggish, freeze more often, or just shut down when you perform certain tasks. When this happens, the system becomes **memory bound**—that is, limited in how fast it can send data to the CPU, because there is not enough memory. If this is the case, then adding more RAM to your system will immediately improve performance.

How do I know whether my system is memory bound? If you don't have enough RAM to hold all of the programs you're currently trying to run, then the operating system will begin to store the data that doesn't fit in RAM in a space on the hard drive called **virtual memory**. When it is using virtual memory, your operating system builds a file called the **page file** on the hard drive to allow processing to continue. This enables the system to run more applications than can actually fit in your computer's RAM.

So far, this system of memory management sounds like a good idea, especially because hard drives are much cheaper than RAM per gigabyte of storage. The drawback

is speed. Remember that accessing data from the hard drive to send it to the CPU is more than one million times slower than accessing data from RAM. Another drawback is that some applications do not run well on virtual memory. Therefore, using virtual memory is a method of last resort.

If your system is often using virtual memory, then adding more RAM will dramatically increase performance. You can monitor how often you are exceeding your installed physical RAM by running the System Information program. In the Search box, type "system information". The System Summary tells you how much physical RAM is installed, how much is free, how much virtual memory is set up, and how much virtual memory is free. Do this at several points during the day and you will build a picture of how memory bound your system is.

Adding RAM

Is there a limit to how much RAM I can add to my computer? Every computer is designed with a maximum limit on the amount of RAM it can support. Each computer is designed with a specific

BITS AND BYTES — The Future of RAM

As the demand for portable computing devices accelerates, researchers are constantly looking for ways to save space and power consumption, thereby increasing battery life. Magnetoresistive Random Access Memory (MRAM) and Nano Random Access Memory (NRAM) are two technologies that may soon provide solutions to these common challenges.

Most RAM used today is DRAM (dynamic RAM). DRAM uses electrical charges to store data, whereas MRAM uses magnetic plates to store data. NRAM uses carbon nanotubes, which are only one carbon atom thick, to store data. A significant advantage of both MRAM and NRAM technologies is that they use almost 99 percent less power, making them ideal for portable computing devices. Imagine a camera with 2 TB of storage—unimaginable today, but perhaps part of the near future.

Figure 15 | DO YOU NEED TO UPGRADE YOUR RAM?*

	Application	Current System	Ideal System
What is the maximum amount of RAM I need in my system for the applications I currently run?			
How much RAM is in my system?			
What is the maximum amount of RAM the system can hold*?			
Would I be willing to upgrade a 32-bit operating system to a 64-bit operating system to support having 4 GB or more of RAM?			

*Check the manufacturer's specifications for your system.

Figure 16

Adding RAM to a computer is quite simple and relatively inexpensive.

number of slots on the motherboard into which the memory cards fit, and each slot may have a limit on the amount of RAM it can support. To determine your specific system limits, check your owner's manual or the manufacturer's Web site.

In addition, the operating system running on your machine imposes its own limit. For example, the maximum amount of RAM for the 32-bit version of Windows 7 is 4 GB, while the 64-bit version of Windows 7 Ultimate can address up to 192 GB.

Once you know how much RAM your computer can support, you can determine the best configuration of memory modules to achieve the greatest amount of RAM. For example, say you have a total of four memory card slots: Two are already filled with 512 MB RAM cards and the other two are empty. The maximum RAM allowed for your system is 4 GB. This means you can buy two more 512 MB RAM modules for the two empty slots, for a total of 2 GB (4 × 512 MB) of RAM. Alternatively, you could throw away the 512 MB cards you have and purchase four new 1 GB cards, filling the system up to its capacity of 4 GB.

Review the considerations presented in Figure 15 to see if your system could benefit from an upgrade of additional RAM.

Is it hard to add RAM? Adding RAM to a computer is fairly easy (see Figure 16). RAM comes with installation instructions, which you should follow carefully. RAM is also relatively inexpensive compared with other system upgrade options. Still, the cost of RAM fluctuates in the marketplace as much as 400 percent over time, so if you're considering adding RAM, you should watch the prices of memory in online and print advertisements.

Joel Gordon Photography

Joel Gordon Photography

Joel Gordon Photography

Understanding and Assessing Hardware: Evaluating Your System

274

Adding RAM to a personal computer is quite simple and relatively inexpensive. You simply line up the notches and push in the memory module. Just be sure that you're adding a memory module that's compatible with your computer. For a video demonstration and more details, watch the Sound Byte, "Installing RAM."

Evaluating the Storage Subsystem

As you've learned, there are two ways data is saved on your computer: temporary storage and permanent storage. RAM is a form of temporary (or volatile) storage. Thus, anything that resides in RAM is not saved permanently. It's critical to have the means to store data and software applications permanently.

Fortunately, several storage options exist within every computer system. Storage devices for a typical personal computer include the hard drive, USB flash drives, optical drives, and external hard drives. When you turn off your computer, the data

stored to these devices is saved. These devices are therefore referred to as *nonvolatile* storage devices. Of all the nonvolatile storage devices, the hard drive is used the most.

The Hard Drive

What makes the hard drive the most popular storage device? With storage capacities exceeding 2 terabytes (TB), a **hard drive** has the largest storage capacity of any storage device. The hard drive is also a much more economical device than other storage options, because it offers the most gigabytes of storage per dollar. Most system units are designed to support more than one internal hard drive. The Apple Mac Pro, shown in Figure 17, has room for four hard drives. Each one simply slides into place when you want to upgrade.

Another reason the hard drive is so useful for storage is that the hard drive's **access time**, the time it takes a storage device to locate its stored data and make it available for processing, is faster than that of other

Figure 17

The Mac Pro allows you to slide a new hard drive into place easily. In all, the Mac Pro can hold up to 4 TB.

Empty cover removed

Moeskau Photography

New 1 TB hard drive

Moeskau Photography

Hard drive #2 slides into place

Moeskau Photography

Evaluating the Storage Subsystem

Device

DVD — 150
Hard drive — 10
USB flash drive | 1
SSD | 0.1

1
0.1

Access Time (ms)

Figure 18

Access times for non-volatile storage options.

permanent storage devices, like optical drives. Hard drive access times are measured in milliseconds (ms), meaning thousandths of seconds. For large-capacity drives, access times of approximately 9.5 milliseconds—that's less than one-hundredth of a second—are typical. A DVD drive can take over 150 milliseconds to access data.

Solid state drives offer even faster access times. A **solid state drive** (SSD) uses the same kind of memory that flash drives use, but whereas flash drives have access times of about 1 ms, SSD drives can reach data in only a tenth of that time (around 0.1 ms). Because there are no spinning platters or motors needed, SSDs run with no noise, very little heat, and require very little power. As the prices for SSDs continue to drop, you'll start to see them in a wide range of systems.

BITS AND BYTES

HDTV on Your Notebook

If you are moving through your day with a notebook in tow, why not use it to pull up your favorite television shows? There are now several USB devices that allow your notebook or desktop to receive the high-definition television (HDTV) signals whizzing by in the airwaves.

Devices like the Hauppauge HDTV stick (see Figure 19) are USB digital TV tuners. One end plugs into any available USB port. The other end connects to the provided digital antenna. Software is included that allows you to schedule shows to record onto your hard drive, so your notebook essentially becomes a time-shifting digital video recorder. If you are at home, you can remove the antenna and connect to your home cable television signal. It's enough to make you think about buying a larger hard drive on your next computer!

Hauppauge Computer Works, Inc.

Figure 19

The Hauppauge HDTV stick allows you to watch and record high-definition television shows on your computer.

Figure 18 provides a listing of the various storage options and compares their access times.

Another key performance specification for a hard drive is the speed at which it can transfer data to other computer components (such as RAM). This speed of transfer is referred to as **data transfer rate**. Depending on the manufacturer, the rate is expressed in either megabits or megabytes per second.

How is data stored on a hard drive? A hard drive is composed of several coated round, thin plates of metal stacked on a spindle. Each plate is called a **platter**. When data is saved to a hard drive platter, a pattern of magnetized spots is created on the iron oxide coating of each platter. When the spots are aligned in one direction, they represent a 1; when aligned in the other direction, the represent a 0. These 0s and 1s are bits (or binary digits) and are the smallest pieces of data that computers can understand. When data stored on the hard drive platter is retrieved (or read), your computer translates these patterns of magnetized spots into the data you have saved.

How do I know how much storage capacity I need? Typically, hard drive capacity is measured in gigabytes (GB), although some high-end systems have a hard drive with capacity in the terabytes (TB). To check how much total capacity your hard drive has, as well as how much is being used, click the Start button and select Computer from the right side of the Start menu. Windows displays the hard drives, their capacity, and usage information, as seen in Figure 20. To get a slightly more detailed view, select a drive; then right-click and choose Properties.

To determine the storage capacity your system needs, calculate the amount of storage required by all the types of files you will be keeping on your system. If you have a large digital music library, that alone could require 30 to 50 GB. Do you keep all of your photographs on your hard drive? You may need another 40 GB or more for them. If you store digital video of television shows and movies, that could easily be 100 to 200 GB more, even higher if the videos are all high definition. Of course, the operating system also requires storage space. The demands on system requirements have grown with new versions of operating systems. Windows 7, the latest Microsoft operating system, can require up to 20 GB of available hard drive capacity, depending on the configuration.

In addition to having space for the operating system, you need enough space to store the software applications you use, such as Microsoft Office, music, and games. Figure 21 shows an example of hard drive requirements for someone storing a few programs on a hard drive.

Are some hard drives faster than others? There are several types of hard drives. Integrated Drive Electronics (IDE), which is also called *parallel advanced technology attachment (PATA)*, is an older style that uses wide cables to connect the hard drive to the motherboard. **Serial Advanced Technology Attachment (Serial ATA)** hard drives use much thinner cables, and can transfer data more quickly than IDE drives. A slower drive is fine if you use your computer primarily for word processing, spreadsheets, e-mail, and the Internet. However, "power users" such as graphic designers and software developers will benefit from the faster Serial ATA hard drive.

Another factor that affects a hard drive's performance is access time (the speed with which it locates data for processing). As noted earlier, access time is measured in milliseconds. The faster the access time the better, although many hard drives have similar access times.

The latest and fastest hard drive option is the solid state drive (SSD). These are popular in the netbook market because they require so little power to run and are so cool and quiet. With access times of merely a tenth of a millisecond, SSDs can deliver data many times more quickly than mechanical hard drives. SSD drives as large as 1 TB are available, but right now, all SSD drives are still much more expensive than mechanical drives. Watch for the integration of SSD drives into most systems as the cost of SSDs continues to drop.

Evaluate hard drive transfer rate when looking for the best performing drive. The **data transfer rate** is the speed at which a hard drive can transfer data to other computer components (such as RAM). Depending on the manufacturer, the rate is expressed in either megabits or megabytes per second. You can compare the average read and write data transfer rates of hard drives at sites that do performance benchmarking, like Tom's Hardware (**tomshardware.com**).

If you are adding an external hard drive to your system, there are two popular ports

to use. Many hard drives use a USB 2.0 port to connect, which limits the transfer rate of data to 400 Mbps. In addition, some computer systems now offer an eSATA port, shown in Figure 22. This is an external SATA port that will connect to some external hard drive models. It allows much faster data transfer—up to 3 Gbps.

Optical Storage

Optical drives are disc drives that use a laser to store and read data. Data is saved to a compact disc (CD), digital video discs (DVD), or **Blu-ray disc (BDs)** within established tracks and sectors, just like on a hard drive. However, unlike hard drives, which store their data on magnetized platters, optical discs store data as tiny pits that are burned into the disc by a high-speed laser. These pits are extremely small. For CDs and DVDs, they are less than 1 micron in

Figure 20

In Windows, the free and used capacity of each device in the computer system are shown in the Computer window. The General tab of the Properties dialog box gives you information that is more detailed.

>To view the Computer window, click **Start**, and click **Computer**. To view the pie chart, right-click the C drive, and select **Properties**.

Figure 21 | SAMPLE HARD DRIVE REQUIREMENTS

Application	Hard Drive Space Required
Windows 7	16–20 GB
MS Office 2007 Professional	2 GB
Adobe Photoshop Elements	2 GB
Roxio Easy Media Creator 9	1 GB installation space and as much as 9 GB to copy CDs or DVDs
Total required	21–33 GB

Optical Storage

diameter, so nearly 1,500 pits fit across the top of a pinhead. The pits on a Blu-ray disc are only 0.15 microns in diameter, more than twice as small as the pits on a DVD. As you can see in Figure 23, data is read from a disc by a laser beam, with the pits and nonpits (called *lands*) translating into the 1s and 0s of the binary code computers understand. CDs and DVDs use a red laser to read and write data. Blu-ray discs get their name because they are read with a blue laser light. All of them collectively are referred to as **optical media**.

ExpressCard - PCMCIA

Figure 22

An eSATA port allows you to connect an external hard drive that can transfer data at much greater speeds than those a USB port supports.

Why can I store data on some discs but not others? All forms of optical media come in prerecorded, recordable, and rewritable formats. The prerecorded discs—known as CD-ROM, **DVD-ROM**, and **BD-ROM discs**—are read-only optical discs, meaning you can't save any data onto them. Pre-recorded CDs usually contain audio content, software programs, or games, whereas DVD-ROMs and BD-ROMs typically contain movies or prerecorded TV shows in regular or high definition, respectively. Recordable formats such as CD-R, DVD-R, and BD-R allow data to be written (saved or burned) to them. If you want to be able to use a form of optical media repetitively, writing and rewriting data to it many times, read/writeable formats such as CD-RW, DVD-RW, and BD-RE are available.

Do I need separate players and burners for CD, DVD, and now BD formats? Although CDs and DVDs are based on the same optical technology, CD drives cannot read DVDs. If your system has only a CD drive, you will need to add a DVD drive to view DVDs. However, if your system has a DVD drive, that is all you need, even just to listen to CDs, because DVD drives can read them. Although Blu-ray discs are read with a different type of laser than CDs and DVDs, most Blu-ray players are backward compatible and can play DVDs and CDs. There are different types of optical drives for playing or recording to discs. If you want to record to CDs, DVDs, or Blu-ray discs, you need to make sure your drive is capable of recording (or burning) and not just playing. Because recording drives are also backward compatible, you do not need separate burners for each form of media. A DVD burner will also record CDs, and a Blu-ray burner will most likely record both CDs and DVDs (although there may be some compatibility issues).

Are there different standards of optical media? Unfortunately, technology experts have not agreed on a standard DVD format. Currently, there are multiple

To read information stored on a disc, a laser inside the disk drive sends a beam of light through the spinning disc.

Laser beam

Non-scattered reflected light = 1

Laser beam

Scattered reflected light = 0

If the light reflected back is scattered in all directions (which happens when the laser hits a pit), the laser translates this into the binary digit 0.

If non-scattered light is reflected back to the laser (which happens when the laser hits an area in which there is no pit), the laser translates this into the binary digit 1.

Spinning CD

In this way, the laser reads the pits and non-pits as a series of bits (0s and 1s), which the computer can then process.

Figure 23

Data is read from a CD using focused laser light.

The thin metal platters that make up a hard drive are covered with a special magnetic coating that enables the data to be recorded onto one or both sides of the platter. Hard drive manufacturers prepare the disks to hold data through a process called *low-level formatting*. In this process, concentric circles, each called a **track**, and pie-shaped wedges, each called a **sector**, are created in the magnetized surface of each platter, setting up a gridlike pattern that identifies file locations on the hard drive. A separate process called *high-level formatting* establishes the catalog that the computer uses to keep track of where each file is located on the hard drive.

Hard drive platters spin at a high rate of speed, some as fast as 15,000 revolutions per minute (rpm). Sitting between the platters are special "arms" that contain read/write heads (see Figure 24). A **read/write head** moves from the outer edge of the spinning platter to the center, as frequently as 50 times per second, to retrieve (read) and record (write) the magnetic data to and from the hard drive platter. As noted earlier, the average total time it takes for the read/write head to locate the data on the platter and return it to the CPU for processing is called its access time. A new hard drive should have an average access time of approximately 10 ms.

Access time is mostly the sum of two factors: seek time and latency. The time it takes for the read/write heads to move over the surface of the disk, moving to the correct track, is called the **seek time**. (Sometimes people incorrectly refer to this as access time.) Once the read/write head locates the correct track, it may need to wait for the correct sector to spin to the read/write head. This waiting time is called **latency** (or *rotational delay*). The faster the platters spin (or the faster the rpm), the less time you'll have to wait for your data to be accessed. Currently, most hard drives for home systems spin at 7,200 rpm. Some people design their systems to have a faster hard drive run the operating system, such as the Western Digital Velociraptor, which spins at 10,000 rpm. They then add a slower drive with greater capacity for storage.

The read/write heads do not touch the platters of the hard drive; rather, they float above them on a thin cushion of air at a height of 0.5 microinches. As a matter of comparison, a human hair is 2,000 microinches thick and a particle of dust is larger than a human hair. Therefore, it's critical to keep your hard drive free from all dust and dirt, because even the smallest particle could find its way between the read/write head and the disk platter, causing a **head crash**—a stoppage of the hard drive that often results in data loss.

Capacities for hard drives in personal computers can exceed 2000 GB (2 TB). Increasing the amount of data stored in a hard drive is achieved either by adding more platters or by increasing the amount of data stored on each platter. How tightly the tracks are placed next to each other, how tightly spaced the sectors are, and how closely the bits of data are placed affect the measurement of the amount of data that can be stored in a specific area of a hard drive platter. Modern technology continues to increase the standards on all three levels, enabling massive quantities of data to be stored in small places.

Read/write head

Arms

Platters

Figure 24

The hard drive is a stack of platters enclosed in a sealed case. Special arms fit in between each platter. The read/write heads at the end of each arm read from and save data to the platters.

recognized formats, **DVD-R/RW** (pronounced "DVD dash") and **DVD+R/RW** (pronounced "DVD plus"). **DVD-RAM** is a third format. You can record, erase, and rewrite on DVD-RAM, as you can with the plus and minus formats, but DVD-RAM discs are generally encased in a plastic cartridge. Web sites such as Video Help (**videohelp. com**) list the compatibility of various DVD players with the various DVD formats.

SOUND BYTE
CD, DVD, and Blu-ray Reading and Writing Interactive

In this Sound Byte, you'll learn about the process of storing and retrieving data from CD-RW, DVD, and Blu-ray discs. You'll be amazed to see how much precision engineering is required to burn MP3 files onto a disc.

Optical Storage

However, you must make sure you purchase blank DVD discs that match the type of drive you own. Most new systems come equipped with a DVD +/− RW drive, that supports both the plus and minus formats.

There were "format wars" like this for high-definition discs as well. Blu-ray competed against another storage format called HD-DVD (high-definition DVD). Some movie companies would only provide their films on HD discs, while other films were exclusive to Blu-ray. Different players were required to view each kind of disc. In 2008, HD-DVDs were retired, and HD discs and players are no longer in production.

Are some CD and DVD drives faster than others? When you buy an optical drive, knowing the drive speed is important. Speeds are listed on the device's packaging. Record (write) speed is always listed first, rewrite speed is listed second (except for CD-R drives and DVD-R, which cannot rewrite data), and playback speed is listed last. For example, a CD-RW drive may have speeds of 52X32X52X, meaning that the device can record data at 52X speed, rewrite data at 32X speed, and play back data at 52X speed. For CDs, the X after each number represents the transfer of 150 KB of data per second. For example, a CD-RW drive with a 52X32X52X rating records data at 52 times 150 KB per second, or 7,800 KB per second.

DVD drives are much faster than CD drives. For example, a 1X DVD-ROM drive provides a data transfer rate of approximately 1.3 MB of data per second, which is roughly equivalent to a CD-ROM speed of 9X. CD and DVD drives are constantly getting faster. If you're in the market for a new CD or DVD burner, then you'll want to investigate the drive speeds on the market and make sure you get the fastest one you can afford.

Blu-ray drives are the fastest optical devices on the market. Blu-ray technology defines 1X speed as 36 MB per second. Because BD movies require data transfer rates of at least 54 MB per second, most Blu-ray disc players have a minimum of 2X speeds (72 MB per second). Many units are available with 6X speeds.

So how do my storage devices measure up? The table in Figure 25 will help you determine if your computer's storage subsystem needs upgrading.

Figure 25 | DO YOU NEED TO UPGRADE YOUR STORAGE SUBSYSTEM?

	Current System	Ideal System
What is my current hard drive capacity?		
Do I have a DVD-ROM drive?		
Can I burn DVDs (i.e., do I have a DVD-/+RW drive)?		
Can I play Blu-ray discs (i.e., do I have a Blu-ray drive)?		
Can I burn my own Blu-ray discs (i.e., do I have a Blu-ray burner installed)?		
Do I have a working data backup solution such as external backup drives or remote data storage?		
Do I use any portable storage devices such as flash drives or portable hard drives?		

Video memory chips

Processor covered
by heat sink and fan

Video memory chip

Connects to
a monitor

HDMI port to
Xbox 360

Video memory chip

Clips into motherboard

S-video port to TV,
stereo, or VCR

Digital Video Interface (DVI)
port to LCD monitor

Figure 26

Video cards have grown
to be highly specialized
subsystems.

Evaluating the Video Subsystem

How video is displayed depends on two components: your video card and your monitor. It's important that your system have the correct monitor and video card to meet your needs. If you are considering loading Windows 7 on your system, or using your computer system to display files that have complex graphics, such as videos on Blu-ray or from your camcorder, or even playing graphics-rich games with a lot of fast action, you may want to consider upgrading your video subsystem.

Video Cards

What is a video card? A **video card** (or **video adapter**) is an expansion card that is installed inside your system unit to translate binary data into the images you view on your monitor. Modern video cards like the ones shown in Figure 26 and Figure 27 are extremely sophisticated. They include ports that allow you to connect to different video equipment such as the DVI ports for digital LCDs, HDMI ports to connect to high-definition TVs or gaming consoles, lower-resolution S-video ports for connecting your computer to a TV, and Super VGA ports for CRT and analog LCD monitors. In addition, video cards include their own RAM, called **video memory**. Several standards of video memory are available, including graphics double data rate 3 (GDDR3) memory and the newer graphics double data rate 5 (GDDR5) memory. Because displaying graphics demands a lot of the

Figure 27

Because of the large amount of graphics memory and the fast graphics processing units on modern video cards, they have their own fan to remove heat.

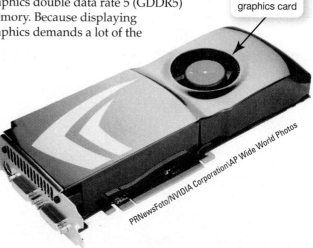

Fan built into
graphics card

PRNewsFoto/NVIDIA Corporation\AP Wide World Photos

Evaluating the Video Subsystem

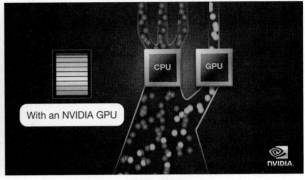

Without a GPU | **With a GPU**

Nvidia

Figure 28

The graphics processing unit (GPU) is specialized to handle processing of photos, videos, and video game images. It frees the CPU to work on other system demands.

Figure 29

These two images show the difference in displayed gaming environments with a basic video card and one with an advanced GPU. The Nvidia GeForce GPU allows more detailed water ripples, shadowing effects, and more realistic terrain texture.

CPU, video cards also come with their own graphics processing units (GPUs). When the CPU is asked to process graphics, those tasks are redirected to the GPU, significantly speeding up graphics processing.

Is a GPU different from a CPU?
The **graphics processing unit (GPU)** performs the same kind of computational work that a CPU performs. However, a GPU is specialized to handle 3-D graphics and image and video processing speedily. Figure 28 shows that the CPU can run much more efficiently when a GPU does all of the graphics computation.

Special lighting effects can be achieved with a modern GPU. Designers can now change the type of light, the texture, and the color of objects based on complex interactions. Some GPU designs incorporate dedicated hardware to allow high-definition movies to be decoded.

Does the GPU live on the motherboard or on the video card? Basic video processing is sometimes integrated into the motherboard. However, high-end video cards that have their own GPUs

are separate from the motherboard. These sophisticated video cards connect through the ultrafast PCI Express bus. The ATI Radeon HD 4870 X2, a top-end card, is a multi-GPU card with two GPUs that work together to add even more processing punch. Cards like this one carry their own processing RAM space, which can range between 512 MB and 2 GB, depending on the model. Together they provide an unprecedented level of realism and detail in gaming environments (see Figure 29).

How can I tell how much memory my video card has? Information about your system's video card can be found in the Advanced Settings of the Screen resolution dialog box. To get to the Screen resolution dialog box, right-click on your desktop and select Screen resolution. In the Screen resolution dialog box, click the Advanced Settings link. A window will appear that shows you the type of graphics card installed in your system, as well as memory information including total available graphics memory, dedicated video memory, system video memory, and shared system memory. The documentation that came with your computer should also contain specifications for the video card, including the amount of video memory it has installed.

How much memory does my video card need? The amount of memory your video card needs depends on what you want to display on your monitor. If you work primarily in Microsoft Word and conduct general Web searches, 128 MB is a realistic minimum. For the serious gamer, a 512 MB or greater video card is essential, although cards with as much as 1 or 2 GB are available in the market and are preferred. These high-end video cards, which have greater amounts

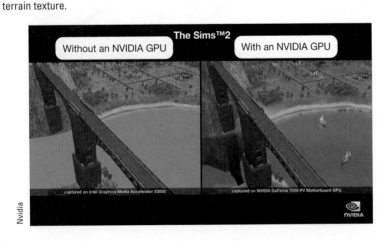

Nvidia

of memory, allow games to generate smoother animations and more sophisticated shading and texture. Before purchasing new software, check the specifications to ensure your video card has enough video memory to handle the load.

How many video cards can I add to a system? For users who are primarily doing text processing or spreadsheet work, one video card is certainly enough. However, computer gamers and users of high-end visualization software often take advantage of the ability to install more than one video card at a time. Two or even three video cards can be used in one system. The two major video card manufacturers, Nvidia and ATI, have each developed their own standards supporting the combining of multiple video cards. For Nvidia this standard is named SLI and for ATI it is called CrossFire. When the system is running at very high video resolutions, such as 1920 × 1200 or higher, multiple video cards working together provide the ultimate in performance. If you are buying a new system and might be interested in employing multiple video cards, be sure to check whether the motherboard supports SLI or CrossFire.

What else does the video card do? The video card also controls the number of colors your monitor can display. The number of bits the video card uses to represent each pixel (or dot) on the monitor, referred to as **bit depth**, defines the color quality of the image displayed. The more bits, the better an image's color detail. A 4-bit video card displays 16 colors, the minimum number of colors your system works with (referred to as Standard VGA). Most video cards today are 24-bit cards, displaying more than 16 million colors. This mode is called *true color mode* (see Figure 30).

Figure 30 | BIT DEPTH AND COLOR QUALITY

Bit Depth	Color Quality Description	Number of Colors Displayed
4-bit	Standard VGA	16
8-bit	256-color mode	256
16-bit	High color	65,536
24-bit	True color	16,777,216
32-bit	True color	16,777,216 plus 8 bits to help with transparency

The most recent generation of video cards can add some great features to your computer if you are a TV fan. Multimedia cards such as the ATI All-In-Wonder X1900 can open a live TV window on your screen, including features such as picture-in-picture. Using this video card, you can record programs to your hard drive or pause a live TV broadcast. The card even comes with a wireless remote control.

So how do I know if I need a new video card? If your monitor takes a while to refresh when you are editing photos, surfing the Web, or playing a graphics-rich game, then the video card could be short on memory. You also may want to upgrade if added features such as television viewing or importing analog video are important to you. If you want to use two monitors at the same time, you also may need to upgrade your video card. Review the considerations listed in Figure 31 to see if it might be time for you to upgrade. On a desktop computer, replacing a video card is fairly simple: just insert the new video card in the correct expansion slot on the motherboard.

Figure 31 | DO YOU NEED TO UPGRADE YOUR VIDEO CARD?

	Current System	Ideal System
Is my video card able to refresh the screen fast enough for the videos and games I play?		
What is the total amount of video memory on my video card?		
How many monitors can this card support?		
Can I import video through my video card?		
Can I send a cable television signal to my video card?		

Decades ago, when the electronic photocopier made its debut, book publishers and others who distributed the printed word feared they would be put out of business. They were worried that people would no longer buy books and other printed matter if they could simply copy someone else's original. Years later, when audiocassette and VCR players and recorders arrived on the market, those who felt they would be negatively affected by these new technologies expressed similar concerns. Now, with the arrival of CD-RW, DVD-RW, and BD-RE technology, the music and entertainment industries are worried because users can copy CDs, DVDs, and Blu-ray discs in a matter of minutes.

Although photocopiers and VCRs certainly didn't put an end to the industries they affected, some people still say the music and entertainment industries will take a significant hit with CD-RW, DVD-RW, and BD-RE technology. Industry insiders are claiming that these technologies are unethical, and they're pressing for increased federal legislation against such copying. It's not just the CD-RW, DVD-RW, BD-RE technology that's causing problems, either, because "copies" are not necessarily of the physical sort. Thanks to the Internet, file transfers of copyrighted works—particularly music and films—is now commonplace. According to Music United (**musicunited.org**), more than 243 million files are downloaded illegally every month, and about one-quarter of all Internet users worldwide have downloaded a movie from the Internet.

In a separate survey, the Recording Industry Association of America (RIAA), a trade organization that represents the interests of recording giants such as Sony, Capitol Records, and other major producers of musical entertainment, reported that 23 percent of music fans revealed they were buying less music because they could download it or copy a CD-ROM from a friend.

As you would expect, the music and entertainment industries want to be fairly compensated for their creative output. They blame the technology industry for the creation of means by which artists, studios, and the entertainment industry in general are being "robbed." Although technology that readily allows consumers to transfer and copy music and videos exists, the artists who produce these works do not want to be taken advantage of. However, others claim that the technology industry should not bear the complete burden of protecting entertainment copyrights. The RIAA sums up the future of this debate nicely: "Goals for the new millennium are to work with [the recording] industry and others to enable technologies that open up new opportunities but at the same time to protect the rights of artists and copyright owners."

Evaluating the Audio Subsystem

Computers output sound by means of speakers (or headphones) and a sound card. For many users, a computer's preinstalled speakers and sound card are adequate for the sounds produced by the computer itself—the beeps and so on that the computer makes. However, if you're listening to music, viewing DVDs, hooking into a household stereo system, or playing games with sophisticated sound tracks, you may want to upgrade your speakers or your sound card.

Sound Cards

What does the sound card do? Like a video card, a **sound card,** is an expansion card that attaches to the motherboard inside your system unit. Just as the video card enables your computer to produce images on the monitor, a sound card enables the computer to produce sounds. Most systems have a separate sound card, although low-end computers often have integrated the job of managing sound onto the motherboard itself.

Can I hook up a surround-sound system to my computer? Many computers ship with a basic sound card, which is often a **3D sound card**. The 3D sound technology advances sound reproduction beyond traditional stereo sound (where the human ear perceives sounds as coming from the left or the right of the performance area) and is better at convincing the human ear that sound is omnidirectional, meaning that you can't tell from which direction the sound is coming. This tends to produce a fuller, richer sound than stereo sound. However, 3D sound is not surround sound.

What is surround sound then? **Surround sound** is a type of audio processing that makes the listener experience sound as if it were coming from all directions. The current surround sound standard is from Dolby. There are many formats available, including Dolby Digital EX and Dolby Digital Plus for high-definition audio. Dolby TrueHD is the newest standard. It features high-definition and lossless technology, in which no data is lost in the compression process. To create surround sound, Dolby takes digital sound from a medium (such as a DVD-ROM) and reproduces it in eight channels. Seven channels cover the listening field with placement to the left front, right front, and center of the audio stage, as well as the left rear and right rear, and then two extra side speakers are added, as shown in Figure 32. The eighth channel holds extremely low-frequency sound data and is sent to a subwoofer, which can be placed anywhere in the room. To set up surround sound on your computer, you need two things: a set of surround-sound speakers and, for the greatest surround-sound experience, a sound card that is Dolby Digital–compatible.

I don't need surround sound on my computer. Why else might I need to buy an upgraded sound card? Most basic sound cards contain the following input and output jacks (or ports): microphone in, speaker out, and line in. This allows you to hook up a set of stereo speakers and a microphone. But what if you want to hook up a right and left speaker individually, or attach other audio devices to your computer? To do so, you need more ports, which are provided on upgraded sound cards like the one shown in Figure 33.

With an upgraded sound card, you can connect portable minidisc players, portable media players, portable jukeboxes, headphones, and CD players to your computer. Musicians also create music on their computers by connecting special devices (such as keyboards) directly to sound card ports. To determine whether your audio subsystem is meeting your needs, review the table in Figure 34.

Evaluating System Reliability

Many computer users decide to buy a new system not necessarily because they need a faster CPU, more RAM, or a bigger hard drive, but because they are experiencing problems such as slow performance, freezes, and crashes. Over time, even normal use can cause your computer to build up excess files and to become internally disorganized. This excess, clutter, and disorganization can lead to deteriorating performance or, far worse, system failure. If you think your system is unreliable, see if the problem is one you can fix before you buy a new machine. Proper upkeep and maintenance also may

Figure 32

Dolby Digital 7.1 surround sound gives you better-quality audio output.

postpone an expensive system upgrade or replacement.

What can I do to ensure my system performs reliably? Here are several procedures you can follow to ensure your system performs reliably:

1. **Clean out your Startup folder.** Some programs install themselves into your Startup folder and run automatically each time the computer reboots, whether you are using them or not. This unnecessary load causes extra stress on RAM. Check your Startup folder by clicking Start > All Programs. Then click on the Startup folder and make sure all the programs listed are important to you. Right-click on any unnecessary program and select Delete to remove it from the Startup folder. Make sure you delete *only* programs you are absolutely

Figure 33

In addition to improving sound quality, upgraded sound cards can provide additional ports for your audio equipment.

Photo courtesy of Creative Labs, Inc. Sound Blaster and Audigy are registered trademarks of CreativeTechnology Ltd. in the United States and other countries.

Analog/Digital Output

Line Input Signal

Microphone Input

Line Output

Rear Speaker Output

FireWire (IEEE 1394)

sure are unnecessary. Another way programs sneak their way in is to load themselves into your system tray. Keep an eye on how many icons are in the system tray and uninstall any that you do not use frequently.

2. **Clear out unnecessary files.** Temporary Internet files can accumulate quickly on your hard drive, taking up unnecessary space. Running the Disk Cleanup utility is a quick and easy way to ensure your temporary Internet files don't take up precious hard drive space. Likewise, you should delete any unnecessary files from your hard drive regularly, because they can make your hard drive run more slowly.

3. **Run spyware and adware removal programs.** These often detect and remove different pests and should be used in addition to your regular antivirus package.

4. **Run the Disk Defragmenter utility on your hard drive.** When your hard drive becomes fragmented, its storage capacity is negatively affected. When you defragment (defrag) your hard drive, files are reorganized, making the hard drive work more efficiently.

The utilities that need to be run more than once, like Disk Cleanup, Disk Defragmenter, and the antivirus and spyware programs, can be configured to run automatically at any time interval you want. You can set up a sequence of programs to run one after the other every evening while you sleep, and wake up each day to a reliable, secure system.

My system crashes often during the day. What can I do? Computer systems are complex. It's not unusual

Figure 34 | DO YOU NEED TO UPGRADE YOUR AUDIO SUBSYSTEM?

	Current System	Ideal System
Is the speaker quality high enough for the way I am using my computer?		
Is my sound card capable of 3D sound?		
Does my sound card support Dolby Digital surround sound?		
Do I have 5.1-channel surround sound or 7.1-channel surround sound?		
Do I have an HDMI port on the audio card?		

Understanding and Assessing Hardware: Evaluating Your System to have your system stop responding occasionally. If rebooting the computer doesn't help, you'll need to begin troubleshooting:

1. Check that you have enough RAM, which you learned how to do in the section "Evaluating RAM: The Memory Subsystem" earlier in this chapter. Systems with insufficient amounts of RAM often crash.

2. Make sure you have properly installed any new software or hardware. If you're using a Windows system, use the System Restore utility to "roll back" the system to a time when it worked more reliably. (To find System Restore, just type "restore" into the Start menu search box.) For Mac systems, Mac OS X Time Machine, shown in Figure 35, provides automatic backup and enables you to look through and restore (if necessary) files, folders, libraries, or the entire system.

3. If you see an error code in Windows, visit the Microsoft Knowledge Base (**support.microsoft.com**), an online resource for resolving problems with Microsoft products. This may help you determine what the error code indicates and how you may be able to solve the problem. If you don't find a satisfactory answer in the Knowledge Base, try copying the entire error message into Google and searching the larger community for solutions.

Can my software affect system reliability? Having the latest version of software products makes your system much more reliable. You should upgrade or update your operating system, browser software, and application software as often as new patches (or fixes) are reported for resolving errors. Sometimes these errors are performance-related; sometimes they are potential system security breaches.

How do I know whether updates are available for my software? You can configure Windows so that it automatically checks for, downloads, and installs any available updates for itself, Internet Explorer, and other Microsoft applications such as Microsoft Office. Many other applications now also include the ability to check for updates. Check under the Help menu of

Figure 35

Mac's Time Machine restores files, folders, libraries and, if necessary, the entire system.

the product, and often you will find a Check for Updates command.

What if none of this helps? Is buying a new system my only option? If your system is still unreliable after these changes, then you have two options:

1. **Upgrade your operating system to the latest version.** There are substantial increases in reliability with each major release of a new operating system. However, upgrading the operating system may require hardware upgrades such as additional RAM, an updated graphics processor, and an even larger hard drive. The Microsoft Windows 7 Upgrade Advisor (a free download from (**microsoft.com**) will scan your system to determine what upgrades might be required before you convert to Windows 7. Be sure to examine the *recommended* (not required) specifications of the new operating system.

2. **Reinstall the operating system.** As a last resort, you might need to reinstall the operating system. To do so, you'll want to back up all of your data files before the installation and be prepared to reinstall all your software after the installation. Make sure you have all of the original discs for the software installed on your system, along with the product keys, serial numbers, and any other activation codes so that you can reinstall them.

What happened to your last computer? If you threw it away hoping it would be safely recycled with your empty water bottles, think again. Mercury in LCD screens, cadmium in batteries and circuit boards, and flame retardant in plastic housings all are toxic. An alarming, emerging trend is that discarded machines are beginning to create an e-waste crisis.

Instead of throwing your computer away, you may be able to donate it to a nonprofit organization. Many manufacturers, such as Dell, offer recycling programs and have formed alliances with nonprofit organizations to help distribute your old technology to those who need it. You can also take your computer to an authorized computer recycling center in your area (see Figure 36). The Telecommunications Industry Association provides an e-cycling information site you can use to find a local e-cycling center (**eiae.org**).

However, before donating or recycling a computer, make sure you carefully remove all data from your hard drive, or you may end up having your good deed turn bad by becoming the victim of identity theft. Credit card numbers, bank information, Social Security numbers, tax records, passwords, and personal identification numbers (PINs) are just some of the types of sensitive information that we casually record to our computers' hard drives. Just deleting files that contain proprietary personal information is not protection enough. Likewise, reformatting or erasing your hard drive does not totally remove data, as was proved by two MIT graduate students. In 2003, they bought more than 150 used hard drives from various sources. Although some of the hard drives had been reformatted or damaged so the data was supposedly irrecoverable, the two students were able to retrieve medical records, financial information, pornography, personal e-mails, and more than 5,000 credit card numbers!

The U.S. Department of Defense suggests a seven-layer overwrite for a "secure erase." In other words, they suggest that you fill your hard drive *seven times over* with a random series of 1s and 0s. Fortunately, several programs exist for PCs running Windows, such as Active@ KillDisk, Eraser, and CyberScrub. Wipe is available for Linux, and Shredit X can be used for OS X. These programs provide secure hard drive erasures, either of specific files on your hard drive or of the entire hard drive.

Keep in mind that even these data erasure programs can't provide the ultimate level in security. Computer forensic specialists or supercyber-criminals can still manage to retrieve some data from your hard drive if they have the right tools. The ultimate level of protection comes from destroying the hard drive altogether. Suggested methods include drilling holes in the hard drive, burning or melting it, or just taking an old-fashioned sledgehammer to it! For large companies that need to upgrade large quantities of computers and have the options of destroying or recycling their old computers, the problem becomes much worse. In these cases, recycling isn't a good option, and throwing the computers away can create an environmental hazard. Companies such as GigaBiter (**gigabiter.com**) eliminate security and environmental risks associated with electronic destruction by first delaminating the hard drive and then breaking down the computer e-waste into recyclable products. The result of the final step is a sandlike substance that is 100 percent recyclable.

Eduardo Contreras/San Diego Union-Tribune/ZUMA Press\Newscom

Figure 36

An electronics scrap recycler "demanufactures" printers, computers, and other electronics and then resells the usable parts.

Making the Final Decision

Now that you have evaluated your computer system, you need to shift to questions of *value*. How closely does your system come to meeting your needs? How much would it cost to upgrade the system you have to match what you'd ideally like your computer to do, not only today but also a few years from now? How much would it cost to purchase a new system that meets these specifications?

To decide whether upgrading or buying a new system has better value for you, you need to price both scenarios. Figure 37

Figure 37 | UPGRADE/NEW PURCHASE COMPARISON WORKSHEET

Needs	Hardware Upgrade Cost	Included on New System?	Additional Expense If Not Included on New System
Portability			
Wireless connectivity			
CPU and Memory Subsystems			
CPU upgrade			
RAM upgrade			
Storage Subsystem			
Hard drive upgrade			
SSD drive			
DVD+/-RW drive			
DVD+/-RW burner			
Blu-ray drive			
Blu-ray burner			
Video and Audio Subsystems			
Video card upgrade			
Sound card upgrade			

provides an upgrade worksheet you can use to evaluate both the upgrade path and the new purchase path. Be sure to consider what benefit you might obtain by having two systems if you were to buy a new computer. Would you have a use for the older system? Would you donate it to a charitable organization? Would you be able to give it to a family member? Purchasing a new system is an important investment of your resources, and you want to make a well-reasoned, well-supported decision.

summary

1. How can I determine whether I should upgrade my existing computer or buy a new one?

To determine whether you need to upgrade your system or purchase a new one, you need to define your ideal system and what you want it to do. Then you need to perform a system evaluation to assess the subsystems in your computer, including the CPU, memory, storage, video, and audio. Finally, you need to determine if it's economical to upgrade, or whether buying a new computer would be better.

2. What does the CPU do, and how can I evaluate its performance?

Your computer's CPU processes instructions, performs calculations, manages the flow of information through the computer system, and is responsible for processing the data you input into information. CPU speed is measured in gigahertz (billions of machine cycles per second). You can tell whether your CPU is limiting your system performance by watching how busy it is as you work on your computer. The percentage of time that your CPU is working is referred to as CPU usage, which you can determine by checking the Task Manager. Benchmarking software offers direct performance comparisons of different CPUs.

3. How does memory work in my computer, and how can I evaluate how much memory I need?

RAM is your computer's short-term memory. It remembers everything that the computer needs to process data into information. However, it is an example of volatile storage. When the power is off, the data stored in RAM is cleared out. The amount of RAM sitting on memory modules in your computer is your computer's physical memory. The memory your OS uses is kernel memory. At a minimum, you need enough RAM to run the OS plus the software applications you're using, plus a bit more to hold the data you will input.

4. What are the computer's main storage devices, and how can I evaluate whether they match my needs?

Storage devices for a typical computer system may include a hard drive, an SSD drive, a flash drive, and CD and DVD drives. Blu-ray drives are gaining in popularity for viewing and burning high-density media. When you turn off your computer, the data stored in these devices is saved. These devices are referred to as *nonvolatile* storage devices. Hard drives have the largest storage capacity of any storage device and are the most economical. Newer SSD drives have the fastest access time and data transfer rate of all nonvolatile storage options. CDs and DVDs have capacities from 700 MB to 17 GB, while Blu-ray discs can hold up to 50 GB. Portable flash drives allow easy transfer of 64 GB or more of data from machine to machine. To determine the storage capacity your system needs, calculate the amount of storage your software needs to reside on your computer. To add more storage or to provide more functionality for your system, you can install additional drives, either internally or externally.

5. What components affect the output of video on my computer, and how can I evaluate whether they match my needs?

How video is displayed depends on two components: your video card and your monitor. A video card translates binary data into the images you see. These cards include their own RAM (video memory) as well as ports that allow you to connect to video equipment. The amount of video memory you need depends on what you want to display on the monitor. A more powerful card will allow you to play graphics-intense games and multimedia.

Understanding and Assessing Hardware: Evaluating Your System

290

6. What components affect the quality of sound on my computer, and how can I evaluate whether they match my needs?

Your computer's sound depends on your speakers and sound card. A sound card enables the computer to produce sounds. Users upgrade their sound cards to provide for 3D sound, surround sound, and additional ports for audio equipment.

7. How can I improve the reliability of my system?

Many computer users decide to buy a new system because they are experiencing problems with their computer. However, before you buy a new system because you think yours may be unreliable, make sure the problem is not one you can fix. Make sure you have installed any new software or hardware properly, check that you have enough RAM, run system utilities such as Disk Defragmenter and Disk Cleanup, clean out your Startup folder, remove unnecessary files from your system, and keep your software updated with patches. If you continue to have troubles with your system, reinstall or upgrade your OS, and, of course, seek technical assistance.

key terms

3D sound card

access time

BD-ROM disc

benchmarks

bit depth

Blu-ray disc

cache memory

clock speed

core

CPU usage

data transfer rate

DVD-RAM

DVD-ROM

DVD-R/RW

DVD+R/RW

External SATA (eSATA)

Express Card

front side bus (FSB)

graphics processing unit (GPU)

hard drive

head crash

hyperthreading

kernel memory

latency

memory bound

memory module (memory card)

Moore's Law

nonvolatile storage

optical media

page file

physical memory

platter

random access memory (RAM)

read/write head

serial advanced technology attachment (SATA)

sector

seek time

solid state drive (SSD)

sound card

surround sound

system evaluation

track

video card (video adapter)

video memory

virtual memory

volatile storage

Word Bank

- access time
- Blu-ray disc
- cache memory
- CPU usage
- data transfer rate
- eSATA
- express cards
- front side bus
- GPU
- hard drive
- memory bound
- memory module
- Moore's law
- sound card
- SSD
- surround sound
- system evaluation

Instructions: Fill in the blanks using the words from the Word Bank above.

Joe already has a PC but just heard about a great deal on a new one. He decides to perform a(n) (1) _____ on his computer to see whether he should keep it or buy the new one. First, he runs the Task Manager in Windows. By doing so, he can check the history of (2) _____ as he works through his day. Because he is often over 90 percent, he begins to suspect his system is (3) _____ memory bound. He has room for an additional two (4) _____ memory module(s) on his motherboard. Adding RAM is something he learned how to do this semester, but would that be enough to make this machine do all he needs?

He visits the Intel Web site to check two other important factors on his model of CPU: the amount of (5) _____ memory and the speed of the (6) _____. It looks like the newer i7 processor would be much faster overall. It seems each generation of processors is so much faster than the last. That rule, (7) _____, is still holding true!

He continues to evaluate his system by checking out which components he has and which ones he'll need. He notes the storage capacity of the (8) _____. Recently, he has been wishing his system had a(n) (9) _____ port because adding an external hard drive would give him enough space to start to record HD television shows. As it is, he is running out of space to store files. But the (10) _____, or the amount of time it takes to retrieve data from the disk drive, on any mechanical drive is slow compared to the (11) _____ in the new computer he's eyeing, which has no moving parts at all. Joe also notes that he is unable to do a complete backup of his music library onto optical media now that he has 40 GB of music data. His current system can't burn a (12) _____, but the new system could. The new system would also include a(n) (13) _____ that would allow him to connect his Xbox 360 using the HDMI cable. It would be great if he could take advantage of the 5.1 (14) _____ that is on the soundtrack of most of the movies he watches on DVD.

He also has a lot of friends who play video games on their computer systems. However, his current system doesn't meet the minimum requirements for a video card. Newer cards have blindingly fast (15) _____, and some cards even have multiple processors. Overall, with prices dropping, it seems like time to go buy that new system!

Jen lives across the hall from you. She heard you worried last semester that your PC wasn't fast enough. Between the simulation program for math, the reports you did for English, and your programming class, your computer was running slowly and you were out of storage space. She's offered to help you upgrade your system, but she needs you to tell her what you want upgraded and why.

Instructions: Using the preceding scenario, write a letter to Jen using key terms from the chapter. Be sure your sentences are grammatically correct and technically meaningful.

Instructions: Answer the multiple-choice and true–false questions below for more practice with key terms and concepts from this chapter.

Multiple Choice

1. The amount of RAM recommended for most systems today is measured in
a. gigabytes. c. megahertz.
b. gigahertz. d. kilobytes.

2. When evaluating CPU performance, which is NOT a feature you need to consider?
a. Amount of cache memory
b. Speed of the processor
c. Speed of the front side bus
d. Size of the processor

3. RAM is classified as what kind of storage in a computer system?
a. Volatile c. Permanent
b. Nonvolatile d. Flash

4. SSD technology involves
a. fast, cool hard drives that have no moving parts.
b. surround-sound devices that support multichannel audio.
c. hard drives that are expandable beyond 2 TB.
d. faster transfer speeds in the front side bus.

5. From which location is it slowest to get data to the CPU for processing?
a. RAM
b. Cache memory
c. Hard drive
d. Virtual memory

6. Multicore CPUs are
a. not common in notebook computers.
b. available in only a dual-core configuration.
c. available in two- or four-core designs.
d. available in seven- or eight-core designs.

7. eSATA is a high-speed port used for
a. video processing.
b. attaching external hard drives.
c. communication with printers.
d. adding RAM.

8. Blu-ray technology is required to store what kind of media?
a. Standard definition video
b. High-definition video
c. Analog audio
d. Digital audio

9. Evaluating your computer system is important when
a. your system has stopped working altogether.
b. you are planning to purchase a new system.
c. you are wondering if you should upgrade your system.
d. All of the above.

10. Which of the following should you do to ensure the reliability of your system?
a. Run Disk Defragmenter.
b. Run Disk Cleanup.
c. Install software upgrades and patches.
d. All of the above.

True–False

_____ 1. The task manager provides information for the windows operating system about programs and processes running on your computer.

_____ 2. Installing a second hard drive in your system will have an immediate impact on system performance if your system is memory bound.

_____ 3. Data is stored using motors and spinning platters on hard drives, CDs, and solid state drives.

_____ 4. A video card has its own memory and its own processor.

_____ 5. CPU performance is affected by the clock speed, the cache size, and the transfer speed of the front side bus.

1. Evaluating Your System

A small worksheet follows the end of each section in this chapter to guide you as you evaluate your own system. These smaller worksheets have been combined into one complete worksheet that is on the book's Companion Website (**pearsonhighered.com/ techinaction**). Download the worksheet and fill it in based on the computer you are currently using.

a. Research the costs of replacement parts for those components you feel should be upgraded.
b. Research the cost of a new system that would be roughly equivalent to your current computer after upgrades.
c. Determine whether it would be more cost effective to upgrade your computer or buy a new one.

2. Your Software Needs

What software do you need for the courses you're taking this semester? Will you need any different software for next semester? How many of these software applications do you run at one time? Examine the requirements for those software packages. Prepare a table that lists the software applications you are currently using as well as any you may need to use in the future. For each, list the minimum RAM and hard drive space requirements. How does your system measure up against those requirements?

3. Campus Computer Use

What kinds of computers do students use in college, and how do different people budget for their computer needs? To find an answer to these questions, interview several people who started college in different years. Ask them the following questions:

a. Did you need your own computing equipment, or did you use your college's equipment when you first started school? Would you recommend I do the same?
b. Did you need to upgrade your computer before you came to college? How did you do this?
c. Was the computer you used in your first year of college able to handle your workload in later years?
d. If you used one computer throughout college, what upgrades did you need to perform?
e. If you had to buy a new computer during college, how much money did you budget and how much did you spend? What did you do with your old computer?

4. Buying Computers Online

Visit an online seller of computer systems and components such as Cool Computing (**coolcomputing.com**), Price Watch (**pricewatch.com**), Newegg (**newegg.com**), or Tiger Direct (**tigerdirect.com**) and answer the following questions:

a. What is the current cost of RAM?
b. How much additional RAM could you add to your system?
c. What are the prices of the most popular CPU chips?
d. How much would you need to spend to upgrade to a new operating system?
e. How would each of these help you in your work?

5. Comparing CPU Benchmark Results

You want to purchase a new system but need to decide which CPU best fits your needs. Using the Web, research several different CPU benchmarking reports. Compare specifications for the CPUs, including number of cores, clock speed, cache size, front side bus transfer rates, and cost. From your list, identify the one CPU you would choose and explain why. Be sure to try to find benchmarking reports that simulate the types of programs you would be using most often.

1. Using Your Computer for Education and Business

As you move from an educational environment to a business environment, how you use your computer will inevitably change. Write one or two paragraphs that describe what your computer system is like now. Then write one or two paragraphs that describe what your ideal computer system would be like after you've graduated and entered the workforce. What different components, if any, would your ideal system need? Could you upgrade your current system to incorporate these new components, or would you need to buy a new system? Make sure you defend the position you take with information covered in this chapter. To help you in your decision, fill out the worksheet, similar to Figure 2, that is available on the companion Website (**pearsonhighered.com/techinaction**).

2. Assessing Memory Use

Your home office computer is running a bit sluggishly, and you want to determine which application is the memory hog so you can either avoid using it or use it without any other programs running to preserve RAM. You've been told you can do this in the Processes tab in the Task Manager utility. On your computer, open the Task Manager utility and determine which currently running application is using the most memory. Can you tell how much it is using? Note that because the names of the programs have been shortened (for example, Microsoft Word is referred to as *winword.exe*), you may not immediately recognize the program names.

3. IT Support at Work

When you are evaluating potential employers, one consideration will be how well they support you as an employee and provide the environment you need to do productive work. What questions would you ask in an interview to determine what kind of IT support you can expect in your new position?

4. Web Programming Software at Home

You are a Web programmer and you often work from home. You need to investigate whether your home computer will be able to run the three programs you use most frequently at work: Adobe Photoshop, Microsoft Visual Basic .NET, and Microsoft Word. Use the Web to research RAM and hard drive requirements for these programs. Will your computer be able to handle the load?

5. Build an Ideal System

Imagine that a client tells you she wants a system that has at least 8 GB of RAM, the fastest processor on the market, and enough storage space to edit hours of video and music files. In table format, compare the components and pricing of three systems that would meet the client's needs by visiting manufacturer Web sites such as Maingear.com (**maingear.com**), Falcon Northwest (**falcon-nw.com**), and Alienware (**alienware.com**). Make a final selection and justify why this is the best solution.

Understanding and Assessing Hardware: Evaluating Your System

Instructions: Albert Einstein used *Gedankenexperiments*, or critical thinking questions, to develop his theory of relativity. Some ideas are best understood by experimenting with them in our own minds. The following critical thinking questions are designed to demand your full attention but require only a comfortable chair—no technology.

1. Your Ideal System

If you could buy any new system on the market, not worrying about the price, what would you buy? What kind of video card(s) would you have? How much RAM would you have installed, and which model of CPU would you request? Which sound card would fit your needs? Would you know how to use your ideal system?

2. Future Systems

Given current trends in technology, what kind of system can you imagine upgrading to or buying new in 10 years? Which components would change the most? Which components would need to stay the same, if any? What do you imagine the entire system would look like?

3. Impacts of New Technology

We are constantly being bombarded with new technology. We hear of new tools and system improvements from our friends, relatives, and advertisements almost daily. This chapter talks about upgrading current systems so that we can take advantage of some of the newer technology. There are some improvements we may absolutely need (more RAM, perhaps), whereas there are others that we may simply want (such as a Blu-ray burner). What do you think are the societal, economic, and environmental impacts of our wanting to have the latest and greatest computers? Do you think the push toward faster and more powerful machines is a good thing?

4. Recycling Computers

Mercury in LCD monitors and switches and cadmium in batteries and circuit boards are environmentally toxic metals. Discarded machines are beginning to create an e-waste crisis. Who do you think should assume the cost of recycling computers? Should it be the consumer, the government, or the industry? What other options are there besides throwing older computers away?

5. System Longevity

If you purchase a computer system for business purposes, the Internal Revenue Service (IRS) allows you to depreciate its cost over five years. The IRS considers this a reasonable estimate of the useful lifetime of a computer system. What do you think most home users expect in terms of how long their computer systems should last? How does the purchase of a computer system compare with other major household appliances in terms of cost, value, benefit, life span, and upgrade potential?

Meeting a Corporation's Computing Needs

Problem

In a large organization, whether it is a company or a college, the IT department often has to install several different types of computing systems. There would be advantages to having every computer be identical, but because different departments have different needs and items are purchased at different times, it is typical for there to be significant differences between two computers in the same corporation.

Process

Split your class into teams.

1. Select a department or computer lab on campus (or one within your company or at the public library). *Note:* If you are physically unable to go to a lab, describe the type of components that would be needed by that particular department. (For example, if you choose the computer art department, you know you will need good graphics software. You also know you will need certain levels of RAM and other functionalities to accommodate that graphics software.)

2. Following the worksheet in Figure 2, analyze the computing needs of that particular computer lab.

3. Using the System Evaluation worksheet (found on the Companion Website at **pearsonhighered.com/techinaction**), develop a complete systems evaluation of the computers at the lab.

4. Consider which upgrades to hardware, software, and peripherals would make this lab better able to meet the needs of its users.

5. Write a report that summarizes your findings. If purchasing a new system is more economical, then recommend which system the lab should buy.

Conclusion

The pace of technological change can make computer science an uncomfortable field for some. For others, it is precisely the pace of change that is exciting. Being able to evaluate a computer system and match it to the current needs of its users is an important skill.

In addition to the review materials presented here, you'll find additional materials featured with the Pearson IT Multimedia Library and the Companion Website (**pearsonhighered.com/ techinaction**), which will help reinforce your understanding of the chapter content. These materials include the following:

Active Helpdesk

In Active Helpdesk calls, you'll assume the role of helpdesk operator, taking calls about the concepts you've learned in this chapter. You'll apply what you've learned and receive feedback from a supervisor to review and reinforce those concepts. The Active Helpdesk calls for this chapter are listed below and can be found on the Pearson IT Multimedia Library:

- Evaluating Your CPU and RAM
- Evaluating Computer System Components

Sound Bytes

Sound Bytes are dynamic multimedia tutorials that help demystify even the most complex topics. You'll view video clips and animations that illustrate computer concepts and then apply what you've learned by reviewing with the Sound Byte Labs, which include quizzes and activities specifically tailored to each Sound Byte. The Sound Bytes for this chapter are listed below and can be found on the Pearson IT Multimedia Library:

- Using Windows 7 to Evaluate CPU Performance
- Memory Hierarchy Interactive
- Installing RAM
- CD, DVD, and Blu-ray Reading and Writing Interactive
- Installing a Blu-ray Drive

Companion Website

The *Technology in Action* Companion Website includes a variety of additional materials to help you review and learn more about the topics in this chapter. The resources available at **pearsonhighered.com/techinaction** include:

- **Online Study Guide.** This chapter features an online true–false and multiple-choice quiz. You can take these quizzes, automatically check the results, and e-mail the results to your instructor.
- **Web Research Projects.** This chapter features several Web research projects that ask you to search the Web for information on computer-related careers, milestones in computer history, important people and companies, emerging technologies, and the applications and implications of different technologies.

networking

connecting computing devices

From Chapter 7 of *Technology in Action Complete*, Seventh Edition, Alan Evans, Kendall Martin, Mary Anne Poatsy. Copyright © 2011 by Pearson Education, Inc. Published by Pearson Prentice Hall. All rights reserved.

networking

connecting computing devices

resources

 Active Helpdesk

- Understanding Networking

 Sound Bytes

- Installing a Home Computer Network
- Securing Wireless Networks

 Companion Website

The Companion Website includes a variety of additional materials to help you review and learn more about the topics in this chapter. Go to: *pearsonhighered.com/techinaction*

how cool is *this*? Configuring a
network using Windows networking tools can often be a **confusing** task
for beginners. Network Magic from Cisco is a software package designed to simplify
configuring network components. The **Network Magic** software guides you
through tasks such as sharing devices, such as printers,
among multiple computers; configuring folders, such
as ones containing music and digital images, for
sharing; setting up **security alerts** to
warn you of intruders on your network; and
repairing damaged network connections.
The software provides a **visual
map** of your network so you can
easily see which devices are online and
change the configuration of any device
quickly and easily.

Anyka\Shutterstock

Networking Fundamentals

Even if you do not have a home network, you use and interact with networks all the time. In fact, every time you use the Internet you're interacting with the world's largest network. But what, exactly, *is* a network? A computer **network** is simply two or more computers that are connected via software and hardware so that they can communicate with each other. Devices connected to a network are referred to as **nodes**. A node can be a computer, a peripheral (such as a printer), a game console (such as an Xbox 360 or a Wii), a digital video recorder (such as a TiVo), or a communications device (such as a modem). The main function for most networks is to facilitate information sharing, but networks provide other benefits.

What are the benefits of networks? There are several benefits to installing a network. First of all, networks

allow users to share peripherals. For example, in Figure 1a, the computers are not networked. Computer 1 is connected to the printer, but Computer 2 is not. To print files from Computer 2, users have to transfer them using a flash drive or another storage medium to Computer 1, or they have to disconnect the printer from Computer 1 and connect it to Computer 2. By networking Computer 1 and Computer 2, as shown in Figure 1b, both computers can print from the printer attached to Computer 1 without transferring files or moving the printer (although Computer 1 must be powered on). Allowing two people to share a printer saves the cost of buying one printer for each computer.

By networking computers, you can transfer files from one computer to another without using external storage media such as flash drives. In addition, you can set up shared folders in Windows or OS X that allow the user of each computer on the

Figure 1

(a) Computers 1 and 2 are not networked, and Computer 2 cannot access the printer. (b) Networking allows sharing of the printer.

Networking: Connecting Computing Devices

network to store files that other computers on the network may need to access, as shown in Figure 2.

This Windows network has two computers attached to it, ALAN-PC and PAT, which are running different Windows operating systems. In this example, both the Public and the SharedDocs folders do the same thing: they enable file sharing. When viewing files in Windows Explorer, Alan can easily access files located in the SharedDocs directory on Pat's computer, such as the file called One Yellow Rose.

Can I use a network to share an Internet connection?   If you install a device called a *router* on your network, you can share broadband Internet connections. Although you could share a dial-up Internet connection, the resulting speed of the networked connection would be painfully slow and would make surfing the Internet almost impossible. We'll discuss routers in detail later in the chapter.

Network Architectures

The term **network architecture** refers to the design of a network. Network architectures are classified according to the way in which they are controlled and the distance between their nodes.

What do we mean by networks being "administered"?   A network can be administered (managed) in either of two main ways: locally or centrally. A peer-to-peer network is the most common example of a locally administered network. The most common type of centrally administered network is a client/server network.

What are peer-to-peer networks? In a **peer-to-peer (P2P) network**, each node connected to the network can communicate directly with every other node on the network instead of having a separate device control the network centrally. Thus, all nodes on this type of network are peers (equals). When printing, for example, a computer on a P2P network doesn't have to go through the computer that's connected to the printer. Instead, it can communicate directly with the printer. Figure 1b shows a very small peer-to-peer network.

Because they are simple to set up, P2P networks are the most common type of home network. We discuss different types of peer-to-peer networks that are popular in homes later in this chapter.

What are client/server networks? Very small schools and offices may have P2P networks. However, most networks that have 10 or more nodes are client/server networks. A **client/server network** contains two different types of computers: clients and servers. A **client** is a computer on which users accomplish specific tasks (such as construct spreadsheets) and make specific requests (such as printing a file). The **server** is the computer that provides information or resources to the client computers on the network. The server on a client/server network also provides central administration for functions on the network (such as printing). Figure 3 illustrates a client/server network in action.

The Internet is an example of a client/server network. When your computer is connected to the Internet, it is functioning as a client computer. When it accesses the Internet through an Internet service provider (ISP), your computer connects to a

Figure 2

Windows Explorer showing shared folders on two computers.

server computer maintained by the ISP. The server "serves up" resources to your computer so that you can interact with the Internet.

Are client/server networks ever used as home networks? Although client/server networks can be configured for home use, P2P networks are more often used in the home because they cost less than

Step 1:
Client computer requests a service.

Computer A (client)

Computer B (server)

Step 2:
Server computer provides service.

Figure 3

In a client/server network, a computer acts either as a client making requests for resources or as a server providing resources.

client/server networks and are easier to configure and maintain. To set up a client/server network in your home, you have to buy an extra computer to act as the server. Although a computer could function both as a server and as a client, its performance would be significantly degraded because of the complexity of the server-related functions it would have to perform. Therefore, it is impractical to use a single computer as both a client and a server. In addition, you need training to install and maintain the special software required by client/server networks. The major benefits a client/server network provides (such as centralized security and administration) are not necessary in most home networks.

However, because of the proliferation of media files from digital cameras, camcorders, and music downloads on home computers, home server options are now being marketed. Windows Home Server and Hewlett Packard's MediaSmart servers, although not as fully featured as servers

used in business networks, are increasingly popular choices for managing an entire family's personal media. We'll discuss servers designed for home networks later in the chapter.

Describing Networks Based on Distance

How does the distance between nodes define a network? The distance between nodes on a network is another way to describe a network. A **local area network (LAN)** is a network in which the nodes are located within a small geographic area. Examples include a network in a computer lab at school or at a fast-food restaurant. A **home area network (HAN)** is a network located in a home. HANs are used to connect all of its digital devices, such as computers, peripherals, phones, cameras, digital video recorders (DVRs), and televisions.

Is it possible to connect LANs together? A wide area network **(WAN)** is made up of LANs connected over long distances. Say a school has two campuses (east and west) located in different towns. Connecting the LAN at the east campus to the LAN at the west campus by telecommunications lines would allow the users on the two LANs to communicate. The two LANs would be described as a single WAN.

Are wireless networks that cover large portions of cities considered WANs? Technically, wireless networks like the one deployed in Minneapolis, which provides Internet access to city residents and visitors, are WANs. However, when a network is designed to provide access to a specific geographic area, such as an entire city, the network is usually called a **metropolitan area network (MAN)**. Many cities in the United States are now deploying MANs to provide Internet access to residents and provide convenience for tourists.

Network Components

To function, all networks must include (1) a means of connecting the nodes on the network (cables or wireless technology),

Networking software running on each computer

Computer 2 network node

Printer network node

Transmission media (wires or radio waves) connecting network nodes

Computer 1 network node

External network adapter

Internal network adapter (network interface card)

Router

Wireless access point

Network adapter attached to or inserted in each network node

Specialized network navigation devices (used on some networks)

Figure 4

Network components.

(2) special devices that allow the nodes to communicate with each other and to send data, and (3) software that allows the network to run. We discuss each of these components next (see Figure 4).

Transmission Media

How are nodes on a network connected? All network nodes (computers and peripherals) are connected to each other and to the network by **transmission media**. A transmission medium establishes a communications channel between the nodes on a network and can take several forms:

1. Networks can use additional cable to connect nodes, such as twisted-pair cable, coaxial cable, or fiber-optic cable. You have probably seen twisted-pair and coaxial cable. Normal telephone wire is **twisted-pair cable**. It is made up of copper wires that are twisted around each other and surrounded by a plastic jacket. If you have cable TV, the cable running into your TV or cable box is **coaxial cable**. Coaxial cable consists of a single copper wire surrounded by

layers of plastic. **Fiber-optic cable** is made up of plastic or glass fibers that transmit data at extremely fast speeds.

2. Wireless networks use radio waves instead of wires or cable to connect nodes.

3. Networks can use existing wiring, such as power lines, to connect nodes.

What media should I use to ensure my network transfers data quickly? Different types of transmission media transmit data at different speeds. **Data transfer rate** (also called **bandwidth**) is the maximum speed at which data can be transmitted between two nodes on a network. **Throughput** is the actual speed of data transfer that is achieved. It is usually less than the data transfer rate. Data transfer rate and throughput are usually measured in megabits per second (Mbps). A megabit, when applied to data transfer rates, represents 1 million bits. Twisted-pair cable, coaxial cable, and wireless media provide enough bandwidth for most home networks, whereas fiber-optic cable is sometimes used in client/server networks.

Network Components

307

Network Adapters

How do the different nodes on the network communicate?

Network **adapters** are devices connected to or installed in network nodes that enable the nodes to communicate with each other and to access the network. Most desktop and notebook computers (and many peripherals) sold today contain network adapters installed *inside* as expansion cards. This type of adapter is referred to as a **network interface card (NIC)**.

What if I don't have a network adapter installed inside my computer or peripheral?

Network adapters are also available as external devices that plug into an available USB port. These are often used to provide older computing devices or other devices (such as TiVo digital video recorders) with wireless connectivity. We discuss network adapters in more detail throughout the chapter.

Network Navigation Devices

How is data sent through a network?

Data is sent over transmission media in bundles. Each bundle is called a **packet**. For computers to communicate, these packets of data must be able to flow between computers. A **network navigation device** helps make this data flow possible. These devices, which are attached to the network, enable the transmission of data. Some simple peer-to-peer networks do not require network navigation devices because the network adapters serve that purpose. Networks that are more sophisticated need specialized navigation devices.

What network navigation devices might I use on my home network?

The two most common specialized navigation devices are routers and switches. A **router** transfers packets of data between

> ❝**What software do home networks require?**❞

two or more networks. For example, if a home network is connected to the Internet, a router is required to send data between the two networks (the home network and the Internet). A **switch** is a "traffic cop" on a network. Switches receive data packets and send them to their intended nodes on the same network (not between different networks). Most routers sold for home use have switches integrated into them. We discuss routers and switches in more detail later in the chapter.

Networking Software

What software do home networks require?

Home networks need operating system (OS) software that supports peer-to-peer networking. The most common versions of Windows used in the home (Windows 7, Vista, and XP) support P2P networking. You can connect computers running any of these OSs to the same network. Mac OS X and the various versions of Linux also support P2P networking. Moreover, computers using OS X and Windows can communicate with each other on the same network.

Is the same software used in client/server networks?

Client/server networks are controlled by a central server that has specialized **network operating system (NOS)** software installed on it. This software handles requests for information, Internet access, and the use of peripherals for the rest of the network nodes. Examples of NOS software include Windows Server 2008 and SUSE Linux Enterprise.

Types of Peer-to-Peer Networks

The most common type of network you will probably encounter in the home is a peer-to-peer network, because this is the type of network you would set up in your home. Therefore, we'll focus on P2P networks in this chapter. There are three main types of P2P networks:

1. Wired Ethernet networks
2. Wireless Ethernet networks
3. Power-line networks

 SOUND BYTE

Installing a Home Computer Network

Installing a network is relatively easy if you've seen someone else do it. In this Sound Byte, you'll learn how to install the hardware and configure Windows for a wired or wireless home network.

The major differences among these networks are the transmission media by which the nodes are connected and the bandwidth each achieves. In the following sections, we will look at these networks and how each one is set up.

Wired Ethernet Networks

What are Ethernet networks? An **Ethernet network** is so named because it uses the Ethernet protocol as the means (or standard) by which the nodes on the network communicate. The Ethernet protocol was developed by the Institute of Electrical and Electronics Engineers (IEEE). This non-profit group develops many standard specifications for electronic data transmission that are adopted throughout the world. Each standard the IEEE develops is numbered, with 802.3 being the standard for wired Ethernet networks. The Ethernet protocol makes Ethernet networks extremely efficient at moving data. However, to achieve this efficiency, the algorithms for moving data through an Ethernet network are complex.

Because of this complexity, Ethernet networks require additional devices such as switches and routers. A **wired Ethernet network** is slightly more complicated to set up than other home network options (such as the direct connection of two Windows computers), but these networks are faster, more reliable, and less expensive, making them the most popular choice for home networks. Although 100 Mbps Ethernet networks are most commonly installed in homes, prices are falling quickly on 1-gigabit-per-second (1 Gbps, or 1,000 Mbps) Ethernet components. The potential high throughput of Gigabit Ethernet is useful if you're moving large files, such as downloaded movies, around your home network.

How do I create an Ethernet network? An Ethernet network requires you to install or attach network adapters to each computer or peripheral you want to connect to the network. Because Ethernet networks are so common, most computers sold today come with Ethernet adapters preinstalled. To see if you have a network adapter installed in your Windows computer

(and check whether the adapter is working), click on the Hardware and Sound Group and then access Device Manager from the Control Panel (see Figure 5). Click on the Network adapters section to display installed adapters.

As noted earlier, such internal network adapters are referred to as *network interface cards (NICs)*. Modern Ethernet NICs are usually 10/100/1000 Mbps cards (see Figure 6a). This means they can handle the old 10 Mbps and 100 Mbps data transfer rates as well as the newer 1 Gbps data transfer rate.

If your computer doesn't have a NIC (or the NIC installed in your motherboard fails), you can buy one and install it or you can use a USB adapter, which plugs into any

Figure 5

This Windows device manager shows a wireless and a wired network adapter installed in a computer.

Figure 6

Ethernet network adapters come in a variety of versions, including (a) a 10/100/1000 NIC, which is installed in an expansion slot inside the system unit, (b) a USB adapter, and (c) an ExpressCard.

Types of Peer-to-Peer Networks

open USB port on the system unit (see Figure 6b). Although you can use USB versions in notebooks, ExpressCard versions of Ethernet NICs are made especially for notebooks (see Figure 6c). ExpressCards are about the size of a flash drive and fit into specially designed slots on a notebook. There are several different configurations of ExpressCards, so make sure you are purchasing the correct one for your computer. However, most new notebooks include built-in wired and wireless Ethernet adapters.

How are nodes connected on wired Ethernet networks? The most popular transmission media option for wired Ethernet networks is **unshielded twisted-pair (UTP) cable**. UTP cable is composed of four pairs of wires that are twisted around each other to reduce electrical interference. You can buy UTP cable in varying lengths with RJ-45 connectors (Ethernet connectors) already attached. RJ-45 connectors resemble standard phone connectors (called *RJ-11 connectors*) but are slightly larger and have contacts for eight wires (four pairs) instead of four wires (see Figure 7). You must use UTP cable with RJ-45 connectors on an Ethernet network because a phone cable will not work.

Do all wired Ethernet networks use the same kind of UTP cable? Figure 8 lists the three main types of UTP cable you would consider using in home-wired Ethernet networks—Cat 5E, Cat 6, and Cat 7—and their data transfer rates. Although Cat 5E cable is the cheapest and is sufficient for many home networking tasks, installing **Cat 6 cable** will allow you to run a Gigabit Ethernet network. Gigabit networks support throughput that is designed to handle data-intensive file transfers, such as digital movies. Cat 7 cable is designed for Ultra-Fast Ethernet (10 Gigabit Ethernet)

networks that run at speeds as fast as 10 Gbps. Installing a 10 Gigabit Ethernet network in the home is probably unnecessary because today's home applications don't require this rate of data transfer. However, if the cost of installing Cat 7 cable is not significantly more than installing Cat 6 cable, you may want to consider using it as a hedge against higher bandwidth requirements of future networking applications.

Is UTP cable difficult to install? UTP cable is no more difficult to install than normal phone cable. You just need to take a few precautions. Avoid putting sharp bends into the cable when running it around corners because this can damage the copper wires inside and lead to breakage. Also, run the cable around the perimeter of the room (instead of under a rug, for example) to prevent damage to wires from foot traffic.

How long can an Ethernet cable run be? Cable runs for Ethernet networks using UTP cable can't exceed 100 meters (328 feet) or the signal starts to degrade. For cable runs of more than 100 meters, you can use a **repeater**, a device that is installed on long cable runs to amplify the signal. In effect, repeaters act as signal boosters. Repeaters can extend run lengths to 600 feet, but they do add to the cost of a network. Whenever possible, use continuous lengths of cable. Although two cables can be spliced together with a connecting jack, this creates a point of failure for the cable, because connectors can loosen in the connecting jack and moisture or dust can accumulate on the contacts. Usually, extending your wired network using wireless technology is a better option than using repeaters or splicing cable.

If I only have notebook computers, why would I even consider using a wired network? Because the whole idea of notebooks is portability, it seems natural to connect them to a network using wireless media. However, most wired networks achieve a much higher rate of data throughput than wireless networks. When engaging in large file transfers (such as downloading digital movies), it may be very desirable to connect your notebook to your network using a cable to take advantage of faster data transfer rates. Fortunately, most wireless routers sold for the home market include an option for creating wired

Figure 7

(a) An RJ-45 (Ethernet) connector, which is used on UTP cables; and (b) a typical RJ-11 connector, which is used on standard phone cords.

connections as well. Therefore, you can get the best of both worlds by using your notebook in wireless mode most of the time and connecting it to your network via a wired connection when you need increased throughput.

Figure 8 | DATA TRANSFER RATES FOR POPULAR HOME NETWORK CABLE TYPES

UTP Cable Category	Data Transfer Rate
Category 5E (Cat 5E)	100 to 1,000 Mbps
Category 6 (Cat 6)	1,000 Mbps (1 Gbps) and higher
Category 7 (Cat 7)	10 Gbps and higher

Ethernet Switches

How do Ethernet networks use switches?
Data is transmitted through the wires of an Ethernet network in packets. Imagine the data packets on an Ethernet network as cars on a road. If there were no traffic signals or rules of the road (such as driving on the right-hand side), we'd see a lot more collisions between vehicles, and people wouldn't get where they were going as readily (or at all). Data packets can also suffer collisions. If data packets collide, the data in them is damaged or lost. In either case, the network doesn't function efficiently. The routers you buy for home networks have a switch integrated into them, so you won't need to buy a stand-alone switch for your home network.

As shown in Figure 9, a switch in an Ethernet network acts like a traffic signal (or a traffic cop) by enforcing the rules of the data road on the transmission media. The switch keeps track of the data packets and, in conjunction with network interface cards, helps the data packets find their destinations without running into each other. This keeps the network running efficiently.

Switches are often mistakenly referred to as *hubs*. A **hub** is a network navigation device that merely retransmits a signal to all other nodes attached to it. Switches are essentially "smart hubs" because they

transmit data only to the node to which it should be sent. When Ethernet networks first came out, switches were much more expensive than hubs, so many home networks used hubs, but today there is virtually no cost difference. Therefore, most navigation devices sold for home networks are switches (even if they are mistakenly referred to as hubs).

How many computers and peripherals can be connected to a switch?
Switches are differentiated by the number of ports they have for connecting network devices. Four- and eight-port switches are often used in home networks. A four-port switch can connect a maximum of four devices to the network, whereas an eight-port switch can handle eight devices. You should buy a switch that has enough ports for all the devices you want to connect to the network. Many people buy switches with more ports than they currently need so that they can expand their network in the future.

A wonderful feature of switches is that you can daisy-chain them together. Usually, one port on a switch is designated for plugging into a second switch. You can chain two four-port switches together to

Figure 9

A simplified explanation is that switches (working in conjunction with NICs) act like traffic signals or traffic cops. They enforce the rules of the data road on an Ethernet network and help prevent data packets from crashing into each other.

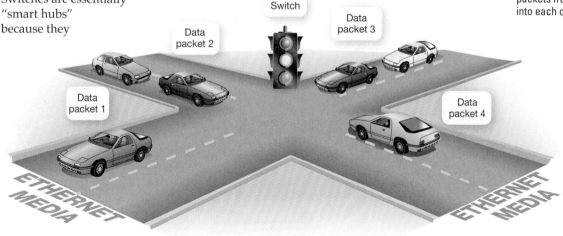

provide connections for a total of six devices. Most switches can be chained to provide hundreds of ports, which would far exceed the needs of most home networks, but may provide you with needed expandability in a small business network.

Ethernet Routers

How is data from an Ethernet network shared with the Internet or another network? As mentioned earlier, routers are devices that transfer packets of data between two or more networks. If a home network is connected to the Internet, you need a router to send data between the home network and the Internet.

Because so many people are sharing Internet access in home networks, manufacturers are making devices that combine switches and routers and are specifically designed to connect to DSL or cable modems. Such devices are often referred to as **DSL/cable routers**. If you want your Ethernet network to connect to the Internet through a DSL or cable modem, obtaining a DSL/cable router is essential. Because you already need a switch to connect multiple devices on an Ethernet network, these routers (which include switching capabilities) fulfill a dual role by controlling your network traffic and allowing your Internet connection to be shared. Figure 10 shows an example of an Ethernet network configured using a DSL/cable router.

Besides computers, what other devices can I attach to a router? Because sharing peripherals is a major benefit of installing a network, many peripheral devices, such as scanners and printers, now come with built-in Ethernet capability. Such devices are usually described as network-ready devices. A **network-ready device** can be connected directly to a router instead of to a computer on the network. These devices can then be accessed by any computer on the network. If a printer were connected

Figure 10

Two desktop computers and a notebook connected to a DSL/cable router.

DSL/Cable modem

DSL/Cable router

Computer #1

Computer #2

Computer #3

Networking: Connecting Computing Devices

directly to another computer on the network instead of to the router, that computer would need to be switched on so other computers could access the printer. With a network-ready printer, only the printer needs to be powered on for any computer on the network to print to it. Many network-ready printers contain wireless NICs so they can be easily installed on wireless networks.

Network attached storage (NAS) devices are also becoming popular in home networks. People are generating tremendous quantities of digital data today with digital cameras and camcorders, and these digital files need to be stored. Although data can always be stored on individual hard drives in computers on a network, NAS devices provide for centralized data storage and access.

Popular for years on business networks, NAS devices are specialized computing devices designed to store and manage data. You can think of them as specialized external hard drives. NAS devices, like the My Book series from Western Digital, connect directly to the network through a router or switch. Specialized software can then be installed on computers attached to the network to ensure that all data saved to an individual computer is also stored on the NAS as a backup.

Aside from creating backups, NAS devices facilitate the sharing of files such as movies, music, and digital photos. Some NAS devices, such as those in the Western Digital My Book line (see Figure 11), are accessible over the Internet, making it possible to retrieve your data wherever you have an Internet connection.

A **digital media receiver (DMR)**, which can also be called a *media extender* or a *media adapter*, is often connected to a home network. DMRs are specialized entertainment devices that are specifically designed to retrieve digital media (music, movies, or pictures) from computers or storage devices on a network and display them on televisions or home theater systems. Some DMRs include their own displays and speakers, while others must be connected to a television or stereo system.

Home network servers, such as a computer configured with Windows Home

Ethernet port for easy connection to a router

Figure 11

The My Book drives from Western Digital feature NAS devices that can store 2 TB of data in a device the size of a small book.

Courtesy Western Digital Corporation; Courtesy Western Digital Corporation

Server, can also be connected to the router on a home network. Home servers do not necessarily convert a home peer-to-peer network into a client/server network, but the servers do take charge of a variety of tasks that are often performed centrally in a client/server network. Home servers often handle the following tasks:

- Back up files for all computers connected to the network.
- Act as a repository for files to be shared across the network (such as music and video files).
- Function as an access gateway to allow any computer on the network to be accessed from a remote location via the Internet.

All of these devices can usually be attached to a network via either wired or wireless transmission media as the situation demands.

Wireless Ethernet Networks

What is a wireless network? A **wireless network** uses radio waves instead of wires or cables as its transmission media. Just as it established the 802.3 standard for wired Ethernet networks, the IEEE has established standards for wireless Ethernet networks. Any current **wireless Ethernet network** in the United States will be based on the **802.11 standard**, which was established in 1997. The 802.11 standard is also known as **Wi-Fi**. Four standards are currently defined under 802.11: 802.11a, 802.11b, 802.11g, and 802.11n. The last of these was ratified in 2009 and is quickly becoming the most popular standard in home networks. The main differences among these standards are the maximum data transfer

Types of Peer-to-Peer Networks

rates and the types of security that they support. For home networking, 802.11g and 802.11n are the standards most commonly used today.

The 802.11g standard, which supports a data transfer rate of 54 Mbps, is a well-established standard for home use because it is much faster than the original 802.11b standard. Devices using the newly ratified 802.11n standard use multiple transmitter and receiver antennas to achieve higher throughput and increased signal range. Devices using the 802.11n standard are more costly than 802.11g devices. However, 802.11n devices usually achieve a data transfer rate that usually exceeds 200 Mbps. Since the signals produced by 802.11n devices also cover a wider area than 802.11g devices, they can be used effectively even in large houses. Therefore, you may want to spend the extra money on 802.11n equipment to achieve good wireless coverage throughout your home.

Do all my devices need to use the same wireless networking standard? When new standards are designed, they are made to be backward compatible with previous standards (work with previous standards). For instance, 802.11n will recognize and work with 802.11g equipment. However, to achieve 802.11n speeds, you need to ensure that your computers have 802.11n network adapters installed in them or connected to them so they can function efficiently with an 802.11n router. A notebook computer with an 802.11g adapter in it can connect to an 802.11n router, but will function at the lower 802.11g speeds. If you were buying 802.11n equipment to upgrade your network, it

would be a good idea to buy all the components (adapters, routers, etc.) from one manufacturer to ensure they work correctly together. Sometimes manufacturers make proprietary tweaks to their equipment, usually to boost throughput. This may keep it from functioning efficiently with another manufacturer's equipment.

What do I need to set up a wireless network? Just like other networks, each node on a wireless network requires a **wireless network adapter**. If not built into the motherboard of the computer, these adapters are available as NICs that are inserted into expansion slots on the computer (see Figure 12a) or as USB devices that plug into an open USB port (see Figure 12b). Most notebooks today come with a built-in 802.11g or 802.11n wireless/wired network adapter.

Wireless network adapters differ from other network adapters in that they contain transceivers. A **transceiver** is a device that translates the electronic data that needs to be sent along the network into radio waves and then broadcasts these radio waves to other network nodes. Transceivers serve a dual function because they also receive the signals from other network nodes. As shown in Figure 12, many add-on wireless network adapters have antennae poking out of them. Antennae are necessary for the transmission and reception of these radio waves.

Do all nodes on the wireless network have to be computers? A node on a wireless network can also be a peripheral device such as a printer, storage device, or scanner. The peripheral will need to be connected to

Figure 12

Wireless network adapters are available as (a) NICs, which are inserted into an open expansion slot on the computer, or (b) USB devices, which plug into an open USB port.

a wireless network adapter so that other nodes on the network can communicate with it.

How do I share an Internet connection on a wireless network?

Just like wired Ethernet networks, wireless Ethernet networks require the installation of a router to share an Internet connection. A **wireless router** (sometimes called a **gateway**) is a device that combines the capabilities of a wired router with the ability to receive wireless signals. Don't buy a wireless access point (which we discuss later) by mistake when you need a wireless router, because a wireless access point does not perform the same function.

What types of problems can I run into when installing wireless networks?

The maximum range of wireless devices under the 802.11g standard is about 250 feet. However, as the distance between nodes increases, throughput decreases markedly. Equipment that meets the 802.11n standard provides greater bandwidth over longer distances.

Note that 802.11g devices work on a bandwidth of 2.4 GHz. This is the same bandwidth that many cordless phones use, so your phone and wireless network may interfere with each other. The best solution is to buy a cordless phone that uses a bandwidth of 5 GHz, or else purchase 802.11n equipment, which uses the 5 GHz band.

Obstacles between wireless nodes also decrease throughput. Walls and large metal objects are the most common sources of interference with wireless signals. For example, placing a computer with a wireless network adapter next to a refrigerator may prevent the signals from reaching the rest of the network. Similarly, a node that has four walls between it and the Internet connection will most likely have lower-than-maximum throughput. The 802.11n devices have a range up to three times as far as 802.11g

devices and are less susceptible (but not immune) to interference.

What if a node on the network can't communicate with other nodes, or with the router?

Repositioning a node or wireless network adapter within the same room (sometimes even just a few inches from the original position) can often affect communication between nodes. If this doesn't work, try moving the computer closer to the router or to other rooms in your house. Many newer routers support the addition of external antennae, which are either directional ones that focus the signal in a certain direction, or omnidirectional ones that spread the signal out over a wide area. If you have a single problem area, plugging a directional antenna into your router, placing the antenna as close to the problem area as possible, and facing directly toward it may solve the reception problem.

If these solutions don't work, then you may need to add a wireless access point. A **wireless access point (WAP)** is a device that attaches to a network and provides wireless nodes (such as a notebook with a wireless NIC installed) with a means of wirelessly connecting to the network. When you have connection problems (for example, the notebook on your porch can't connect to the wireless router), adding a WAP to the network will often solve the problem. Essentially, you're extending the range of the wireless network by providing a second point at which nodes can connect to the network. The WAP must be connected to the network either directly to the switch on the router or to another node within range of the router.

For example, as you can see in Figure 13, Notebook C on the back porch and the wireless router (connected to Computer

---

BITS AND BYTES

Wireless Hot Spots: How to Find One on the Go

Wireless hot spots are places where you can connect to the Internet via a computing device with wireless networking capability (such as your notebook computer). Providers of wireless hot spots may provide free access, or they may charge a fee, which is usually based on connection time (such as a set fee per hour of access). So aside from randomly cruising around searching for a place to connect, how do you find out where the hot spots are? Directories have popped up on the Internet to help you locate hot spots in the areas in which you'll be traveling. Check out JiWire (**jiwire.com**), Wi-Fi FreeSpot (**wififreespot.com**), and Wi-Fi Hotspot List (**wi-fihotspotlist.com**) to locate a hot spot near you.

Types of Peer-to-Peer Networks

Bedroom   Den   Back porch

Wireless router

Information from A to C

Information from A to C

Wireless access point

Computer A with
wireless network adapter

Computer B with
wireless access point

Notebook C with
wireless network adapter

Figure 13

Because a wireless access point is installed on Computer B, data can travel from Notebook C on the back porch to the wireless router in the bedroom.

A in the bedroom) can't make contact. However, Notebook C can connect to Computer B in the den. By connecting a WAP to Computer B, all traffic from Notebook C is relayed to the wireless router through the WAP connected to Computer B. It is a good idea to set up appropriate wireless security for your WAP so that strangers can't connect to your network without your knowledge. (We cover wireless security later in this chapter.)

Can I have wired and wireless nodes on one network? Many users want to create a network in which some computers (such as desktops) connect to the network with wires, whereas other computers (such as

notebooks) connect to the network wirelessly. Most wireless DSL/cable routers allow you to connect wireless and wired nodes to the same network. This type of router contains both a WAP and ports that allow you to connect wired nodes to the router. Figure 14 shows an example of a network with a wireless DSL/cable router attached. As you can see, the notebook maintains a wireless connection to the router, whereas the other two computers are connected by wires. Using this type of router is a cost-effective way to have some wireless connections while preserving the high-speed attributes of wired Ethernet where needed.

Figure 14

Wired and wireless connections in the same home network.

INTERNET

Wireless DSL/Cable router

Computer in bedroom
with wired connection

Notebook on back
porch with wireless
connection

Computer in den with
wired connection

Networking: Connecting Computing Devices

Power-Line Networks

What are power-line networks?

Power-line networks use the existing electrical wiring in your home to connect the nodes in the network. Thus, in a power-line network, any electrical outlet provides a network connection. The HomePlug Power Line Alliance (**homeplug.org**) sets standards for home power-line networking. The original power-line networks had a maximum data transfer rate of 14 Mbps. However, currently available power-line networks have data transfer rates approaching 200 Mbps, which can make them a viable alternative to wireless or wired Ethernet in certain situations.

How do I create a power-line network? To create a power-line network, you connect a power-line network adapter (similar to a network adapter in an Ethernet network) to each computer or peripheral that you're going to attach to the network (see Figure 15). You can buy power-line network adapters in either USB or Ethernet versions. After you attach a network adapter to each node on the network, you plug the adapters into an electrical outlet. Most power-line network adapters will be recognized automatically by the Windows operating system.

Why would I use a power-line network instead of an Ethernet network? Because of the low bandwidth of the original power-line networks and the lower costs of Ethernet networks, power-line networks declined in popularity. However, with the introduction of power-line equipment that supports much higher data throughput, power-line networks are becoming popular again. Modern power-line networks can sometimes exceed speeds of wireless Ethernet networks, especially where there is a lot of interference on the wireless network. Therefore, if you're in a situation in which running new wires is impractical and you're experiencing too much interference to run a wireless network, you may want to consider installing a power-line network.

Choosing a Peer-to-Peer Network

If you're setting up a home network, the type of network you should choose will depend on your particular needs. In general, consider the following questions in determining your network type:

- Is existing wiring available?
- Do you want wireless communications?
- How fast do you want your network connection to be?
- How much money can you spend on your network?

What if I want to use existing wiring for my home network? As noted earlier, you can use power lines (electrical wiring) as media for a home network. Obviously, you need to have an electrical outlet available in each room in which you want to connect a node to the network. Because you have to plug most nodes (computers, printers, and so on) into an electrical outlet to operate them anyway, connecting a power-line network is usually convenient. However, these networks might be more expensive than wired or wireless Ethernet networks.

What are the pros and cons of wireless networks? Wireless networks free you from having to run wires in your home. In addition, your ability to move around is not impaired or restricted by wires. However, wireless networks may not work effectively in every home, so you need to install and test the wireless network to figure out whether it will work. To avoid unnecessary expenses, make sure you can

Twilight Images\Alamy Images; Twilight Images\Alamy Images

Plug into electrical outlet

Ethernet connection

Figure 15

Power-line adapters plug into any electrical outlet and can then connect to your computer (or peripheral) via an Ethernet cable.

return equipment for a refund if it doesn't work properly in your home.

Which network type provides the highest data transfer rate? Most routine home computing tasks such as Web browsing and e-mailing require minimal throughput (less than 10 Mbps is sufficient). However, if high-speed data transmission is important (for example, if you play computer games or exchange large files), then you may want a network with high throughput. With data transfer rates as high as 1,000 Mbps, wired Ethernet networks are the fastest home networks. You may want to consider a Gigabit network if you engage in a lot of multiplayer gaming or video transfer. Without high throughput, streaming video can appear choppy, games can respond slowly, and files can take a long time to transfer.

What cost factors do I need to consider in choosing a network? You may need to consider your budget when deciding what type of network to install. Figure 16 lists the approximate costs of installing the various types of peer-to-peer networks and their advantages and disadvantages.

Do I need to consider the type of broadband connection I have? Whether you connect to the Internet by DSL, cable, or satellite makes no difference in terms of the type of network you select. The differences occur with your particular network's hardware and software requirements.

Configuring Software for Your Home Network

Once you install the hardware for your network, you need to configure your operating system software for networking on your computers. In this section, you'll learn how to do just that using special Windows tools. Although configuration is different with Mac OS X, the setup is quick and easy. Linux is the most complex operating system to configure for a home network, though the difficulties are not insurmountable.

Is configuring software difficult? Windows makes configuring software relatively simple by virtually automating the entire process of setting up a network using various wizards. A wizard is a utility program included with software that you can use to help you accomplish a specific task. You can launch the Windows wizards from the Network and Sharing Center, which can be accessed via the Network and Internet group in the Control Panel. Before running any wizards, you should do the following:

1. Install network adapters on each node.

2. For a wired network, plug all the cables into the router, network adapters, and so on.

Figure 16 | COMPARISON OF MAJOR TYPES OF HOME NETWORKS

	Wired			Wireless	
	100 Mbps Ethernet	Gigabit Ethernet	Power Line	802.11g	802.11n
Maximum data transfer rate (bandwidth)	100 Mbps	1,000 Mbps or 1 Gbps	200 Mbps	54 Mbps	540 Mbps
Actual expected throughput	50 to 60 Mbps	500 to 600 Mbps	100 Mbps	15 to 25 Mbps	150 to 200 Mbps
Operational frequency	N/A	N/A	N/A	2.4 GHz	5 GHz
Cost of basic access point, router or switch	$40 to $60 (switch)	$100 to $200 (switch)	$100 to $200 (adapter or router)	$30 to $60	$80 and up
Pros	Mature, proven technology; low cost	Fastest practical home technology available	No additional wiring required	Mature, proven technology; low cost	Significantly faster than 802.11g
Cons	Can be expensive to install hidden wiring.	Cat 6 wiring required. Can be expensive to install hidden wiring.	May not have outlets in the correct locations.	Interference from walls and other structures can cause signal to degrade (especially over greater distances).	Same as 802.11g, but to a lesser extent.

Source: Table adapted from "Pump Up Your Home Network" by Erik Rhey, *PC Magazine*, October 3, 2006.

Networking: Connecting Computing Devices

3. Make sure your cable/DSL modem is connected to your router and that it is connected to the Internet.

4. Turn on your equipment in the following order (allowing the modem and the router about one minute each to power up and configure):
   a. your cable/DSL modem,
   b. your router, and

   c. all computers and peripherals (printers, scanners, and so on).

By completing these steps, you enable the wizards to make decisions about how best to configure your network. After you have completed these steps, open the Network and Sharing Center from the Control Panel (see Figure 17a). You can see the network to which you are currently connected on

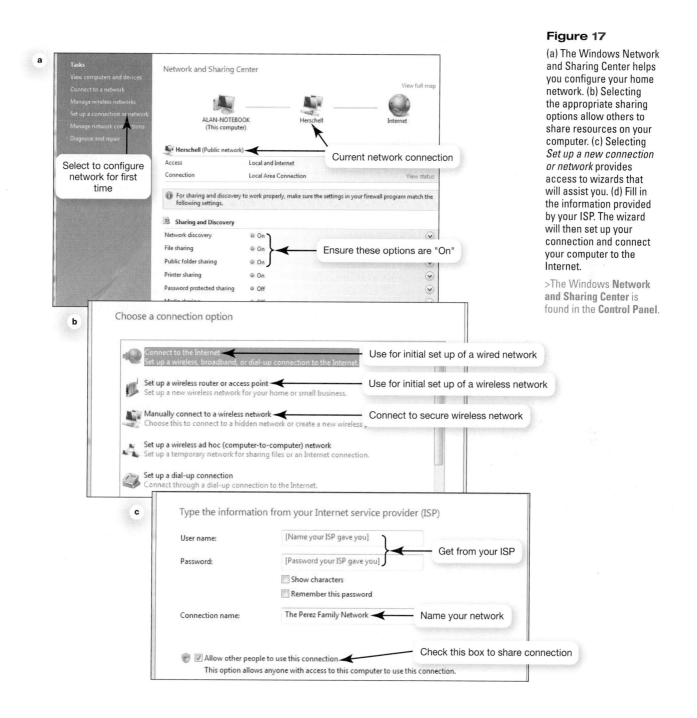

Figure 17

(a) The Windows Network and Sharing Center helps you configure your home network. (b) Selecting the appropriate sharing options allow others to share resources on your computer. (c) Selecting *Set up a new connection or network* provides access to wizards that will assist you. (d) Fill in the information provided by your ISP. The wizard will then set up your connection and connect your computer to the Internet.

>The Windows **Network and Sharing Center** is found in the **Control Panel**.

this screen. On the lower portion of the Network and Sharing Center screen, you can set sharing options for your network. Ensure that network discovery is shown as "on," because this allows your computer to locate other computers and peripherals on the network. You should also verify that the options for file and printer sharing and public folder sharing are shown as "on" to enable file and printer sharing with other computers. From the Network and Sharing Center, select *Set up a new connection or network* to access the Windows networking wizards (see Figure 17b). *Note:* If you already have a wired network set up and are connected to the Internet, plugging your Windows computer into the router is all you need to do. Windows will automatically detect an existing wired network.

Select the Connect to the Internet wizard to configure your network to use your cable/DSL modem to connect to the Internet for the first time. This wizard also configures your wired network. On the information screen (see Figure 17c) enter and access information provided by your ISP. Enter a memorable name for your network and check the box to allow other people to use the Internet connection you are establishing. This will allow all users on the network to use the same connection.

After running this wizard, run the Set Up a Wireless Router wizard to configure your wireless network. If you set up a secured wireless network, use the Manually Connect to a Wireless Network wizard to connect computers to the secure network.

What if I don't have the same version of Windows on all my computers? Windows 7, Windows Vista, and Windows XP are the most common OSs for home use that support P2P networking. Fortunately, you can network computers using any of these versions of Windows. If you have one computer with Windows 7 but your other computers run on other versions of Windows, then you should set up your Windows 7 computer first. Windows 7 and Vista can automatically detect computers running other versions of Windows on your network; however, you may have to make adjustments to the Windows XP computers on your network (such as installing Windows XP Service Pack 3) to enable them to see the networked Windows 7 and Vista computers. Check the Microsoft Web site for instructions.

How do I differentiate the computers on my network? When you set up your Windows computer, you gave it a name. Each computer on a network needs a name that is different from the names of all other computers on the network so that the network can identify it. This unique name ensures that the network knows which computer is requesting services and data and can deliver data to the correct computer.

Figure 18

Accessing the System screen allows you to check your computer and workgroup names and change them if necessary.

>The **Windows System** screen can be accessed by clicking the **System** and **Security** link in the **Control Panel**.

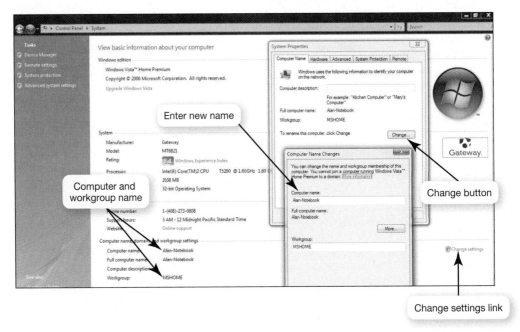

Computers on a network can be located in various workgroups. For simplicity on a home network, you should assign all your computers to the same workgroup. If you don't recall your computer's name or the workgroup to which it is assigned, open the Control Panel, click the System and Security link and then click the System icon (see Figure 18). The current name of your computer and the workgroup to which it belongs is shown. You can change the name of the computer or the workgroup by clicking the Change Settings link, which launches the System Properties dialog box. Clicking the Change button on the Computer Name tab will launch the Computer Name Changes dialog box, where you can rename your computer or assign it to a different workgroup.

Is that it? Assuming you installed and configured everything properly, your home network should now be up and running, allowing you to share files, Internet connections, and peripherals. Most routers will work right out of the box. However, with some routers you may have to alter the configuration to connect to the Internet. Check the instructions that came with your router or refer to the router manufacturer's Web site for guidance.

How do I set up my router so that I can use it to connect to the Internet? First, contact your ISP and find out about any special settings that you may need to configure your router to work with your ISP. Next, access your router from Internet Explorer (or another Web browser) by entering the router's IP address or default URL. You can usually find this information in the documentation that came with the router. You'll also need a username and password to log on to the router. You'll probably find these, too, in the documentation that came with the router.

Many routers feature their own wizard (different from the Windows Networking wizards) that takes you through special configuration screens. A sample screen from a router is shown in Figure 19. The documentation that came with your router will provide a URL to use to log on to the router. If you're unsure of any information that needs to be entered to configure the router (such as whether IP addresses are assigned dynamically—meaning you are assigned a new IP address by your ISP each time you connect to the Internet), contact your ISP and ask for guidance.

How can I test my Internet connection speed? Your ISP may have promised you certain speeds of downloading and uploading data. How can you tell if you are getting what was promised? There are numerous sites on the Internet, such as **Speedtest.net** (see Figure 20), where you can test the speed of downloading files to your computer and uploading files to other computers. You can then see how your results compare to those of

Figure 19

Although setups differ from router to router, you will need basic information such as the logon information and the type of IP addressing to configure the router to work with your network and your ISP.

Figure 20

Speed test showing a download speed of 8.38 megabits, which is fast for a home Internet connection.

other users in your state and across the United States. Many factors can influence your Internet speeds, so be sure to run the test at several different times during the day over the course of a week before complaining to your ISP about not getting your promised speed.

Securing Wireless Networks

All computers that connect to the Internet (whether or not they are on a network) need to be secured from intruders. This is usually accomplished by using a **firewall**, which is a hardware or software solution that helps shield your network from prying eyes. Wireless networks present special vulnerabilities; therefore, you should take additional specific steps to keep your wireless network safe.

Why is a wireless network more vulnerable than a wired network?
With a wired network, it is fairly easy to tell if a **hacker** (someone who breaks into computer systems to create mischief or steal valuable information) is using your network. However, wireless networks, especially those using 802.11n equipment, have wide ranges that may extend outside of your house. This makes it possible for a hacker to access your network without your knowledge.

Why should I be worried about someone logging onto my wireless network without my permission?
Some use of other people's wireless

networks is unintentional. Houses are built close together. Apartments are clustered even closer together. Wireless signals can easily reach a neighbor's residence. Most wireless network adapters are set up to access the strongest wireless network signal detected. If your router is on the east side of your house and you and your notebook are on the west side, then you may get a stronger signal from your neighbor's wireless network than from your own. **Piggybacking** is connecting to a wireless network (other than your own) without the permission of the owner. This practice is illegal in many jurisdictions but often happens inadvertently between neighbors.

Your neighbor probably isn't a hacker, but he might be using a lot of bandwidth—your bandwidth! If he's downloading a massive movie file while you're trying to do research for a term paper, he's probably slowing you down. In addition, when some less-than-honest neighbors discover they can log onto your wireless network, they may cancel their own Internet service to save money by using yours. Some neighbors might even be computer savvy enough to penetrate your unprotected wireless network and steal personal information, just as any other hackers would.

In addition, because computer criminal activities are traceable, hackers love to work their mischief from public computers (such as those in a library or college) so they can't be identified. If a hacker is sitting in her car outside your house and logging on to your wireless network, any cyberattacks she launches might be traced back to your computer, and you might find law enforcement officials knocking on your door.

How is my wireless network vulnerable? Packets of information on a wireless network are broadcast through the airwaves. Savvy hackers can intercept and decode information from your transmissions that may allow them to bypass any standard protections, such as a firewall, which you have set up on your network. Therefore, to secure a wireless network, you should take the additional precautions described in the Sound Byte "Securing Wireless Networks" and as summarized below:

1. **Change your network name (SSID).**
   Each wireless network has its own name to identify it. Unless you change this name when you set up your router,

SOUND BYTE

Securing Wireless Networks

In this Sound Byte, you'll learn what "war drivers" are and why they could potentially be a threat to your wireless network. You'll also learn some simple steps to secure your wireless network against intruders.

the router uses a default network name (also known as the **service set identifier** or **SSID**) that all routers from that manufacturer use (such as "Wireless"). Hackers know the default names and access codes for routers. If you haven't changed the SSID, it's advertising the fact that you probably haven't changed any of the other default settings for your router, either.

2. **Disable SSID broadcast.** Most routers are set up to broadcast their SSIDs so that other wireless devices can find them. If your router supports disabling SSID broadcasting, turn it off. This makes it more difficult for a hacker to detect your network.

3. **Change the default password on your router.** Hackers know the default passwords of most routers, and if they can access your router, they can probably break into your network. Change the password on your router to something hard to guess. (Use at least eight characters that are a combination of letters, symbols, and numbers.)

4. **Turn on security protocols.** Most routers ship with security protocols such as Wired Equivalent Privacy (WEP) or Wi-Fi Protected Access (WPA). Both use encryption (a method of translating your data into code) to protect data in your wireless transmissions. WPA is a much stronger protocol than WEP, so enable WPA if you have it; enable WEP if you don't. When you enable these

protocols, you are forced to create a security encryption key (passphrase). When you attempt to connect a node to a security-enabled network for the first time, you'll be required to enter the encryption key. The encryption key (see Figure 21) is the code that computers on your network need to decrypt (decode) data transmissions. Without this key, it is extremely difficult, if not impossible, to decrypt the data transmissions from your network (see Figure 22). This prevents unauthorized access to your network because hackers won't know the correct key to use. The Windows 7 Connect to a network dialog box shows all wireless networks within range (see Figure 22). Clicking on one allows you to connect to it, or prompts you for more information such as the SSID name and security key.

5. **Implement media access control.** Each network adapter on your network has a unique number (like a serial number) assigned to it by the manufacturer. This is called a **media access control (MAC) address**, and it is a number printed right on the network adapter. Many routers allow you to restrict access to the network to only certain MAC addresses. This helps ensure that only authorized devices can connect to your network.

6. **Limit your signal range.** Most modern routers allow you to adjust the

Figure 21

By running your router configuration wizard, you can configure the security protocols available on your router and change the SSID, which helps protect your wireless network.

Create and enter unique SSID here

Select a security protocol

Create hard-to-guess passphrase

Figure 22

(a) The Windows 7 Connect to a network dialog box. (b) Manually connecting to a wireless network allows you to establish a connection if you know the network encryption key and the SSID name.

>You can access the **Connect to a network** dialog box by right-clicking the **Network Connection** icon on the taskbar and selecting **Connect to a network** from the shortcut menu. You can access the **Manually connect to a wireless network** dialog box by accessing the **Control Panel**, clicking on **Network and Internet**, selecting **Network and Sharing Center**, choosing the **Set up a connection or network** option, and then clicking on **Manually connect to a wireless network**.

transmitting power to low, medium, or high. Cutting down the power to low or medium could prevent your signal from reaching too far away from your home, making it tougher for interlopers to poach your signal.

7. **Apply firmware upgrades.** Your router has read-only memory that has software written to it. This software is known as **firmware**. As bugs are found in the firmware (which hackers might exploit), manufacturers issue patches, just as the makers of operating system software do. Periodically check the manufacturer's Web site and apply any necessary upgrades to your firmware.

If you follow these steps, you will greatly improve the security of your wireless network.

Ethics: Sharing Your Internet Connection with Your Neighbors: Legal? Ethical? Safe?

With the advances in wireless equipment, signals can travel well beyond the range of your home. This makes it possible in an apartment or single family home (where homes are close together) for a group of neighbors to share a wireless signal and potentially save money by splitting the cost of one Internet connection among them. However, before jumping into this venture, you need to weigh a few issues carefully.

You probably aren't legally prohibited from sharing an Internet connection, but you should check on the state and local laws. Most laws are designed to prohibit piggybacking, which is using a network without the account holder's consent. However, if you are giving neighbors permission to share your connection, you probably don't violate any piggybacking laws.

Of course, your ISP might not permit you to share your Internet access with anyone. You probably have a personal account that is designed for one household. The terms of your agreement with the cable company might prohibit you from sharing your connection with people outside your household. If you aren't allowed to share the type of account you have now, your ISP probably offers a type of account (such as a small business account) that will allow you to share a connection, but it will most likely be more expensive. The ISPs know that the more people that share an account, the more likely that account is to use bandwidth; so they price their accounts accordingly. You might be able to share a personal account without being detected by your ISP, but that certainly would be unethical because you should be paying for a higher level of access. Therefore, make sure to check with your ISP to determine that you have the right account.

The next thing you need to consider is whether the shared access should be open to all neighbors, or just to the neighbors that are contributing to the cost of the Internet connection. You could leave the connection open (like the connections at Panera Bread are) and let anyone who finds it log on and surf. You might consider this a very ethical action, because you are providing free Internet access for anyone who needs it. You could register your free hot spot with a service like JiWire, and then people would know where it is. However, your neighbors who are helping pay the cost might have a different viewpoint and not want to fund free surfing for everyone. Make sure you work this out before proceeding.

If you are going to host a free and open hot spot, you still need to make sure that you set it up safely. You want to maintain a secure network for you and your neighbors while still allowing the occasional visiting surfer to use the connection. There are Wi-Fi sharing services (see Figure 23) such as Fon (**fon.com/en**), Whisher (**whisher.com**, now owned by **wifi.com**), and WeFi (**wefi.com**) that can provide you with special hardware (a router) or software that allows you to configure your hot spot so your network remains secure.

While offering free access to anyone will earn you lots of good karma, additional risks exist because you don't know what mischief or criminal activities someone might engage in while connected to the Internet through your account. Think very carefully before you proceed down the sharing path, and make sure you set your hot spot up to protect your internal network.

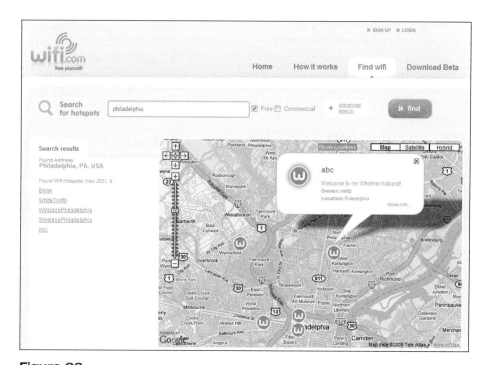

Figure 23

At Wifi.com you can search and find free hot spots hosted by other Whisher users.

1. What is a network, and what are the advantages of setting one up?

A computer network is simply two or more computers that are connected using software and hardware so that they can communicate. Networks allow users to (1) share peripherals, (2) transfer files easily, and (3) share an Internet connection.

2. What is the difference between a client/server network and a peer-to-peer network?

In peer-to-peer networks, each node connected to the network can communicate directly with every other node instead of having a separate device exercise central control over the network. P2P networks are the most common type of network installed in homes. Most networks that have 10 or more nodes are client/server networks. A client/server network contains two types of computers: a client computer on which users perform specific tasks and a server computer that provides resources to the clients and central control for the network.

3. What are the main hardware components of every network?

To function, any network must contain four components: (1) transmission media (cables or radio waves) to connect and establish communication between nodes, (2) network adapters that allow the nodes on the network to communicate, (3) network navigation devices (such as routers and switches) that move data around the network, and (4) software that allows the network to run.

4. What are the most common home networks?

The two most common home networks are wired Ethernet and wireless Ethernet. Modern power-line networks, boasting faster data throughput, are now a viable option in certain situations. The major difference among these network types is the transmission media by which the nodes are connected.

5. What are wired Ethernet networks, and how are they created?

Ethernet networks use the Ethernet protocol as the means by which the nodes on the network communicate. This protocol makes Ethernet networks efficient but also slightly complex. Because of this complexity, additional devices (switches or routers) are required in Ethernet networks. To create a wired Ethernet network, you connect or install network adapters or NICs to each network node. Network adapters connect via cables to a central network navigation device such as a switch or a router. Data flows through the navigation device to the nodes on the network.

6. What are wireless Ethernet networks, and how are they created?

A wireless network uses radio waves instead of wires or cable as its transmission medium. Current wireless protocols provide for networks with data transfer rates in excess of 100 Mbps. To create a wireless network, you install or attach wireless network adapters to the nodes that will make up the network. If the nodes are unable to communicate because of distance, you can add a wireless access point to the network to help relay data between nodes. Wireless networks are susceptible to interference from other wireless devices such as phones.

7. How are power-line networks created, and are they a viable alternative to Ethernet networks?

Power-line networks use the electrical wiring in your home to connect the nodes in the network. To create a power-line network, you connect special network adapters to each node on the network. These adapters are then plugged into an electrical outlet, and data is transmitted through the electrical wires. Modern power-line networks can often exceed the throughput achieved in wireless Ethernet networks, making them a viable option when interference with wireless signals is present.

Networking: Connecting Computing Devices

8. How do I configure my computer's software to set up a network?

Windows 7, Vista, and XP all feature software wizards that facilitate the setup of both wired and wireless networks. Plug in the modem, routers, and all cables, and then switch on the modem, router, and computers (in that order). Run the wizards, which should guide you through the process. Make sure each computer has a distinct name and ensure that all computers are in the same workgroup.

9. Why are wireless networks more vulnerable than wired networks, and what special precautions are required to ensure my wireless network is secure?

Wireless networks are even more susceptible to hacking than wired networks because the signals of most wireless networks extend beyond the walls of your home. Neighbors may unintentionally (or intentionally) connect to the Internet through your wireless connection, and hackers may try to access it. To prevent unwanted intrusions into your network, you should change the default password on your router to make it tougher for hackers to gain access, use a hard-to-guess SSID (network name), turn off SSID broadcasting to make it harder for outsiders to detect your network, and enable security protocols such as WPA or WEP.

key terms

802.11 standard (Wi-Fi)
Cat 6 cable
client
client/server network
coaxial cable
data transfer rate (bandwidth)
digital media receiver (DMR)
DSL/cable router
Ethernet network
fiber-optic cable
firewall
firmware
hacker
home area network (HAN)
hub
local area network (LAN)
media access control (MAC) address
metropolitan area network (MAN)
network
network adapter
network attached storage (NAS) device
network architecture
network interface card (NIC)
network navigation device
network operating system (NOS)

network-ready device
node
packet
peer-to-peer (P2P) network
piggybacking
power-line network
repeater
router
server
service set identifier (SSID)
switch
throughput
transceiver
transmission media
twisted-pair cable
unshielded twisted-pair (UTP) cable
wide area network (WAN)
Wi-Fi
wired Ethernet network
wireless access point (WAP)
wireless Ethernet network
wireless network
wireless network adapter
wireless router (gateway)

buzzwords

Word Bank

- Cat 6 cable
- client/server
- data transfer rate
- hacker(s)
- hub
- LAN
- network adapter(s)
- network-ready
- peer-to-peer (P2P)
- coaxial cable
- piggybacking
- router
- switch
- throughput
- WAN
- wired Ethernet
- wireless access point
- wireless Ethernet

Instructions: Fill in the blanks using the words from the Word Bank above.

Cathi needed to network three computers for herself and her roommates, Sharon and Emily. She decided that a(n) (1) _____ network was the right type to install in their dorm suite because a (2) _____ network was too complex. Because they all liked to download digital movies, they needed high (3) _____. Because they knew that they would never achieve the promised (4) _____ in any network they installed, they decided to use the fastest type of home network, a(n) (5) _____ network. However, because they wanted to use their notebooks wherever they were in their suite, they needed their network to also be a(n) (6) _____ network. Therefore they needed to buy a (7) _____ with wireless capability that would allow them to share the high-speed Internet access that Sharon already had through the cable TV company. This device would also double as a(n) (8) _____, preventing the need to purchase a separate device. Fortunately, all their computers already had (9) _____ installed, making it easy to connect the computers to the network. Cathi knew they would need to purchase some (10) _____ for the wired part of the network because this would provide them with a fast data transfer medium.

Cathi's roommate Emily wanted to know if they could hook into the (11) _____ (small network) that was already deployed for the students in the dorm. This student network was already hooked into the college's (12) _____ (large network), which spanned all three of the college's campuses. She knew they would need to be careful when connecting to the network, because some students from the dorm had accidentally been illegally (13) _____ on a network from the deli across the street. As the connectivity for notebooks in the lounge at the end of the hall was very poor, they needed to consider purchasing a (14) _____ to extend the range of the wireless signal. As a final detail, Emily suggested they get a (15) _____ printer that would plug right into the router and allow them all to print whenever they needed to do so.

becoming computer literate

While attending college, you are working at the Snap-Tite company, a small manufacturer of specialty fasteners. Currently, the employees must copy files to flash drives to transfer them among the four PCs the company owns. Only the company president has access to the Internet. The accounts payable clerk is the only one who has a printer. He is constantly being interrupted by other employees when they want to print their files. Your boss heard that you were taking a computer course and asked you to create a solution.

Instructions: Using the preceding scenario, draft a networking plan for Snap-Tite, using as many of the keywords from the chapter as you can. Be sure that the company president, who is unfamiliar with many networking terms, can understand the report.

Instructions: Answer the multiple-choice and true–false questions below for more practice with key terms and concepts from this chapter.

Multiple Choice

1. Which type of sharing is not a benefit of installing a home network?
   a. Peripheral
   b. Router
   c. Media
   d. Internet connection

2. Which of the following is a reason peer-to-peer networks are generally installed in homes?
   a. Peer-to-peer networks are more expandable than client/server networks.
   b. Client/server networks aren't designed to handle wireless networking, which is required by most home users.
   c. Client/server networks do not provide the level of security needed in a home network.
   d. The expense of a server is difficult to justify for most home networks

3. All networks contain the following elements except
   a. hubs.
   b. networking software.
   c. network adapters.
   d. transmission media.

4. Which is an example of a network navigation device required to move data around a single network?
   a. Wireless signal sender
   b. Switch
   c. Router
   d. Cat 6 cable

5. Wired Ethernet networks are superior to wireless networks because
   a. they generally provide faster data throughput.
   b. they have fewer security vulnerabilities.
   c. they are less susceptible to signal interference.
   d. they are significantly cheaper to install.

6. Power-line networks are desirable to install for all of the following reasons except
   a. Running Cat 6 cable would be too expensive.
   b. They are considerably cheaper to deploy than wireless networks.
   c. There is significant wireless signal interference.
   d. Lower throughput is acceptable.

7. A wireless network set up by a city to provide access to residents and visitors is usually referred to as a:
   a. LAN   c. HAN
   b. MAN   d. WAN

8. The throughput of a network
   a. is usually lower than the data transfer rate.
   b. is usually higher than the data transfer rate.
   c. is equal to the data transfer rate.
   d. is equal to the data transfer rate divided by bandwidth.

9. Which network navigation device is designed to move data between two networks?
   a. Hub   c. Router
   b. Repeater   d. Switch

10. The newest wireless Ethernet standard, which also provides the fastest data transfer rate, is
    a. 802.11g.   c. 802.11a.
    b. 802.11n.   d. 802.11b.

True–False

_____ 1. Actual data throughput is usually lower on wireless networks.

_____ 2. All home networks require each computer on the network to be equipped with its own network navigation device.

_____ 3. To facilitate sharing an Internet connection between computers on an Ethernet network, you should install a router.

_____ 4. LANs cover a larger geographic area than WANs.

_____ 5. Modern wireless Ethernet networks are immune to signal interference.

Networking: Connecting Computing Devices

1. Dormitory Networking

Dave, Jerome, and Thomas were sitting in the common room of their campus suite staring at $100 piled up on the coffee table. Selling last semester's books back to the bookstore had been a good idea. As they waited for Phil, their other roommate, to come home, Dave said, "Wouldn't it be cool if we could network our notebooks? Then we could play Ultra Super Robot Kill-Fest in team mode!" Jerome pointed out it would be even more useful if they could all have access to Dave's laser printer because he owned the only one. "And Jerome's always bugging me to use my scanner when I'm trying to sleep," remarked Thomas. "And I can't believe the only high-speed Internet connection is out here in the lounge!" The three roommates ran down the hall and rapped on your door looking for some guidance. Consider how you would answer their questions:

a. Is $100 enough to set up a wireless network for four notebooks in four separate rooms? (Assume each computer contains a wireless network adapter already.)

b. Can the roommates share a printer and a scanner if they set up a wireless network? Will they need any additional equipment for the printer and the scanner to share them across the network if they are already connected to one of the notebook computers?

c. How would they share the one high-speed Internet connection wirelessly?

d. Phil just returned from the campus post office with a check from his aunt for $75. Do the roommates now have enough money to set up a network attached storage (NAS) device that would allow them to have their files automatically backed up?

To answer these questions, use the chapter text and the following resources: **coolcomputing.com**, **pricewatch.com**, **westerndigital.com**, **netgear.com**, **bestbuy.com**, and **tigerdirect.com**.

2. Connecting Your Computer to Public Networks

In the course of your education, you are constantly connecting your notebook to various wireless public networks such as those in the school library and the neighborhood coffee shop. As you know from reading this chapter, you are more vulnerable to hackers when connected to a wireless network. Conduct research on the Internet about surfing at public hot spots and prepare a list of sensible precautions for you and your classmates to take when surfing on an open network.

3. Adding a Hard Drive for Backups to Your Network

You know that adding a network-ready external hard drive to your network would facilitate sharing of your digital media and would make backing up data files easier. You need to consider the following questions when selecting an appropriate hard drive:

1. What is the volume of shared media that you need to store? (In other words, how many MP3 files, movies, and other media files do you have?)

2. What are the sizes of the hard drives of the computers on your network (for backup purposes)?

3. Do you need to access files on the hard drive when you are away from home?

Research network-ready hard drives using sites such as **wdc.com** and **buffalotech.com** to select one that is appropriate for your home network. Prepare a summary of your findings. Include the reasons for your selection.

1. **Wireless LAN for a Small Business**

   You are working for a local coffee shop. The owner of the shop thinks that adding a wireless network and providing free Internet access to customers would be a good way to increase business. The owner has asked you to research this idea and prepare a report of your findings. Consider the following:

   a. Price out business Internet connectivity with local phone and cable providers. Which vendor provides the most cost effective solution for a coffee shop? Are there any limitations on bandwidth or the number of people that can access the Internet at one time through the business account connection?

   b. What potential problems could you foresee with providing unrestricted free access to the Internet? What policies would you suggest to keep people from abusing the free Internet access? (An example of abuse is someone who sits all day and surfs for free without purchasing any coffee.)

2. **Public Wireless Access**

   Many corporations are using wireless technology to enhance or drive their businesses. Assume you are opening a local coffee shop in your town. Investigate the following:

   a. Starbucks (**starbucks.com**) currently provides wireless access (for a fee) in many of its locations. Using **jwire.com** or **wi-fihotspotlist.com**, find the closest Starbucks to your home that features wireless access. Will this store compete with your proposed store, or is it too far away?

   b. Visit your local Starbucks (or check **starbucks.com**) and find out the cost of its wireless access. Use the Internet to research whether wireless access is profitable for Starbucks and whether it drives customers to their stores. (Many articles have been written about this.) Compare Starbucks' model with that of Panera Bread, which offers free wireless access to its customers. Why does one company charge for Internet access while another does not?

   c. As part of your business plan, write one or two paragraphs explaining why you will (or will not) offer wireless connectivity at your coffee shop and whether it will be a pay service or a free service.

   d. Can you find any free wireless access points within a 10-mile radius of your proposed store location? How will this affect your decision to offer wireless connectivity at your business?

3. **Testing Your Internet Connection Speed**

   Visit **speedtest.net** and **speakeasy.net/speedtest** and test the speed of your Internet connection at your home and in the computer lab at your school. Try to repeat the test at two different times during the day.

   a. What did you find out about download speeds at your home? Are you getting as much speed as was promised by your ISP? Would this speed be sufficient for a home-based business? What type of business packages does your ISP offer, and what speeds could you expect when paying for a business package?

   b. How does the connection speed at your school compare to the speed at your home? Where do you think you should have a faster connection—at your school or at your home? Why might the connection speed at your school be slower than you think it should be?

Networking: Connecting Computing Devices

Instructions: Albert Einstein used *Gedankenexperiments*, or critical thinking questions, to develop his theory of relativity. Some ideas are best understood by experimenting with them in our own minds. The following critical thinking questions are designed to demand your full attention but only require a comfortable chair—no technology.

1. Protecting Your Wireless Home Network

Many people have installed wireless networks in their homes. Consider the wireless network installed in your home (or in a friend's home if you don't have wireless).

a. Is your network set up to provide adequate protection against hackers? If not, what would you need to do to make it secure?

b. Are there other wireless networks within range of your home? If so, are they set up with an adequate level of security, or can you connect to them easily? How would you go about informing your neighbors that their networks are vulnerable?

2. Upgrading Your Wireless

You have just finished purchasing and installing a new wireless network in your home. A new wireless standard of networking will be launched next month that is 10 times as fast as the wireless network you installed.

a. What types of applications would you need to be using heavily to make it worth upgrading to the new standard?

b. Suppose your neighbor upgraded to the new standard but does not have his network secured. Is tapping into your neighbor's wireless connection ethical? Is it illegal where you live?

3. Evaluating Your Home Networking Needs

You might have a network installed in your home already, or perhaps you are still considering whether it is necessary to install one. Consider these issues:

a. Who uses computing devices in your home? How many computers (notebooks and desktops) are currently in your home? Are the computers networked? If not, should they be networked? What advantages would your family gain by networking its computers?

b. Which computer peripheral devices does your family own? Which family members need to use which peripherals? Are the peripherals network-ready or are they connected to individual computers? How easy is it to share these peripherals? Which peripherals don't your family own that would be beneficial? (Make sure to explain why.) How would you go about connecting new peripherals to your network?

c. Does your home network have network attached storage or a home server? Would your family benefit from having this technology on your home network? What types of media do your family members routinely share? What other types would they share if they had the means?

4. Sharing a Home Internet Connection

Perhaps you have considered whether sharing a home Internet connection with your neighbors would save you money. Consider the following issues:

a. How many neighbors would be within range (say, within 350 feet of your router) of an 802.11n signal that came from your house or apartment? Do you think your neighbors would be amenable to sharing the cost of your Internet connection and your bandwidth? Why or why not?

b. Is it permissible to share an Internet connection with neighbors under your ISP's terms of use for the type of connection you purchased? If not, what type of plan would you need to upgrade to in order to share a connection with your neighbors? Would the increased cost of upgrading your connection still make it economically feasible to share a connection?

c. Do you think any of your neighbors would use significantly more bandwidth than others would? If so, do you think they should pay for a greater portion of the monthly Internet fees? What would you do if one of the neighbors were constantly hogging most of the bandwidth that you all were sharing?

team time

Creating a Wireless Network

Problem

Wireless technology is being adopted by leaps and bounds, both in the home and in the workplace. Offering easy access free of physical tethers to networks seems to be a solution to many problems. However, wireless computing also has problems, ranging from poor reception to hijackers stealing your bandwidth.

Task

You are volunteering for a charity that installs wireless networks in homes for needy families. Many of these installations are done in older homes, and some recipients of the networks have reported poor connectivity in certain areas of their residences and extremely low bandwidth at other times. You have volunteered to research the potential problems and to suggest solutions to the director of the program.

Process

Break the class into three teams. Each team will be responsible for investigating one of the following issues:

1. **Detecting poor connectivity:** Research methods that can be used to find areas of poor signal strength, including signal sniffing software (**netstumbler.com**) and handheld scanning devices such as Wi-Fi Finder (**us.kensington.com**). Investigate maximum distances between access points and network nodes and make appropriate recommendations. (Equipment manufacturers such as **netgear.com** and **linksys.com** provide guidelines.)

2. **Signal boosters:** Research ways to increase signal strength in access points, antennae, and wireless cards. Signal boosters are available for access points. You can purchase or construct replacement antennae or antenna enhancements. Wi-Fi cards that offer higher power than conventional cards are now available.

3. **Security:** "War drivers" (people who cruise neighborhoods looking for open wireless networks from which to steal bandwidth) may be the cause of the bandwidth issues. Research appropriate measures to keep wireless network traffic secure from eavesdropping by hackers. In your investigation, look into the new Wi-Fi Protected Access (WPA) standard developed by the Wi-Fi Alliance. Check out the security section on the Wi-Fi Alliance Web site to start (**weca.net**).

Present your findings to your class and discuss possible causes of and ways to prevent the problems encountered at the residences. Provide your instructor with a report suitable for eventual presentation to the CEO of the charity.

Conclusion

As technology improves, wireless connectivity should eventually become the standard method of communication between networks and network devices. As with any other technology, security risks exist. Understanding those risks and how to mitigate them will allow you to participate in the design and deployment of network technology and provide peace of mind for your network users.

Networking: Connecting Computing Devices

In addition to the review materials presented here, you'll find additional materials featured with the Pearson IT Multimedia Library and the Companion Website (**pearsonhighered.com/techinaction**), which will help reinforce your understanding of the chapter content. These materials include the following:

Active Helpdesk

In Active Helpdesk calls, you'll assume the role of helpdesk operator, taking calls about the concepts you've learned in this chapter. You'll apply what you've learned and receive feedback from a supervisor to review and reinforce those concepts. The Active Helpdesk call for this chapter is listed below and can be found on the Pearson IT Multimedia Library:

• Understanding Networking

Sound Bytes

Sound Bytes are dynamic multimedia tutorials that help demystify even the most complex topics. You'll view video clips and animations that illustrate computer concepts and then apply what you've learned by reviewing with the Sound Byte Labs, which include quizzes and activities specifically tailored to each Sound Byte. The Sound Bytes for this chapter are listed below. They can be found on the Pearson IT Multimedia Library.

• Installing a Home Computer Network
• Securing Wireless Networks

Companion Website

The *Technology in Action* Companion Website includes a variety of additional materials to help you review and learn more about the topics in this chapter. The resources available at **pearsonhighered.com/techinaction** include:

• **Online Study Guide.** This chapter features online true–false and multiple-choice quizzes. You can take these quizzes, automatically check the results, and e-mail the results to your instructor.
• **Web Research Projects.** This chapter features several Web research projects that ask you to search the Web for information on computer-related careers, milestones in computer history, important people and companies, emerging technologies, and the applications and implications of different technologies.

produced by the analog-to-digital conversion process gives us the digital form of the wave. Figure 3 shows analog and digital versions of the same wave. In Figure 3a, you see the original, continuous analog wave. You could draw that wave without lifting your pencil from the page. In Figure 3b, the wave has been digitized and is no longer a single line; instead, it is represented as a series of points or numbers.

How has the change from analog to digital technologies affected our lifestyle? When the market for communication devices for entertainment media—like photographs, music, and video—switched over to a digital standard, we began to have products with new and useful capabilities. Small devices can now hold huge collections of a variety of types of information. We can interact with our information any time we like, in ways that, prior to the conversion to digital media, had been too expensive or too difficult to learn. The implications of the shift to digital media are continually evolving. Let's examine the many ways in which digital media has already changed our lifestyles.

Figure 2

(a) This is an analog wave showing the simple, pure sound of a piano playing middle C. (b) This is the complex wave produced when a person says "Hello."

Figure 3

(a) A simple analog wave. (b) A digitized version of the same wave.

A Digital Lifestyle

Digital Telephony: Communicating with Bits

Communication has changed radically in the digital age. Wikis, blogs, RSS feeds, and other Web-based tools for connecting people and their ideas are dependent on digital information.

Hardware devices that support communication also have evolved because of digital technologies. **Telephony**, the use of equipment to provide voice communications over a distance, has shifted from an analog science to a digital one. In this section, we examine cell phones, smartphones, and Voice over Internet Protocol (VoIP) devices to see how they are changing to meet modern communication needs.

What are cell phones and smartphones? The **cellular phone** (or **cell phone**) has evolved from a clunky, boxlike device to a compact, fully featured communication and information storage device. Cell phones offer all of the features available on a traditional telephone system, including automatic redial, call timers, and voice mail capabilities. Some cell phones also feature voice-activated dialing, which is important for hands-free operation. In addition, many cell phones offer Internet access, text messaging, personal information management (PIM) features, voice recording, GPS services, and digital image

and video capture. The most fully featured and powerful cellular phones are found in the **smartphone** category. A smartphone often requires a data plan from the provider. This is logical because a smartphone user is likely to spend a lot of time accessing the Internet to upload and download e-mail and data. Some smartphones have enough computing power to run versions of programs like Microsoft Excel and PowerPoint.

How do cell phones use digital signals? When you speak into a cell phone, the sound enters the microphone as a sound wave. Because analog sound waves need to be digitized (that is, converted into a sequence of 1s and 0s that the cell phone's processor can understand), an **analog-to-digital converter chip** converts your voice's sound waves into digital signals. Next, the digital data must be compressed, or squeezed, into the smallest possible space so that it will transmit more quickly to another phone. The processor cannot perform the mathematical operations required at this stage quickly enough, so a specialized chip called the **digital signal processor** is included in the cell phone to handle the compression work. Finally, the digital data is transmitted as a radio wave through the cellular network to the destination phone.

When you receive an incoming call, the digital signal processor decompresses the incoming message. An amplifier boosts the signal to make it loud enough, and it is then passed on to the speaker.

What's "cellular" about a cell phone? A set of connected "cells" makes up a cellular network. Each cell is a geographic area centered on a **base transceiver station**, which is a large communications tower with antennas, amplifiers, receivers, and transmitters. When you place a call on a cell phone, a base station picks up the request for service. The station then passes the request to a central location called a **mobile switching center**. (The reverse process occurs when you receive an incoming call on a cell phone.) A telecommunications company builds its network by constructing a series of cells that overlap in an attempt to guarantee that its cell phone customers have coverage no matter where they are.

As you move during your phone call, the mobile switching center monitors the strength of the signal between your cell phone and the closest base station. When the

Figure 4

Inside your cell phone, you'll find a CPU, a memory chip, input devices such as a microphone and a keypad, and output devices such as a display screen and a speaker.

Memory chip

Speaker

Liquid crystal display

Keypad

CPU

Microphone

signal is no longer strong enough between your cell phone and the base station, the mobile switching center orders the next base station to take charge of your call. When your cell phone "drops out," it may be because the distance between base stations was too great to provide an adequate signal.

Are cell phones and smartphones considered to be computers?   Cell phones and smartphones are so advanced that they have many of the same components as a computer: a processor (central processing unit, or CPU); memory; and input and output devices, as shown in Figure 4. Cell/smartphones also require software and have their own operating systems (OSs).

What does the processor inside a cell/smartphone do?   Although the processor inside a cell/smartphone is obviously not as fast or as high-powered as a processor in a desktop computer, it is still responsible for a great number of tasks. The processor coordinates sending all of the data among the other electronic components inside the phone. It also runs the cell/smartphone's operating system, which provides a user interface so that you can change phone settings, store information, play games, and so on. Popular processors for cell/smartphones include the Samsung SC, the Texas Instruments OMAP, and the Marvell XScale processor. Some processors use dual-core processing technology, which is also used in some desktop processors.

Remember to be well prepared when shopping, and use published mobile phone benchmarking results to compare performance. These are often published on the PC Magazine Web site (**pcmag.com**) or at Wired (**wired.com**).

Is there a standard operating system for cell/smartphones?   Each cell/smartphone manufacturer makes its own tweaks to an operating system and designs its own user interface. This can make switching phones daunting because you have to learn how to use a different set of commands and icons for each cell/smartphone you use.

There are a number of operating systems in the cell/smartphone market now. One popular OS is the Symbian, from the Symbian Foundation. Many smartphones use the Windows Mobile operating system. Apple's iPhone uses a version of the OS X operating system that is used in Apple's personal computers, while the Palm Pre uses its own Palm-developed webOS. These operating systems are required to translate the user's commands into instructions for the processor.

There now are free operating systems that a manufacturer can use as a base for its cell/smartphone operating system. One open source project to develop a free cell/smartphone operating system is Openmoko. Another is the Android collection developed by Google. The goal of an open source mobile operating system is to leverage the creativity of many developers in creating great applications and new phone designs. Figure 5 illustrates some of the different and creative user interfaces

Figure 5

(a) Openmoko, (b) Windows Mobile, and (c) Android are all cell/smartphone operating systems.

OpenMoko, Inc.

Nidesoft

Digital Telephony: Communicating with Bits

David Young-Wolff\PhotoEdit Inc.

Figure 6

You can insert additional memory by installing a micro SD flash card in a smartphone.

featured in modern cell/smartphone operating systems.

What does the memory chip inside a cell/smartphone do? The operating system and the information you save in your cell/smartphone (such as phone numbers and addresses) need to be stored in memory. The operating system is stored in read-only memory (ROM) because the phone would be useless without that key piece of software. As you learned earlier, there are two kinds of memory used in computers: volatile memory, which requires power to save data, and non-volatile memory, which stores data even when the power is turned off. ROM is nonvolatile, or permanent, memory. This means that when you turn off your phone, the data that is stored in ROM (including the operating system) remains in memory.

Other phone data, such as ring tones, is stored in separate internal memory chips. Full-featured cell

phones have as many as 200 MB of internal memory (with some smartphones carrying 1 GB internally) and support additional memory through micro SD flash cards that can store up to 32 GB. Micro SD cards are easy to install in a phone, as shown in Figure 6. You can use that storage for contact data, ring tones, images, songs, videos, and even software applications such as a currency converter or a world clock. Not every cell/smartphone allows memory upgrades in this way, however. For example, the iPhone series does not allow you to add any memory.

What input and output devices do cell/smartphones use? The primary input devices for a cell/smartphone are a microphone and a keypad. Some phones, such as the Samsung Impression (see Figure 7), feature both a hidden keyboard (to make sending e-mail or text messages more efficient) and a touch-sensitive screen. The Apple iPhone uses its touch-sensitive screen to offer a software-based keyboard (see Figure 7) that supports more than 40 languages.

Cell/smartphones often include a digital camera. The Sony Ericsson Cyber-Shot C510 offers a high-quality 3.2-megapixel camera with flash and smile shutter feature. (The shutter goes off once the camera detects a smile.) Most cameras on cell/smartphones can record video as well as take still shots. Picture and video messaging is popular with many cell/smartphone users. They can transmit photos and video files via e-mail, post the files to Web sites such as Facebook, or send them directly to other cell/smartphones.

Cell/smartphone output devices include a speaker and a liquid crystal display (LCD). Higher-end models include full-color, high-resolution LCD screens. Newer on the market are OLED (organic light-emitting diode) displays, which allow very bright, sharp imaging and draw less power. High-resolution displays are becoming increasingly popular because more people are using their cell phones to send and receive the digital images included in multimedia text messages and e-mail, and even to watch TV (see Figure 8). Cell phone and cable providers are teaming up to deliver broadcast TV programs directly to cell phones through services such as Verizon V Cast and Sprint TV Live. A developing standard named Mobile DTV allows

MWW Group

Courtesy of Apple

Figure 7

(a) The Samsung Impression includes a touch screen and a built-in QWERTY keyboard. (b) The Apple iPhone has a touch keyboard that supports over 40 languages and a range of character sets.

Digital Lifestyle: Managing Digital Data and Devices

cell/smartphones to receive free broadcasts from television stations using the M-DTV technology. At the time of this writing, affiliates of NBC, CBS, and PBS are testing this system.

What cell phone and smartphone software is available? Most devices come with a standard collection of software such as a to-do list, contact manager, and calendar. Modified versions of application software such as Microsoft Word, Excel, Outlook, and PowerPoint are available for some high-end smartphones. A variety of games, tools, and reference applications are available from numerous software companies. A good source to locate software applications for your phone is PDA Street (**pdastreet.com**). In addition, Web sites such as download.com (**download.com**) and Tucows (**tucows.com**) feature plenty of shareware and freeware applications for mobile platforms. Some manufacturers have Web-based software stores, like iTunes for the Apple iPhone and the BlackBerry App World for RIM's BlackBerry devices (see Figure 9). The Android developer community has held competitions to spur the creation of new software applications for Android-based phones. Many software applications are available for Android though the Web and the Android Market.

How do I move music from my computer to my cell/smartphone? On the 32 GB micro SD cards available for smartphones, there is room for thousands of songs, videos, or data files. You can transfer files between your phone and your computer easily. Some phones are designed with a flash card that can be easily removed

LG Electronics, Inc.

Figure 8

Mobile DTV receiver chips are appearing in a number of phones, like this model from LG.

and slipped directly into a flash card reader on the computer. Almost all phones are designed with a USB port. Some have a mini-USB connector, while other models require a special cable to connect the phone to a standard USB port (see Figure 10). Once connected using a USB data cable, your phone will appear on your computer like an additional flash drive, and you can drag and drop files to it. You can also charge your cell/smartphone through the USB cable.

How do I synchronize a cell phone with a computer? Cell/smartphones let you coordinate the changes you make to your to-do lists, schedules, and other files with the files on your home or office computer. This process of updating your data so that the files on your cell phone and computer are the same is called **synchronizing**. To synchronize your computer and the device, simply place the cell phone in its cradle (or attach it to the computer via a USB cable) and touch a "sync" button. This begins the process of data transfer that updates both sets of files to the most current version.

Microsoft has recognized the vast increase in portable computing devices by integrating synchronization into the

Figure 9

The Blackberry App World is one of many online stores delivering software for smartphones.

Digital Telephony: Communicating with Bits

Figure 10

A USB data synch cable connects your cell phone to your computer for data transfer.

Figure 11

The Windows Sync Center makes it easy to arrange for synchronization of all your mobile devices.

> To launch Sync Center, click the **Start** button, select **Control Panel**, and double-click the **Sync Center** icon.

Windows operating system. The Sync Center (see Figure 11), which is accessed from the Control Panel, allows you to set up automatic or manual synchronization. Ensure that the device for which you are trying to set up synchronization parameters is connected to your computer and then launch the Sync Center. Select the *Set up new sync partnerships* option to view available devices and configure their synchronization options.

Can I transfer files wirelessly? **Bluetooth** technology uses radio waves to transmit data signals over short distances (approximately 30 feet for Bluetooth 1 and 60 feet for Bluetooth 2 and 3). Bluetooth 3 devices is expected to hit the market in 2010. Distance is expected to be about the same, but throughput is increased. Most cell phones on the market today are Bluetooth-enabled, meaning they include a small Bluetooth chip that allows them to transfer data wirelessly to any other Bluetooth-enabled device. One benefit Bluetooth has over infrared, a wireless connection used in the past, is that a direct line of sight does not have to be present between two devices for them to communicate. You also can use Bluetooth to synchronize your device with your computer. Bluetooth accessories such as earpieces, mice, keyboards, and even stereo headsets are now available.

Text Messaging

What is text messaging? Short message service (SMS)—often just called *text messaging*—is a technology that allows you to send short text messages (comprising up to 160 characters) over mobile networks. To send SMS messages from your cell phone, you use the keypad or a pre-saved template and type your message. You can send SMS messages to other mobile devices (such as cell phones or pagers) or to any e-mail address. You also can use SMS to send short text messages from your home computer to mobile devices such as your friend's cell phone.

How does SMS work? SMS uses the cell phone network to transmit messages. When you send an SMS message, an SMS calling center receives the message and delivers it to the appropriate mobile device using something called *store-and-forward* technology. This technology allows users to send SMS messages to any other SMS device in the world.

Many SMS fans like text messaging because it can be cheaper than a phone call and allows the receivers to read messages when it is convenient for them. In fact, in some countries such as Japan, text messaging is more popular than voice messaging. There are several companies that provide useful services based on text messaging (see Figure 12).

If you plan to do a lot of texting, look for a phone with a good text prediction algorithm. With such an algorithm, typing a single letter pulls up a list of popular words beginning with that letter, saving you typing time. For example, the T9 algorithm also "learns" from your usage patterns and displays the most-used word first.

The Apple iPhone offers some unique services. You can rent movies from the iTunes store and have them delivered directly to your phone. In addition, Apple and Starbucks have teamed up to develop the Now Playing service. When in a participating Starbucks, iPhone users can enter the iTunes store online and identify, purchase, and download the song they are currently listening to at their Starbucks location.

Can I send and receive multimedia files over a cell/smartphone? SMS technology allows you to send only text messages. However, an extension of SMS called **multimedia message service (MMS)** allows you to send messages that include text, sound, images, and video clips to other phones or e-mail addresses. MMS messages actually arrive as a series of messages; you view the text, then the image, and then the sound, and so on. You can then choose to save just one part of the message (such as the image), all of it, or none of it. MMS users can subscribe to financial, sports, and weather services that will "push" information to them, sending it automatically to their phones in MMS format.

411 for Answers

Most phone services charge as much as $2.00 for a 411 call for information on a phone listing or address. Now there is competition. The Google 411 service is a free way to find out the address of, directions to, or phone number of a business or person. A call to 1-800-GOOG-411 gets you this information at no charge. If you say "text" into the phone, it kicks back a text message with the address and a map.

If you are looking for a different kind of information, try the ChaCha service. You can either call (1-800-2chacha) or text (242 242) with any kind of question, and real human "guides" will find the answer and send it back to you. So, answers to questions like

- How many calories are there in a slice of pizza?
- When is *American Idol* on tonight?
- Is there a way to get acrylic paint out of jeans?

are just a free call or text away!

Internet Connectivity

How do I get Internet service for my cell/smartphone? Just as you have an Internet service provider (ISP) for Internet access for your desktop or notebook computer, you must have a **wireless Internet service provider** (or **wireless ISP**) to connect your cell/smartphone to the Internet. Phone companies that provide cell/smartphone calling plans (such as T-Mobile, Verizon, and AT&T) usually double as wireless ISPs. An Internet connectivity plan or text messaging plan is usually known as a **data plan**. Data charges are separate from phone calling charges and are provided at rates different from voice calls. Before subscribing to a data plan, you should assess your data needs: How often do you download new wallpaper, ring tones, or games? Do you use your cell/smartphone's Internet access to download

---

Figure 12 | TEXT MESSAGING SERVICES

SMS Code	Service Name	Web Site	Description
466453 (google)	Google SMS	**google.com/sms**	Obtains information such as addresses, phone numbers, driving directions, sports scores, and movie listings from the Google search engine.
44636 (4Info)	4INFO	**4info.net**	Similar to Google SMS, but also handles flight information and horoscopes.
242 242 (cha cha)	ChaCha	**chacha.com**	Human "guides" provide answers to any question in conversational English.
3109043113	411sms	**411sms.com**	Offers many services, including address and phone listings, turn-by-turn directions, movie show times, stock quotes, hot spot locations, dictionary definitions, horoscopes, and foreign language translations.

Make Your Cell/Smartphone Deliver

Carriers offer many additional services for your cell/smartphone. MusicID, for example, allows you to identify a song easily. Just hold your phone close to the radio's speaker for 15 seconds. You will then receive a text message with the name of the artist and the song. MusicID has a database of more than 3 million songs, so you can be the first to grab those new titles.

Other services can be added to your cell/smartphone plan. For example, you can subscribe to high-definition radio stations over your cell phone. The extra fee allows you to stream more than 50 channels of commercial-free digital radio through your phone. Many phones are equipped for navigation services such as TeleNav Navigator. TeleNav delivers turn-by-turn instructions to you over your phone and displays real-time traffic information.

downloading information (such as from a company intranet or the Internet) can take place much more quickly. Of course if you are in range of a WiFi signal, that is going to be a much faster transfer option. EDGE and 3G have advantages over WiFi, however. They are more reliable and less susceptible to interference. Moreover, you won't have to hunt for a WiFi hot spot, because these technologies are used to blanket major urban areas with connectivity.

As of this writing, 4G networks are beginning to be tested in two cities. The promise of 4G is incredible: mobile connection speeds of up to 100 Mbps. The expansion of 4G will usher in a new generation of mobile devices and applications that will continue to expand how we think of mobile computing.

How is the Internet displayed on a cell/smartphone? On cell/smartphones that have a limited amount of screen space, it is difficult to view Web pages without a great deal of horizontal scrolling. This is because most Web sites are designed for viewing on desktop monitors, which have much wider pixel widths than mobile screens. To enhance your Internet browsing experience on mobile devices, special microbrowser software runs on your phone. **Microbrowser** software provides a Web browser that is optimized to display Web content effectively on the smaller screen (see Figure 14). Popular versions of microbrowser software include Internet Explorer Mobile (included with the Windows Mobile OS) and Opera Mobile. Opera Mobile uses special small-screen rendering technology to reformat the Web images to fit on your cell/smartphone screen, eliminating the need for horizontal scrolling. For the best Web experience, consider a phone that has a large screen, such as the Samsung Omnia 2, which boasts a 3.7-inch diagonal measure screen.

More and more Web sites are being created with content specifically designed for wireless devices. This specially designed content, which is text based and contains no graphics, is written in a format called **Wireless Markup Language (WML)**. Content is designed so that it fits the smaller display screens of handheld mobile devices.

Can I keep my e-mail up to date using my cell/smartphone? A popular feature of cell/smartphones with Internet access lets users check e-mail. BlackBerry

files from e-mails or from your company Web site? Begin by estimating how many kilobytes of data you transfer up and down from the Internet each month. Then select a plan that provides adequate service at a good price.

At what speed is digital information transferred to my cell/smartphone? A cell/smartphone connection often is slower than the one you have at your home. Although broadband speeds of 50 megabits per second (Mbps) are achievable at home using a cable or fiber-optic connection, your cell/smartphone will connect at a much lower speed (see Figure 13).

Providers have introduced many cell/smartphones based on two standards that support faster data transfer technologies: EDGE (short for enhanced data rate for global evolution) and 3G. EDGE and 3G have brought mobile devices much faster data transfer—as high as 1.7 Mbps (or more) under ideal conditions. If you use a cell/smartphone that supports EDGE or 3G, and have a phone plan that allows data transfer, both uploading information (such as e-mail messages that include photos) and

Figure 13 | CELLULAR CONNECTION SPEEDS

Network	Availability	Connection Speed (Mbps)
Edge	13,000 cities	0.1
3G	300 major markets	1.7
WiFi	WiFi hot spots	5.0
4G	2 cities in trial	50.0

Note: Speeds will vary. This data was measured using an iPhone over the AT&T network.

handhelds were the first devices that were optimized to check e-mail. BlackBerry pioneered the "push" technology that delivers your e-mail automatically to your phone, whether you want it or not. Now many other systems also offer "push" technology. BlackBerry devices are still an excellent option, but they aren't the only option. With Internet access, users can always e-mail through Web-based e-mail accounts like Gmail or Yahoo!

If checking and sending e-mail while on the go is mission critical for you, check out cell/smartphones with larger displays and integrated keyboards that make it easier to read and respond to messages.

Voice over Internet Protocol

Cell phone service is still not 100 percent reliable. Dropped calls and poor reception are a problem in many areas. In addition, the call quality of landline phone service is often superior to cell phone call quality. Therefore, many people who run home businesses or make business calls from their home maintain a landline to ensure high voice quality of calls. In many instances, landline phone plans can be cheaper than cell phone plans, especially for international calls. Therefore, you may want to consider a style of landline phone service called VoIP (voice over Internet protocol).

How is VoIP different from regular telephone service? Voice over Internet Protocol (VoIP) is a form of voice-based Internet communication that turns a standard Internet connection into a means to place phone calls, including long-distance calls. Traditional telephone communications use analog voice data and telephone connections. In contrast, VoIP uses technology similar to that used in e-mail to send your voice data digitally over the Internet.

What do I need to use VoIP? For the simplest and least costly VoIP service, you need speakers, a microphone, an Internet connection, and a VoIP provider (see Figure 16). Depending on the provider you choose, you also may need to install software or a special adapter. Creating a VoIP account with Skype (**skype.com**) is similar to creating an instant messaging account. Skype requires that both callers and

Figure 14

Microbrowser software on phones like the Palm Pre let you work with (a) one window or (b) several live browser windows.

BITS AND BYTES

How Do You Find Your WiFi?

Detecting a nearby WiFi signal is important if you are looking for Internet connectivity while you are on the move. Some notebooks have a built-in WiFi scanner that displays a row of lights on the case whenever a WiFi signal is available. Keychain fobs that light up when they detect WiFi signals in the vicinity are also available.

If you are running Windows 7, the Connect to a Network dialog box (accessible from the Network and Sharing Center) shows the strength of all wireless networks within range of your computer.

At ThinkGeek (**thinkgeek.com**), you may find the most easy-to-use WiFi detector ever. The WiFi Detector t-shirt has a logo that lights up to indicate the signal strength of a nearby WiFi network (see Figure 15). Find your WiFi and look . . . well, look geeky while doing so!

Figure 15

The WiFi Detector T-shirt makes a statement—a geeky statement.

---

receivers have the company's free software installed on their computers. Another similarity to IM is that with Skype you can change your online status, look at your contact list, and decide whom you want to talk to. Other VoIP services, such as Vonage (**vonage.com**), are a bit more complicated to set up and are not free. You can use your own telephone by connecting your phone to a special adapter that the company provides, or you can buy a special IP phone that connects to your broadband Internet connection or to a USB port on your computer.

One limitation of VoIP used to be that when you made a call, you had to be at your computer. WiFi (wireless Internet) IP phones, however, make it possible to place VoIP calls from any WiFi hot spot location.

What are the advantages and disadvantages of VoIP?
For people who make many long-distance phone calls, the advantage of VoIP is its free or low cost. Portability is another advantage because all

you need is an Internet connection. With Internet accessibility so abundant, you can keep in touch with friends and family no matter where you are. As long as you are covered by a WiFi signal, you can plug in your headset or IP phone, sign on to your VoIP service, and make your call.

Although VoIP is affordable and convenient, it does have drawbacks. Some people regard sound quality and reliability issues as VoIP's primary disadvantages. Another drawback is the loss of service if power is interrupted. Although many traditional phones do not depend on electricity, your Internet connection and IP phone do. One serious drawback when VoIP service was first offered to the public was the inability for 911 calls to be traced back to the caller, unlike with a traditional phone. The FCC now requires all VoIP providers to provide traceable 911 services.

Another issue with VoIP is security. Security risks are similar to the risks associated with e-mail (such as spam) and fraud (such as where a hacker breaks into a VoIP system to make unauthorized calls). These are real risks but they are avoidable if you take proper precautions. In addition, encryption services (similar to those used with e-mail) that convert data into a form that is not easily understood by unauthorized people are being deployed to help protect the very nature of calls made over the Internet. Despite these concerns, VoIP continues to enjoy explosive growth, and the technology will continue to improve.

Figure 16

Depending on your VoIP service, you can hold conversations through a computer, a special VoIP telephone, or a regular telephone with an adapter.

What new features come with having an Internet-based digital phone at home? Once you are using an Internet-based digital phone system, new features become possible. You can have your telephone messages automatically bundled up as e-mails and sent to your account. If you are watching television and a call comes in, it can be displayed on the screen with caller ID information. Many cable delivery companies are bundling digital phone services in for free if you already purchase cable and television through them, so the price may be attractive.

Cell Phone/Smartphone Security

Can I get a virus on my cell/ smartphone? Although viruses can already infect cell phones, manufacturers and software engineers are bracing themselves for a tidal wave of viruses targeted to cell/smartphones. With half of users reporting that they send confidential e-mails using their phones and one-third of users indicating that they access bank account or credit card information, cell/smartphones are the next most likely realm of attack by cybercriminals. The potential of cell/smartphone viruses ranges from the mildly annoying (certain features of your phone stop working) to the expensive (your phone is used without your knowledge to make expensive calls).

How can I prevent cell/smartphone viruses? Symantec, McAfee, and F-Secure are the leading companies currently providing antivirus software for mobile devices. Products are designed for specific cell/smartphone operating systems; for example, Symantec Mobile Security for Symbian is designed for cell/smartphones running the Symbian OS. Often businesses will have their information technology department install and configure an antivirus solution like this for all the phones used in the organization. Although viruses plaguing cell/smartphones have not yet reached the volume of viruses attacking PC operating systems, with the proliferation of mobile devices it is expected that such virus attacks will increase. If no antivirus program is available for your phone's operating

system, the best precautions are common sense ones. Check the phone manufacturer's Web site frequently to see whether your cell/smartphone needs any software upgrades that could patch security holes. In addition, remember that you should not download ring tones, games, or other software from unfamiliar Web sites.

How do I keep my cell/smartphone number private? It seems that every time you fill out a Web form someone is asking for your phone number. If you are concerned about widely distributing your cell/smartphone number and potentially inviting lots of unwanted solicitation calls, you should consider using a virtual phone number. A virtual phone number is a phone number you create that can be assigned to ring on existing phone numbers (such as your cell phone). Companies such as Telusion (**tossabledigits.com**) provide these virtual numbers. Then, when you are filling out a registration form for some Web service, you can input your virtual phone number in the Web form instead of giving out your number. When you set up the virtual account, you can restrict the hours that you will receive calls from that number (no more 2:00 A.M. telemarketing calls), and if you are receiving many unwanted calls, you can disable the virtual number without affecting your cell/ smartphone service.

> **"How do I keep my cell/ smartphone number private?"**

Digital Media

The entertainment industry has become an all-digital field. Today, videos, music, and photographs are created using digital recording devices, processed using digital software systems, and delivered over digital distribution channels. What does this mean

Digital Media

351

Singer playing music

Analog wave

ADC

Digital format
28,36,42,
84,120,126,
120,98,98...

CD or DVD

DAC

Speaker

28,36,42,
84,120,126,
120,98,98...

Figure 17

During the complete recording process, information changes from analog form to digital data and then back again to analog sound waves.

for you and your use of music, photography, and video?

How is digital media created? All digital media, whether an image, a song, or a video, has the same basis—digitized information. Figure 17 shows the process of creating digital information for a musical selection. This process is described below:

1. Playing music creates analog waves.

2. A microphone feeds the sound waves into a chip called an *analog-to-digital converter (ADC)* inside the recording device.

3. The ADC digitizes the waves into a series of numbers.

4. This series of numbers can be recorded onto CDs and DVDs or sent electronically.

5. On the receiving end, a playback device such as a CD player or DVD player is fed that same series of numbers. Inside the playback device is a digital-to-analog converter (DAC), a chip that converts the digital numbers to a continuous analog wave.

6. That analog wave tells the receiver how to move the speaker cones to reproduce the original waves, resulting in the same sound as the original.

More precisely, the digital wave will be *close* to exact. How accurate it is, or how close the digitized wave is in shape to the original analog wave, depends on the sampling rate of the ADC. The **sampling rate** specifies the number of times the analog

wave is measured each second. The higher the sampling rate, the more accurately the original wave can be recreated. However, higher sampling rates also produce much more data, and therefore result in bigger files. For example, sound waves on CDs are sampled at a rate of approximately 44,000 times a second. This produces a huge list of numbers for even a single minute of a song!

When sounds or image waves are digitized, it means that analog data is changed into digital data—from a wave into a series of numbers. The digital data is perfectly reproducible and can be distributed easily on CDs and DVDs or through the airwaves. The data also can be easily processed by a computer.

Digital Music

How can I carry music files easily? **Portable media players (PMPs)** are small portable devices (such as an iPod) that enable you to carry your MP3 files around with you. Many PMPs handle video and still images, as well as music files. Many smartphones are capable of storing and playing media files, but for the best experience, a dedicated media player, such as a portable media player, is often the optimal choice because PMPs tend to offer more features and storage.

Depending on the player, you can carry several hours of music or video—or possibly your entire CD collection—in an incredibly small device. For example, an Apple iPod classic with a 160 GB hard drive is 4.1 inches by 2.4 inches (and only 0.41 inch thick), yet it can hold as many as 40,000 songs, or 200 hours of video. The most compact players are slightly larger than a flash drive (although they hold far less music than the iPod). Figure 18 shows several models of PMPs, all of which connect to computers via USB 2.0 ports.

Are all music files MP3 files? The letters at the end of a file name (the file extension) indicate how the data in the file is organized. MP3 is the name of just one type of file format used to store digital music, but many others exist, such as AAC and WMA. There are also many video formats such as DivX, MPEG-4 (which usually has an .mp4 extension), WMV, and XviD. All file

Figure 18 | SOME PORTABLE MEDIA PLAYERS AND THEIR CHARACTERISTICS

	Media Capacity	Built-In Flash Memory	Hard Drive Capacity	Connection to Computer	Other Features
Sansa® Fuze™ Player	2000 songs or 24 hours of video	512 MB to 1 GB	None but 16 GB mSD card supported	USB 2.0 port	FM radio, voice recorder and available "radio" cards prefilled with 1000 songs
Oregon Scientific MP121	Up to 32 hours of music	1 GB	None	USB 2.0 port	Waterproof to 3 feet, built-in pedometer, built-in FM radio, and equalizer.
Apple iPod touch	As many as 14,000 songs or 80 hours of video	8 GB to 64 GB	None	USB 2.0 port	Weighs only 4.05 ounces; flash memory enables skip-free playback.
Apple iPod classic	As many as 40,000 songs or 200 hours of video	None	160 GB	USB 2.0 port	Has calendar feature that syncs with Outlook; can serve as a small, portable hard drive.
Archos 7	As many as 190,000 songs or 400 movies	None	320 GB	USB 2.0 port	Includes 7" screen display, Wi-Fi, and touch screen.

SanDisk and Sanza FUZE are trademarks of SANDISK Corporations; Courtesy of Apple; Apple Computer, Inc.; Archos, Inc.

formats compete on sound and video quality and *compression*, which relates to how small the file can be and still provide high-quality playback. If you buy a song from the iTunes Music Store, for example, you receive an .aac format file. AAC files can be played only on iPods but can be converted to the more widely seen MP3 or Windows Media Audio (WMA) formats. WMA files can be played on a wide variety of MP3 players. Most PMPs that support video playback can play a wide range of video formats.

Are PMP devices the only choice for portable media management?

PMP devices are not the only choice for portable media management. A number of electronic devices now incorporate the capability to carry electronic files and play music and video files. Some models of digital cameras, such as the Samsung NV3, have support for playing both music and videos. Gaming devices such as the Sony PlayStation Portable (PSP) allow you to play video games, play music and video files, and browse the Internet.

In the last few years, stand-alone **GPS (global positioning system)** devices have dropped dramatically in price and size. Now these small, handheld units organize music and photos as well as deliver turn-by-turn instructions and real-time traffic

Figure 19

The Garmin Nuvi series GPS devices are also able to provide Internet services.

information. Full-featured GPS models such as the Garmin Nuvi 705 series include MP3 players, audio book players, and the capability to display photos and connect to the Internet (see Figure 19). Using Internet services such as MSN Direct, your GPS can keep you informed about the weather, traffic backups, local movie times, and even local gas prices.

How do I know how much digital media a PMP can hold? The number of songs or hours of video a portable media

ETHICS IN IT

The Power of GPS … and the Threats

Most people know where the closest supermarket is in relation to their home. But if you are out of town, how can you find a local supermarket when you get a craving for potato chips? Many people aren't whizzes at geography, but knowing your current location and the location of your destination can often come in handy. Luckily for those who are "directionally impaired," GPS technology enables users to carry a powerful navigational aid in a pocket.

You've probably heard of GPS, but what is it exactly and how does it work? Built and operated by the U.S. Department of Defense, the global positioning system is a network of 21 satellites (plus 3 working spares) that constantly orbit the Earth. GPS devices use an antenna to pick up the signals from these satellites and use special software to transform those signals into latitude and longitude. Using the information obtained from the satellites, GPS devices can tell you what your geographical location is anywhere on the planet to within 10 feet (see Figure 20). Because they provide such detailed positioning information, GPS devices are now used as navigational aids for aircraft, recreational boats, and automobiles, and they even come in handheld models for hikers.

Although this precise positioning information clearly redefines the fields of surveying and search-and-rescue operations, it also has changed other fields. Wildlife researchers now tag select animals, watch their migration patterns, and observe how populations are distributed. GPS also was important to the two teams that created the Chunnel, the tunnel under the English Channel that connects England to France. One team worked from France toward England and the other from England toward France. They used GPS information along the way to make sure they were on target. In 1990, the two sections were joined to become the first physical link between England and the continent of Europe since the Ice Age.

GPS units are available with a wide range of features. Garmin, for example, offers a wide range of services on its line of GPS units. A Map mode displays your location on a map that is updated in real time as you drive. Enter a series of destinations, and an optimal route is developed for you. A voice warns you of lane changes and approaching turns, giving you directions using the actual street name ("Turn right on Hancock

Figure 20

GPS computes your location anywhere on Earth from a system of orbiting satellites.

Avenue"). If you miss a turn, the unit automatically recalculates the required route and gives you directions to get back on course. Flip to player can hold depends on how much storage space it has. Most PMPs use built-in **flash memory**, a type of nonvolatile memory, to store files. Most PMPs that support video use a hard drive instead of flash memory and can store a much greater amount of music and video. Less expensive PMPs use flash memory (ranging from 1 GB to 32 GB), whereas models that are more expensive use built-in hard drives, which provide as much as 160 GB of storage. Some of the PMPs that use flash memory allow you to add storage capacity by purchasing removable flash memory cards.

Another factor that determines how much music a player can hold is the quality of the MP3 music files. The size of an MP3 file depends on the digital sampling of the song. The same song could be sampled at 320 kbps or 64 kbps. The size of the song file will be five times larger if it is sampled at 320 kbps rather than the lower sampling rate of 64 kbps. The higher the sampling rate, the better quality the sound— but the larger the file size.

How do you control the size of an MP3 file? If you are *ripping*, or converting, a song from a CD into a digital MP3 file,

Telefonica O2 UK Limited

Figure 21

A cell/smartphone can now use a GPS service to give you turn-by-turn directions and current traffic conditions.

another screen, and it shows you how far you have to drive to the next gas station, restaurant, or hospital. Some models automatically mark the location of your car when you remove them from the vehicle, and can give you step-by-step directions back to your car.

Most automotive companies now offer GPS systems as installed options in their vehicles. However, GPS navigation can be added to any vehicle using a portable GPS device or a PDA/smartphone equipped with GPS (see Figure 21), or by adding GPS software and accessories to your notebook.

But Who Is Watching?

Having the ability to locate and track an object anywhere on Earth does bring with it societal implications, however. The Federal Communications

Commission (FCC) mandated that every cell/smartphone had to include a GPS chip by the end of 2005. This enabled the complete rollout of the Enhanced 911 (E911) program. E911 automatically gives dispatchers precise location information for any 911 call. It also means your phone records may include this precise tracking information, which indicates where you are when you make a call. Is that information something you would want the government, or other people, to know? Consider if you were at a park playing baseball with your friends and you made a phone call. At the same time, in another part of the park, an organization with suspected terrorist ties was holding a rally. Would you want the government to assume that because you made a phone call from the park, you are a member of that organization?

Because phones now have GPS chips, cellular phone providers offer plans (for a monthly fee) that allow you to track where a phone is at any given time via a Web site. This could be a real boon for tracking a lost child who wandered off into the woods during a group hike. But are other uses of the technology ethical? Did your daughter really go to the library, or is she actually at the local skate park hanging with her friends? Is your spouse really working late at the office—or at the ballpark watching the baseball game with friends? Now, with a few clicks of the mouse, you can tell where a family member's phone is located. Is this an invasion of privacy? Is it ethical to track the whereabouts of your family members? This is something that you need to decide.

GPS technology begs several questions: What limits and supervision of the government need to be in place to ensure the ethical use of GPS technologies? In what ways could the tracking information provided by GPS devices be used unethically? If GPS tracking information is recorded in people's phone data, should the criteria for allowing government agencies to subpoena phone records be changed? Should users be allowed to disable the location information feature on their phones? Location records such as these were used to determine that *New York Times* reporter Jayson Blair had been fabricating stories, a determination that resulted in his resignation. Car rental companies such as Acme Car Rental of New Haven, Connecticut are using GPS records to fine customers for speeding violations. As a nation, we now need to decide how we should balance the benefits and costs (to our privacy) of using this new level of tracking information.

you can select the sampling rate yourself. You decide by considering what quality sound you want, as well as how many songs you want to fit onto your MP3 player. For example, if your player had 1 GB of storage and you have ripped songs at 192 kbps, you could fit about 694 minutes of music onto the player. The same 1 GB could store 2,083 minutes of music if it were sampled at 64 kbps. Whenever you are near your computer, you can connect your player and download a different set of songs, but you always are limited by the amount of storage your player has.

What if I want to store more music or video than the memory on my PMP allows? Some PMPs allow you to add memory by inserting removable flash memory cards. Flash memory cards are noiseless and featherlight, use tiny amounts of power, and slide into a special slot in the player. If you've ever played a video game on PlayStation or Xbox and saved your progress to a memory card, then you have used flash memory. Because flash memory is nonvolatile, when you store data on a flash memory card, you won't lose it when you turn off the player. In addition, flash memory can be erased and rewritten with new data. PMPs use a variety of different types of flash cards. Check your manual and then review information coverage on flash media for more details.

How do I transfer media files to my portable media player? All portable media players come with software that enables you to transfer audio and video files from your computer to the player. As noted earlier, players that hold thousands of songs and hours of video use internal hard drives to store the files. For example, devices such as Apple iPods can hold several gigabytes of data. To move large volumes of data between your computer and your PMP, you want a high-speed port. Most PMPs use a USB 2.0 port, but some players may use FireWire ports, which provide comparable throughput. Using a USB 2.0 port, you can transfer two dozen MP3 files to the iPod in less than 10 seconds.

What if I want a lot of people to listen to my digital music? PMPs are great for individual listening, but to share

music from a PMP, you have to connect it to an alternative device. Many audio receivers now come with a port or a dock so that you can connect a PMP device directly to them as another audio input source, like a CD player or a television. Most new cars are equipped with at least an auxiliary input to the speaker system to support connecting a PMP; others have a fully integrated software system that displays and runs the PMP playlists. There are alarm clocks and home speaker docks that can mate with a PMP and broadcast brilliant sound.

How did the shift to digital music impact the music industry? The initial MP3 craze was fueled by sites such as MP3.com, which originally stored its song files on a public server with the permission of the original artists or recording companies. Therefore, you were not infringing on a copyright by downloading songs from sites such as MP3.com (which still exists and now provides free music in streaming format).

> **"Audio receivers now come with a port to connect a PMP device directly. "**

Napster was a file exchange site created to correct some of the annoyances found by users of MP3.com. One such annoyance was the limited availability of popular music in MP3 format. With the MP3 sites, if you found a song you wanted to download, the link to the site on which the file was found often no longer worked. Napster differed from MP3.com because songs or locations of songs were not stored in a central public server, but instead were "borrowed" directly from other users' computers. This process of users transferring files between computers is referred to as **peer-to-peer (P2P) sharing**. Napster also provided a search engine dedicated to finding specific MP3 files. This direct search and sharing eliminated the inconvenience of searching links only to find them unavailable.

The problem with Napster was that it was so good at what it did. Napster's convenient and reliable mechanism to find and download popular songs in MP3 format became a huge success. The rapid acceptance and use of Napster—at one point, it had nearly 60 million users—led the music industry to sue the site for copyright infringement, and Napster was closed in June 2002. Napster has since reopened as a music site that sells music downloads and is sanctioned by the recording industry.

The reaction of the record industry was to continue to enforce its absolute ownership over digital forms of its music. The industry even filed legal actions against individuals who had downloaded large amounts of music from Internet sites. This heavy-handed reaction to the new era of digital music ultimately backfired and left the music industry scrambling. Overall music sales in 2009 were about half what they were at the industry's peak. The record industry is still trying to counter losing CD sales to digital forms of music. The approach they took early on did not allow them to adapt quickly enough to the new business models required by the shift to digital technologies.

So if I don't pay for a music download, is it illegal? Although you need to pay for most music you download, some artists post songs for free. Business models are still evolving as artists and recording companies try to meet audience needs while also protecting their own intellectual property rights. Several different approaches exist. One is to deliver something called *tethered downloads* in which you pay for the music and own it, but are subject to restrictions on its use.

Another approach is to offer *DRM-free* music, which is music without any digital rights management. These song files can be moved freely from system to system. For example, Apple's iTunes store currently sells only DRM-free types of music. A DRM-free song can be placed on as many computers or players as you wish. Other sites offer subscription services. For a monthly fee, Napster to Go allows you to download as many songs as you like to your MP3 player. These songs will be usable, however, only as long as you are paying the monthly subscription fee.

Why buy any music if peer-to-peer (P2P) sharing sites are still operating? When Napster was going through its legal turmoil, other P2P Web sites were quick to take advantage of a huge opportunity. Napster was "easy" to shut down because it used a central index server that queried other Napster computers for requested songs. Current P2P protocols (such as LimeWire and BearShare) differ

ACTIVE HELP-DESK

Using Portable Media Players

In this Active Helpdesk call, you'll play the role of a helpdesk staffer, fielding calls about portable media players, what they can carry, and how they store data.

from Napster in that they do not limit themselves to sharing only MP3 files. Video files are obtainable easily on P2P sites. More importantly, these sites don't have a central index server. Instead, they operate in a true P2P sharing environment in which computers connect directly to other computers. This makes them a prime source of unwanted viruses and spyware.

The argument these P2P networks make to defend their legality is that they do not run a central server like the original Napster, but only facilitate connections between users. Therefore, they have no control over what the users choose to trade. Note that not all P2P file sharing is illegal. For example, it is legal to trade photos or movies you have created with other folks over a P2P site.

People who oppose such file-sharing sites contend that the sites know their users are distributing files illegally and breaking copyright laws. Be aware that having illegal content on your computer, deliberately or by accident, is a criminal offense in many jurisdictions.

Will PMPs eliminate radio stations? Radio stations have always had certain advantages: early access to new music, and personalities and conversations that add to the listening experience.

BITS AND BYTES

Trick Out Your iTouch

There are over 75,000 Web apps available for the iPhone and iTouch. Some are games, some are just gimmicks, but many are great tools for a student. iFlipr is an app that connects you to 2.7 million flash cards. You can study for the MCAT exam or build and share your own custom flash card deck. iHomework organizes your teacher contact info, due dates for assignments, and research materials. iProRecorder lets your iPhone record audio from your classes. Can't find the app you are dreaming of? The iPhone Developer University program is free and supports students and faculty in designing and coding Web apps.

Digital Media

However, the Internet allows artists to release new songs to their fans immediately (on sites such as mp3.com) and without relying on radio airtime. This opens up new channels for artists to reach an audience and changes the amount of power radio stations have in the promotion of music. Many radio stations have increased listenership by making their stations available through Internet sites and by broadcasting in high-definition quality.

Another development that competes with radio (and television) is *podcasting*, which allows users to download audio and video content and then listen to those broadcasts on their PMPs whenever they want. Podcasting is paving the way for anyone to create a radio or television show at home and distribute it easily to an audience. Using free software such as Audacity (**audacity. sourceforge.net**) and a microphone, you can record voice-overs, sequence songs, and "publish" your show to the Internet. Loyal fans can use podcasting software such as Juice (**juicereceiver.sourceforge.net**) or iTunes (for Windows or Mac) to find a podcast's latest episode and automatically transfer it to their portable media players. Plugging your iPod into a data port on your computer causes the iPod to search iTunes for new content and automatically transfers the new files to your iPod. Podcasts are easy to subscribe to and download using iTunes (see Figure 22).

Digital Photography

What is "analog" photography?
Before digital cameras hit the market, most people used some form of 35-mm single-lens reflex (SLR) camera. When you take a picture using a traditional SLR camera, a shutter opens, creating an aperture (a small window in the camera) that allows light to hit the 35-mm film inside. Chemicals coating the film react when exposed to light. Later, additional chemicals develop the image on the film, and the image is printed on special light-sensitive paper. A variety of lenses and processing techniques, special equipment, and filters are needed to create printed photos from traditional SLR cameras.

What is different about digital photography?
Digital cameras do not use film. Instead, they capture images on electronic sensors called *charge-coupled device (CCD) arrays* and then convert those images to digital data, long series of numbers that represent the color and brightness of millions of points in the image. Unlike traditional cameras, digital cameras allow you to see your images the instant you shoot them. Most camera models can now record digital video as well as digital photos.

How do I select a digital camera?
With hundreds of models to choose from, where do you begin? The first question to answer is whether you want a compact "point-and-click" model camera or a more serious digital SLR. The larger digital SLR cameras allow you to switch among different lenses and offer features important to serious amateur and professional photographers (such as depth-of-field previewing). Although having such flexibility in moving up to a larger zoom lens is a great advantage, these cameras are also larger, heavier, and use more battery power than the tiny point-and-click models. Think about how you will be using your camera and decide which model will serve you best in the long run.

Figure 22

iTunes makes it easy to subscribe to and manage podcasts.

Consider this scenario: You were in Washington, D.C. over spring break and you took a lovely photograph of the Washington Monument at sunset. You posted the photo on your Facebook page so your family and friends could see it. One morning you pop open your e-mail and there is an offer from a magazine to feature your photo on the cover. (An editor saw it on Facebook.) Before accepting the offer, you need to be aware of your digital rights concerning your photograph.

Copyright is a bundle of rights that are granted to creators of original works such as literary materials, music, and photographs. For photographs, the photographer usually owns the copyright to the photo. The rights you have over your photograph of the Washington Monument include the right to publish, to display (such as on your Facebook page), or to sell copies of the work. Therefore, posting the photograph on your Facebook page, as well as selling it to the magazine, are probably within your rights.

In the United States, you are free to take photographs in public places such as streets, public parks, or sidewalks without asking anyone's permission. However, property owners can prohibit photography on their premises or place restrictions on the use of photographs taken on their property. For instance, museums usually restrict the photographic rights of buildings and works of art on display. If you had taken a photograph of *Coast of Normandy* (a painting by Claude Monet), which is displayed at the Philadelphia Museum of Art, you would not be able to use the photograph for commercial purposes (for example, sell it to a magazine) without the consent of the museum. When taking photographs on private property, you should always inquire about restrictions on the use of photographs.

In the case of a national monument, which is a public place, there are generally no restrictions to copyright on photographs you take. Nevertheless, for our example, you should check with the National Park Service (which administers the Washington Monument) just to be on the safe side.

But what if two of your friends and three complete strangers, who were all standing in front of the Washington Monument, are prominently featured in your photograph? Generally speaking, people in photographs do not have any rights or partial ownership of the copyright of the photo.

However, in the United States, the Fourth Amendment to the Constitution and various other laws and court cases have recognized Americans' rights to certain amounts of privacy. Being photographed without your consent is considered a violation of privacy. Your friends essentially gave their permission to be photographed by jumping in front of your camera and posing. However, the three strangers didn't give their permission.

Usually, when photographers know they will use a photograph for commercial purposes, they have all people in the photograph sign a *model release*. A model release grants the photographer the rights to use an image of the model (the person in the photo) commercially. Be aware there are many instances where you grant your approval to have your image used commercially. For example, most tickets to amusement parks have a clause on the back that states that by entering the park you grant the park permission to use your image in marketing and publicity materials.

On the other hand, if a picture of you is published without your consent, you may have the basis for a lawsuit. Consider the case of teenager Alison Chang, who was photographed at a church-sponsored car wash. The photographer posted the photograph on Flickr, stating that anyone was free to use his photos as long as they identified him as the photographer. An advertising agency in Australia saw the photograph on Flickr and used it in a billboard advertising campaign for a cell phone company. All of a sudden, Alison was the "friend" you could dump when you became cool and bought a cell phone. When Alison found out about this unauthorized use of her image, her family promptly filed a lawsuit seeking damages. Although the photographer was able to give away his rights to the photograph, he couldn't give away Alison's rights without her permission.

Therefore, for your Washington Monument photo, you should obtain model releases from your friends before selling the photo to the magazine. You should also inform the magazine that you do not possess model releases for the three strangers in the photo so the magazine can remove those people from the image before publication. You need to respect the rights of others, and exercise discretion when taking and displaying photographs, so you don't end up on the wrong side of a lawsuit.

Next, you'll want to evaluate the quality of the camera on a number of levels. One great resource to use is Digital Photography Review (**dpreview.com**). The site's camera reviews evaluate a camera's construction as well as its features, image quality, ease of use, and value for the cost. In addition, the site provides comparisons to similar camera models by other manufacturers and feedback from owners of those models. Links are provided to several resellers, making it easy to compare prices as well.

Why not just use the camera on my cell/smartphone? Many cell/smartphones include a digital camera. These cameras often provide lower resolutions than stand-alone models and inferior lenses. Many features that photographers rely on are not often available in the cameras included on phones, such as different types of autofocus, image stabilization algorithms, and *smile shutter*, which waits to take a shot until your subject is smiling.

What determines the image quality of a digital camera? Part of what determines the image quality of a digital camera is its **resolution**, or the number of data points it records for each image captured.

Digital Media

359

Canon Lumix G1 (12.1 MP)

Kodak V1273 (12 MP)

Canon EOS-1Ds (21.9 MP)

Sony Cybershot
DSC-T900R (12.1 MP)

Panasonic Corporation of North America

Courtesy of Sony Electronics Inc.

Figure 23

Digital camera resolutions.

A digital camera's resolution is measured in megapixels (MP). The prefix *mega* is short for millions. The word *pixel* is short for picture element, which is a single dot in a digital image. Point-and-click models typically offer resolutions from 8 MP to 15 MP. Professional digital SLR cameras, such as the Canon EOS-1Ds Mark III, can take photos at resolutions as high as 21.1 MP, but they sell for thousands of dollars. Figure 23 shows some popular digital camera models and the number of pixels they record at their maximum resolution.

If you're interested in making only 5″ × 7″ or 8″ × 10″ prints, a lower-resolution camera is fine. However, low-resolution images become grainy and pixelated when pushed to make larger-size prints. For example, if you tried to print an 11″ × 14″ enlargement from a 2 MP image taken using your cell phone's camera, the image would look grainy; you would see individual dots of color instead of a clear, sharp image. The 8 MP to 15 MP cameras on the market now have plenty of resolution to guarantee sharp, detailed images even with enlargements as big as 11″ × 14″.

What file formats are used for digital images? To fit more photos on the same size of flash memory card, digital cameras allow you to choose from several different file types in order to compress, or squeeze, the image data into less memory space. When you choose to compress your images, you will lose some of the detail, but in return, you'll be able to fit more images on your flash card. The most common file types supported by digital cameras are raw uncompressed data (RAW) and Joint Photographic Experts Group (JPEG). Raw files have different formats and extensions depending on the manufacturer of a particular camera. The raw file records all of the original image information, so it is larger than a compressed JPEG file. JPEG files can be compressed just a bit, keeping most of the details, or compressed a great deal, losing some detail. Most cameras allow you to select from a few different JPEG compression levels.

Often cameras also support a very low-resolution storage option, enabling you to create files that you can easily attach to e-mail messages. This low-resolution setting typically provides images that are not useful for printing but are so small in size that they are easily e-mailed. Even people who have slow Internet connections are able to quickly download and view such images on-screen.

How do I move photos to my computer? If you just want to print your photos, you may not need to transfer them to your computer. Many photo printers can make prints directly from your camera or from a flash memory card, and many retailers, like CVS and Wal-Mart, provide photo printing machines that can read directly from your memory card. However, transferring the photos to your computer does allow you to store them and frees your flash card for reuse.

Digital cameras have a built-in USB 2.0 port. (Some high-end models may also include a FireWire port.) Using a USB 2.0 cable, you can connect the camera to your computer and copy the converted images as uncompressed files or in a compressed format as JPEG files. Another option is to transfer the flash card from your camera directly to the built-in memory card reader on your computer. Some camera models support wireless network connections so that you can transfer the images without the fuss of putting a cable in place. The Panasonic Lumix TZ50 goes a step further. It uses its integrated WiFi to connect to Google's online photo service, Picasa, and uploads your images to a Picasa Web photo album automatically.

Can I make my old photos digital?

Obviously, not every document or image you have is in an electronic form. What about all the photographs you have already taken? What about an article from a magazine or a hand-drawn sketch? How can these be converted into digital format?

Digital scanners such as the ones shown in Figure 24 convert paper text and images into digital formats. You can place any flat material on the glass surface of the scanner and convert it into a digital file. Most scanner software allows you to store the converted images as RAW files or in compressed form as JPEG files. Some scanners include hardware that allows you to scan film negatives or slides as well or even insert a stack of photos to be scanned in sequence.

Scanner quality is measured by its resolution, which is given in dots per inch (dpi). Most modern scanners can digitize a document at resolutions as high as 4,800 × 9,600 dpi, in either color or grayscale mode. You can easily connect a scanner to your computer using USB 2.0 or FireWire ports. Scanners also typically come with software that supports optical character recognition (OCR). OCR software converts pages of handwritten or typed text into electronic files. You can then open and edit these converted documents with traditional word processing programs such as Microsoft Word. In addition, many scanners have a copy function that allows you to scan and print documents, taking the place of a copy machine.

How do I print a digital image?

You can print a digital image using a professional service or your own printer. Most photo printing labs, including the film processing departments at stores such as Wal-Mart and Target, offer digital printing services, as do many high-end online processing labs. The paper and ink used at processing labs are higher quality than what is available for home use and produce heavier, glossier prints that won't fade. You can send your digital photos directly to local merchants such as CVS and Walgreens for printing using Windows Live Photo Gallery. Online services, such as Flickr (**flickr.com**) and Shutterfly (**shutterfly.com**), store your images and allow you to organize them into photo albums or to create hard-copy prints, mugs, T-shirts, or calendars.

Photo printers for home use are available in two technologies: inkjet and dye sublimation (see Figure 25). The most popular and

The Neat Company

inexpensive ones are inkjet printers. Some inkjet printers are capable of printing high-quality color photos, although they vary in speed and quality. Some include a display window so that you can review the image as you stand at the printer, whereas others are portable, allowing you to print your photos wherever you are. Some printers even allow you to crop the image right at the printer without having to use special image editing software.

Unlike inkjet printers, which use an inkjet nozzle, dye-sublimation printers produce images using a heating element. The heating element passes over a ribbon of translucent film that has been dyed with bands of colors. Depending on the temperature of the element, dyes are vaporized from a solid into a gas. The gas vapors penetrate the photo paper before they cool and return to solid form, producing glossy, high-quality images. If you're interested in a printer to use for printing only

Figure 24

Scanners are available in a variety of shapes, but all of them can convert paper documents, photo prints, and strips of film negatives into digital data.

Figure 25

(a) The Kodak EasyShare inkjet system allows you to transfer and print pictures quickly and easily. (b) The Sony DPP-FP90 dye-sublimation printer produces professional-quality images that resist fading, water stains, and fingerprints.

photographs, a dye-sublimation printer is a good choice. However, some models print only specific photo sizes, such as 4" × 6" prints, so be sure the printer you buy will fit your long-term needs.

Transferring images to a printer is similar to transferring them to your computer. If you have a direct-connection camera, you can plug the camera directly into the printer with a cable. Some printers have slots that accept different types of flash memory cards. Of course, you also can transfer your images to the printer from your computer if you have stored them there.

Do I need to print out my photos?
You may decide not to print your photos at all. As noted earlier, online albums let you share your photos without having to print them. Portable devices, such as Apple's iPod and cell phones, also enable you to carry and display your photos. The iPod, for example, can be connected to a TV and deliver slide shows of your photographs, complete with musical soundtracks you have selected.

Digital Video

Where does digital video come from?
Digital video that you watch comes from several sources, but now people often create their own digital videos. As a video creator, you may purchase dedicated digital camcorders to record digital video. Most cell phones can record video, and digital cameras take video as well as digital still shots. Webcams also work as inexpensive devices for creating digital video.

There are many other sources of digital video available to you now. Television is broadcasting in digitally formatted signals.

The Internet delivers a huge amount of digital video through Google Video, YouTube, communities like Vimeo (**vimeo.com**), and webcasting sites like Ustream (**ustream.tv**). Many pay services are available to deliver digital video to you. These include on-demand streaming from cable providers, iTunes, Netflix's Instant Watch films, and Amazon's Video On Demand download service.

How do I record my own digital video? Video equipment for home use stores information in the digital video (DV) format. This allows the cameras to be incredibly small and light. Such cameras don't require any tapes at all; they store hours of video on built-in hard drives or flash cards. Some models even record directly to DVD discs.

You can easily transfer video files to your computer and, using video editing software, edit the video at home, cutting out sections, resequencing segments, and adding titles. To do the same with analog videotape would require expensive and complex audio/video equipment available only in video production studios. You can save (or *write*) your final product on a CD or DVD and play it in your home DVD system or on your computer. For true videophiles, cameras and burners are now available for high-definition video format.

What if I decide to add some special effects and a sound track?
Video editing software presents a storyboard or *timeline* with which you can manipulate your video file, as shown in Figure 26. You can review your clips frame by frame or trim them at any point. You can order each segment on the timeline in whichever sequence you like and correct segments for color balance, brightness, or contrast.

In addition, you can add transitions to your video such as those you're used to seeing on TV—fades to black, dissolves, and so on. Just select the type of transition you want from the drop-down list and drag that icon into the timeline where you want the transition to occur.

Video editing software also lets you add titles, animations, and audio tracks to your video, including background music, sound effects, and additional narration. You can adjust the volume of each audio track to switch from one to the other or have both playing together. Finally, you can preview all of these effects in real time.

There is a lot to learn about digital video editing, and with the number of choices available, it is easy to be overwhelmed. Examine online tutorial resources such as Izzy Video podcasts (**izzyvideo.com**) to learn how to make the most impact with the editing and effects you apply to your raw video footage.

What kinds of files will I end up with? Once you're done editing your video file, you can save (or export) it in a variety of formats. Figure 27 shows some of the popular video file formats in use today, along with the file extensions they use.

Your choice of file format for your finished video will depend on what you want to do with your video. For example, the QuickTime streaming file format is a great choice if your file is really large and you plan to post it on the Web. The Microsoft AVI format is a good choice if you're sending your file to a wide range of users, because it's extremely popular and is commonly accepted as the standard video format for the Windows Media Player.

You also can try different compression choices to see which one does a better job of compressing your particular file. A **codec** (**co**mpression/**dec**ompression) is a rule,

Effects · Transitions · Titles · Themes · Clip Art

Video track · Audio track · Music track

Christian Musat\Shutterstock; Jan Martin Will\Shutterstock; kwest\Shutterstock

Figure 26

Adobe Premiere Elements allows you to build a movie from video clips and add sound tracks and special effects.

Figure 27 | TYPICAL FILE FORMATS FOR DIGITAL VIDEO

Format	File Extension	Notes
QuickTime	.mov .qt	You can download QuickTime player without charge from **apple.com/quicktime**. The pro version allows you to build your own QuickTime files.
Moving Picture Experts Group (MPEG)	.mpg .mpeg .mp4	MPEG-4 video standard adopted internationally in 2000; recognized by most video player software.
Windows Media Video	.wmv	Microsoft file format recognized by Windows Media Player (included with the Windows OS).
Microsoft Video for Windows	.avi	Microsoft file format recognized by Windows Media Player (included with the Windows OS).
RealMedia	.rm	Format from RealNetworks; popular for streaming video. You can download the player for free at **real.com**.
Adobe Flash Video	.flv	Adobe Flash video format, sometimes embedded in Shockwave files (*.swf).

Digital Media

So you just returned from your trip to the Grand Canyon and all your friends are raving about the high quality of the photographs you took. You decide to put the photographs out on Flickr so your friends can see them. You also think that maybe someone might see your photos and want to use them in a commercial publication such as a magazine. Wouldn't that be cool? Because you own the copyright to your photos, you control how they can be used—and you want to protect your rights. You add a disclaimer to Flickr indicating that all rights are reserved on your photos. Anyone who wants to use them will need to contact you and request permission.

All of a sudden, you are bombarded by dozens of requests for permission to use your photographs for all sorts of purposes. A high school student in Illinois wants to feature one of your photos on her travel blog. A church in Georgia wants to use a photo for their newsletter to illustrate a story about a church member's trip to Arizona. An advertising agency in Seattle wants to modify your sunrise photo by inserting a family on a camping trip into the photo. You want to protect your rights (maybe the ad agency might even pay you!), but isn't there an easier way to manage photo permission requests?

Copyleft, a play on the word copyright, is designed for this situation. Copyleft is a term for various licensing plans that enable copyright holders to grant certain rights to the work while retaining other rights. The GNU General Public License is a popular copyleft license that is used for software. For other works, the Creative Commons, a nonprofit organization, has developed a range of licenses that can be used to control rights to works.

Creative Commons has various types of licenses available based on the rights you wish to grant. The company provides a simple form to assist you with selecting the proper license for your work. Creative Commons provides two licenses at **creativecommons.org/about/licenses** that could simplify your life. An *attribution license* permits others to copy, distribute, and display your copyrighted work, but only if they give you credit in the way you specify. Under this license, the high school student could use one of your photos as long as he or she gave you credit.

A *noncommercial license* allows anyone to copy, distribute, and display your work, but only for noncommercial purposes. The church in Georgia could use one of your photos under this license because it is not profiting from its use.

Both of these licenses can also be used to cover derivative works. A **derivative work** is based on the original work (one of your photos) but is modified in some way. The ad agency that wants to modify one of your photos is seeking permission to create a derivative work. If you had used an attribution license, the ad agency could use your work for a derivative purpose, but only if it attributed the original work to you as the author. If you had used a noncommercial license, the ad agency could not use your work to make a profit for itself.

The obvious advantage to using these Creative Commons licenses is that people won't constantly annoy you with permission requests to use your work. These licenses explain exactly how you are willing to have your work be used. Also, many advocates of copyleft schemes feel that creativity is encouraged when people are free to modify other people's work instead of worrying about infringing on copyright.

Opponents of Creative Commons licenses often complain that these licenses have affected their livelihoods. If millions of images are out on Flickr with Creative Commons licenses that permit free commercial use, professional photographers might have a tougher time selling their work. Furthermore, Creative Commons licenses are irrevocable. If you make a mistake and select the wrong license for your work, or you later find out a work is valuable and you've already selected a license that allows commercial use, you're out of luck.

Many people find listings of Creative Commons licenses confusing. If there is a Creative Commons disclaimer at the bottom of a group of photos, does that mean all the photos are available under that license, or just some of them? What actually constitutes commercial use? Is displaying Google Adsense ads on your blog commercial use?

You need to carefully consider the value of your intellectual property and decide how best to protect your rights. You should proceed carefully before giving up some of your rights under any copyleft license, especially if it is irrevocable. Nevertheless, using a copyleft scheme may be appropriate if it greatly simplifies your life in regards to managing permission requests.

implemented in either software or hardware, that squeezes the same audio and video information into less space. Some information will be lost using compression, and there are several different codecs to choose from, each claiming better performance than its competitors. Commonly used codecs include MPEG-4, H.264, and DivX. There is no one codec that is always superior—a codec that works well for a simple interview may not do a good job compressing a live-action scene.

What if I want a DVD with a menuing system? If you want a DVD with a menuing system, you can use special DVD authoring software such as Pinnacle Studio or Adobe Encore DVD. These DVD software packages often include preset selections for producing video for mobile devices (like the Apple iPod or the Sony PSP). These programs can also create final DVDs that have animated menu systems and easy navigation controls, allowing the viewer to move quickly from one movie or scene to another. Home DVD players as well as gaming systems such as PlayStation and Xbox can read these DVDs.

What is the quickest way to get my video out to viewers? Because of the popularity of videos on the Web, products and services are now available that let you quickly upload your videos. One such product is the Flip video camcorder from Pure Digital Technologies, shown in Figure 28.

The Flip camcorder, which retails at about $200, can record 60 minutes of video. After recording, simply flip out the USB connector and plug it into your computer. Flip has built-in software that lets you transfer the video file directly to YouTube (**youtube.com**) or e-mail the file. It's a simple solution that takes advantage of the easy Web-based distribution of video.

YouTube has a special Mobile Upload Profile that you can set up for your account. Once your unique e-mail address has been assigned, you can submit a video that you have on your phone to YouTube by e-mailing the file to the account address. Of course, it is illegal for you to upload videos you do not own. You also cannot take a piece of a copyrighted video and post it publicly. The Ethics in IT section in this chapter presents several legal and ethical situations that it is important for you to be aware of as a content creator in the digital age.

Webcasting, or broadcasting your video live to an audience, is another option that has become simpler. Inexpensive webcams (costing from $25 to $100) can be easily attached to your desktop or notebook computer. Many models of monitors have built-in webcams. Webcam models that are more expensive have motors that allow you to automatically rotate to track the sound, so you are always in the frame even if you are moving around the room. Services such as YouTube offer Quick Capture buttons, so with one click, your video can be shot and delivered to the Internet.

How can I distribute my video to the greatest number of viewers?
Sites like **justin.tv** or **ustream.tv** let you quickly set up to webcast your video as it is captured to a live Internet audience. You can also display an interactive chat next to the video feed. Both the chat and the video are captured and archived for viewers who

Pure Digital Technologies Inc.

Figure 28

The Flip video camcorder is an inexpensive way to capture 60 minutes of HD video and post it on YouTube.

missed the live broadcast. iTunes offers free distribution of video podcasts, so you can build a following there for your video work.

Are the television shows and movies I watch digital?
There are a number of ways you can create video content yourself; but probably most of the video you consume in a typical week was created by someone else— movie studios, television studios, or other students. The number of sources we have for video has increased dramatically since digital video appeared. Because the hardware for capturing video and the software for doing professional-level editing have become so inexpensive, there are few barriers to anyone making video. Further, because the opportunities for distributing video have broadened so much and become so instantaneous, there is an ever-growing market for more video.

Is all video digital video now?
The switch to digital video as a broadcasting medium has happened over the past few years. As of June 13, 2009, all television stations were required to make the move to digital signal broadcasting. **DTV.gov** is a site that keeps consumers current on using conversion boxes to allow older television sets to operate with the new digital signal.

Movie production studios have also been moving toward digital video for many years. George Lucas, a great proponent of digital technology, filmed *Star Wars Episode II: Attack of the Clones* completely in digital format way back in 2002. It played in a special digital release at digital-ready theaters. And in January 2005, the digital film *Rize*, by David LaChapelle, premiered at the Sundance Film Festival. It was streamed from computers in Oregon to a full-size cinema screen in Park City, Utah, beginning a new age of movie distribution.

Since the conversion to digital TV signals, are there any more "free" television signals?
Digital television signals now flood the air around you and can be picked up by a digital antenna. If you live in an area with good "over-the-air"

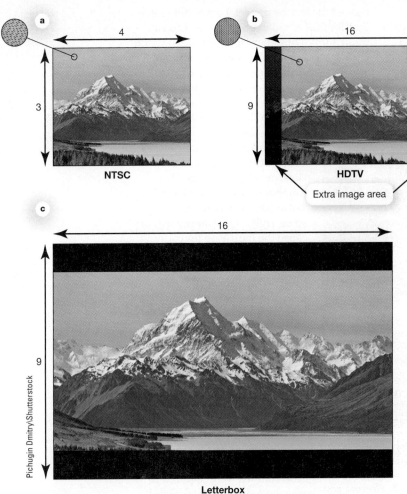

Figure 29

(a) Standard definition television has a more "square" aspect ratio, while (b) high-definition television matches the 16:9 ratio used in the motion picture industry without resorting to (c) letterboxing.

the number and types of connectors on a television. A typical HD set has at least three HDMI connectors, allowing game consoles, Blu-ray players, and cable boxes to be connected and produce the highest-quality output. HDMI is a single cable, with just one plug, that carries all of the video and all of the audio information. That means there is one connector, not three for different parts of the video signal and another two for the stereo sound signals!

Many sets have a built-in SD card reader. This allows users to display slide shows of photographs captured by their digital cameras. A PC VGA port is also included on most sets. This allows you to feed your computer's output video signal directly to the television so you can display an Internet browser or work on your files on the big screen. Some sets are now incorporating a wireless network adapter so the set can stream video from the Internet without having a separate computer connected. The Sony Bravia Internet Video link can deliver content on demand from a number of free sources (see Figure 30).

What advantages are there to watching digital video? Because the signal can be stored into computer memory as it is delivered, a digital video television show can be paused, or can be rewound in real time. Other information services can be integrated with the broadcast; so if a telephone call came through during the show, a pop-up could appear identifying the caller. The Sony Bravia series of televisions, for example, has Internet video capabilities that let you select "widgets" you can position on the screen to display the latest news, weather, sports, or other Internet downloads. In the future, there will be more interactivity integrated so you can participate in live polls or chats onscreen as the show is broadcast.

In movie studios, digital video is ushering in the age of "remixable" films. The components of these feature films—from production footage to soundtrack, dialogue, and sound effects—are available to the audience online, and each person is able to interact with and modify the film, creating a new plotline or a different ending. The MOD

(OTA) reception, you can pick up crisp, high-quality digital versions of all the shows on local network affiliates for free.

How is HD different from "plain" digital? HD stands for *high definition*. It is a standard of digital television signal that guarantees a specific level of resolution and a specific *aspect ratio*, which is the rectangular shape of the image. A 1080 HD TV displays 1,920 vertical lines and 1,080 horizontal lines of video on the screen, which is over six times as many pixels as standard definition. The aspect ratio used is 16:9, which makes the screen wider, giving it the same proportions as the rectangular shape of a movie theater screen (see Figure 29). This allows televisions to play movies in the widescreen format that they were created for, instead of "letterboxing" the film with black bars on the top and the bottom of the screen.

What types of connectivity are provided on modern television sets? As video sources have increased, so have

Films site (**modfilms.com**) is one place where remixers gather.

Can I record the digital video that comes over my television? There are a variety of digital video recorders (DVRs) available to record the digital video from your television. These can record in either standard or HD quality and store the information on a hard drive. Useful features include being able to record two shows at once, being able to download movie purchases or rentals from the Internet directly to the DVR unit, and easily moving stored content to a mobile device like an iPod or a notebook. Using a DVR, you can pause live TV or set up a schedule to capture every episode of a series, no matter when it airs. Models like TiVo even recommend new shows you might like based on what you have been watching. If you don't want to purchase a DVR or pay the monthly subscription fee for DVR service, you can install PVR (personal video recording) software on your computer. When connected to your cable signal, programs like BeyondTV (**snapstream.com**) and SageTV (**sagetv.com**) turn your computer itself into a DVR.

How else can I get digital video to my TV? In addition to the broadcast content coming in to your TV, there are a number of streaming sources of digital video. Cable providers offer a wide range of on-demand video services. Many older films, as well as shows such as exercise classes, are offered free of charge. Other premium content, like new-release movies, is offered for a fee. Just one click and you can instantly watch any offered movie for 24 hours, with full control—stopping, starting, and rewinding. Other providers, like Netflix, also offer streaming video content. While Netflix's basic business model is to ship members DVDs physically in the mail, they now also offer Watch Instantly. Thousands of movies and TV series are available with just a click. You can view these shows on a television through an Xbox gaming console, a PC, or a specialized device like the Roku digital video player.

Can I get digital video to watch on my portable device? Yes. Many DVR units, like TiVo, support software that allows you to transfer recorded shows to files on your PC and format them for viewing on an iPod, a PlayStation Portable, or another mobile device. There are also devices like Slingbox that take the video from your television and broadcast it to you over the Internet. With Slingbox, you can be in another room, or another country, and control and watch your home television on your notebook or your smartphone (see Figure 31).

Sling Media, Inc.

Figure 31
Slingbox can send your digital television content to your notebook or phone, wherever that may be.

Figure 30
Sony Bravia televisions use a wireless network adapter to stream digital video from a number of online sources.

Digital Mobility and Access

Once you are comfortable with digital communication and digital media, you'll want to be able to communicate and to access your music, files, and videos whether you are in front of a desktop at home or in an airport while traveling. Access to your digital assets is required in a modern business environment and is a great benefit for personal lifestyles. There is a wide range of devices that grant you access to your media and data wherever you are.

Selecting the Right Device

Do I need access to my digital assets all the time? Figure 32 presents a checklist of the factors you need to consider

Figure 32 | HOW IMPORTANT IS ACCESS TO DIGITAL ASSETS TO YOU?

Consideration	Yes	No
When I'm away from my desk, I need to **communicate** with others using both voice and e-mail.		
I need access to **my electronic files** wherever I am.		
I need access to **the Internet** wherever I am.		
The added **convenience and productivity** of mobile devices are important to me.		
My needs match the **limitations** of mobile devices (such as short battery life, small display screens, and slower Internet connection speeds).		
Most of my living and travel locations are **covered** by wireless Internet access.		
It is worth the added **expense** for me to go mobile.		

when deciding if you need a digital device when you are on the go. Do your needs to communicate and to access electronic information and the Internet when you're away from your desk make mobile devices a good investment?

How do I select the right device for my needs? There are a wide range of computing devices on the market today that give you varying access to digital

communication and digital media. A **netbook** runs a fully featured operating system but weighs in at 2 pounds or less. An **Internet tablet** is another type of very light, very portable device. Internet tablets do not offer full-size keyboards. Netbooks and Internet tablets can carry files, music, and videos as well as providing specialized services. Then there is the full range of notebooks and tablet computers. Figure 33 lists

Figure 33 | MOBILE DEVICES: PRICE, SIZE, WEIGHT, AND CAPABILITIES

Device	Relative Price	Approximate Size	Approximate Weight	Standard Capabilities
Cell phone	$$ (Includes cost for the phone, a monthly plan, and Internet access)	5″ × 2″ × 0.5″	0.25 lb.	Voice, e-mail, some application software, and Internet connectivity
PMP	$$–$$$	3″ × 2″ × 0.5″	0.25 lb. or more	Storage of digital music, video, and other digital files
Smartphone	$$–$$$	4.5″ × 2″ × .75″;	0.25 lb.	PIM capabilities, access to application software, and access to the Internet
Internet tablet	$$	3″ × 5″ × 0.5″	0.5 lb	Webcam, GPS, phone calls using Skype, sharp resolution, and widescreen display
Netbook	$$$$	7″ × 5″	1–2 lbs.	8″ to 10″ screens and run full-featured operating systems and applications
Tablet PC	$$$$$	10″ × 8″ × 1″	3 lbs.	PIM capabilities, access to application software, access to the Internet, and special handwriting- and speech-recognition capabilities
Notebook	$$$$–$$$$$	10″ × 13″ × 2″	5 to 8 lbs.	All the capabilities of a desktop computer plus portability

Emerging Technologies: Nanotubes—The Next Big Thing Is Pretty Darn Small!

In the classic 1967 film *The Graduate*, Dustin Hoffman is a young man uncertain about which career he should embark on. At a cocktail party, an older gentleman provides him with some career advice, telling him, "I've got just one word for you ... plastics!" This made sense at the time because plastics were coming on strong as a replacement for metal. If *The Graduate* were remade today, the advice would be, "I've got just one word for you ... nanotubes!"

Nanoscience involves the study of molecules and structures (called *nanostructures*), whose size ranges from 1 nanometer to 100 nanometers (or one-billionth of a meter). Using nanotechnology, scientists are hoping to one day build resources from the molecular level by manipulating individual atoms instead of using raw materials already found in nature (such as wood or iron ore). This would allow us to create microscopic computers—the ultimate in portable devices. Imagine nano-sized robotic computers swimming through your arteries, clearing them of plaque. Consider carrying a supercomputer the size of a pencil eraser—or, even better, having the power of your desktop computer implanted in your body as a nano-sized chip.

The possibilities of miniaturization are endless, but what materials would be used to construct the computer circuits for these devices? Carbon nanotubes are poised to be the building blocks of the future. You're familiar with carbon from pencils. The graphite core in a pencil is composed of sheets of carbon atoms laid out in a honeycomb pattern. Individual sheets of graphite are extremely strong but don't bond well to other sheets. This makes them ideal for use in a pencil because, as you write, the graphite flakes off and leaves marks on the paper. Unfortunately, graphite doesn't conduct electricity well. This inability, coupled with the lack of strong bonding principles, makes graphite unsuitable as a material to manufacture circuits.

There needs to be a way to rearrange the carbon to give it just the behaviors we want. Carbon nanotubes, discovered in the 1950s, are the answer. A nanotube is essentially a sheet of carbon atoms (much like graphite) laid out in a honeycomb pattern but rolled into a spherical tube, as shown in Figure 34. Arranging the carbon in a tube increases its strength astronomically. It is estimated that carbon nanotubes are as much as 10 to 100 times stronger per unit of weight than steel. This should make them ideal for constructing many types of devices and building materials. Someday we may have earthquake-proof buildings constructed from nanotubes or virtually indestructible clothing woven from nanotube fibers.

How does this help us build a computer? Aside from strength, the most interesting property of nanotubes is that they are good conductors of electricity. Nanotubes are actually classified as *semimetal,* meaning they can have properties that are a cross between semiconductors (such as silicon, which is used to create computer chips) and metals. In fact, depending on how a nanotube is constructed, it can change from a semiconductor to a metal along the length of the tube. These properties make nanotubes vastly superior to silicon for the construction of transistor pathways in computer chips because they provide engineers with more versatility.

In addition, although the smallest silicon transistors that are likely to be produced in the future will be millions of atoms wide, scientists believe that transistors constructed of nanotubes would be only 100 to 1,000 atoms wide. This represents a quantum leap in miniaturization that surpasses even the original invention of the transistor. Just imagine what can be done when nanotube transistors replace silicon transistors!

So, when can you buy that pencil eraser–sized computer? Not for quite a while. At this point, researchers can manufacture nanotubes only in extremely small quantities at a large cost. However, the U.S. government and many multinational corporations are expected to pour billions of dollars into nanoscience research over the next decade. It is hoped that the ongoing research will lead to breakthroughs in manufacturing technology that will result in nano-scale computers within your lifetime.

Figure 34

Here is a highly magnified close-up of a carbon nanotube. Rolling the sheets of carbon atoms into a tube shape gives them incredible strength.

the main features of several different mobile devices.

What if I don't need a phone but do need Internet access? New offerings are hitting the market regularly. Tiny Internet-enabled devices are appearing that don't bother to include cell phone features at all. The Nokia N810 Internet tablet series

Nokia

Figure 35

The Nokia N810 series Internet tablet features a touch screen and keypad and is designed primarily for Web surfing and sending e-mail.

(see Figure 35), for example, uses Skype or Gizmo for voice communications instead of a cell phone service. It has a high-resolution screen and WiFi connectivity so you can stream audio and video, use Web e-mail clients, and access Web sites. It features an RSS reader so you can peruse the latest from the sites you are following. Memory expands with SD expansion cards.

What if I need a larger screen and keyboard? If you require a larger screen and more processing power, then look at a category of emerging computer systems known as *netbooks* or *subnotebooks*. Examples include the Asus Eee PC and the Dell Inspiron Mini 9 (see Figure 36). Netbooks pack major computing power into a tiny package, and manufacturers try to extend battery life as long as possible. Screen sizes are typically between 8" to 10", and keyboards are less than full sized. No optical drive is integrated but one can be connected as a separate peripheral via the USB port. Netbooks often come with a Windows operating system. Some users opt to install a flavor of Linux, however, because Linux requires fewer resources than Windows. Solid-state hard drives are a good choice because they use

ExpressCard - PCMCIA

Figure 36

Subnotebooks like the Asus Eee PC weigh in at less than two pounds but run fully featured operating systems.

less power and produce less heat. Many models include integrated webcams as well as Bluetooth, so while netbooks are small and light, they still can serve many functions.

What if all I really need is to bring my books with me? For avid readers of e-books (books stored as electronic files), the Amazon Kindle DX (see Figure 37) or the Sony Reader Digital Book could be what you are looking for. These feature internal RAM, but also support flash memory cards for more storage. You can get approximately 7,500 turned pages on one charge, so on long plane flights this may be the device you use most. Color e-books are appearing as well. The Fujitsu FLEPia e-book reader has a color touch screen that can display 260,000 colors. It also can support e-mail, spreadsheets, and Web browsing, so it is part e-book and part computer.

Are portable gaming systems able to do any real work? Many portable gaming systems are very sophisticated. The Sony PlayStation Portable (PSP) can play video games but also includes a Web browser, Skype, and an RSS reader. It uses Sony Memory Sticks to store data files, videos, music, and images. The screen is a 4.3" widescreen design with great clarity and brightness. The PSP can even connect over the Internet to your PlayStation 3 system at home and display the videos or music stored there for you wherever you are.

Ubiquitous Computing

What is in the future for our digital lifestyles? Mark Weiser, a researcher at Xerox's PARC laboratories, has predicted that "computing will be woven into the fabric of everyday life until it is indistinguishable from it." This concept is called

Figure 37

The Amazon Kindle DX is designed to store as many as 3,500 e-books and is about 1/3″ thick.

ubiquitous computing (or *ubicom*). More and more styles of digital devices are being introduced, but there is a second force at work. Digital computing devices are increasingly embedded in appliances, clothing, cars—all the items we physically interact with in our day. The era of "smart things" is just beginning.

How will our lifestyles change as computing becomes everywhere and invisible? Researchers and inventors like

Mike Kuniavsky of ThingM are creating devices that exploit the new digital nature of our world to make tasks easier. The WineM product from ThingM is a good example (see Figure 38). WineM is a "smart" wine rack. Each bottle is labeled with a radio frequency identification (RFID) tag when it is stored by the owner. When it is time to pick the perfect bottle for dinner, the owner can ask the wine rack to show just the Chardonnay, and LEDs light up just those bottles. WineM can also display which wines are ready to drink, or if any of your friends has a similar wine collection, or if the winery is having a sale. It updates information automatically and will e-mail or text you an alert when a bottle of wine is removed from the rack.

The evolution of information to a digital form is allowing us to change our relationship to objects. Items like bicycles and cars can become "subscriptions" instead of large one-time purchases. Call a Bike is a program run in Germany. At most major street corners, there is a rack of Call a Bikes

Figure 38

The smart WineM Rack answers queries from its controller, (a) like "Show me all of the California wines I have that are ready to drink and under $50 in value." (b) In response WineM lights up the bottles that fit the criteria.

Figure 39

Call a Bike uses digital
technology to change our
lifestyle from one of
ownership to one of
"subscription."

Superbass\Wikipedia, The Free Encyclopedia

(see Figure 39). Place a call to the phone number printed on the bike, and it texts you a code you can use to unlock the bike lock. Ride the bike to where you're going. When you arrive, re-lock it. The amount of time you rode it automatically is billed (by the minute) to your phone.

City CarShare is another system using the digital communication of information to change our lifestyle habits. Many cities, like San Francisco and Philadelphia, now offer a City CarShare program. Residents sign up for the program and receive a key that has an RFID chip in it. All cars are connected to a central network. You can open a City CarShare car and start the engine only when your specific key is scheduled to open and start it. GPS technology is used to track where the car is, whether it has been dropped off at the right location, and how far it has been driven. The entire process is transparent to City CarShare members. Members have 24/7 access to a vehicle—a truck, a hybrid, a convertible—when they need it, with very little advance notice, for a cost of about $6.00 an hour. Gas and insurance are included.

Ubiquitous Networking: Wherever You Go, There You Are

With the rise of portable computing devices, the idea of ubiquitous networking has been generating a lot of interest. Ubiquity in computing essentially means (a) being able to have access to and exchange information wherever you happen to be, and (b) having access to the key information that you need when you need it. How can networking move us closer to that goal? There are two popular approaches.

The Network Is Watching You (Hello, Big Brother!)

Instead of having to move the files and programs you need onto mobile devices, how about having a network that "watches" your movements and moves the data so that it follows you? Researchers at telecommunications companies such as the AT&T Laboratories at Cambridge University are attempting to make this possible by creating a detection system that can track your location within a building, moving your files wherever you go. To take advantage of the network, users will carry a small device called a "bat," shown in Figure 40. This device will have a unique ID number and contain a radio transceiver and transmitter. A detection system (or central controller) installed in the building will keep track of the physical location of the bats (and of the people who carry them).

How does this system work? Suppose you go into a conference room that contains a computer and a phone. The controller is tracking the bat you have in your pocket, so it knows you have entered the conference room and therefore routes all your phone calls to the phone in the conference room. It also sends your files and desktop settings to the computer in the conference room.

What if two people are in the conference room at the same time? The controller assigns available devices to the first person who enters the room. However, using interactive buttons on your bat, you can indicate to the controller that you wish to take temporary possession of a device assigned to another person.

Take Your Computer's Soul with You

Another option would be to take not just your data files with you (say, on a flash drive), but instead to take your entire computer with you (virtually, of course). IBM is conducting a research project called SoulPad that attempts to achieve this miracle of portability. Using a portable storage device (IBM has used iPods in its testing), you save a suspended image of your computer, including all desktop settings and data files (essentially the "soul" of your computer), before leaving your main computer. When you arrive at another computer, you attach the portable storage device. Your computer data and settings then are loaded onto the remote computer so that you can pick up exactly where you left off. In testing, this has been piloted on computers running Windows and Linux. What is making this technology possible is the availability of tiny, high-capacity storage devices, high-speed data transfer (via FireWire or USB 2.0), and virtualization software. Eventually, it will probably be possible to deploy the SoulPad on a smartphone. This is convergence at the next level!

As we achieve ubiquity in computing, we will have to rethink our territorial approach to work and living spaces, as well as some of our ideas about privacy. In the future, because our data might follow us around (or we'll take it all with us), access to our personal information may always be right where we are.

Figure 40

Bats are about the size of a pager and therefore are small enough to be carried comfortably. They allow the detection system to locate the bat owners wherever they roam in the facility.

summary

1. What are the changes that have brought us a digital lifestyle?

The increased use of digital information has led to a period of greater creativity and control of our data. In a digital format, information is easy to carry, manipulate, and exchange. This has led to revolutionary changes in communication, entertainment media, and mobile computing.

2. How has the move to digital information affected the communication tools important to both the business world and life outside of work?

The age of digital information has brought new opportunities and challenges to businesses. Some have had to struggle to shift their business models to the new style of information. Because information can be shared so easily, issues of copyright and intellectual property have become critical. In our personal lives, we see products that allow us to interact with information in ways that had been too expensive or difficult before.

3. How do cell/smartphone components resemble a traditional computer, and how do they work?

Like a traditional computer, a cell/smartphone has a central processor, memory, and an operating system. These components work in the same way as in a computer to process information and support communications, software applications, and other services.

4. Why would I use VoIP, and what does it offer that is unique?

VoIP allows inexpensive communication using a computer or a WiFi-enabled phone. Because it is based on a digital format for information, it can support services like on-screen caller ID with your television or automatic delivery of phone messages to an e-mail account.

5. How is digital media different from analog?

Digital media is based on a series of numeric data comprising number values that were measured from the original analog waveform. As a string of numbers, a digital photo or video file can be easily processed by modern computers.

6. What can I carry in a portable media player, and how does it store data?

Most PMPs can store any kind of digital information—photos, videos, or music files as well as data files. Some PMPs store data on a hard drive, while others use flash memory. Some also allow the amount of memory to be upgraded, while others have a fixed amount of memory.

1. Choosing Devices to Fit Your Needs

As a student, which devices discussed in this chapter would have the most immediate impact on the work you do each day? Which would provide the best value (that is, the greatest increase in productivity and organization per dollar spent)? Consider the full range of devices, from cell phones to notebook systems.

2. Keeping Your Content

As a student, you create large numbers of products each semester—papers, videos, software programs, presentations. How do you organize and display them? Will they be available to you if you transfer to another school or apply for a job? How do you store, organize, and use those files to show the growth of your skills and abilities? Are there devices or services discussed in this chapter that would support you in doing that?

3. Do You Still Need a Phone?

Explore Skype (**skype.com**) as an alternative to paid telephone service. What equipment would you need to use Skype as your everyday communication medium? Skype now works on the iPhone. When would this be useful? What telephone services and features would you lose if you went to Skype?

4. Choosing the Best Phone

Your friend wants to trim down the number of different devices that she carries. Visit the most popular cellular providers' Web sites and research options. Which phone would you recommend to your friend, and why? Compare at least three different models of phones and list their price, music storage capacity, built-in memory, and expandability options.

a. Which of the three models you compared is the best value for your friend?
b. What special features does the phone you chose have? What accessories would you recommend your friend buy to make the phone more useful?
c. Would you suggest buying a refurbished phone? Why or why not?

5. iTunes U

Download a free copy of iTunes software. In the iTunes Store, explore the iTunes U podcast directory, which contains free audio and video lectures published by major universities.

a. Look for the MIT Open Courseware video podcasts. How many lectures are available from MIT (Massachusetts Institute of Technology)?
b. If each lecture were 90 minutes on average and approximately 200 MB in size, how much storage would it take to save all of the video lectures in every course published by MIT?
c. Is there a mobile device that can store and play that much content? What devices could store the lectures from all of the courses in mathematics offered by MIT Open Courseware?

1. **Corporate Mobile Communications Needs**

   Imagine your company is boosting its sales force and looking to the future of mobile technology. Your manager has asked you to research the following issues surrounding mobile communications for the company:

   a. Do mobile communication devices present increased security risks? What would happen if you left a cell phone at a meeting and a competitor picked it up? Are there ways to protect your data on mobile devices?

   b. Can viruses attack cell phones? Is there any special software on the market to protect mobile devices from viruses? How much would it cost to equip 20 devices with virus protection?

   c. Is there a role for mobile communication devices even if employees don't leave the building? Which devices would be important for a company to consider for use within corporate offices? Are there software solutions that would work as well?

   d. Should employees be allowed to use mobile phones provided by the company for personal use even though files related to personal use might eat up potentially valuable memory and space? What restrictions should be put on personal use to protect the privacy of proprietary company information contained on the devices?

2. **3G Communications**

   The current generation of telecommunications (nicknamed "3G" for third generation) allows the speed of cellular network transmissions to hit 3 Mbps. How does that compare to dial-up and cable modem access over wired networks? What implications does it have for information access and e-commerce? What download speed would be ideal? Upload speed?

3. **Subscription versus Ownership**

   Consider the examples of Call-a-Bike and CarShare. Are there other businesses you can identify that would be able to take advantage of digital information and become subscription services instead of vendors of a physical product? What are the advantages to the consumer of subscription over ownership? What are the drawbacks?

4. **Too Much Media?**

   Imagine you are a manager of 18 employees, all of whom work with constant Internet access. As a manager, what concerns might you have about their use of corporate bandwidth to download and view media files? Do you think it would benefit your business to block any MP3 file transfers? Should you put in place a block to prevent access to sites that store huge numbers of streaming videos? As a manager, are there concerns you might have if employees have digital cameras on their cell phones? What would you do if an employee records a meeting with you on his cell phone without your knowledge?

5. **Mobile Devices on the Highway**

   Mobile devices used in vehicles are becoming the norm in today's society. Consider the following:

   a. Several car manufacturers provide Bluetooth option packages for their vehicles. What advantages are there to having Bluetooth connectivity in your car? Are there any disadvantages?

   b. Examine the Microsoft Sync software package. List the features and services it provides. If you were a salesperson with a territory that you covered by car, how would Sync help you?

Digital Lifestyle: Managing Digital Data and Devices

Instructions: Albert Einstein used *Gedankenexperiments*, or critical thinking questions, to develop his theory of relativity. Some ideas are best understood by experimenting with them in our own minds. The following critical thinking questions are designed to demand your full attention but require only a comfortable chair—no technology.

1. Digital Entertainment

Can you name a style of media that has not made the shift to digital? What advantages does digital photography offer? Digital video? What disadvantages come along with a digital format for entertainment media? Has the growth in digital media promoted an increased understanding between people or has it created more isolation?

2. The Ultimate Style

As ubiquitous computing continues to evolve, devices become lighter and smaller, and we are beginning to see a convergence of computing and clothing.

  a. What would the ultimate convergent mobile clothing be for you? Is there a limit in weight, size, or complexity?

  b. Can you imagine uses for technology in fashion that would support better health? Better social relationships? A richer intellectual life?

3. Protecting Intellectual Property

The recording industry, recording artists, the motion picture industry, and consumers find themselves in a complex discussion when the topic of peer-to-peer sharing systems is brought up.

  a. Have you ever downloaded music, movies, or software from the Web? Did you download in a legal manner? Did the media you downloaded have any associated DRM (digital rights management)? Do you think peer-to-peer download sites should be allowed to exist in their current form?

  b. Now, imagine yourself as a video creator. You spend hours on your home computer producing a short weekly cartoon video that you are hoping will lead to a career in animation. How can you build an audience for your work? How could you expand your audience and still garner some income from the cartoon series?

4. Next Wave Is Nano

As nanotechnology continues to mature as a science, what impacts will we begin to see on our digital lifestyle? How will communications change? How might our consumption of digital media change? What new privacy and intellectual property rights challenges may appear?

5. Privacy Concerns: GPS Tracking at Home

Consider the following questions related to GPS security risks:

  a. Your spouse carries a GPS-enabled cell phone. The GPS chip inside allows a private service (**ulocate.com**) to gather information on your spouse's last location, the path he or she took to get there, and his or her average speed from point to point. Would you use the service to check on your spouse's activities? What if your spouse was monitoring you?

  b. Would you agree to insert a GPS-enabled tracking device into your pet? Your child? What legislation do you think should be required if tracking data was available about you? Would you be willing to sell that information to marketing agencies? Should that data be available to the government if you were suspected of a crime?

6. Electronic Publishing

Explore the specifications of the Sony Portable Reader and the Amazon Kindle. How would your study habits change if your textbooks were only delivered to you in electronic format on one of these E-reader machines? What unique advantages would there be? What disadvantages would there be? How would using an E-reader compare with just receiving the book as an electronic file, such as a PDF document?

Assisting with the Move to a Digital Lifestyle

Problem

You have formed a consulting group that advises clients on how to move their businesses and personal lives into the age of the digital lifestyle.

Task

Each team will be defined as an expert resource in one of the digital areas presented in this chapter: digital communication, digital media, or digital mobility. For each scenario described by a client, the group should assess the kinds of technologies that will meet and enhance the client's needs.

Process

Divide the class into three or four teams and assign each group a different digital lifestyle focus (communication, media, or mobility).

1. Research the current digital technologies emerging in the area your team has been assigned.
2. Consider the following three clients:
    - A retired couple who now travel for pleasure a great deal. They want to be involved in their grandchildren's lives and will need support for their health and personal care as they age.
    - A young family with two children, two working parents, and a tight budget.
    - A couple in which each individual is a physician and both adore technology.
3. Make two recommendations for your client in terms of digital technologies that will enhance their business or their lifestyle. Discuss the advantages and disadvantages of each technology. Consider value, reliability, computing needs, and communication needs, as well as expandability for the future.
4. As a group, prepare a final report that considers the costs, availability, and unique features of the recommendations you have made for each client.
5. Bring the research materials from the individual team meetings to class. Looking at the clients' needs, make final decisions as to which digital technologies are best suited for each client.

Conclusion

Digital information has allowed the development of a new style of living, both at home and at work. With so many digital solutions on the market today, recommending digital communication, media management, and mobility options depends on factors such as value, reliability, expandability, and the needs of the client.

In addition to the review materials presented here, you'll find additional materials featured with the Pearson IT Multimedia Library and the Companion Website (**pearsonhighered.com/ techinaction**), which will help reinforce your understanding of the chapter content. These materials include the following:

Active Helpdesk

In Active Helpdesk calls, you'll assume the role of helpdesk operator, taking calls about the concepts you've learned in this chapter. You'll apply what you've learned and receive feedback from a supervisor to review and reinforce those concepts. The Active Helpdesk calls for this chapter are listed below and can be found on the Pearson IT Multimedia Library:

- Keeping Your Data on Hand
- Using Portable Media Players

Sound Bytes

Sound Bytes are dynamic multimedia tutorials that help demystify even the most complex topics. You'll view video clips and animations that illustrate computer concepts and then apply what you've learned by reviewing with the Sound Byte Labs, which include quizzes and activities specifically tailored to each Sound Byte. The Sound Bytes for this chapter are listed below and can be found on the Pearson IT Multimedia Library.

- Smartphones Are Really Smart
- Connecting with Bluetooth

Companion Website

The *Technology in Action* Companion Website includes a variety of additional materials to help you review and learn more about the topics in this chapter. The resources available at **pearsonhighered.com/techinaction** include

- **Online Study Guide.** This chapter features an online true–false and multiple-choice quiz. You can take these quizzes, automatically check the results, and e-mail the results to your instructor.
- **Web Research Projects.** This chapter features several Web research projects that ask you to search the Web for information on computer-related careers, milestones in computer history, important people and companies, emerging technologies, and the applications and implications of different technologies.

digital lifestyle:

protecting digital data and devices

digital lifestyle:
protecting digital data and devices

how cool

is this?

how cool is *this?*

Protect your surfing like a pro. When you use **public hotspots** to surf, your Internet activity is subject to **snooping** by prying eyes. Hotspot Shield (**hotspotshield.com**) is a free **software utility** that ensures all of your data is transmitted across the Internet through a virtual private network (VPN). A VPN is a secure Internet pathway that large corporations use to protect sensitive data. Using the VPN **shields your data**, such as information in forms you fill out, credit card data, instant messages, and Web browsing activities, from the prying eyes of hackers. So install Hotspot Shield today and surf with confidence.

Keeping Your Data Safe

The media is full of stories about computer viruses damaging computers, criminals stealing people's identities online, and attacks on corporate Web sites that have brought major corporations to a standstill. These are examples of **cybercrime**, which is defined as any criminal action perpetrated primarily through the use of a computer. The existence of cybercrime means that computer users must take precautions to protect themselves (see Figure 1).

Who perpetrates computer crimes? **Cybercriminals** are individuals who use computers, networks, and the Internet to perpetrate crime. Anyone with a computer and the wherewithal to arm him- or herself with the appropriate knowledge can be a cybercriminal.

What kind of cybercrimes are conducted over the Internet? The Internet Crime Complaint Center (IC3) is a partnership between the Federal Bureau of Investigation (FBI) and the National White Collar Crime Center (NW3C). In 2008, the latest year for which data is available, IC3 processed more than 275,000 complaints related to Internet crime. Many complaints were fraud-related, such as auction fraud, nondelivery of ordered items, and credit and debit card fraud. Non-fraud–related complaints pertained to issues such as computer intrusions, unsolicited e-mail, and child pornography. The majority of complaints (more than 58 percent) were related to three key areas: Internet auction fraud, nondelivery of merchandise, and failure to pay. Much of this credit card fraud was perpetrated when credit card numbers were stolen by phishing (tricking people into revealing sensitive information) or by virus programs that gather credit card data.

Are computer viruses a type of cybercrime? Creating and disseminating computer viruses is one of the most widespread types of cybercrimes. Tens of thousands of new viruses or modified versions of old viruses are released each year. The effect of a computer virus varies widely. Some cause only minor annoyances, while others cause wanton destruction of data. Many viruses are now designed to gather sensitive information such as credit card numbers. The Conficker virus that broke out in late 2008 infected an estimated 15 million computers in a few weeks, which illustrates how serious a threat a virus can pose to your digital security. You need to make sure your data is protected from viruses and other malicious software attacks.

Does cybercrime include the theft of computing devices? Although theft of computer equipment is not classified as a cybercrime (rather, it is considered larceny), the theft of notebook computers, cell phones, iPods, and other portable computing devices is on the rise. The resale value for used electronic equipment is high, which contributes to demand for stolen merchandise. The ease with which equipment can be sold online also fuels this problem.

In this chapter, we discuss serious threats to your digital security (such as computer viruses and other activities of cybercriminals), less serious annoyances (such as spyware and spam), and good security practices to keep yourself from undermining your digital security. We also discuss methods for protecting your digital assets from attacks and damage.

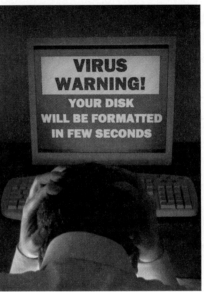

Mauro Bighin\Shutterstock

Figure 1

Cybercrimes, including virus attacks, are a serious problem for Web surfers.

Computer Threats: Computer Viruses

One of the most serious threats to digital security is computer viruses. A computer **virus** is a computer program that attaches itself to another computer program (known as the *host program*) and attempts to spread to other computers when files are exchanged. Viruses normally attempt to hide within the code of a host program to avoid detection.

What do computer viruses do? A computer virus's main purpose is to replicate itself and copy its code into as many other files as possible. Although virus replication can slow down networks, it is not usually the main threat. The majority of viruses have secondary objectives or side effects, ranging from displaying annoying messages on the computer screen to destroying files or the contents of entire hard drives. Because computer viruses cause disruption to computer systems, including data destruction and information theft, virus creation and deployment is a form of cybercrime.

How does my computer catch a virus? If your computer is exposed to a file infected with a virus, the virus will try to copy itself and infect a file on your computer. If you never expose your computer to new files, it will not become infected. However, this would be the equivalent of a human being living in a bubble to avoid catching viruses from other people—quite impractical.

Downloading infected audio and video files from peer-to-peer file sharing sites is a major source of virus infections. Shared disks or flash drives are also a common source of virus infection, as is e-mail, although many people have misconceptions about how e-mail infection occurs. Just opening an e-mail message will not infect your computer with a virus. Downloading or running a file that is attached to the e-mail is how your computer becomes infected. Thus, be extremely wary of e-mail attachments, especially if you don't know the sender. Figure 2 illustrates the steps by which computer viruses are often passed from one computer to the next.

1. A hacker writes a virus program disguised as an MP3 file of a popular music group's new hit song to a file sharing site.

Figure 2

Computer viruses are passed from one unsuspecting user to the next.

Step 1: Virus creation.

Hacker's computer

File sharing server

Step 2: Initial virus infection.

Bill's computer

Coworker's computer

Step 3: Virus spreads to another computer.

Fred's work computer

Step 4: Virus spreads to work computer.

Coworker's computer

Step 5: Other computers susceptible to infection.

Fred's home computer

Computer Threats: Computer Viruses

2. Unsuspecting Bill downloads the "music file" and infects his computer.

3. Bill sends his cousin Fred an e-mail with the infected "music file" and contaminates Fred's computer.

4. Fred saves the MP3 file to a flash drive and then copies it to his work computer and infects that machine as well.

5. Everyone who copies files from Fred's infected computer at work, or whose computer is networked to Fred's computer, is at risk to spread the virus.

Types of Viruses

Although thousands of computer viruses and variants exist, they can be grouped into six broad categories based on their behavior and method of transmission.

Boot-Sector Viruses

What are boot-sector viruses? A **boot-sector virus** replicates itself into a hard drive's master boot record. The **master boot record** is a program that executes whenever a computer boots up, ensuring that the virus will be loaded into memory immediately, even before some virus protection programs can load. Boot-sector viruses are often transmitted by a flash drive left in a USB port. When the computer boots up with the flash drive connected, the computer tries to launch a master boot record from the flash drive, which is usually the trigger for the virus to infect the hard drive. Boot-sector viruses can be extremely destructive.

Logic Bombs and Time Bombs

What is a logic bomb? A **logic bomb** is a virus that is triggered when certain logical conditions are met—such as opening a file, or starting a program a certain number of times. A **time bomb** is a virus that is triggered by the passage of time or on a certain date. For example, the Michelangelo virus, first launched in 1992, was a famous time bomb that was set to trigger every year on March 6, Michelangelo's birthday. The BlackWorm virus (otherwise known as Kama Sutra, Mywife, or CME-24), another time bomb, spreads

through e-mail attachments. Opening the attachment infects the computer, and on the third day of every month, the virus seeks out and deletes certain file types (such as executable or EXE files) on Windows computers. The effects of logic bombs and time bombs range from display of annoying messages on the screen to reformatting of the hard drive, which causes complete data loss.

Worms

What is a worm? A **worm** is slightly different from a virus in that a worm attempts to travel between systems through network connections to spread an infection. A virus infects a host file and waits until that file is executed on another computer to replicate. A worm, however, works independently of host file execution and is much more active in spreading itself. The Conficker worm broke out in November 2008 and quickly infected an estimated 9 to 15 million individual computers. This worm spread through vulnerabilities in the Windows code and compromised computers by disabling certain software services and utility programs (such as Windows Update). Fortunately, it is easy to protect yourself from most worms. Installing antivirus software and a firewall is a good start. You also should apply software patches (code issued by the manufacturers of software such as Windows that repairs known security problems) to your computer whenever they are issued. We discuss protective measures later in the chapter.

Script and Macro Viruses

What are script and macro viruses? Some viruses are hidden on Web sites in the form of scripts. A **script** is a series of commands—actually, a miniprogram—that is executed without your knowledge. Scripts are often used to perform useful, legitimate functions on Web sites such as collecting name and address information from customers. However, some scripts are malicious. For example, say you receive an e-mail encouraging you to visit a Web site full of useful programs and information. When you click a link to display a video on the Web site you were directed to, a script runs that infects your computer with a virus without your knowledge

A **macro virus** is a virus that attaches itself to a document (such as a Word or Excel file) that uses macros. A macro is a short series of commands that usually automates repetitive tasks. However, macro languages are now so sophisticated that viruses can be written with them. In March 1999, the Melissa virus became the first major macro virus to cause problems worldwide. It attached itself to a Word document.

The Melissa virus was also the first practical example of an **e-mail virus**. E-mail viruses use the address book in the victim's e-mail system to distribute the virus. Anyone opening an infected document triggered the virus, which infected other Word documents on the victim's computer. Once triggered, the Melissa virus sent itself to the first 50 people in the address book on the infected computer. This helped ensure that Melissa became one of the most widely distributed viruses ever released.

Encryption Viruses

What are encryption viruses?

Encryption viruses are the newest form of virus. When these viruses infect your computer, they run a program that searches for common types of data files (such as Microsoft Word and Excel files) and compresses them using a complex encryption key that renders your files unusable. You then receive a message that asks you to send money to an account if you want to receive the program to decrypt your files. The flaw with this type of virus, which keeps it from being widespread, is that law enforcement officials can trace the payments to an account and may possibly be able to catch the perpetrators. Still, we see these types of viruses from time to time.

ACTIVE HELP-DESK — Avoiding Computer Viruses

In this Active Helpdesk call, you'll play the role of a helpdesk staffer, fielding calls about different types of viruses and what users should do to protect their computer from them.

BITS AND BYTES — Virus Symptoms

If your computer displays any of the following symptoms, it may be infected with a virus:

1. Existing program icons or files suddenly disappear. (Viruses often delete specific file types or programs.)
2. Changes appear in your browser. If you fire up your browser and it takes you to an unusual home page (one you didn't set) or it has new toolbars, then you may have a virus.
3. Odd messages or images are displayed on the screen or strange music or sounds play.
4. Data files become corrupt. Although files become corrupt for many reasons, a virus is one cause.
5. Programs don't work properly. This could be caused by either a corrupted file or a virus.

If you think you have a virus, boot up your computer with an antivirus software DVD (or CD) in your DVD/CD drive. This allows you to run the antivirus software before potential viruses load on the computer. Are you looking for free antivirus software? Consider downloading AVG Antivirus Free Edition (**free.avg.com**).

Virus Classifications

How else are viruses classified?

Viruses can also be classified by the methods they take to avoid detection by antivirus software:

- A **polymorphic virus** changes its own code (or periodically rewrites itself) to avoid detection. Most polymorphic viruses infect one type of file (.exe files, for example).
- A **multipartite virus** is designed to infect multiple file types in an effort to fool the antivirus software that is looking for it.
- **Stealth viruses** temporarily erase their code from the files where they reside and then hide in the active memory of the computer. This helps them avoid detection if only the hard drive is being searched for viruses. Fortunately, antivirus software developers are aware of, and have designed software to watch for, these tricks.

Given the creativity of virus programmers, you can be sure we'll see other types of viruses emerge in the future. In the next section, we discuss preventing virus infections.

Computer Threats: Computer Viruses

Computer Safeguard: Antivirus Software and Software Updates

Certain viruses merely present minor annoyances, such as randomly sending an ambulance graphic across the bottom of the screen, as is the case with the Red Cross virus. Other viruses can significantly slow down a computer or network, or destroy key files or the contents of entire hard drives. The best defense against viruses is to install **antivirus software**, which is specifically designed to detect viruses and protect your computer and files from harm. Norton, Kaspersky, AVG, and McAfee are among the companies that offer highly rated antivirus software packages.

Although you can buy stand-alone antivirus software, antivirus protection is included in comprehensive Internet security packages such as Norton Internet Security, Kaspersky Internet Security, or McAfee Total Protection. These software packages will help protect you from other threats as well as from computer viruses.

Antivirus Software

How often do I need to run antivirus software?
Although antivirus software is designed to detect suspicious activity on your computer at all times, you should run an active virus scan on your entire system at least once a week. By doing so, all files on your computer will be checked for

undetected viruses. Because these checks take time, you can configure the software to run them automatically when you aren't using your system—for example, late at night (see Figure 3). Alternatively, if you suspect a problem, you can launch a scan and have it run immediately.

How does antivirus software work?
Most antivirus software looks for virus signatures in files. A **virus signature** is a portion of the virus code that is unique to a particular computer virus. Antivirus software scans files for these signatures and thereby identifies infected files and the type of virus that is infecting them.

The antivirus software scans files when they're opened or executed. If it detects a virus signature or suspicious activity (such as the launch of an unknown macro), it stops the execution of the file and virus and notifies you that it has detected a virus. It also places the virus in a secure area on your hard drive so that it won't spread infection to other files. This procedure is known as **quarantining**. Usually the antivirus software then gives you the choice of deleting or repairing the infected file. Unfortunately, antivirus programs can't always fix infected files to make them usable again. You should keep backup copies of critical files so that you can restore them in case a virus damages them irreparably.

Most antivirus software will also attempt to prevent infection by inoculating key files on your computer. In **inoculation**, the antivirus software records key attributes about files on your computer (such as file size and date created) and keeps these statistics in a safe place on your hard drive. When scanning for viruses, the antivirus software compares the files to the attributes it previously recorded to help detect attempts by virus programs to modify your files.

Does antivirus software always stop viruses?
Antivirus software catches known viruses effectively. Unfortunately, new viruses are written all the time. To combat unknown viruses, modern antivirus programs search for suspicious viruslike activities as well as virus signatures. However, virus authors know how antivirus software works. They take special measures to disguise their virus code and hide the effects of a virus until just the right moment. This helps ensure that the virus spreads faster and farther. Thus, your computer can be attacked by a virus that your antivirus

Figure 3

In Norton Internet Security, complete virus scans can be set up to run automatically. This computer will be scanned every Tuesday at 8 P.M.

Click to display dialog box

Click to schedule a scan

Click to launch scan immediately

software doesn't recognize. To minimize this risk, you should keep your antivirus software up to date.

How do I make sure my antivirus software is up to date? Most antivirus programs have an automatic update feature that downloads updates for virus signature files every time you go online (see Figure 4).

What should I do if I think my computer is infected with a virus? Boot up your computer with the antivirus installation DVD/CD in your DVD drive. (Note: If you download your antivirus software from the Internet, it is a good idea to copy your antivirus software to a DVD in case you have problems in the future.) This should prevent most virus programs from loading and will allow you to run the antivirus software directly from the DVD drive. If the software does detect viruses, you may want to research them further to determine whether your antivirus software will eradicate them completely or whether you will need to take additional manual steps to eliminate the virus. Most antivirus company Web sites, such as the Symantec site (**symantec.com**), contain archives of information on viruses, and provide step-by-step solutions for removing viruses.

Are instant messenger programs safe from virus attacks? Virus attacks and other forms of malicious hacking are being perpetrated at an alarming rate via instant messenger (IM) programs such as AOL Instant Messenger and Windows Live Messenger. Even if you have antivirus protection installed, people still could contact you for the purposes of trying to trick you into revealing sensitive information. Therefore, you should try to hide your instant messaging activity from everyone except people that you know. To keep your IM sessions safe, follow these precautions:

1. **Allow contact only from users on your Buddy or Friends List.** This prevents you from being annoyed by unknown parties. On the settings screen for your IM program (Figure 5), select Allow only users on my Buddy List. And, of course, don't put anyone you don't know and trust on your buddy list.

2. **Never automatically accept transfers of data.** Although file and video transfers are potentially useful for swapping files over IM (see Figure 5), they are a common way of transmitting malicious

Figure 4

files, which can then infect your computer with viruses. Enabling auto-acceptance of data transfers is never a good idea.

3. **Avoid using instant messaging programs on public computers.** If you use a shared computer, such as one in a computer lab at school, be sure you don't select any features that remember your password or connect you automatically. The next person who uses the computer might be able to connect to the instant messaging service with your screen name and impersonate you.

Software Updates

Is there anything else I should do to protect my system? Many viruses exploit weaknesses in operating systems. Malicious Web sites can be set up to attack your computer by downloading harmful software

Figure 4

Antivirus software, such as Norton Internet Security, provides for automatic updates to the software installed on the computer.

SOUND BYTE Protecting Your Computer

In this Sound Byte, you'll learn how to use a variety of tools to protect your computer, including antivirus software and Windows utilities.

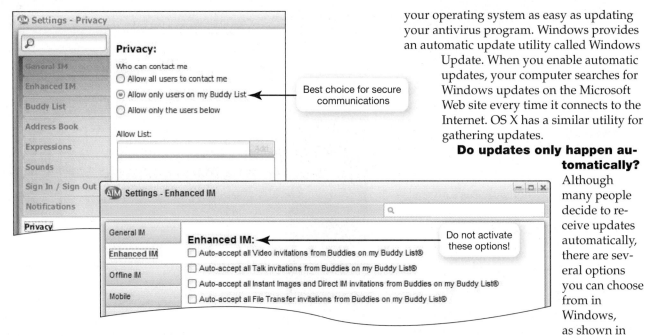

Best choice for secure communications

Do not activate these options!

your operating system as easy as updating your antivirus program. Windows provides an automatic update utility called Windows Update. When you enable automatic updates, your computer searches for Windows updates on the Microsoft Web site every time it connects to the Internet. OS X has a similar utility for gathering updates.

Do updates only happen automatically?

Although many people decide to receive updates automatically, there are several options you can choose from in Windows, as shown in

Figure 5

When you use instant messenger programs, check all of the preference screens for appropriate settings.

onto your computer. According to research conducted by Google, this type of attack, known as a **drive-by download**, is common and affects almost one in one thousand Web pages. To combat these threats, make sure your antivirus software and your operating system are up to date and contain the latest security patches. You can make updating

Figure 6. The following options are noteworthy:

- Option 1: **Install updates automatically:** Selecting this option will automatically download and install updates at a time you have specified. We strongly recommend that you select this option.

- Option 2: **Download updates but let me choose whether to install them:** Although this option automatically downloads updates, they are not installed until you instruct Windows to install them. We don't usually recommend this option because you may forget to install important updates.

- Option 3: **Check for updates but let me choose whether to download and install them:** This is an appropriate choice if you have low bandwidth Internet access. Because downloads over dial-up can take a long time due to low bandwidth, you need to control when downloads will occur so they don't interrupt your workflow.

- Option 4: **Give me recommended updates:** This option ensures you receive recommended (optional) updates as well as critical (necessary) updates.

- Option 5: **Microsoft Update:** This option ensures you receive updates for other Microsoft products besides Windows (such as Microsoft Office).

Option 1
Option 2
Option 3
Option 4
Option 5

Figure 6

The Windows Update screen makes it easy for users to configure Windows to update itself.

>To enable automatic updates, click **Start**, select **Control Panel**, select **System and Security**, click the **Windows Update** link, and then click the **Change Settings** link.

In the next section, we explore another major threat to your digital security—hackers.

Computer Threats: Hackers

Although there is a great deal of disagreement as to what a hacker actually is (especially among hackers themselves), a **hacker** is most commonly defined as anyone who unlawfully breaks into a computer system—either an individual computer or a network (see Figure 7).

Are there different kinds of hackers?
Some hackers are offended by being labeled as criminals and therefore attempt to classify different types of hackers. A hacker who breaks into systems just for the challenge of it (and who don't wish to steal or wreak havoc on the systems) may refer to him- or herself as a **white hat hacker**. These individuals tout themselves as experts who are performing a needed service for society by helping companies uncover the vulnerabilities in their systems.

White hat hackers look down on those hackers who use their knowledge to destroy information or for illegal gain. A term for these more villainous hackers is **black hat hacker**. (The terms *white hat* and *black hat* are references to old Western movies in which the heroes wore white hats and the outlaws wore black hats.) Regardless of the hackers' opinions, the laws in the United States and in many other countries consider any unauthorized access to computer systems a crime.

What about the teenage hackers who are caught every so often?
These amateur hackers are often referred to as **script kiddies**. Script kiddies don't create the programs they use to hack into computer systems; instead, they use tools created by skilled hackers that enable un-skilled novices to wreak the same havoc as professional hackers. Although these tools can be found on the Web, using such tools (even ones created by someone else) to penetrate computer systems is a crime.

Fortunately, because the users of these programs are amateurs, they're usually not proficient at covering their electronic tracks. Therefore, it's relatively easy for law enforcement officials to track them down and prosecute them. Script kiddies nevertheless can cause a lot of disruption and damage to computers, networks, and Web sites before they're caught.

Why would a hacker be interested in breaking into my home computer?
Some hackers just like to snoop. They enjoy the challenge of breaking into systems and seeing what information they can find. Other hackers are hobbyists seeking information about a particular topic wherever they can find it. Because many people keep proprietary business information on their home computers, hackers bent on industrial espionage may break into home computers. For other hackers, hacking is a way to pass time.

What Hackers Steal

Could a hacker steal my credit card number? If you perform financial transactions online, such as banking or buying goods and services, then you probably do so using a credit (or debit) card. Credit card

BRINGING CIVILIZATION TO ITS KNEES...

Goths — HACK HACK HACK HACK

Vandals — HACK HACK HACK

Huns — HACK HACK

Geeks — HACK HACK HACK HACK

Figure 7

Although they do not necessarily destroy civilization, hackers can cause problems for corporations and individuals alike.

Be Careful When Joining Social Networking and Video Sites

Making contacts and meeting friends online has never been easier. Social networking services such as MySpace (**myspace.com**) and Facebook (**facebook.com**) are signing up users at a rapid pace. Another site, YouTube (**youtube.com**), allows you to post videos of yourself and your friends. These services have you list personal information about yourself (interests, hobbies, photos, what school you attend, and so on) and encourage you to list connections to your friends. When your friends log on and view your profile, they can see themselves and long chains of other acquaintances. The idea is that your friends can see who else you know and get you to make appropriate introductions (or do it themselves).

Although the sites offer fairly tight protection of personal information (such as not revealing last names), think carefully about making your personal information visible on a site and be wary of disclosing additional information to people you meet online. Often children and young adults, who account for a large percentage of the users on these sites, are too trusting about revealing personal information. Cybercriminals are combing these sites with the sole purpose of using the information to perpetrate identity theft. Therefore, always avoid giving out personal information such as your full name, address, Social Security number, or financial information to people you have never met. Also, be careful when uploading videos of yourself or your friends. Identity thieves often like to steal younger people's identities because the identity theft of minors takes longer to detect.

Finally, be wary of accepting computer files from people you've met online, because these files could contain viruses or other destructive software. Just because you meet someone who is a friend of a friend of your second cousin doesn't mean that person isn't a hacker or a scam artist. So, enjoy meeting new people, but exercise the appropriate amount of caution.

not enable encryption of data when they set up their wireless networks. This makes it easy for hackers to intercept and read sensitive information transmitted in plain text, such as credit card numbers or the contents of e-mails.

What do hackers do with the information they "sniff"? Once a hacker has your credit card information, he or she can either use it to purchase items illegally or sell the number to someone who will. If a hacker steals the login ID and password to an account where you have your credit card information stored (such as eBay or Amazon), he or she can also use your account to purchase items and have them shipped to him- or herself instead of to you. If hackers can gather enough information in conjunction with your credit card information, they may be able to commit identity theft. **Identity theft** is characterized by someone using personal information about you (such as your name, address, or Social Security number) to assume your identity for the purpose of defrauding others.

Although this sounds scary, you can easily protect yourself from packet sniffing by installing a firewall (which we discuss later in this chapter) and using data encryption on a wireless network.

and bank account information can thus reside on your hard drive and may be detectable by a hacker. Also, many sites require you to provide a login ID and password to gain access. Even if this data is not stored on your computer, a hacker may be able to capture it when you're online by using a packet sniffer.

What's a packet sniffer? Data travels through the Internet in small pieces, each called a **packet**. The packets are identified with an IP address, in part to help identify the computer to which they are being sent. Once the packets reach their destination, they are reassembled into cohesive messages. A **packet sniffer** is a program that looks at (or sniffs) each packet as it travels on the Internet—not just those that are addressed to a particular computer, but all packets. Some packet sniffers are configured to capture all the packets into memory, whereas others capture only packets that contain specific content (such as credit card numbers). Wireless networks can be particularly vulnerable to this type of exploitation because many people do

Trojan Horses

Besides stealing information, what other problems can hackers cause if they break into my computer? Hackers often use individuals' computers as a staging area for mischief. To perpetrate widespread computer attacks, for example, hackers need to control many computers at the same time. To this end, hackers often use Trojan horses to install other programs on computers. A **Trojan horse** is a program that appears to be something useful or desirable (like a game or a screen saver), but while it runs does something malicious in the background without your knowledge. The term *Trojan horse* derives from Greek mythology and refers to the wooden horse that the Greeks used to sneak into the city of Troy and conquer it. Therefore, computer programs that contain a hidden (and usually dreadful) "surprise" are referred to as Trojan horses.

What damage can Trojan horses do? Often, the malicious activity perpetrated by a Trojan horse program is the installation of a **backdoor program** that allows hackers to take almost complete control of your computer without your knowledge. Using a backdoor program, hackers can access and delete all the files on your computer, send e-mail, run programs, and do just about anything else you can do with your computer. A computer that a hacker controls in this manner is referred to as a **zombie**. Zombies are often used to launch denial-of-service attacks on other computers.

Denial of Service Attacks

What are denial-of-service attacks?

In a **denial-of-service (DoS) attack**, legitimate users are denied access to a computer system because a hacker is repeatedly making requests of that computer system through a computer he or she has taken over as a zombie. A computer can handle only a certain number of requests for information at one time. When it is flooded with requests in a denial-of-service attack, it shuts down and refuses to answer any requests for

information, even if the requests are from a legitimate user. Thus, the computer is so busy responding to the bogus requests for information that authorized users can't gain access.

Couldn't a DoS attack be traced by to the computer that launched it?

Launching a DoS attack on a computer system from a single computer is easy to trace. Therefore, most savvy hackers use a **distributed denial-of-service (DDoS) attack**, which launches DDoS attacks from more than one zombie (sometimes thousands of zombies) at the same time. Figure 8 illustrates how a DDoS attack works. A hacker creates many zombies (sometimes hundreds or thousands) and coordinates them so that they begin sending bogus requests to the same computer at the same time. Administrators of the victim computer often have a great deal of difficulty stopping the attack because it comes from so many computers. Often the attacks are coordinated automatically by botnets. A **botnet** is a large group of software programs (called *robots* or *bots*) that runs autonomously on zombie computers. Some botnets have been known to span 1.5 million computers.

DDoS attacks are a serious problem. In January 2008, Scientology Web sites became the victims of DDoS

Figure 8

Zombie computers are used to facilitate a distributed denial-of-service (DDoS) attack.

Hacker launches DDoS by activating zombies (red lines)

Hacker's computer

Academic computer (zombie)

Government computer (zombie)

Home computer (zombie)

Corporate computer (zombie)

ISP computer (zombie)

Zombie computers attack target system (blue lines)

Victim of DDoS

Computer Threats: Hackers

Prevention of Identity Theft . . . Don't Overlook Photocopiers!

We are constantly bombarded with identity theft warnings regarding suspicious e-mail, phishing sites, and telephone scams. Many people are unaware that photocopiers, too, present a risk of identity theft. This is because most photocopiers manufactured today contain hard drives, just as computers do. Documents are scanned, stored on the hard drive, and then printed by the copier. So, unless the copier has been specially configured to have the hard drive overwritten to destroy data or to use encryption, copies of your tax return may be lurking on the public copier at your local library or copy shop that you used before you mailed your return to the Internal Revenue Service. A clever hacker could retrieve a wealth of potential information off just one public copy machine.

So what should you do to protect yourself? Ask the local copy shop or public library, or the IT department at your office, about the security measures they have set up on their copiers before you use them to copy sensitive documents. If you are buying a copier for your business, investigate security options that are available to protect your employees. For small copying jobs (such as your tax return), consider buying an all-in-one device (combining a printer, copier, scanner, and fax machine) for your home office because you can more easily keep that machine protected from wily hackers.

attacks by a group that called itself "Anonymous," and whose members were linked to an anti-Scientology campaign called Project Chanology. In April 2009, the International Federation of the Phonographic Industry (IFPI) and Motion Picture Association of America (MPAA) Web sites were subjected to DDoS attacks in protest of the conviction of the owners of The Pirate Bay (a notorious file-sharing site) on charges of assisting in copyright infringement. Because many Web sites receive revenue from users, either directly (such as via subscriptions to online games) or indirectly (such as when Web surfers click on advertisements), DDoS attacks can be financially distressing for the owners of the affected Web sites.

How Hackers Gain Access

How exactly does a hacker gain access to a computer? Hackers can gain access to computers directly or indirectly. Direct access involves sitting down at a computer and installing hacking software. It is unlikely that such an attack would occur in your home. However, to deter unauthorized use, you may want to lock the room that your computer is in or remove key components (such as the power cord) when strangers such as repair personnel are in your house and may be unobserved for periods of time. You might also set up your computer so that it requires a password for a user to gain access to your desktop.

The most likely method a hacker will use to access a computer is to enter indirectly through its Internet connection. When connected to the Internet, your computer is potentially open to attack by hackers. Many people forget that their Internet connection is a two-way street. Not only can you access the Internet; people on the Internet can also access your computer.

Think of the computer as a house. Common sense tells you to lock your doors and windows to deter theft when you aren't home. Hooking your computer up to the Internet is like leaving the front door to your house wide open. Anyone passing by can access your computer and poke around for valuables. Your computer obviously doesn't have doors and windows like a house, but it does have logical ports.

What are logical ports? Logical ports are virtual—that is, not physical—communications gateways or paths that allow a computer to organize requests for information (such as Web page downloads or e-mail routing) from other networks or computers. Unlike physical ports (USB, FireWire, and so on), you can't see or touch a logical port; it is part of a computer's internal organization.

Logical ports are numbered and assigned to specific services. For instance, logical port 80 is designated for hypertext transfer protocol (HTTP), the main communications protocol (or standard) for the Internet. Thus, all requests for information from your browser to the Web flow through logical port 80. E-mail messages sent by simple mail transfer protocol (SMTP), the protocol used for sending e-mail on the Internet, are routed through logical port 25. Open logical ports, like open windows in a home, invite intruders, as illustrated in Figure 9. Unless you take precautions to restrict access to your logical ports, other people on the Internet may be able to access your computer through them.

Fortunately, you can thwart most hacking problems by installing a firewall.

Restricting Access to Your Digital Assets

Keeping hackers at bay is often just a matter of keeping them out. This can be achieved either by preventing them from accessing your computer (usually through your Internet connection), by protecting your digital information in such a way that it can't be accessed (with passwords, for example), or by hiding your activities from prying eyes. In the next section, we explore strategies for protecting access to your digital assets and keeping your Internet surfing activities from being seen by the wrong people.

FTP (Port 21)   YOUR COMPUTER   DNS (Port 53)

HTTP (Port 80)

E-mail (Port 25)   Telnet (Port 23)

WEB SITE REQUEST

Figure 9

Open logical ports are an invitation to hackers.

Firewalls

A **firewall** is a program or hardware device designed to keep computers safe from hackers. A firewall specifically designed for home networks is called a **personal firewall**. Personal firewalls are made to be easy to install. By using a personal firewall, you can close open logical ports to invaders and potentially make your computer invisible to other computers on the Internet.

Firewalls are named after a housing construction feature. When houses were first being packed densely into cities, they were attached to each other with common walls. Fire was a huge hazard because wood (the major construction component for houses) burns readily. An entire neighborhood could be lost in a single fire. Thus, builders started building common walls of nonflammable or slow-burning material to stop, or at least slow, the spread of fire. These came to be known as firewalls.

Types of Firewalls

What kinds of firewalls are there?
As noted earlier, firewalls can be configured using either software or hardware devices.

Although installing either a software or a hardware firewall on your home network is probably sufficient, you should consider installing both for maximum protection.

What software firewalls are there?
Firewalls for home networks are mostly offered through comprehensive security packages such as Norton Internet Security, McAfee Internet Security, and ZoneAlarm Internet Security Suite. Most current operating systems also include reliable firewalls. These products are easy to set up and include options that allow the software to make security decisions for you based on the level of security you request. These programs also come with monitoring systems that alert you if your computer is under attack. The newest versions of these programs have "smart agents" that automatically stop attacks as they are detected by closing the appropriate logical ports or disallowing the suspicious activity.

What are hardware firewalls?
You can also buy and configure hardware firewall devices. For example, when buying a router for your network, make sure to buy one that also acts as a firewall. Manufacturers such as Linksys, Belkin, and Netgear make routers that double as firewalls. Just like software firewalls, the setup for

ACTIVE HELP-DESK   Understanding Firewalls

In this Active Helpdesk call, you'll play the role of a helpdesk staffer, fielding calls about how hackers can attack networks and what harm they can cause, as well as what a firewall does to keep a computer safe from hackers.

How Firewalls Work

Firewalls are designed to restrict access to a network and its computers. Firewalls protect you in two major ways: by blocking access to logical ports and by keeping your computer's network address secure.

To block access to logical ports, firewalls examine data packets that your computer sends and receives. Data packets contain information such as the address of the sending and receiving computers and the logical port the packet will use. Firewalls can be configured so that they filter out packets sent to specific logical ports. This process is referred to as **packet filtering**.

For example, file transfer protocol (FTP) programs are a typical way in which hackers access a computer. Hackers can disguise their requests for information as legitimate packets that appear to be FTP requests authorized by your computer. If a firewall is configured to ignore *all* incoming packets that request access to port 21 (the port designated for FTP traffic), no FTP requests will get through to your computer. This process is referred to as **logical port blocking**. If port 21 were a window at your home, you : would probably lock it so that a burglar 'couldn't get in. If you needed port 21 for a legitimate purpose, you could instruct the firewall to allow access to that port for a specified period of time or by a certain user.

For the Internet to share information seamlessly, data packets must have a way of getting to their correct locations. Therefore, every computer connected to the Internet has a unique address called an **Internet Protocol address** (or **IP address**). As noted earlier, data packets contain the IP address of the computer to which they are being sent. Routing servers on the Internet make sure the packets get to the correct address. This is similar to the way addresses work on a conventional letter. A unique street address (such as 123 Main St., Anywhere, CA 99999) is placed on the envelope and the postal service routes it to its correct destination. Without such addressing, data packets, like letters, would not reach the intended recipients.

IP addresses are assigned in a procedure known as **dynamic addressing** when users log on to their Internet service provider (ISP). This is illustrated in Figure 10. IP addresses are assigned out of a pool of available IP addresses licensed to the ISP in this manner:

1. When you connect to your ISP, your computer requests an IP address.
2. The ISP's Web server consults its list of available IP addresses and selects one.
3. The selected IP address is communicated to your computer. The address remains in force for as long as you are connected to the ISP.
4. Once on the Internet, your Web browser requests access to ABC Company's Web site.
5. The ABC Company server consults an IP address listing and determines that the IP address of your computer is assigned to your ISP. It then forwards the requested information to the ISP's Web server.
6. The ISP's Web server knows to whom it assigned the IP address and, therefore, forwards the requested information to your computer.

Because hackers use IP addresses to find victims and come back to their computers for more mischief, frequently switching IP addresses helps make users less vulnerable to attacks. Periodically switching off your modem and rebooting it will cause a different IP address to be assigned dynamically to your

Figure 10

How dynamic addressing works.

---

hardware firewalls is designed for novices, and the default configuration keeps unnecessary logical ports closed. Documentation accompanying the firewalls can assist users with more experience in adjusting the settings to allow access to specific ports if needed.

Knowing Your Computer Is Secure

How can I tell if my computer is at risk? For peace of mind (and to ensure that your firewall setup was successful), you can visit several Web sites that offer free services that test your computer's vulnerability. One popular site is Gibson Research (**grc.com**). The company's ShieldsUP and LeakTest programs are free, easy to run, and can pinpoint security vulnerabilities in a system that is connected to the Internet. If you get a clean report from these programs, your system is probably not vulnerable to attack. Figure 12 shows the results screen

Router IP address:
111.22.3.44

Your computer's internal
IP address: 112.11.4.13

ABC Company
Web server

Hacker

Figure 11

Network address
translation in action.

modem by your ISP. This tends to enhance your security.

However, because many broadband (cable and DSL) users leave their modems on for long periods of time (consecutive days or weeks), their IP addresses tend to change less frequently than those of dial-up users. This is similar to having an IP address assigned by **static addressing**. In static addressing, your IP address is always the same and is assigned by your ISP. This process is often used by businesses who are hosting a Web site. When a broadband user has a static address, the user is more vulnerable to hackers because the hackers have a more permanent IP address with which to locate the computer. It also makes it easier for hackers to make repeated visits to a computer.

To combat the problems associated with static addressing, firewalls use a process called **network address translation (NAT)** to assign internal IP addresses on a network. These internal IP addresses are only shared with devices that are part of the network, so the addresses are safe from hackers. Figure 11 shows how NAT works. Your computer's internal IP address is assigned to your computer by the router. This IP address is used only on the internal network and therefore cannot be detected by other Internet users. Here's how it works:

1. Your computer's Web browser requests access to the ABC Company's Web site. This request travels through the router, which is configured as a firewall.

2. The router forwards the browser request to the ABC Company Web server and directs that server to send the data back to the router IP

address (in this example, 111.22.3.44). The internal IP address of your computer (assigned by NAT) is not revealed to computers outside your network.

3. The ABC Company Web server processes the request and sends the data back to the router IP address (111.22.3.44). This is the IP address the ISP assigned to your router, and it can be detected by other users on the Internet.

4. The router then passes the requested data to the IP address of the computer that requested it (in this example, 112.11.4.13).

The router's IP address is assigned by your ISP. Only the router's IP address can be detected by other users on the Internet. For hackers to access your computer, they must know your computer's IP address. With a NAT capable router/firewall installed on your network, hackers are unable to access the internal IP address assigned to your computer, so your computer is safe.

You can use NAT in your home by purchasing a hardware firewall with NAT capabilities. As noted earlier, many routers sold for home use are also configured as firewalls, and many feature NAT as well.

143	IMAP	Closed	Your computer has responded that this port exists but is currently closed to connections.
389	LDAP	Closed	Your computer has responded that this port exists but is currently closed to connections.
443	HTTPS	Closed	Your computer has responded that this port exists but is currently closed to connections.
445	MSFT DS	Stealth	There is NO EVIDENCE WHATSOEVER that a port (or even any computer) exists at this IP address!
1002	ms-ils	Closed	Your computer has responded that this port exists but is currently closed to connections.
1024	DCOM	Closed	Your computer has responded that this port exists but is currently closed to connections.
1025	Host	OPEN!	One or more unspecified Distributed COM (DCOM) services are opened by Windows. The exact port(s) opened can change, since queries to port 135 are used to determine...

Ports safe from attack

Port subject to attack

Figure 12

ShieldsUP common ports
test results

Restricting Access to Your Digital Assets

from a ShieldsUP port probe test, which checks which logical ports in your computer are vulnerable. This test was run on a computer connected to the Internet with no firewall installed. Ports reported as closed or in stealth mode are safe from attack. Ports reported as open (such as port 1025) are subject to exploitation by hackers. Installation of a hardware or software firewall should close any open ports.

What if I don't get a clean report from the testing program? If the testing program detects potential vulnerabilities and you don't have a firewall, you should install one as soon as possible. If the firewall is already configured and common ports (such as those shown in Figure 13) are identified as being vulnerable, consult your firewall documentation for instructions on how to close or restrict access to those ports.

Preventing Bluetooth Attacks

What are the security vulnerabilities of Bluetooth devices? Bluetooth is a transmission medium for exchanging data wirelessly over short distances. Most smartphones are Bluetooth enabled. Although progress is being made, Bluetooth hardware and software still are riddled with security holes, especially on smartphones. If you have a Bluetooth-enabled device, you are susceptible to two severe types of mischief:

- **Bluesnarfing:** Bluesnarfing involves exploiting a flaw in the Bluetooth access software for the purpose of accessing a Bluetooth device and stealing the

information contained on it. Think how much valuable information is contained on your smartphone (names, contact information, and meeting notes) that might be valuable to a business competitor. Unfortunately, Bluesnarfing is relatively easy (and cheap) because a lot of Bluesnarfing software is available on the Internet.

- **Bluebugging:** Although much more difficult and expensive to execute, Bluebugging presents more serious dangers. The process involves a hacker actually taking control of a Bluetooth-enabled device. Once a hacker gains control of the device, he or she can make phone calls; establish Internet connections; read phonebook entries; set call forwarding; or send, receive, and read short message service (SMS) messages.

- This is a major risk in Europe because Bluetooth and SMS are wildly popular there, but the rise of Bluetooth usage in the United States is making it a risk here as well. Many cars in the United States are now equipped with Bluetooth so that owners can connect their mobile devices (such as phones and GPS units) to the car's systems. Many Europeans use their phones to make micropayments (small purchases from merchants that eventually appear on their cell phone bill) by a process known as *reverse SMS*. If a hacker Bluebugs your phone, he could potentially send payments to fake accounts he or she controls, using reverse SMS.

How can I protect myself from Bluetooth attacks? Most devices with Bluetooth capability give you the option of making your device invisible to unauthorized Bluetooth devices. This does not affect your ability to use two Bluetooth devices you own together (such as a wireless headset paired with a phone). When you pair your headset with your phone, the headset (which has a unique serial number) becomes an authorized Bluetooth device for your phone. Moreover, by making your device invisible to unauthorized devices (such as hackers' headsets), you prevent hackers from connecting to your equipment (your phone) because their headsets are not

Figure 13 | COMMON LOGICAL PORTS

Port Number	Protocol Using the Port
21	FTP (file transfer protocol) control
23	Telnet (unencrypted text communications)
25	SMTP (simple mail transfer protocol)
53	DNS (domain name system)
80	HTTP (hypertext transfer protocol)
443	HTTPS (HTTP protocol with transport layer security [TLS] encryption)

authorized devices for your phone. When vulnerabilities are discovered, smartphone manufacturers issue software patches. Antivirus software is also available for mobile devices, so you may wish to purchase this for your smartphone. You must ensure that you update the software in your mobile devices just as you do your computer's OS and antivirus software. For more information on securing your Bluetooth devices, go to the Bluetooth Technology Web site (**bluetomorrow.com**).

Password Protection and Password Management

Passwords, used in conjunction with login IDs, are the major way we restrict access to computers, networks, and online accounts. You no doubt have many passwords that you need to remember to access your digital life. However, creating strong passwords—ones that are difficult for hackers to guess—is an essential piece of security that individuals sometimes overlook. Password cracking programs have become more sophisticated lately. In fact, some commonly available programs, such as John the Ripper, can test more than 1 million password combinations per second! Creating a secure password is therefore more important than ever.

Creating Passwords

What constitutes a strong password? Strong passwords are difficult for someone to guess. They should not contain easily deduced components related to your life such as parts of your name, your pet's name, your street address, or your telephone number. To create strong passwords, follow the basic guidelines shown here:

- Your password should contain at least 14 characters and include numbers, symbols, and upper- and lowercase letters.

- Your password should not be a single word or any word found in the dictionary.
- Ideally, it should be a combination of several words with strategically placed uppercase characters.
- Your password should not be easily associated with you (such as your birth date, the name of your pet, or your nickname).
- Use a different password for each system or Web site you need to access. This prevents access to other accounts you maintain if one of your passwords is discovered. (If you can't remember them all, use the password management feature of Windows or of the Firefox browser.)
- Never tell anyone your password or write it down in a place where others might see it.
- Change your password on a regular basis (say every month) and change it sooner if you think someone may know it.

Figure 14 shows some possible passwords and explains why they are strong or weak candidates.

How can I check the strength of my passwords? You can use online password strength testers, such as The

---

BITS AND BYTES Connecting to Wireless Networks on the Road? Beware of "Evil Twins"!

When you are at the airport or Starbucks, you may need to connect to a wireless network and check your e-mail. You switch on your notebook, and the wireless network adapter finds a network called "starbucks" or "airport wireless." You connect, enter your credit card information to pay for your airtime, and start merrily surfing away. Three days later, your credit card company calls asking about the $4,800 big screen TV you just bought at the local electronics store and the $6,300 of power tools charged at the home improvement store. You didn't make either of these purchases, but you probably fell prey to an "evil twin" wireless hotspot.

Hackers know the areas where people are likely to seek access to wireless networks. They will often set up their own wireless networks in these areas with sound-alike names to lure unsuspecting Web surfers and get them to enter credit card information to gain access. Other times these "evil twins" offer free Internet access and the hackers monitor traffic looking for sensitive information they can use.

So how can you protect yourself? Check with authorized personnel at places where you will be connecting to hotspots to determine the names of the legitimate hotspots. If you run across "free" access to a hotspot that isn't provided by a legitimate merchant, you are better off not connecting at all because you can't be sure your information won't be used against you or that malicious files won't be downloaded to your computer.

Are Klingonese Passwords Safe?

Many computer users are diehard science fiction fans. *Star Trek*, *Star Wars*, and *Battlestar Galactica* have provided computer users with loads of planet names, alien races, alien vocabulary (Klingon words from the *Star Trek* series are especially popular), and starship names to use as passwords. Unfortunately, hackers are onto this ploy. Recently developed hacking programs use dictionaries of "geek-speak" to attempt to break passwords. Although "Qapla" (Klingonese for "success"; also used as "goodbye") might seem like an unbreakable password, don't bet your data on it! You can still use these words if you incorporate multiple words into a password that also contains symbols and numbers.

Password Meter (**passwordmeter.com**) or Microsoft's test (**microsoft.com/protect/yourself/password/checker.mspx**), to evaluate your passwords (see Figure 15). The Password Meter provides guidelines for good passwords and shows you how integrating various elements (such as symbols) affects the strength score for your password.

You should make sure you change your passwords on a regular basis (such as monthly or quarterly). Your school or your employer probably requires you to change your password regularly. This is also a good idea for your personal passwords. You should also not use the same password for every account that you have. Because remembering constantly changing strong passwords for numerous accounts can be a

challenge, you should use password management tools, as described below, to make the process easier to handle. If you have trouble thinking of secure passwords, there are many password generators available for free, such as Perfect Passwords (**grc.com/passwords.htm**) and the Bytes Interactive Password Generator (**goodpassword.com**).

Can I use a password to restrict access to my computer? Windows has built-in password protection for files as well as the entire desktop. If your computer is set up for multiple users with password protection, the Windows login screen requires you to enter a password to gain access to the desktop. You are also asked to enter a password hint to remind you in case you forget your password. The computer can be set to default back to the Welcome screen after it is idle for a set period of time. This forces a user to reenter a password to regain access to the computer. If someone attempts to log on to your computer without your password, that person won't be able to gain access. It is an especially good idea to use passwords on notebook computers or any computer that may be unattended for periods of time. Figure 16 shows the Control Panel screen used to set up a password on a user account.

There are two types of users in Windows: administrators and standard users. Setting up a password on a standard user account prevents other standard users from being

Figure 14 | STRONG AND WEAK PASSWORD CANDIDATES

Strong Password	Reason
L8t2meGaNDalf351	Uses letters and numbers to come up with memorable phrase "Late to me" and adds it to a character name from *Lord of the Rings* plus a random number.
IwaLR8384GdY	First initials of first line of Green Day song *I Walk a Lonely Road* plus a random number and an abbreviation for Green Day
P1zzA244WaterShiPDowN	Easily remembered word with mix of alphanumeric characters and upper- and lowercase letters, your locker number at your gym, plus the title of a book that you like (with upper- and lowercase letters)
S0da&ICB3N&J3RRY	Mix of numbers, symbols, and letters. Stands for soda and ice cream and the names of famous ice cream makers with the number 3 instead of the letter E
Weak Password	Reason
Jsmith	Combination of first initial and last name
4smithkids	Even though this has alphanumeric combination, it is too descriptive of a family.
Brown5512	Last name and last four digits of phone number are easily decoded.
123MainSt	A street address is an easily decoded password.

able to access that user's files. However, users with administrator privileges can still see your files if you are a standard user. So be aware that your files may not be safe from all prying eyes!

Managing Your Passwords

How can I remember all of my complex passwords? Good security practices suggest that you have different passwords for different Web sites that you access and that you change your passwords frequently. The problem with well-constructed passwords is that they can be hard to remember. Fortunately, password management tools are now widely available. This takes the worry out of forgetting passwords because the password management software does the remembering for you.

Where can I obtain password management software? Windows, Norton 360 (and other Internet security packages), and the Firefox browser make it easy to keep track of passwords by providing password management tools. From the Tools menu in Firefox, select Options, and then click the Security icon (the closed padlock) shown in Figure 17. In the Passwords section, check **Remember passwords for sites** to have Firefox remember passwords when you log onto Web sites. Check **Use a master password**, which causes a dialog box to appear, and enter a well-designed, secure password. The next time you go to a Web site that requires a login, Firefox will a dialog box prompting you to have Firefox remember the login name and password for this site. Then, when you return to the site and select a login option, enter the master password and the Firefox Password Manager will fill in the login and password information for you.

You also can see a list of sites maintained by the Firefox Password Manager by clicking the Show Passwords button, which displays the Remember Passwords dialog box (see Figure 17). Passwords for each site are displayed after you click the Show Passwords button and enter the master password.

Even though you only need to remember the master password, you still need to make sure that is a secure password (according to the rules we discussed earlier) and that you change it on a regular basis. Password

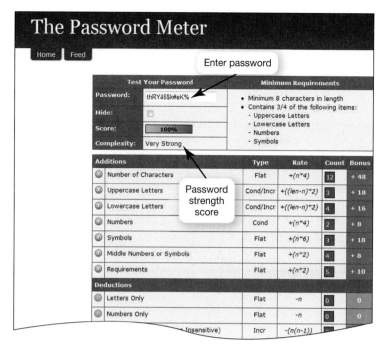

Figure 15

The Password Meter objectively evaluates your passwords.

Figure 16

Windows provides additional security for your files by locking unauthorized users out of your account.

>Click **Start**, click **Control Panel**, click **User Accounts and Family Safety**, click **User Accounts**, and then click **Create a password for your account**.

managers are useful on the machine that you use on a regular basis. However, if you need to access your accounts from another computer (such as one at school), you will still need to know the individual passwords for each site you wish to access.

So start using secure passwords and let your browser relieve you of the problem of trying to remember them all.

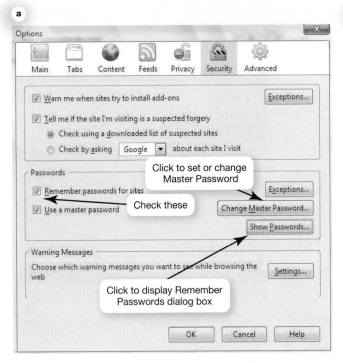

Figure 17

(a) The security tab in the Firefox browser options screen provides access to password management tools.

(b) The Firefox Remember Passwords dialog box displays all sites for which login information is saved.

>From the **Tools** menu, select **Options**. In the **Options** dialog box, click the **Show Passwords** button.

Anonymous Web Surfing: Hiding from Prying Eyes

Should I be concerned about surfing the Internet on shared or public computers?
If you use shared computers in public places such as libraries, coffee shops, or college student unions, you should be concerned about a subsequent user of a computer spying on your surfing habits. You never know what nefarious tools have been installed by hackers on a public computer. When you browse the Internet, traces of your activity are left behind on that computer, often as temporary files. A wily hacker can glean sensitive information long after you have finished your latte and your surfing session.

What tools can I use to protect myself when using public computers?
Google Chrome and Internet Explorer 8 both include privacy tools that help you surf the Internet anonymously. Google Chrome's Incognito feature allows you to open a special version of the Google browser window. When surfing in this window, records of

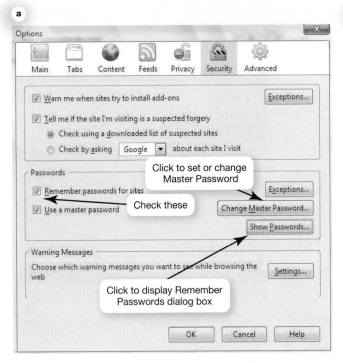

Ironkey

Figure 18

Portable privacy devices help to protect your privacy when you work on computers away from your home or office.

Web sites you visit and files you download do not appear in the Web browser's history files. Furthermore, any new cookies that were generated in that browsing session are deleted when you exit the Incognito window. The InPrivate feature of Internet Explorer 8 offers similar security features.

Portable privacy devices, such as the IronKey (**ironkey.com**) shown in Figure 18, provide an even higher level of surfing privacy. Simply plug the device into an available USB port on the machine on which you will be working. All sensitive Internet files, such as cookies, Internet history, and browser caches, then will be stored on the privacy device, not on the computer you are using. Privacy devices such as these often come preloaded with software such as Anonymizer Safe Surfing Suite (**anonymizer.com**), which shields your IP address from prying eyes, making it difficult (if not impossible) for hackers to tell where you are surfing on the Internet. These privacy devices also have password management tools that store all of your login information and encrypt it so it will be safe if your privacy device falls into someone else's hands.

Another free practical solution is to take the Linux OS with you on a flash drive and avoid using the public computer's operating system. The interfaces of many Linux builds,

Figure 19

Ubuntu is a version of Linux that has a Windows-like interface and familiar browser tools like Firefox.

such as Ubuntu (see Figure 19), look almost exactly like Windows and are easy to use.

There are several advantages to using a Linux-based operating system on a public computer. First, your risk of picking up viruses and other malware is significantly reduced because when you boot a public computer from a flash drive, you completely eliminate any interaction with the public computer's operating system. This, in turn, significantly reduces the chance that your flash drive will become infected by any malware running on the public computer.

Next, virus and hacking attacks against Linux are far less likely than attacks against Windows. Because Windows has an over 90 percent share of the operating system market, people who write malware tend to target Windows systems. Finally, when you run software from your own storage medium (flash drive), you avoid reading and writing to the hard disk of the public computer. This significantly enhances your privacy because you don't leave traces of your activity behind.

Pendrivelinux.com (**pendrivelinux.com**) is excellent resource that offers many different versions of Linux for download and includes step-by-step instructions on how to install them on your flash drive. If you are a Mac user, there is an option for you, too! gOS is a version of Linux that provides

a close approximation of OS X, so you can feel right at home.

Biometric Authentication Devices

Besides passwords, how else can I restrict the use of my computer? A biometric authentication device is a device that reads a unique personal characteristic such as a fingerprint or the iris pattern in your eye and converts its pattern to a digital code. When you use the device, your pattern is read and compared to the one stored on the computer. Only users having an exact fingerprint or iris pattern match are allowed to access the computer.

Because no two people have the same biometric characteristics (fingerprints and iris patterns are unique), these devices provide a high level of security. They also eliminate the human error that can occur in password protection. You might forget your password, but you won't forget to bring your fingerprint to the computer! Some notebooks feature built-in fingerprint readers, and Figure 20a shows a mouse that includes a fingerprint reader. Another useful device is the APC Touch Biometric Pod Password Manager (see Figure 20b); after it identifies you by your fingerprint, the device provides login information to password-protected Web sites you need to access. The device also stores all your login names and passwords so that you don't have to keep track of them. As many as 20 users can use the same device, making it perfect for shared computers. Other biometric devices, which include voice authentication and face pattern–recognition systems, are now widely offered in notebook computers.

Make sure to utilize some (or all) of these methods to keep your activities from prying eyes and to restrict access to your digital information.

Managing Online Annoyances

Surfing the Web, sending and receiving e-mail, and chatting online have become a common part of most of our lives.

SecuGen Corporation

American Power Conversion Corporation

Fingerprint
reader

Figure 20

(a) The SecuGen Opti-Mouse III is a two-button mouse with a scroll wheel that includes a digital fingerprint reader. (b) The APC Touch Biometric Pod Password Manager employs a fingerprint reader to recognize authorized users.

What is adware? Adware is software that displays sponsored advertisements in a section of your browser window or as a pop-up ad box. It is considered a legitimate (though sometimes annoying) means of generating revenue for those developers who do not charge for their software or information. Pop-up windows (small boxes that open up automatically on your screen) have been referred to as the billboards of the Internet because they appear and display advertisements or other promotional information when you install freeware programs or access certain Web sites. These pop-up windows, at one point, were so common that they were incredibly irritating and annoying.

Some pop-ups, however, are legitimate and increase the functionality of the originating site. For example, your account balance may pop up on your bank's Web site. Fortunately, because Web browsers such as Firefox, Safari, and Internet Explorer have pop-up blockers built into their browsers, the occurrence of annoying pop-ups has been greatly reduced. You can access the pop-up blockers settings in your browser (see Figure 21) and add Web sites for which you will allow pop-ups. Whenever a pop-up is blocked, the browser displays an information bar at the top of the browser window or plays a sound to alert you. If you feel the pop-up is legitimate, you can then choose to accept it.

Unfortunately, the Web has become fertile ground for people who want to advertise their products, track our Web browsing behaviors, or even con people into revealing personal information. In this section, we'll look at ways in which you can manage, if not avoid, these and other online headaches.

Malware, Adware, and Spyware

What is malware? Malware is software that has a malicious intent (hence the prefix *mal*). There are three primary forms of malware: adware, spyware, and viruses (which we have already discussed). Adware and spyware are not destructive like viruses and worms are. Known collectively as grayware, most are intrusive, annoying, or objectionable online programs that are downloaded to your computer when you install or use other online content such as a freeware program, game, or utility.

Pop-up Blocker Settings

Exceptions

Pop-ups are currently blocked. You can allow pop-ups from specific websites by adding the site to the list below.

Address of website to allow:

Add sites here   Add

Allowed sites:

*.mail.yahoo.com
affiliate-program.amazon.com
games.yahoo.com
jtams.tix.com
www.broadwayoffers.com
www.southparkstudios.com
www.usairways.com

Remove

Remove all...

Will permit pop-ups from these sites

Notifications and filter level

☑ Play a sound when a pop-up is blocked.
☑ Show Information Bar when a pop-up is blocked.

Level of blocking

Filter level:

Medium: Block most automatic pop-ups

Pop-up Blocker FAQ   Close

Figure 21

The Internet Explorer pop-up blocker settings dialog box.

>Pop-up Blocker is found in the **Tools** menu on the Internet Explorer toolbar.

What is spyware? Some adware programs are more intrusive than the ones just discussed. Without your knowledge, they transmit information about you, such as your Internet surfing habits, to the owner of the adware program so that the information can be used for marketing purposes. In these

ETHICS IN IT

Ethics: Big Brother Is Watching . . . But Should He Be Allowed to Do So?

Think you aren't being closely watched by your employer? Think again! A survey of employers by the American Management Association and the ePolicy Institute revealed that of the employers surveyed:

- 73 percent monitored e-mail messages
- 66 percent monitored Web surfing
- 48 percent monitored activities using video surveillance
- 45 percent monitored keystrokes and keyboard time
- 43 percent monitored computer files in some other fashion

There is a high probability that you are being monitored while you work and when you access the Internet via your employer's Internet connection.

The two most frequently cited reasons for employee monitoring are to prevent theft and to measure productivity. Monitoring for theft isn't new, because monitoring cameras have been around for years, and productivity monitoring has been a consistent process for assembly line workers for decades. However, the rise of the Internet has led to a new type of productivity drain that is of concern to employers. **Cyberloafing**, or cyberslacking, means doing anything with a computer, while you are being paid to do your job, that is *not* an approved function of your job. Examples of cyberloafing activities are playing games, reading personal e-mail, checking sports scores, watching videos, and buying personal-use products on e-commerce sites. Estimates of business productivity losses due to cyberloafing top $50 billion annually. While many employers don't mind if workers answer the occasional personal e-mail while at work, they would probably not appreciate it if they spent four hours of their workday playing World of Warcraft online!

Like most other Americans, you probably feel you have a right to privacy in the workplace. Unfortunately, the laws in the United States don't support a worker's right to privacy. Laws such as the 1986 Electronic Communications Privacy Act (ECPA), which prohibits unauthorized monitoring of electronic communications, have been interpreted by the courts in favor of employers. The bottom line is that when the employer is paying for equipment and software (such as Internet access and e-mail), the employer has the legal right to monitor its usage.

Is it ethical for employers to monitor employees? Just because an action is *legal* doesn't mean it is *ethical*. It is difficult to argue that an employer doesn't have the right to take measures to prevent theft and detect low productivity. The ethical issue here is whether or not the employees are made aware that they are being monitored. An ethical employer should treat employees with respect and dignity and inform the employees that they are being monitored. Employers have an ethical responsibility (and a legal one as well, depending on the jurisdiction) not to place monitoring devices in sensitive locations such as bathrooms and dressing areas. However, in many states, the employer does not need to inform the employees in advance that they are being monitored. Conscientious employers include monitoring disclosures in published employee policies to avoid confusion and conflict. If you aren't sure whether your employer monitors employees, check with the company's human resources department.

Employers use a variety of software programs to monitor employee computer usage. Certain software packages keep track of every Web site you visit and the duration of your stay. Checking the baseball scores might take only three seconds and go unnoticed, but spending two hours updating your fantasy football team may be flagged. Keystroke loggers were originally used to monitor performance for people with input-intensive jobs, like clerks and secretaries. Now these programs have the potential to be used to invade your privacy, because they can record everything you type, even that nasty e-mail about the boss that you thought better of sending and deleted!

In addition to monitoring keystrokes, computer software can also be used to monitor the contents of your hard drive, so you don't want to collect 4,823 illegal MP3 files on your work computer. Some programs even keep track of how long your computer is idle, which can give your manager a good idea of whether you were working or taking a three-hour lunch.

Since your employer might not tell you that your computer use is being monitored, you should assume that anything you do on your company-provided computer is subject to scrutiny. If you need to do personal work on your lunch hour or other breaks, you may be able to use your personal laptop to avoid the monitoring. Check with your employer to be sure you can connect personal computers to the corporate network or Internet connection. Note that courts in some jurisdictions have ruled that e-mails sent from third-party systems, such as Yahoo! and Gmail, are subject to monitoring if they are sent from employer-provided computer systems. Instant messaging is also subject to monitoring. Therefore, the best defense against monitoring of personal instant messaging or e-mail is to use your own computing device to send the communications.

People who monitor employees have a duty to protect their right to privacy and not to disclose any information that they may inadvertently see during the course of monitoring. The acceptable computer use policies at most companies include guidelines for network administrators and other people who have high levels of access to sensitive information. When monitoring employees' work habits, management must ensure that compliance with the policies is tested periodically. Periodic reviews of procedures and compliance help ensure that established company policies are working as designed. An ethical employer strives to prevent misuse of personal data and accidental data loss. This helps a company maintain the trust of its employees. However, you can't always be certain that everyone who monitors you will behave in an ethical manner. Therefore, you need to think very carefully about exactly what personal tasks you are willing to risk engaging in on company computer systems.

So, do your employers have an ethical right to monitor your activities? Certainly, they have a right to ensure they are getting a fair day's work from you, just as you have an ethical obligation to provide a fair effort for a fair wage. However, employers should also be willing to respect the privacy rights of their employees and treat them as professionals, unless there is some indication of wrongdoing. Because employers may have a legal right to monitor you in the workplace, you should work under the assumption that everything you do on your work computer is subject to scrutiny, and behave accordingly. Do your online shopping at home!

instances, such adware is more malicious in intent and can be considered spyware. **Spyware** is an unwanted piggyback program that usually downloads with other software you want to install from the Internet. It runs in the background of your system. Many spyware programs use tracking cookies to collect information, whereas others are disguised as benign programs that are really malicious programs (such as Trojan horses). One type of spyware program (known as a **keystroke logger**) monitors keystrokes with the intent of stealing passwords, login IDs, or credit card information.

Can I prevent spyware? Many Internet security suites now include antispyware software. However, you can also obtain stand-alone spyware removal software and run it on your computer to delete unwanted spyware. Because there are so many variants of spyware, your Internet security software may not detect all types that attempt to install themselves on your computer. Therefore, it is a good idea to install one or two additional stand-alone antispyware programs on your computer.

Because new spyware is created all the time, you should update and run your spyware removal software regularly. Windows comes with a program called Windows Defender, which scans your system for spyware and other potentially unwanted software. Ad-Aware and Spybot–Search & Destroy (both available from **download.com**) and CA Anti-Spyware (**ca.com**) are other programs that are easy to install and update. Figure 22 shows an example of Ad-Aware and Spybot in action. They detect unwanted programs and allow you to delete the offending software easily.

Spam

How can I best avoid spam? Companies that send out **spam**—unwanted or junk e-mail—find your e-mail address either from a list they purchase or with software that looks for e-mail addresses on the Internet. (Unsolicited instant messages are also a form of spam, called *spim.*) If you've used your e-mail address to purchase anything online, open an online account, or participate in a social network such as Facebook, your e-mail address eventually will appear on one of the lists that spammers get.

One way to avoid spam in your primary account is to create a free Web-based e-mail address that you use only when you fill out forms or purchase items on the Web. For example, both Office Live Mail and Yahoo! allow you to set up free e-mail accounts. If your free Web-based e-mail account is saturated with spam, then you can abandon that account with little inconvenience. It's much less convenient to abandon your primary e-mail address.

Another way to avoid spam is to filter it. A **spam filter** is an option you can select in your e-mail account that places known or suspected spam messages into a folder other than your inbox. Most Web-based e-mail

Figure 22

After performing a routine scan of a computer, Ad-Aware and Spybot each return a log of problems found on the system.

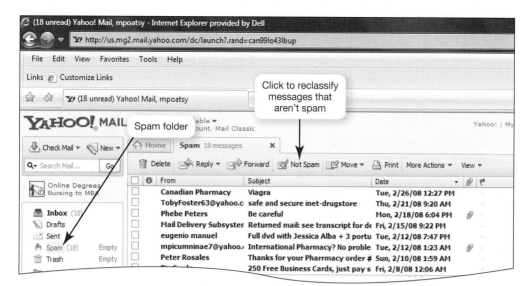

Figure 23

In Yahoo! Mail, messages identified as spam are directed into a folder called "Spam" for review and deletion.

services, such as Office Live Mail and Yahoo!, offer spam filters (see Figure 23). Files perceived to be spam are segregated in a special folder (often named "Spam"). Microsoft Outlook also features a spam filter. Third-party programs that provide some control over spam include SPAMfighter and Cactus Spam Filter, both of which can be obtained at download.com.

How do spam filters work? Spam filters and filtering software can catch as much as 95 percent of spam by checking incoming e-mail subject headers and senders' addresses against databases of known spam. Spam filters also check your e-mail for frequently used spam patterns and keywords (such as "for free" and "over 21"). E-mail that the filter identifies as spam does not go into your inbox, but rather to a folder set up for spam. Spam filters aren't perfect, and you should check the spam folder before deleting its contents because legitimate e-mail might end up there by mistake. Most programs provide you with a tool to reclassify e-mails that have been misidentified as spam.

How else can I prevent spam? There are several additional ways you can prevent spam.

1. Before registering on a Web site, read its privacy policy to see how it uses your e-mail address. Don't give the site permission to pass on your e-mail address to third parties.

2. Don't reply to spam to remove yourself from the spam list. By replying, you are confirming that your e-mail address is active. Instead of stopping spam, you may receive more.

3. Subscribe to an e-mail forwarding service such as Emailias (**emailias.com**) or Sneakemail.com (**sneakemail.com**). These services screen your e-mail messages, forwarding only those messages you designate as being okay to accept.

Cookies

What are cookies? Cookies are small text files that some Web sites automatically store on your computer's hard drive when you visit them. When you log on to a Web site that uses cookies, a cookie file assigns an ID number to your computer. The unique ID is intended to make your return visit to a Web site more efficient and better geared to your interests. The next time you log on to that site, the site marks your visit and keeps track of it in its database.

What do Web sites do with cookie information? Cookies provide Web sites with information about your browsing habits, such as the ads you've opened, the products you've looked at, and the time and duration of your visits. Companies use this information to determine the traffic flowing through their Web site and the effectiveness of their marketing strategy and placement on Web sites. By tracking such information, cookies enable companies to identify different users' preferences.

Managing Online Annoyances

Can companies get my personal information when I visit their sites?

Cookies do not go through your hard drive in search of personal information such as passwords or financial data. The only personal information a cookie obtains is the information you supply when you fill out forms online.

Do privacy risks exist with cookies?

Some sites sell the personal information their cookies collect to Web advertisers that are building huge databases of consumer preferences and habits, collecting personal and business information such as phone numbers, credit reports, and the like. The main concern is that advertisers will use this information indiscriminately, thus infiltrating your privacy.

Should I delete cookies from my hard drive?

Because cookies pose no security threat (it is virtually impossible to hide a virus or malicious software program in a cookie), take up little room on your hard drive, and offer you small conveniences on return visits to Web sites, there is no great reason to delete them. Deleting your cookie files could actually cause you the inconvenience of reentering data you have already entered into Web site forms. However, if you're uncomfortable with the accessibility of your personal information, you can periodically delete cookies or configure your browser to block certain types of cookies, as shown in Figure 24. Software such as Cookie Pal (**kburra.com**) also can help you monitor cookies.

Figure 24

Tools are available, either through your browser (Internet Explorer is shown here) or as separate applications, to distinguish between cookies you want to keep and cookies you don't want on your system.

>On the Internet Explorer menu toolbar, click **Tools**, and then click **Internet Options**. The cookie settings are on the **Privacy** tab.

Protecting Yourself . . . From Yourself!

People are often too trusting or just plain careless when it comes to protecting private information about themselves or their digital data. When was the last time you created a copy of your digital data (such as the thousands of photographs you have stored on your hard drive)? The hard drive in your computer is likely to fail at some point, which may render all the data on it useless. What strategy do you have in place to protect your data from damage?

If you have a MySpace or Facebook account, you are probably constantly revealing information about your likes and dislikes, such as what movie you saw this weekend, which concert you attended last night, the presents you received for your birthday, and so on. You might even be revealing information about where you live. Have you ever filled out an online form to enter a contest? Have you ever applied for a customer loyalty card at your local supermarket or electronics store? Think about how much information you voluntarily give up all the time in the course of running your digital life. Con artists and scammers take advantage of people's tendency to reveal information freely to compromise their privacy and commit theft.

In this section, we discuss ways to keep your data safe from damage (either accidental or intentional) and to keep unscrupulous individuals from tricking you into revealing sensitive information.

Backing Up Your Data

How might I damage the data on my computer?   The data on your computer faces three major threats: unauthorized access, tampering, and destruction. As noted earlier, a hacker can gain access to your computer and steal or alter your data. However, a more likely scenario is that you will lose your data unintentionally. You may accidentally delete files. You may drop your notebook on the ground, causing the hard drive to break down, resulting in complete data loss. A virus from an e-mail attachment you opened may destroy your original file. Your house or dorm many catch fire and your computer be destroyed. Because many of these factors are beyond your control, you should have a strategy for backing up your files. Backups are especially important if you are running a small business. (The backup strategy for small businesses is quite similar to the procedures recommended for individuals.)

What exactly is a meant by backing up data?   Backups are copies of files that you can use to replace the originals if they are lost or damaged. To be truly secure, backups must be stored away from your home or office. You wouldn't want a fire or a flood destroying the backups along with the original data. Removable storage media, such as external hard drives, DVDs, CDs, and flash drives, are popular choices for backing up files because they hold a lot of data and can be transported easily.

Do I need to back up all the files on my computer?   Two types of files need backups—program files and data files.

A **program file** is used to install software and usually comes on CDs or DVDs or is downloaded from the Web. If any programs came preinstalled in your computer, then you may have received a CD or DVD that contains the original program. As long as you have the original media in a safe place, you shouldn't need to back up these files. If you have downloaded a program file from

the Internet, however, you should make a copy of the program installation files on a removable storage device as a backup. If you didn't receive discs for installed programs with your computer, then see the next section for suggested strategies for backing up your entire computer.

A **data file** is a file you have created or purchased. Data files include such files as research papers,, spreadsheets, music files, movies, contact lists, address books, e-mail archives, and your Favorites list from your browser.

How often should I back up my files?   You should back up your data files frequently. How frequently will depend on how much work you cannot afford to lose. You should always back up data files when you make changes to them, especially if those changes involve hours of work. It may not seem important to back up your history term paper file when you finish it, but do you really want to do all that work again if your computer crashes before you have a chance to turn in your paper?

> "The data on your computer faces three major threats: unauthorized access, tampering, and destruction."

To make backups easier, store all your data files in one folder on your hard drive. For example, in Windows and most other operating systems, on your hard drive you will find a folder called Documents. You can create subfolders (such as History Homework, Music Files, and so on) within the Documents folder. If you store all your data files in one place, to back up your files, you simply copy the Documents folder and all of its subfolders onto an alternative storage medium.

For Mac OS X users, backups are much easier. The Time Machine feature (in Mac OS X Snow Leopard and previous versions) detects when an external hard drive is attached to the computer. You are then asked if you want this to be your backup drive. If you answer yes, all of your files (including operating system files) are automatically backed up to the external drive. You even have the option to go back in time and see what your computer looked like on a specific date. This is very handy for recovering a file that you wish you hadn't deleted.

Figure 25

(a) The General tab in Cobian Backup lets you choose the type of backup. (b) The Schedule window makes it easy to schedule backups on a regular basis. (c) You simply drag and drop files or folders that need to be backed up from Windows Explorer to the storage location.

How do I actually perform a file backup? The simplest method would be to open Windows Explorer and copy the files you need to back up to another medium, such as an external hard drive. Of course, this method relies on your remembering to back up files and update the backups when you make changes to the original file. Many people use backup software with features that allow them to schedule backups of key files or directories automatically at specified times. Additionally, some backup software can be configured to make backups of data files automatically as soon as they are created or when they are changed. This resolves the problem of forgetting to perform backups. Many external hard drives are sold with backup software.

Windows 7 includes a backup utility that provides a quick and easy way to schedule backups of files on a regular basis. This utility allows you to select certain folders or directories for backup, although it does not allow you to select individual files. A better choice for Windows users is backup software such as Norton Ghost, Genie Backup Manager, or a free product called Cobian Backup (which you can download from the CNet download site (**download.cnet.com/windows/**), shown in Figure 25. Cobian allows you to easily configure backup tasks and select directories or individual files to back up on a regular basis. A **full backup** will back up all files in a specified location. An **incremental backup** will back up only files that have changed since the last time a backup was performed on the files.

What backups should I perform in case of a total hard drive failure? Your OS and software applications also need to be protected by backups. Although you can create restore points in Windows to take your system back to the time before it had a problem, this doesn't help in the case of a hard drive failure. If you have the media to reinstall Windows and your application programs, then you should be in good shape—although this process may take more time than you think. Windows has many settings that may need to be reinstated to get your machine functioning the way you had it set up. Working with these settings can be intimidating for the average user and just plain time consuming for experienced users. In addition, all of your applications would need to be reinstalled, which could take hours (or days), assuming you can locate all of the CDs and DVDs for your software and re-download all of the applications you purchased over the Internet. If you are running a small business, the time you lose reconfiguring the computers probably means lost revenue.

For complete protection, you should use backup software such as Genie Backup Manager (**genie-soft.com**) or Safety Drill, which comes with Maxtor external hard drives. These products create an **image backup** of your entire system. Windows 7 backup utilities also give you the option of making a copy of your system image for restoration purposes. Taking an image of your entire system and storing it on another hard drive provides you with the ultimate protection. With a backup of your entire hard drive, including your system image, you won't need to reinstall all of the program software from the original media. Instead, you just replace the broken hard drive with the backup hard drive (or copy the contents of the backup drive to a new drive).

Where is a safe place to store my backups? Taking the backup media (external hard drive, DVDs, etc.) to a location other than where the original files are located is usually a sufficient solution. You could store the backups at a friend's house or dorm room. However, if you want an extremely secure location you can store backups of your files online, which is often the most convenient solution for small businesses. For a fee, companies such as Iron Mountain (**backup.ironmountain.com**) and IBackup (**ibackup.com**) can provide you with such online storage. If you store a backup of your entire system on the Internet, then you won't need to buy an additional hard drive for backups. This method also takes the worry out of finding a safe place to keep your backups because they're always stored in an area far away from your computer (on the backup company's server). However, if you'd like to store your backups online, make sure you have high-speed Internet access.

Should I back up my files that are stored on my school's network? Most likely, if you're allowed to store files on your school's network, these files are backed up on a regular basis. You should check with your school's network administrators to determine how often they're backed up and how you would go about requesting that files be restored from the backup media if they're damaged or deleted. But don't rely on these network backups to bail you out if your data files are lost or damaged. It may take days for the network administrators to get around to restoring your files. It is better to keep backups of your data files yourself (especially homework and project files) so that you can immediately restore them. Buy a large-capacity flash drive and carry it with you!

> " Where is a safe place to store my backups? "

Social Engineering: Fooling the Unwary

What is social engineering? Social engineering is any technique that uses social skills to generate human interaction that entices individuals to reveal sensitive information. Social engineering often doesn't involve the use of a computer or face-to-face interaction. For example, telephone scams are a common form of social engineering because it is often easier to manipulate someone when you don't have to look at them.

How does social engineering work? Most social engineering schemes use a pretext to lure their victims. **Pretexting** involves creating a scenario that sounds legitimate enough that someone will trust you. For example, you might receive a phone call during which the caller says he is from the bank and that someone tried to use your account without authorization. The caller then tells you he needs to confirm a few personal details such as your birth date, Social Security number, bank account number, and whatever other information he can get out of you. The information he obtains can then be used to empty your bank account or commit some other form of fraud. Often pretexting is used to gain access to corporate computer networks. People will sometimes call random extensions in a large business, claiming to be from technical support. Eventually, the caller will find someone who has a problem and is happy that someone is willing to help. The scam artist will then elicit information such as logins and passwords from the victim as part of the

Computers in Society: Identity Theft—Is There More Than One You Out There?

You've no doubt heard of identity theft. A thief steals your name, address, Social Security number, and bank account and credit card information and runs up debts in your name. This leaves you holding the bag, and you're hounded by creditors collecting on the fraudulent debts. It sounds horrible—and it is. In fact, one of the authors of this text had his identity stolen and spent about 50 hours filing police reports, talking to credit agencies, closing bogus accounts, and convincing companies that the $25,000 of debt run up on six phony credit card accounts was done by an identity thief. Many victims of identity theft spend months (or even years) trying to repair their credit and eliminate fraudulent debts. Worse yet, if an identity thief uses your identity to obtain medical services at a hospital, you may be denied coverage at a later date because the thief's treatment has exceeded the limit of covered services on your policy.

Stories of identity thieves—such as the New York. Man accused of stealing more than 30,000 identities—abound in the media, and should serve to make the public wary. However, many media pundits would have you believe that the only way your identity can be stolen is by a computer. This is simply not true. The Federal Trade Commission (**ftc.gov**) has identified other methods thieves use to obtain others' personal information. These include (1) stealing purses and wallets, in which people often keep unnecessary valuable personal information such as their ATM PIN codes, (2) stealing mail or looking through trash for bank statements and credit card bills, which provide valuable personal information; and (3) posing as bank or credit card company representatives and tricking people into revealing sensitive information over the phone.

Obviously, you're at risk from online attacks, too, such as phishing and pharming. Once identity thieves obtain your personal information, they can use it in many different ways. Identity thieves often request a change of address for your credit card bill or bank statement. By the time you realize that you aren't receiving your statements, the thieves have rung up bogus charges on your account or emptied your bank account.

The thieves can open new credit card and bank accounts in your name. They then will write bad checks and not pay the credit card bills, which will ruin your credit rating.

Even worse, the identity thieves may counterfeit debit cards or checks for your legitimate accounts and empty them of funds. They might even take out a mortgage in your name and then disappear with the proceeds, leaving you with the debt.

Although foolproof protection methods don't exist, there are precautions that will help you minimize your risk. You should never reveal your password or your PIN code to anyone or place it in an easy-to-find location. Also, never reveal personal information unless you're sure that a legitimate reason exists for a business to know the information, and you can confirm you're actually dealing with a legitimate representative (don't fall for phishing schemes). If someone calls or e-mails asking you for personal information, decline and call the company with which you opened your account.

Obviously, you should create secure passwords for your online accounts. When shopping online, be wary of unfamiliar merchants that you can't contact through a mailing address or phone number, or businesses whose prices are too good to be true. These can be attempts to collect your personal information for use in fraudulent schemes.

If you have been the victim of identity theft, most states now allow you to freeze your credit history so that no new accounts can be opened until you lift the credit freeze. Even if you live in a state where you can't freeze your account, you can still place an extended fraud alert on your credit history for seven years, which also warns merchants that they should check with you (at your home address or phone number) before opening an account in your name.

Using common sense and keeping personal information in the hands of as few people as possible are the best defenses against identity theft. For additional tips on preventing identity theft or for procedures to follow if you are a victim, check out the U.S. government site on identity theft (**consumer.gov/idtheft**).

---

process for "solving the problem." The most common form of pretexting in cyberspace is phishing.

Phishing and Pharming

How are phishing schemes conducted? **Phishing** (pronounced "fishing") lures Internet users to reveal personal information such as credit card numbers, Social Security numbers, or other sensitive information that could lead to identity theft. The scammers send e-mail messages that look like they are from a legitimate business such as an online bank. The e-mail states that the recipient needs to update or confirm his or her account information. When the recipient clicks the provided link, he or she goes to a Web site. The site looks like a legitimate site but is really a fraudulent copy the

scammer has created. Once the e-mail recipient confirms his or her personal information, the scammers capture it and can begin using it.

Is pharming a type of phishing scam? Pharming is much more insidious than phishing. Phishing requires a positive action by the person being scammed, such going to a Web site mentioned in an e-mail and typing in your bank account information. **Pharming** is when malicious code is planted on your computer that alters your browser's ability to find Web addresses. Users are directed to bogus Web sites even when they enter the correct address of the real Web site or follow a bookmark that they previously had established for the Web site. So instead of ending up at your bank's Web site when you type in its address, you end up at a fake Web site that looks like your bank's site but is expressly set up for the purpose of gathering information.

How can I avoid being caught by phishing and pharming scams? You should never reply directly to any e-mail asking you for personal information. Never click on a link in an e-mail to go to a Web site. Instead, type the Web site address in the browser. Check with the company asking for the information and only give the information if you are certain it is needed.

Also, never give personal information over the Internet unless you know the site is secure. Look for the closed padlock, https, or a certification seal such as VeriSign to indicate that the site is secure. The latest versions of Firefox, Chrome, and Internet Explorer have phishing filters built in, so each time you access a Web site, the phishing filter checks for the site's legitimacy and warns you of possible Web forgeries.

Finally, make sure you have Internet security software installed on your computer and that it is constantly being updated. Most Internet security packages can detect and prevent pharming attacks. The major Internet security packages—for example, McAfee and Norton (see Figure 26)—also offer phishing protection tools. When you have the Norton Toolbar displayed in your browser, you are constantly informed about the legitimacy of the site you are visiting. In fact, if you have an Internet security package installed, you can turn off the phishing filter in your browser to speed up the loading of Web pages.

Another way to protect yourself is never to use your credit card number when you shop online. Although it sounds impossible, credit card providers such as Citibank are offering services such as "Virtual Account Numbers" for their customers. Before purchasing a product online, you visit an online site, where you are assigned a new virtual account number each time you visit. This number looks like a regular credit card number and is tied to your real credit card account. However, the virtual account number can be used only once. That means that if the number is stolen, it's no good to thieves. They can't use the virtual account number, because you've already used it.

Hoaxes

What is a hoax? A **hoax** is an attempt to make someone believe something that is

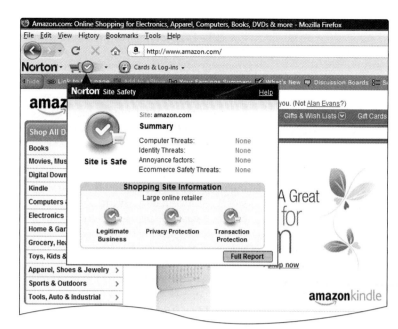

untrue. Hoaxes target a large audience and are generally perpetrated as practical jokes, instruments of social change (which poke fun at an established norm in an effort to change it), or merely ways to waste people's valuable time. Although there are hoax Web sites such as Pacific Northwest Tree Octopus (**zapatopi.net/treeoctopus/**), most cyberspace hoaxes are perpetrated by e-mail.

Why do people concoct e-mail hoaxes? As opposed to garnering financial rewards (like in a phishing fraud), the motives of e-mail hoax creators can be more complex. Many people start an e-mail hoax just for the challenge of seeing if their "brainchild" can be spread globally. Other hoaxes start as innocent practical jokes between friends but then take on a life of their own via the fast communication available on the Internet. Many hoaxes become so well known that they are accepted by society as true events even though they are false. Once this happens to a hoax, it becomes known as an **urban legend**. An example is the phony story about the man who woke up in a bathtub full of ice water and found he had had his kidney stolen. Hoaxes may be compared to acts of real-world vandalism like graffiti. Graffiti artists "make their mark" on the world, physically; hoaxers may consider they are making a similar mark when a bogus e-mail they have created becomes widespread.

Sometimes hoaxes are based on misinformation or are a way to vent frustration. An

Figure 26

Not sure whether you are on the Amazon Web site or a cleverly disguised phishing site? Norton Site Safety reassures you that all is well.

e-mail hoax that reappears every time there is a spike in gasoline prices is the Gas Boycott (Gas War) hoax. To boost the scheme's credibility, the e-mail touts it as having been invented by reputable businesspeople. The e-mail explains how boycotting certain gasoline companies will drive the price of gasoline down and urges recipients of the e-mail to join the fight. The originator of this hoax was probably frustrated by high gas prices and, armed with a poor understanding of economics, distributed this brainstorm. Unfortunately, this tactic can have no effect on gasoline prices because it only shifts demand for gasoline from certain oil companies to other sources. Because it does not reduce the overall demand for gasoline, the price of gas will not decline. Did you receive this e-mail and think it sounded like a plausible idea? How many people did you forward it to?

How can I tell if an e-mail is a hoax? Sometimes it is difficult to separate fact from fiction. Many hoax e-mails are well written and crafted in such a way that they sound very real. Before using the Forward button and sending an e-mail to all your friends, check it out at one of the many Web sites that keep track of and expose e-mail hoaxes. Check sites such as Snopes (**snopes.com**), Hoax Slayer (**hoax-slayer.com**, shown in Figure 27), or TruthOrFiction.com (**truthorfiction.com**). These sites are searchable, so you can enter a few keywords from an e-mail you suspect may be a hoax and quickly find similar e-mails, with an explanation of whether they are true or false. Checking out e-mails before

forwarding them on to friends, family, and co-workers will save other people's time and help end the spread of these time wasters.

Protecting Your Physical Computing Assets

Your computer isn't useful to you if it is damaged. Therefore, it's essential to select and ensure a safe environment for it. This includes protecting it from environmental factors, power surges, power outages, and theft.

Environmental Factors

Why is the environment critical to the operation of my computer equipment? Computers are delicate devices and can be damaged by the adverse effects of being kept in a poor environment or abused. Sudden movements (such as a fall) can damage your notebook computer or mobile device's internal components. You should make sure that your computer sits on a flat, level surface, and, if it is a notebook, carry it in a padded case to protect it. If you do drop your computer, have it professionally tested by a computer repair facility to check for any hidden damage.

Electronic components do not like excessive heat or excessive cold. Unfortunately, computers generate a lot of heat, which is why they have fans to cool their internal components. Make sure that you place your computer where the fan's input vents (usually found on the rear of the system unit) are unblocked so that air can flow inside. And don't leave computing devices in a car during especially hot or cold weather, because components can be damaged by extreme temperatures. Naturally, a fan drawing air into a computer also draws in dust and other particles, which can wreak havoc on your system. Therefore, keep the room in which your computer is located as clean as possible. Even in a clean room, the fan ducts can become packed with dust, so vacuum it periodically to keep a clear airflow into your computer. Finally, because food crumbs and liquid can damage keyboards and other computer components, consume food and beverages away from your computer.

Figure 27

Sites like Hoax-Slayer help you research potential hoaxes.

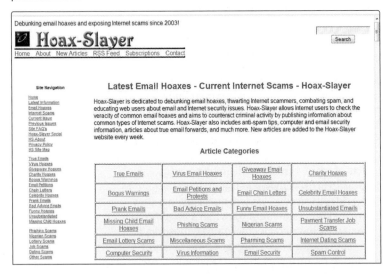

Power Surges

What is a power surge? Power surges occur when electrical current is supplied in excess of normal voltage (120 volts in the United States). Old or faulty wiring, downed power lines, malfunctions at electric company substations, and lightning strikes can all cause power surges. A **surge protector** is a device that protects your computer against power surges (see Figure 28). To use a surge protector, you simply plug your electrical devices into the outlets of the surge protector, which in turn plugs into the wall.

How do surge protectors work? Surge protectors contain two components that are used to protect the equipment that is connected to them. Metal-oxide varistors (MOVs) bleed off excess current during minor surges and feed it to the ground wire, where it harmlessly dissipates. The MOVs can do this while still allowing normal current to pass through the devices plugged into the surge protector. Because the ground wire is critical to this process, it is important to plug the surge protector into a grounded (typically 3-prong) power outlet.

During major surges that overwhelm the MOVs, a fuse inside the surge protector blows, which stops the flow of current to all devices plugged into the surge protector. After a major surge, the surge protector will no longer function and must be replaced.

Over time, the MOVs lose their ability to bleed off excess current, which is why you should replace your surge protectors every 2 to 3 years. Buy a surge protector that includes indicator lights. Indicator lights illuminate when the surge protector is no longer functioning properly. (Don't be fooled by old surge protectors that can still function as multiple-outlet power strips,

delivering power to your equipment without protecting it.) A power surge could ruin your computer and other devices if you don't protect them. At $20 to $40, a quality surge protector is an excellent investment.

Besides my computer, what other devices need to be connected to a surge protector? All electronic devices in the home that have solid-state components, such as TVs, stereos, computers, printers, and phones, should be connected to a surge protector. Printers and other computer peripherals all require protection. However, it can be inconvenient to use individual surge protectors on everything. A more practical method is to install a **whole-house surge protector** (see Figure 29). Whole-house surge protectors function like other surge protectors, but they protect *all* electrical devices in the house. Typically, you will need an electrician to install a whole-house surge protector, which will cost $200 to $300 (installed).

Data lines (transmission media), such as the coaxial cable that attaches to your modem, also can carry surges. Installing a **data line surge suppressor** for each data line connected to your computer through another device (such as a modem) will provide additional protection (see Figure 30). A data line surge suppressor is connected to the data line at a point before it reaches the modem or

Figure 28

Anatomy of a surge protector.

Metal-oxide varistors (MOVs) bleed off excess current

Fuse blows during major surges

Surge protector

Figure 29

A whole-house surge protector usually is installed at the breaker panel or near the electric meter.

other device. In this way, it intercepts surges on the data line before they reach sensitive equipment.

Is my equipment 100 percent safe when plugged into a surge protector? Surge protectors won't necessarily guard against all surges. Lightning strikes can generate such high voltages that they can overwhelm a surge protector. As tedious as it sounds, unplugging computers and peripherals during an electrical storm is the only way to achieve absolute protection.

How can I prevent my computers from losing power during a power outage? Like power surges, power outages can wreak havoc on a system. Computers can develop software glitches caused by a loss of power if not shut down properly. Mission-critical computers such as Web servers often are protected by an **uninterruptible power supply**

Figure 30

American Power Conversion (APC), a large manufacturer of surge protection devices, makes a wide range of data line surge suppressors to accommodate almost any type of data line.

(UPS), as shown in Figure 31. A UPS is a device that contains surge protection equipment and a large battery. When power is interrupted (such as during a blackout), the UPS continues to send power to the attached computer from its battery. Depending on the battery capacity, you have between about 20 minutes and 3 hours to save your work and shut down your computer properly.

Deterring Theft

Because they are portable, notebooks are easy targets for thieves. Common sense dictates that you shouldn't leave your notebook unattended or in a place where it can be stolen easily (such as in a hotel room or coffee shop). Even though they are not considered portable, desktop computers are also subject to theft. Three approaches to deterring computer theft include alarming them, locking them down, or installing devices that alert you (or destroy data) when the computer is stolen.

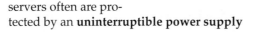

Figure 31

A UPS device should not be mistaken for a fat surge protector!

Alarms

What type of alarm can I install on my notebook computer? To prevent your notebook from being stolen, you can attach a motion alarm to it (see Figure 32). When you leave your notebook, you use a small device called a *key fob activator* to activate the alarm. If your notebook is moved while the alarm is activated, it emits a wailing 85-decibel sound. The fact that the alarm is visible acts as an additional theft deterrent, just like a "Beware of Dog" sign in a front yard.

Figure 32

A notebook alarm sends out an ear-piercing sound if your notebook is moved before you deactivate the alarm.

Alarm

Locks and Surrounds

How can I lock up a notebook computer? Chaining a notebook to your work surface can be another effective way to prevent theft. As shown in Figure 33, a special locking mechanism is attached to the notebook (some notebooks are even manufactured with locking ports), and a hardened steel cable is connected to the locking mechanism. The other end of the cable is looped around something large and heavy, such as a desk. The cable lock requires the use of a key or combination to free the notebook. You should consider taking a cable lock with you when traveling to help deter theft from hotel rooms.

Many people associate computer theft only with notebooks or mobile devices. Desktop computers are

Figure 33

Cable locks are an effective deterrent to theft.

vulnerable to theft also, especially theft of internal components such as RAM. Your school most likely has the desktop computers in the lab secured in some fashion. Cable locks connect through special fasteners on the back of desktop computers, but components can still be stolen because these cables often don't prevent the system unit case from being opened. A more effective theft deterrent for desktops is a surround (or cage) such as the one shown in Figure 34. A surround is a metal box that encloses the system unit, making it impossible to remove from the cage while still allowing access to ports and devices such as DVD players.

Software Alerts

How can my computer alert me when it is stolen? You've probably heard of LoJack, the theft-tracking device used in cars. Car owners install a LoJack transmitter somewhere in their vehicle. If the vehicle is stolen, police activate the transmitter and use its signal to locate the car. Similar systems now exist for computers. Tracking software such as Computrace Complete, Computrace LoJack for Laptops (**absolute.com**), PC PhoneHome, and Mac PhoneHome (**pcphonehome.com**) enables the computer it is installed on to alert authorities as to the computer's location if it is stolen. This software can be installed in either notebook or desktop computers.

To enable your computer to help with its own recovery, install the tracking software on your hard drive. The software contacts a server at the software manufacturer's Web site each time you connect to the Internet. If your computer is stolen, you notify the software manufacturer. The software manufacturer instructs your computer to transmit tracking information (such as an IP address) that will assist authorities in locating and retrieving the stolen computer.

What if the thieves find the tracking software and delete it? The files and directories holding the software are not visible to thieves looking for such software, so they probably won't know the software is there. Furthermore, the tracking software is written in such a way that even if the thieves tried to reformat the hard drive, it would detect the reformat and hide the software code

Figure 34

Computer surrounds deter theft by making access to the internal components of the computer difficult while still allowing access to ports and drives.

in a safe place in memory or on the hard drive. (Some sectors of a hard drive are not rewritten during most reformattings.) That way, it can re-install itself after the reformatting is completed.

Are there ways to protect data contained on mobile devices? Smartphones can be vulnerable to unauthorized access if they are left unattended or are stolen. Although some devices offer basic protection features (such as password protection), sensitive business information often requires an additional level of protection. Security software such as TealLock from TealPoint Software (**tealpoint.com**) offers additional protection features such as data encryption and protection against attempts to break into a device through "brute force" attacks (running a program to guess all possible passwords). Most programs feature optional data self-destruct modes (sometimes known as **bomb software**) that destroy data on both internal memory and external data cards if repeated attempts are made to crack passwords.

How can I ensure that I've covered all aspects of protecting my computer? The checklist in Figure 35 is a guide to ensure you didn't miss any critical aspects of security. If you've addressed all of these issues, you can feel reasonably confident that your Internet access will be secure and free from problems.

Taking a few precautions regarding your data security can provide huge benefits such as peace of mind and the avoidance of time spent correcting problems. So enjoy your computing experiences, but do so safely.

Figure 35 | COMPUTER SECURITY CHECKLIST

	Yes	No
Virus and Spyware Protection		
Is antivirus and antispyware software installed on all your computers?		
Is the antivirus and antispyware software configured to update itself automatically and regularly?		
Is the software set to scan your computer on a regular basis (at least weekly) for viruses and spyware?		
Firewall		
Do all your computers have firewall software installed and activated before connecting to the Internet?		
Is your router also able to function as a hardware firewall?		
Have you tested your firewall security by using the free software available at **grc.com**?		
Wireless Security		
Have you changed the default password for your router?		
Have you changed the name (SSID) of your network and turned off SSID broadcasting?		
Have you enabled WPA or WEP encryption for your network?		
Software Updates		
Have you configured your operating systems (Windows, OS X) to install new software patches and updates automatically?		
Is other software installed on your computer (such as Microsoft Office) configured for automatic updates?		
Is the Web browser you are using the latest version?		

With billions of dollars spent on e-commerce initiatives every year, companies have a vested interest in keeping their information technology (IT) infrastructures humming along. The rise in terrorism has shifted the focus slightly—from protecting virtual assets and access, to protecting these plus physical assets and access points. The increased need for virtual and physical security measures means there should be a robust job market ahead for computer security experts.

The National Security Agency and the Office of Homeland Security are both encouraging information security professionals to be proficient in information assurance. As defined by the NSA, **information assurance** is "the set of measures intended to protect and defend information and information systems by ensuring their availability, integrity, authentication, confidentiality, and non-repudiation. This includes providing for restoration of information systems by incorporating protection, detection, and reaction capabilities." The five key attributes of secure information systems are as follows:

1. **Availability:** The extent to which a data-processing system is able to receive and process data. A high degree of availability is usually desirable.

2. **Integrity:** A quality that an information system has if the processing of information is logical and accurate and the data is protected against unauthorized modifications or destruction.

3. **Authentication:** Security measures designed to protect an information system against acceptance of a fraudulent transmission of data by establishing the validity of a data transmission or message, or the identity of the sender.

4. **Confidentiality:** The assurance that information is not disclosed to unauthorized persons, processes, or devices.

5. **Nonrepudiation:** A capability of security systems that guarantees that a message or data can be proven to have originated from a specific person and was processed by the recipient. The sender of the data receives a receipt for the data, and the receiver of the data gets proof of the sender's identity. The objective of nonrepudiation is to prevent either party from later denying having handled the data.

The Global Information Assurance Certification, or GIAC (**giac.org**), is an industry-recognized certification that provides objective evidence (through examinations) that security professionals have mastered key skills in various aspects of information assurance.

What skill sets will be most in demand for security professionals? In addition to information assurance technical skills (with an emphasis on network engineering and data communications), broad-based business experience is also extremely desirable. IT security professionals need to understand the key issues of e-commerce and the core areas of their company's business (such as marketing, sales, and finance). Understanding how a business works is essential to pinpointing and correcting security risks that could be detrimental to a company's bottom line. Because of the large number of attacks by hackers, security and forensic skills and related certifications also are in high demand. Working closely with law enforcement officials is essential to rapidly solving and stopping cybercrime.

Another important attribute of security professionals is the ability to lead and motivate teams. Security experts need to work with diverse members of the business community, including customers, to forge relationships and understanding among diverse groups. Security professionals must conduct skillful negotiations to ensure that large project implementations are not unduly delayed by security initiatives or pushed through with inadequate security precautions. Diplomacy is therefore a sought-after skill.

Look for more colleges and universities to roll out security-based degree and certificate programs as the demand for security professionals increases. These programs will most likely be appropriate for experienced networking professionals who are ready to make the move into the IT security field. If you're just starting to prepare for a career, consider a degree in network engineering, followed by network security training while you're working at your first job. A degree program that is also designed to prepare you for security certification exams is particularly desirable. Networking and security degrees, combined with passing grades on certification exams, should help you make a smooth transition into the exciting world of cybersecurity.

Protecting Your Physical Computing Assets

summary

1. From which types of viruses do I need to protect my computer?

A computer virus is a program that attaches itself to another program and attempts to spread to other computers when files are exchanged. Computer viruses can be grouped into five categories: (1) boot-sector viruses, (2) logic bombs and time bombs, (3) worms, (4) scripts and macros, and (5) encryption viruses. Once run, they perform their malicious duties in the background, and are often invisible to the user.

2. What can I do to protect my computer from viruses?

The best defense against viruses is to install antivirus software. You should update the software on a regular basis and configure it to examine all e-mail attachments for viruses. You should periodically run a complete virus scan on your computer to ensure that no viruses have made it onto your hard drive.

3. How can hackers attack my computing devices, and what harm can they cause?

A hacker is defined as anyone who breaks into a computer system unlawfully. Hackers can use software to break into almost any computer connected to the Internet (unless proper precautions are taken). Once hackers gain access to a computer, they can potentially (1) steal personal or other important information; (2) damage and destroy data; or (3) use the computer to attack other computers.

4. What is a firewall, and how does it keep my computer safe from hackers?

Firewalls are software programs or hardware devices designed to keep computers safe from hackers. By using a personal firewall, you can close open logical ports to invaders and potentially make your computer invisible to other computers on the Internet.

5. How do I create secure passwords and manage all of my passwords?

Secure passwords contain a mixture of upper- and lowercase letters, numbers, and symbols, and are at least 14 characters long. Passwords should not contain words that are in the dictionary or easy-to-guess personal information (like your pet's name). Online password checkers can be used to evaluate the strength of your passwords. Utilities built into Web browsers and Internet security software can be used to manage your passwords and alleviate the need to remember numerous complex passwords.

6. How can I surf the Internet anonymously and use biometric authentication devices to protect my data?

The current versions of the popular browsers include tools (such as Chrome's Incognito feature) that hide your surfing activities by not recording Web sites that you visit, or files that you download, in your browser's history files. Biometric authentication devices use a physical attribute (such as a fingerprint) that is not easily duplicated to control access to data files or computing devices. Some notebooks today feature fingerprint readers and facial recognition software to control access.

7. How do I manage online annoyances such as spyware and spam?

The Web is filled with annoyances such as spam, pop-ups, cookies, spyware, and scams such as phishing that make surfing the Web frustrating and sometimes dangerous. Software tools help to prevent or reduce spam, adware, and spyware, while exercising caution can prevent serious harm caused by phishing, pharming, and other Internet scams and hoaxes.

Digital Lifestyle: Protecting Digital Data and Devices

8. What data do I need to back up, and what are the best methods for doing so?

Data files created by you (such as Word and Excel files) or purchased by you (such as music files) need to be backed up in case they are inadvertently deleted or damaged. Application software (such as Microsoft Office) may need to be reinstalled if files are damaged, so backups (usually the DVDs or CDs the application came on) must be maintained. External hard drives are popular choices for holding backup copies of files. Various backup software packages are available to automate the backup tasks.

9. What is social engineering, and how do I avoid falling prey to phishing and hoaxes?

Social engineering schemes use human interaction, deception, and trickery to fool people into revealing sensitive information such as credit card numbers and passwords. Phishing schemes usually involve e-mails that direct the unwary to a Web site that appears to be legitimate (such as a bank site) but is specifically designed to capture personal information for committing fraud. To avoid phishing scams, you should never reply directly to any e-mail asking you for personal information, and never click on a link in an e-mail to go to a Web site. You can research topics you believe to be hoaxes at sites such as Snopes (**snopes.com**).

10. How do I protect my physical computing assets from environmental hazards, power surges, and theft?

Computing devices should be kept in clean environments free from dust and other particulates and should not be exposed to extreme temperatures (either hot or cold). You should protect all electronic devices from power surges by hooking them up through surge protectors, which will protect them from most electrical surges that could damage the devices. Notebook computers can be protected from theft either by attaching alarms to them or by installing software that will help recover the computer, if stolen, by reporting the computer's whereabouts when it is connected to the Internet.

key terms

adware

antivirus

backdoor program

backup

biometric authentication device

black hat hacker

bomb software

boot-sector virus

botnet

cookie

cybercrime

cybercriminal

cyberloafing

data file

data line surge suppressor

denial-of-service (DoS) attack

distributed denial-of-service (DDoS) attack

drive-by download

dynamic addressing

e-mail virus

encryption virus

firewall

full backup

hacker

hoax

identity theft

image backup

incremental backup

information assurance

inoculation

Internet protocol address (IP address)

keystroke logger

logic bomb

logical port

logical port blocking

macro virus

malware

master boot record

multipartite virus

network address translation (NAT)

packet

packet filtering

packet sniffer

personal firewall

pharming

phishing

polymorphic virus

pretexting

program file

quarantining

script

script kiddy

social engineering

spam

spam filter

spyware

static addressing

stealth virus

surge protector

time bomb

Trojan horse

uninterruptible power supply (UPS)

urban legend

virus

virus signature

white hat hacker

whole-house surge protector

worm

zombie

Word Bank

- adware
- antivirus software
- backup(s)
- distributed denial-of-service (DDoS)
- firewall
- hacker(s)
- identity theft
- information assurance
- keystroke logger(s)
- logical port(s)
- phishing
- social engineering
- spyware
- virus
- zombie(s)

Instructions: Fill in the blanks using the words from the Word Bank above.

Emily learned a lot about computer security in her computer literacy class. She already knew it was important to exercise caution when using the Internet because she had been the victim of (1) _____, which destroyed her credit rating. A(n) (2) _____ had obtained her credit card information by posing as an employee of her bank, using a method known as (3) _____. In her class, Emily learned that hackers could install (4) _____, a type of software that will capture everything she types, to steal her personal information. And one of Emily's classmates received a (5) _____ e-mail that directed her to a fake Web site that looked like her bank's Web site and resulted in her bank account information being stolen. The computers in the lab at school had just been cleaned of (6) _____ software that was displaying annoying pop-up advertisements. The computer technician who fixed this problem indicated that (7) _____ software, which was monitoring computer user activity, was often inadvertently installed on lab computers by students downloading files.

Emily found out that her router could be configured as a(n) (8) _____ to repel malicious hacking mischief and assist in providing (9) _____ for the data on her computer. Turning off the unused (10) _____ would repel most attacks on her home network. With this protection, it was unlikely that a hacker would turn her PC into a(n) (11) _____ to launch (12) _____ attacks. However, after the scare with the Conficker (13) _____, Emily was careful to warn her family not to open files from untrusted sources. She also made sure all of the computers in her home had (14) _____ installed to protect them from viruses. For extra security, Emily installed an external hard drive so that she could create (15) _____ of her data files.

becoming computer literate

While attending college, you are working at the Snap-Tite company, a small manufacturer of specialty fasteners. Recently, the company computers have been behaving strangely and running slowly. You suspect that viruses and spyware might be present on the computers, as it appears most of the computers lack any sort of protection. Your boss heard that you are taking a computer course and has asked you to suggest a solution.

Instructions: Using the preceding scenario, draft an antivirus and antispyware plan for Snap-Tite using as many of the keywords from the chapter as you can. Be sure that the company president, who is unfamiliar with many computer terms, can understand the report.

Instructions: Answer the multiple-choice and true–false questions below for more practice with key terms and concepts from this chapter.

Multiple Choice

1. Computer viruses that are triggered when a certain condition is met are known as
   a. logic bombs.
   b. time bombs.
   c. stealth viruses.
   d. multipartite viruses.

2. Viruses that periodically change their code to avoid detection are called
   a. stealth viruses.
   b. script viruses.
   c. polymorphic viruses.
   d. macro viruses.

3. Portions of virus code that are unique to a particular computer virus are known as
   a. master boot records.
   b. virus signatures.
   c. virus footprints.
   d. virus traces.

4. Hackers who break into systems just for the challenge, or to bring system vulnerabilities to light for the greater good, are called
   a. black hat hackers.
   b. script kiddies.
   c. valiant hackers.
   d. white hat hackers.

5. Programs that allow hackers to take almost complete control of a computer without the owner's knowledge are known as
   a. Trojan horses.
   b. backdoor programs.
   c. stealth viruses.
   d. None of the above.

6. Techniques that use verbal or written communication to generate human interaction that tricks individuals into revealing sensitive information are collectively known as
   a. phishing.
   b. pharming.
   c. pretexting.
   d. social engineering.

7. When hackers use computers to launch an attack on another computer, the computers used to stage the attack are known as
   a. drones.
   b. zombies.
   c. packet sniffers.
   d. Trojan horses.

8. Which is NOT a benefit of firewalls?
   a. They make it harder for a hacker to locate specific computers on a network.
   b. They repeatedly change the IP address of the router.
   c. They close unused logical ports to decrease network vulnerability.
   d. They filter out unauthorized requests for data.

9. Planting code on your computer that alters your browser's ability to find Web addresses is a type of cyberannoyance known as
   a. phishing.
   b. keystroke logging.
   c. logic bombing.
   d. pharming.

10. Viruses that attempt to travel between systems through network connections to spread their infections are called
    a. worms.
    b. stealth viruses.
    c. logic bombs.
    d. macro viruses.

True-False

_____ 1. Viruses that render your files unusable in an attempt to extort money to have them restored are known as stealth viruses.

_____ 2. A properly installed surge protector will protect a computer from all power surges.

_____ 3. Installing a firewall on your network will not stop most viruses from being planted on your network.

_____ 4. E-mails designed to trick you into revealing information (such as bank account numbers) are a type of phishing scam.

_____ 5. If you have designed strong passwords, there is never a need to change them.

1. Backup Procedures

After reading this chapter, you know you should have a good backup strategy in place for your key data. Consider the following and prepare answers in an appropriate format as directed by your instructor.

a. How often do you back up critical data files such as homework files? What type of device do you use for backing up files? Where do you store the backups to ensure they won't be destroyed if a major disaster (such as a fire) destroys your computer?

b. List the applications (such as Microsoft Office) that are currently installed on your computer. Where is the media (DVDs, CDs) for your application software stored? For any software you purchased in an Internet download, have you burned a copy of the installation files to DVD/CD in case you need to reinstall the software?

c. Have you ever made an image backup of your entire system? If so, what software do you use for image backups, and where are the image backups stored? If not, research image backup software on the Internet and find an appropriate package to use. Will you need to purchase an additional backup device to hold your image backup or does your current device have room for an image backup? If you need a new device, find one on the Internet that is appropriate. What is the total cost of the software and hardware you will need to implement your image backup strategy?

2. Connecting Your Computer to Public Networks

In the course of your education, you are constantly connecting your notebook to various wireless public networks such as those in the school library and neighborhood coffee shop. As you know from reading this chapter, you are more vulnerable to hackers when connected to a wireless network in a public place such as a coffee shop. Conduct research on the Internet about surfing at public hot spots and prepare a list of sensible precautions for you and your classmates to take when surfing on an open network.

3. Identity Theft Awareness

Two students in your residence hall have recently been the victims of identity theft. You have been assigned to create a flyer telling students how they can protect themselves from identity theft in their residence hall. Using the information found in this chapter, materials you find on the U.S. government Web site on identity theft (**consumer.gov/idtheft**), and other Web resources, create a flyer that lists 5 to 10 ways in which students can avoid having their identities stolen.

1. Antivirus Protection

Your employer recently installed high-speed Internet access at the office where you work. There are 50 workstations connected to the network and the Internet. Within a week, half the computers in the office went down because of a virus that infected a screen saver. In addition, network personnel from a university in England contacted the company, claiming that your employer's computer systems were being used as part of a denial-of-service (DDoS) attack on their Web site.

a. Price security suite software on the Internet and determine the most cost-effective package for the company to use to implement protection on 50 workstations.

b. Write a "virus prevention" memo to all employees that suggests strategies for avoiding computer virus infections.

c. Draft a note to the CEO to explain how a firewall could prevent DDoS attacks from being launched on the company network.

2. Securing Customer Data

Many corporations are collecting vast amounts of sensitive data (such as credit card numbers, birth dates, etc.) about their customers. Assume you are working for a business that accepts orders for merchandise through a Web site. Answer the following questions:

a. What security measures should you implement on your Web site to ensure that customers' data is protected (or encrypted) from the prying eyes of hackers?

b. Your company would like to send e-mails to customers on their birthdays, offering them a special discount on merchandise purchased within one week of their birthday. How would you explain to customers why you are collecting their birthdates, and what measures would you need to take to keep this data secure?

c. How would you ensure that information shared with third parties (such as delivery companies) is kept secure?

3. Testing Your Computer

Visit Gibson Research (**grc.com**) and run the company's ShieldsUP and LeakTest programs on your computer.

a. Did your computer get a clean report? If not, what potential vulnerabilities did the testing programs detect?

b. How could you protect yourself from the vulnerabilities these programs can detect?

Digital Lifestyle: Protecting Digital Data and Devices

Instructions: Albert Einstein used *Gedankenexperiments*, or critical thinking questions, to develop his theory of relativity. Some ideas are best understood by experimenting with them in our own minds. The following critical thinking questions are designed to demand your full attention but only require a comfortable chair—no technology.

1. Protecting Your Home Network

Many people have networks in their homes. Consider the network installed in your home (or in a friend's home if you don't have a network).

a. Is your network set up to provide adequate protection against hackers? If not, what would you need to do to make it secure?

b. Are the computers on your home network protected against viruses and malware? Is the software used for protection updated on a regular basis? Have you ever had problems from a virus or spyware infestation? If so, how did you resolve the problem?

2. Password Protection

You know from reading this chapter that secure passwords are essential to protecting your digital information. Consider the following:

a. How many online accounts do you have that have passwords? List them. Are the passwords for these accounts secure, based on the suggestions proposed in this chapter? Do you change your passwords on a regular basis?

b. How do you keep track of all of your passwords? Do you use password management software? If so, what product are you using? How often do you change your master password? If you don't use password management software, what methodology do you use for remembering and tracking your passwords? Do you think password management software would improve your password security?

3. Ethical Hacking?

Hackers and virus authors cause millions of dollars worth of damage to PCs and networks annually. However, hacking is a highly controversial subject. Many hackers believe they are actually working for the "good of the people" or "exercising their freedom" when they engage in hacking activities. However, in most jurisdictions in the United States, hacking is punishable by stiff fines and jail terms.

a. Hackers often argue that hacking is for the good of all people because it points out flaws in computer systems. Do you agree with this? Why or why not?

b. What should the punishment be for convicted hackers? Why?

c. Who should be held accountable at a corporation whose network security is breached by a hacker?

4. Keeping Networks Safe from Cyberterrorists

Many of us rely on networks every day, often without realizing it. Whether you are researching a term paper on the Internet, ordering a book from Amazon.com, or accessing your college e-mail from home, you are relying on networks to relay information. But what if terrorists destroyed key components of the Internet or other networks on which we depend?

a. What economic problems would result from DDoS attacks launched by terrorists on major e-commerce sites?

b. Research the precautions that the U.S. military and intelligence agencies such as the Departments of Homeland Security and Commerce, the FBI, and the CIA are taking to ensure that networks involving national defense remain secure from terrorist attacks. What else should they do?

Protecting Your Local Real Estate Office

Problem

Computer networks with high-speed connections to the Internet are common in most businesses today. However, along with easy access to computing devices and the Web comes the danger of theft of digital assets.

Task

A recent graduate of your school has opened a 15-person real estate office in a neighboring town. He approached your instructor for help in assuring that his computers are adequately protected from viruses, malware, and hackers. Because he is currently low on funds, he is hoping that there may be free software available that can adequately shield his company from harm.

Process

Break the class into three teams. Each team will be responsible for investigating one of the following issues:

1. **Firewalls:** Research free firewall software and locate at least three software options that can be deployed at the business. Be sure to concentrate on software that is easy to configure and requires little or no user interaction to be effective.

2. **Antivirus software:** Research alternatives that can be used to protect the computers in the office from virus infection. Find at least three alternatives and support your recommendations with reviews (from publications such as *PC Magazine* or *Consumer Reports*) that evaluate the free packages and compare them to commercial solutions.

3. **Anti-malware software:** Research free packages that will offer protection from malware. Locate at least three alternatives and determine whether the recommended software can be updated automatically. (Many free versions require manual updates.) Most companies that provide free malware protection also offer commercial packages (for a fee) that provide automatic updates. You may need to recommend that the company purchase software to ensure that a minimum of employee intervention is needed to keep the software up to date.

Present your findings to your class and discuss the pros and cons of free and commercial software. Provide your instructor with a report suitable for eventual presentation to the owner of the real estate office.

Conclusion

With the proliferation of viruses and malware, it is essential to protect business (and home) computers and networks from destruction and disruption. Free alternatives might work, but you should ensure that you have done adequate research to determine the best possible protection solution for your particular situation.

multimedia

In addition to the review materials presented here, you'll find additional materials featured with the Pearson IT Multimedia Library and the Companion Website (**www.pearsonhighered.com/techinaction**), which will help reinforce your understanding of the chapter content. These materials include the following:

Active Helpdesk

In Active Helpdesk calls, you'll assume the role of helpdesk operator, taking calls about the concepts you've learned in this chapter. You'll apply what you've learned and receive feedback from a supervisor to review and reinforce those concepts. The Active Helpdesk calls for this chapter are listed below and can be found on the Pearson IT Multimedia Library:

- Avoiding Computer Viruses
- Understanding Firewalls

Sound Bytes

Sound Bytes are dynamic multimedia tutorials that help demystify even the most complex topics. You'll view video clips and animations that illustrate computer concepts and then apply what you've learned by reviewing with the Sound Byte Labs, which include quizzes and activities specifically tailored to each Sound Byte. The Sound Bytes for this chapter are listed below and can be found on the Pearson IT Multimedia Library:

- Protecting Your Computer
- Installing a Personal Firewall
- Surge Protectors

Companion Website

The *Technology in Action* Companion Website includes a variety of additional materials to help you review and learn more about the topics in this chapter. The resources available at **www.pearsonhighered.com/techinaction** include:

- **Online Study Guide.** This chapter features an online true–false and multiple-choice quiz. You can take these quizzes, automatically check the results, and e-mail the results to your instructor.
- **Web Research Projects.** This chapter features several Web research projects that ask you to search the Web for information on computer-related careers, milestones in computer history, important people and companies, emerging technologies, and the applications and implications of different technologies.

Index